CAMBRIDGE TEXTS IN THE
HISTORY OF POLITICAL THOUGHT

———

THE RADICAL REFORMATION

CAMBRIDGE TEXTS IN THE HISTORY OF POLITICAL THOUGHT

Series editors

RAYMOND GEUSS *Columbia University*
QUENTIN SKINNER *Christ's College, Cambridge*
RICHARD TUCK *Jesus College, Cambridge*

The series is intended to make available to students the most important texts required for an understanding of the history of political thought. The scholarship of the present generation has greatly expanded our sense of the range of authors indispensable for such an understanding, and the series will reflect those developments. It will also include a number of less well-known works, in particular those needed to establish the intellectual contexts that in turn help to make sense of the major texts. The principal aim, however, will be to produce new versions of the major texts themselves, based on the most up-do-date scholarship. The preference will always be for complete texts, and a special feature of the series will be to complement individual texts within the compass of a single volume, with subsidiary contextual material. Each volume will contain an introduction on the historical identity and contemporary significance of the text concerned.

For titles already published in the series, see end of book.

THE RADICAL REFORMATION

EDITED AND TRANSLATED BY

Michael G. Baylor
Professor of History
Lehigh University
Bethlehem, Pennsylvania

CAMBRIDGE
UNIVERSITY PRESS

Published by the Press Syndicate of the University of Cambridge
The Pitt Building, Trumpington Street, Cambridge CB2 1RP
40 West 20th Street, New York, NY 10011-4211 USA
10 Stamford Road, Oakleigh, Melbourne 3166, Australia

First published 1991
Reprinted 1995

Printed in Great Britain by Athenæum Press Ltd, Gateshead, Tyne & Wear

British Library cataloguing in publication data
The radical reformation.
1. Germany. Christian church, history
I. Baylor, Michael G.
274.306

Library of Congress cataloging in publication data
The Radical Reformation / edited and translated by Michael G. Baylor.
p.   cm – (Cambridge texts in the history of political thought)
Translated from German.
Includes bibliographical references and index.
ISBN 0 521 37073 6. – ISBN 0 521 37948 2 (pbk.)
1. Anabaptists – Doctrines – History – 16th century – Sources.
2. Church and state – Anabaptists – History – 16th century – Sources.
3. Church and state – Europe – History – 16th century – Sources.
4. Reformation – Sources.   5. Peasants' War. 1524–1525 – Sources.
I. Baylor, Michael G., 1942–   .   II. Series.
BX4931.1.R23   1991
270.6–dc20   90–20416   CIP

ISBN 0 521 37073 6 hardback
ISBN 0 521 37948 2 paperback

Contents

Preface   *page* vii
List of abbreviations   x
Introduction   xi
Chronology 1521–1528   xxvii
Bibliographical note   xxxiii

 1 Thomas Müntzer, *The Prague Protest*   1
 2 Thomas Müntzer, *Sermon to the Princes*
       (or *An Exposition of the Second Chapter of Daniel*)   11
 3 Andreas Karlstadt, *Letter from the Community of*
       Orlamünde to the People of Allstedt   33
 4 Conrad Grebel, *Letter to Thomas Müntzer*   36
 5 Andreas Karlstadt, *Whether One Should Proceed Slowly*   49
 6 Thomas Müntzer, *A Highly Provoked Defense*   74
 7 Felix Manz, *Protest and Defense*   95
 8 Anonymous, *To the Assembly of the Common Peasantry*   101
 9 Hans Denck, *On the Law of God*   130
10 Hans Hut, *On the Mystery of Baptism*   152
11 Michael Sattler, *The Schleitheim Articles*   172
12 Balthasar Hubmaier, *On the Sword*   181
13 Hans Hergot, *On the New Transformation of the*
       Christian Life   210

Appendices: Programs of the Peasants' War   227

a   *The Eleven Mühlhausen Articles*   227

v

Contents

b   *The Twelve Articles of the Upper Swabian Peasants*   231

c   *The Memmingen Federal Constitution*   239

d   *The Document of Articles of the Black Forest Peasants*   243

e   *The Forty-six Frankfurt Articles*   246

f   Michael Gaismair's *Territorial Constitution for Tyrol*   254

Biographical notes   261

Index of subjects   272

Index of proper names   282

Index of biblical references   289

Preface

This work brings together a variety of writings – published and unpublished tracts, letters, declarations, and lists of articles – illustrative of both the rich diversity and the fragile unity that existed in the political thinking of some major radical reformers of the early Reformation in Germany. To give the volume a coherent focus, the texts selected for translation have been drawn from a single decade, the 1520s. They concern the central event of that decade for German society, the Peasants' War of 1524–26, the most massive European popular upheaval before the French Revolution. During the period 1521–27, as Reformation radicals confronted the issue of revolution, and subsequently had to deal with the reality of a failed revolt, the basic patterns of the radicals' thought about society and politics were established.

Politics for the radical reformers was inseparable from religion, as it was for the vast majority of sixteenth-century Europeans. The texts assembled here are "premodern" in the sense that their criticisms of existing social and political arrangements, their legitimations of change, and their visions of an alternative society are animated by Christian ideas and values. But rather than attempting to categorize the writings in terms of a theological typology (Anabaptist, Spiritualist, etc.), I have presented them in roughly chronological order. This arrangement is appropriate to the inchoate nature of Reformation radicalism during the 1520s and to the evolution that radical thought underwent over the decade. Before 1525 no radical aimed at establishing a separatist church or "sect." This alternative emerged only after the failure of the Peasants' War. The sole exception to a chronological ordering comes at the end. Hans Hergot's *On the New Transformation of the Christian Life* was published a few months before Balthasar Hubmaier's *On the Sword*; presenting Hergot's writing last allows Hubmaier's work to be juxtaposed with *The Schleitheim Articles*, which set forth a position that Hubmaier sought to refute, and allows Hergot's work to serve as a recapitulation of some central themes of the collection. The documents appended to the writings present some of the programs of the peasantry and the urban artisan classes during the upheaval of 1525. They show the relationship between the religio-political convictions of the radical reformers and the concrete aspirations of the commoners during the Peasants' War. In many cases the radicals directly participated in, or influenced the framing of these programs.

Some of the writings presented here have been translated before, but all these translations are new, done from the best German editions of the texts. The combination of accuracy and readability in translating is elusive. In the interest of readability I have felt free to divide sentences, alter punctuation, add paragraph divisions, and occasionally eliminate redundancies.

The radicals usually cited Scripture in a general way – ordinarily their references are to whole chapters or psalms. Often I have offered more specific verse references, which have been enclosed in square brackets, as has editorial material in the texts. But the radicals insisted that specific scriptural verses must be understood in context; sometimes they wanted a reader to examine whole chapters or psalms. The Vulgate's nomenclature has been modernized according to *The New English Bible with the Apocrypha*.

This book owes much to the generous help I have received from several individuals and institutions. The preparation of the volume was made possible in part by a grant from the National Endowment for the Humanities, whose support enabled me to spend the academic year 1988–89 in Germany. While there I benefited from the library resources of the University of Tübingen, both the main library and that of the Historisches Seminar. All the personnel of the Historisches Seminar were kind and helpful, but I owe a particular debt of gratitude to Professor Dr. Hans-Christoph Rublack, who did a great deal to make my year enjoyable and profitable. He facilitated the move from the U.S., shared office space, suggested secondary literature, and offered his expertise in translating difficult passages.

The seminar we taught together in the summer of 1989 on the political theory of the radical reformers was a pleasure. I worked through first drafts of the translations with Dieter Jellinghaus of Stuttgart, who offered numerous corrections and suggestions. My wife, Carol Baylor, and my parents, Murray and Elisabeth Baylor, also suggested many stylistic improvements. Dr. Robert W. Scribner of Clare College, Cambridge, shared with me a draft translation of *To the Assembly of the Common Peasantry*. Professor Ulrich Bubenheimer of Heidelberg gave generously of his great knowledge of Thomas Müntzer, and I profited from our discussions about Karlstadt. I also discussed Müntzer with Dr. Dieter Fauth, who lent me source materials. Dr. Gerhard Günther of Mühlhausen encouraged me and provided me with a copy of his manuscript analyzing *The Eleven Mühlhausen Articles*. Professor Joe Dowling, chair of Lehigh University's Department of History, reduced my teaching load to give me more time to work on the book.

Abbreviations

The following abbreviations are used in the notes:

FB   *Flugschriften der Bauernkriegszeit*, ed. Adolf Laube and Hans Werner Seiffert, 2nd revised edn. (Cologne/Vienna, 1978)

MSB   *Thomas Müntzer, Schriften und Briefe. Kritische Gesamtausgabe*, ed. Günter Franz with the collaboration of Paul Kirn (Quellen und Forschungen zur Reformations-geschichte, 33) (Gütersloh, 1968)

QGTS   *Quellen zur Geschichte der Täufer in der Schweiz*, vol. I, Zurich, ed. Leonhard von Huralt and Walter Schmidt (Zurich, 1952, 1974); vol. II, Ostschweiz, ed. Heinold Fast (Zurich, 1973)

PSMB   *Thomas Müntzer: Politische Schriften, Manifeste, Briefe*, ed. Manfred Bensing and Bernd Rüdiger (Leipzig, 1973)

WA   *D. Martin Luthers Werke, Kritische Gesamtausgabe*, vol. Iff. (Weimar, 1883ff.)

WA Br   *D. Martin Luthers Werke, Briefwechsel*, 18 vols. (Weimar, 1930–85)

Introduction

I. The radical Reformation

Radicalism in the sixteenth-century Reformation first appeared in the stormy early years of the movement in Germany and Switzerland. Especially from 1521, the year when Luther was condemned at the Diet of Worms, a powerful current of popular evangelicalism convulsed society. During the early 1520s a cause which had begun with the defense of Luther in his conflict with Rome entered a phase of rapid proliferation. Evangelical preachers appeared in numerous towns, gaining a widespread following among the laity. And, contrary to popular stereotype, the laity did not always follow clerical leaders. From urban bases the Reformation quickly spread to the countryside. With this rapid growth, the reform movement inevitably became more diversified and its message more diffuse. Influential new centers of evangelical theology appeared, such as Zurich where Ulrich Zwingli emerged as the dominant figure. In addition to those of Wittenberg and Zurich, a variety of other Reformation programs were also initiated at the local level. Here preachers and laymen advanced their own understanding of slogans initially made popular by Wittenberg theologians ("the pure gospel," "Christian liberty," "the priesthood of all believers," etc.). As the Reformation spread – through a flood of printed literature, but, more importantly for lay commoners, through sermons, public debates, and less formal oral channels – it also absorbed preexisting socio-economic grievances and political aspirations, and gained a revolutionary momentum. This popular movement culminated in the Peasants' War of 1524–26, or, as it has also been termed, the Revolution of the Common Man.

Reformation radicalism must be considered in the fluid context of this powerful social movement. The radicals are commonly viewed as a fringe element in the Reformation – "marginal" reformers or "reformers in the wings." But during the early 1520s they were the ideologists of the popular evangelicalism that swept Germany and Switzerland. Like the popular Reformation, the radical reformers were driven by a fervent, impatient desire to see sweeping reforms made on the basis of religion. The radicals also insisted that Reformation meant much more than changes in devotional practices and ecclesiastical institutions; public life as a whole was urgently in need of Christianization. Two other important features of this popular evangelicalism are reflected in the themes of Thomas Müntzer's *Prague Protest*: bitter anticlericalism and apocalypticism. The clergy as a whole – but especially prelates, theologians, and monks – were held responsible for the pervasive corruption of Christendom. Müntzer, like many commoners, charged the clergy with preaching a false faith designed to sustain their privileged position in the decayed social order. The social counterpart of this anticlericalism was an exaltation of the "common man" – a term which the popular Reformation and the radical reformers used to designate, not the destitute lower classes, but the modestly propertied peasants and artisans who had no share in government. Radicals held that the common man, rather than the monk or priest, was the better Christian, a model of simple but genuine piety, better able than the clergy to understand the essential message of the gospel. Secondly, *The Prague Protest* and the popular Reformation were suffused with apocalyptic expectations, a conviction that history had reached its "harvest time," and that God was about to intervene directly in the culmination of human affairs. Anticlericalism and apocalypticism were both strong emotional forces, contributing to the urgency of the commoners' demands for change. But it is doubtful if either can explain the distinctive politics of the radical Reformation.

As a popular movement, radicals stood at the center, not at the periphery of the Reformation. But the commoners' cause was not the whole of the Reformation. The radicals came to differ with other, more moderate, "magisterial" reformers over matters of scope and strategy, as well as in their underlying attitude toward the popular movement and the prevailing structure of politics. The magisterial reformers rejected traditional ecclesiastical authority but did not question the authority of existing secular governments. They wanted reform with the approval and backing of princes and urban magistrates. They hoped, as Luther did, for a princely authorization that would leave much control in the hands of the clergy, or they felt it legitimate, as Zwingli did in Zurich, to pressure an oligarchical city council to institute change. But in the last analysis the magisterial reformers asserted a basic Erastianism. Rejecting traditional ecclesiastical authority, they clung more firmly to existing secular authority, which they held to be ordained by God. They also deeply distrusted the common man and feared that his participation in politics would lead to anarchy. They were willing to proceed only as far as authorization would allow. The ecclesiastical counterpart to this view of secular authority was the magisterial reformers' view that the power to proclaim the meaning of the gospel – and to advise secular authorities about the interpretation of Scripture – should remain in the hands of a university-trained, properly ordained clergy. Reformation radicalism was, in the first instance, "internal dissent" within the Reformation – opposition to the paradigm for change set forth by such magisterial reformers as Luther and Zwingli.

Nowhere was this internal opposition more forcefully expressed than in Müntzer's savage criticism of Luther. Beginning with his *Sermon to the Princes*, and reaching a climax with his *Highly Provoked Defense*, Müntzer's attack on Luther was simultaneously personal, theological and political. Although his final work acknowledged Luther as having inaugurated the Reformation, Müntzer excoriated him as a vain academic who led a pampered life, as the theologian of a morally flaccid faith which relied on a literal view of Scripture, and as the toadying accomplice of secular rulers whose primary aim was the exploitation of their subjects. In Müntzer's view, and in that of the radicals generally, a Reformation guided by the magisterial reformers did not go far enough; it was incapable of bringing about the sweeping improvement of society which they sought. By remaining at the disposal of existing elites, the magisterial vision of reformation failed to perceive how deeply Christian society was flawed.

Recently it has been suggested that while there were Reformation radicals – a heterogeneous group of internal critics and dissenters –

there was no "radical Reformation" in the sense of a positive movement with any cohesiveness of thought and action. Was there no more to Reformation radicalism than a heuristically useful but negative "unity in opposition"? There does not seem to be an identifiable set of theological doctrines that radicals shared and that set them apart. What are commonly claimed as distinctive emphases in radical theology – biblical literalism, opposition to sacerdotal and sacramental thinking, moral earnestness, and reliance on personal experience and direct revelations – do not clearly distinguish the radicals from the magisterial reformers. The same is true for the notion that the magisterial reformers sought to reform an existing institutional church, while the radicals aimed to reinstitute an apostolic church. In addition, efforts to construct a theological typology of the radical Reformation commonly emphasize its fundamental internal differences and tensions – e.g. those between so-called "Spiritualists" (such as Müntzer and Andreas Karlstadt in Saxony), who held that the believer may receive divine revelations independently of Scripture, and "Anabaptists" (such as Conrad Grebel or Felix Manz in Zurich), who were committed to a biblical literalism. But such categories fail to do justice to an early Reformation theological context that was as fluid as the social context. Anabaptism, formerly regarded as the most unified strand of the radical Reformation, is now seen as emerging from diverse origins, and for some early Anabaptists (e.g. Hans Hut and Hans Denck) Müntzer's influence was formative. In recent research Karlstadt too has emerged as an important influence on the Zurich radicals who were among the progenitors of Anabaptism. In short, distinctions between Spiritualists and Anabaptists are of doubtful value, especially during the early and mid-1520s, and the possibility of constructing a distinctive theology for the radical Reformation as a whole seems remote.

Despite the absence of theological unity, the radical Reformation had more cohesiveness than that of a common opposition to magisterial reformers. In the first place, many radicals thought of themselves as constituting a unified movement or informal party. At a time when communication and transportation were slow and uncertain, they sought contact and dialogue with one another. The *Letter to Thomas Müntzer* from the Zurich radicals around Conrad Grebel, for all the disagreements it mentioned, also expressed a striking awareness of a shared identity, a sense of solidarity with

Müntzer and other radicals in Saxony and Thuringia that overrode theological differences. Müntzer himself developed a network of contacts and communications with fellow radicals. He was in contact with Karlstadt and sought to win him for a political alliance. When Müntzer left Thuringia in the fall of 1524 he met with Hans Hut, probably with Hans Denck, and perhaps with his Nuremberg publisher Hans Hergot. After leaving Nuremberg, Müntzer traveled to southwestern Germany and Switzerland where he made contact with other radicals, including Balthasar Hubmaier. Similar networks of mutual contacts can be established for other radicals, suggesting that they had a sense of common identity.

In some cases this subjective sense of unity was no doubt misguided. Müntzer's efforts to win Karlstadt to a political alliance is a case in point. Nevertheless, on certain basic issues it is possible to find agreement among radicals that provided the basis for their sense of identity. This agreement was not monolithic, of course. It lacked the ideological uniformity that an organized political party or church can provide. As a political movement rather than an institution, the identity of the radical Reformation is to be found primarily in terms of two issues. Radicals were in rough agreement about a strategy for bringing about Reformation and an underlying conception of politics which it implied.

In contrast to the magisterial reformers' reliance on the support of the secular authorities and on postponing change until it was won, the radical reformers were the theorists and executors of immediate Reformation through direct action from below, a strategy which is defended in Karlstadt's tract, *Whether One Should Proceed Slowly*. Radicals took the view that each community had the right to restructure its life immediately according to the gospel as understood by the community. Like Karlstadt, the radicals also held that zealous Christians (the "elect" in the community, whether the pastor or pious laymen) had the obligation to initiate changes even if others disagreed – or, as the radicals saw it, did not "yet" understand the reasons for change. They embarked on a campaign of Reformation through provocation: shouting down sermons by those they held to be preaching something other than the pure word of God; engaging in iconoclastic assaults on images and shrines they regarded as embodying blasphemous practice and superstitious belief; transforming old usages and initiating new ones without asking the permission of superior authorities. Some refused to have their children baptized or to pay tithes and other dues, demanding that laws be changed so as to conform to the gospel.

This strategy contained no principle for compromising or adjudicating differences with those who disagreed. The radicals were convinced of the righteousness of their cause and, like the popular reformation for which they spoke, assumed that collective forms of decision-making would bear them out. But despite their image as wild-eyed fanatics, some radicals took the view that everything need not be changed at once. Müntzer at Allstedt and Hubmaier at Waldshut were critical of infant baptism yet retained the practice for parents who wanted it. Nevertheless, Müntzer at Allstedt, Karlstadt at Orlamünde, and the radicals around Grebel at Zurich all identified the magisterial reformers' justification of a gradualist approach – postponing reforms in order not to offend the weak – as a pious hypocrisy contrived to conceal their subservience to secular authorities.

The strategic differences between magisterial and radical reformers were symptomatic of a more fundamental difference in their politics, especially in their attitudes toward the authority of existing secular rulers. Above all, what gave the radicals their coherence as the Reformation's "left wing" was the rejection of a hierarchical conception of politics in which legitimate authority, whether secular or ecclesiastical, devolved from the top down. Instead, the radicals' vision of politics was rooted in notions of local autonomy and community control which also implied an egalitarianism. The radicals were the most articulate theorists of a "grass-roots" paradigm of Reformation, one based on principles of communalism that grew out of the late Middle Ages. In addition to asserting traditional communal rights to administer certain local affairs, the radical Reformation stood for the right of each local community to hear the gospel preached in pure form and regulate its life according to the gospel. The radical Reformation also advocated community control over the local church, including the rights of each congregation to choose its own minister and to control the use of ecclesiastical payments. In 1522 Luther had indicated support for this kind of communal Reformation; by 1524 he opposed it.

At first the radicals did not explicitly repudiate the existing authorities. Both Müntzer's *Sermon to the Princes* and Felix Manz's *Protest and*

Defense were appeals set before secular rulers to do what God had ordained for them. But the radicals also made the legitimacy of government conditional. The most characteristic feature of the radical Reformation was that, unlike the magisterial reformers, radicals made the legitimacy of existing political authority contingent on its willingness to serve the gospel and the needs of the community. Müntzer's *Sermon to the Princes* was also an ultimatum: if existing rulers did not carry out the proper functions of government, the community would assume the power to do this. Müntzer's final treatises of 1524 document how this contingent acceptance of secular authorities was, for some radicals, transformed into support for popular insurrection.

II. Politics and religion in radical thought

The radical reformers saw themselves as pious Christians seeking to live their faith. But it would be false to stress the religious character of their thinking in opposition to the political. The Christian faith and church were so integral to social life that thinking about religion was also inherently political thinking. Religious discourse in the sixteenth century had an unavoidable dimension of political reference, just as ideas about political authority and the polity were articulated in religious language. To say that the radical reformers saw themselves as "religious" rather than "political" in the modern sense is inaccurate; the distinction is anachronistic.

The sacrament of baptism, for example, became a focal issue for early Reformation radicals. Their opposition to infant baptism was based on more than rigorous biblicism. Baptism was a sacrament with socio-political implications. It was a rite of admission into the polity of Christians, an agreement to a social contract. The practice of infant baptism became, for radicals, compelling evidence of how corrupt Christendom had become. To admit infants to the polity transformed the Christian community into something infantile. To refuse to have one's child baptized, as did Hans Hut and others, was to repudiate the bonds connecting both parent and child with church and society. An opponent of infant baptism such as Felix Manz might protest to the Zurich council that he had never taught rebellion; but the authorities saw him as propagating subversive ideas that threatened the whole structure of authority and obedience.

Few radicals shared Luther's notion, designed to meet the political situation in Saxony, that there was a sharp division between "spiritual" and "worldly" kingdoms, and that secular rulers performed functions which had nothing to do with the Christian faith. More typical for the radicals was the view expressed by Hans Hergot that there should be "one shepherd and one flock": God's religious and political commandments were one; authority should be Christian, derived from and governing the community; and the existing divisions of "temporal" and "spiritual" authority should be done away with. State and society were not clearly separated in radical thought. Society was seen in religio-political terms, without a notion of "civil society" anterior to politics.

Nor were the radicals interested in political theory as an abstract set of doctrines about government. Instead, their writings contained a set of norms for living, practical values and principles about how socio-political life should be conducted among people who call themselves Christians. In this sense, their political theory was implicit, a sense of social morality embedded in everyday life. In its essentials this moral economy was simple and conservative, constructed from traditional notions. Christians should live together in harmony and peace (*Friede*) as brothers and sisters, and practice charity (*brüderliche Liebe*) toward one another; the well-being of the commonweal should take precedence over the private advantage of the individual (*Gemeinnutz geht vor Eigennutz*); and if disputes arise they should be settled by divine law (*das göttliche Recht*), a standard of justice derived from Scripture.

Such principles were hegemonic values, shared by virtually all in the society. But they had a different specific meaning for the radical reformers and the commoners than for the magisterial reformers and the governing authorities. What gave the ideas of the radicals political force was that many commoners shared their view that the moral economy of society was dislocated, and that the behavior of the clergy and secular rulers contradicted the values they professed. Many commoners shared both the radicals' ideal of an egalitarian and autonomous local community as the place where these traditional values were to be realized, and shared their strategy of reforming the local community without the authorization of superior authorities. By 1524 this popular communal Reformation was being realized in several places, with or without the consent of local authorities. As the popular Reformation also came to articulate social and economic grievances, some authorities sought to suppress it. In this context the radical Reformation faced the political issue that generated the greatest tension, that of the legitimacy of "active resistance," i.e. illegal or revolutionary violence. Here the fragile unity of the radical Reformation came apart. Some radicals rejected any use of coercion as a violation of Christian norms and urged the commoners to resolve differences with their lords peacefully, through negotiation. Others adopted a position they regarded as justified by the Bible, or natural law, or common sense – the right of self-defense. Christians need not always turn the other cheek; repressive violence may be met with counter-violence. Radicals holding this view provided the Peasants' War with its ideological leadership.

The question that divided the radicals was not that of revolutionary violence in the modern sense. Those who sanctioned violence, like Müntzer or the author of *To the Assembly of the Common Peasantry*, justified it on defensive grounds rather than in terms of creating a new social order. Some commoners in 1524 and 1525 may have had little need for this legitimation of their rebellion; but one should not assume that those who participated in the Peasants' War were a monolithic, revolutionary party completely certain of the rightfulness of their actions. And those radical reformers who supported the rebellion performed other ideological functions beyond supplying a justification for violence.

The apocalyptic dimension in the thought of Müntzer and other radicals, often taken as the central, determining feature of their political thought, may have been important mainly for its function in mobilizing the commoners. Müntzer's convictions that history had entered the Last Days, that the corruption of Christendom had reached an ultimate peak, and that the time had arrived for the elect, the commoners, to rise up and separate themselves from the godless, their ecclesiastical and secular rulers – all this lent a powerful sense of urgency to action, but that may be all. There is scant evidence that either Müntzer or other leaders of the uprising were motivated by specifically millenarian dreams of a perfect society, the earthly realization of the kingdom of God, which would endure for a thousand years. Beyond their function as mobilizers, Reformation radicals sought to provide spiritual and moral guidance for the insurrection, sometimes acting as secretaries, chaplains, and charismatic spiritual advisers to peasant armies. They cautioned troops to be mindful that they were fighting for the honor of God and not for selfish, material or "creaturely" motives. And, as in the case of *To the Assembly of the Common Peasantry*, they presented arguments for the necessity of solidarity. Their warnings about what the failure of the uprising would lead to – an even harsher system of arbitrary princely oppression – were an accurate prediction of German politics in the age of absolutism.

Radical reformers, both those who defended violence and those opposing it, also made a significant contribution to individual political programs which were drawn up during the Peasants' War. In late 1524, in the spring of 1525 – and in the case of Michael Gaismair in Tyrol, in 1526 – the political vision of some radicals solidified as they began to think about alternatives to existing institutions and political principles. Some radical reformers developed political theories that promoted the principles of popular sovereignty, republicanism, and civil equality.

Müntzer's final treatises presented no proposals about government beyond an implicit theory of popular sovereignty in temporal and ecclesiastical affairs: God gave both the power of the sword and the power to remit sin to the community of Christians. As the Peasants' War unfolded, the principle of popular sovereignty led to a variety of republican constitutional theories. For the author of *To the Assembly of the Common Peasantry* the clear alternative to existing principalities ruled by hereditary monarchs – associated, in the work, with both tyranny and blasphemy – was a Swiss-style republicanism, a decentralized polity with elected leaders. Gaismair also proposed a republican constitution for Tyrol, one with a hierarchy of elective government that extended from the local community to the central government of the territory. Unlike the Tyrol, some regions in Upper Germany lacked an existing territorial assembly that could serve as an institutional model to be recast on popular lines. In these territories republicanism took the form of a *Bund* – a covenant, federation or league that would link the local communities of a territory. *The Memmingen Federal Constitution* and *The Document of Articles of the Black Forest Peasants* set forth the fundamentals of such a *Bund* and the penalties for refusing to adhere to it.

The principle of civil equality also emerged during the Peasants' War. Radicals moved from rejecting clerical privilege to the rejection of noble privilege as well; their republicanism led them to break with a concept of authority based on social estate. A basic feature of Gaismair's Tyrolean constitution, in particular, was the elimination of all "freedoms" – i.e. privileges and immunities – which some individuals enjoyed at the expense of others. Hans Hergot as well as Gaismair described publicly financed social welfare systems that local government should provide to care for the needy. But the civil equality envisaged by radicals did not mean the elimination of economic inequalities. Gaismair's program, for example, did not call for the expropriation of noble property. Although he set forth statesmanlike plans for the economic development of the whole territory, Gaismair nowhere mentioned land reform or redistribution. Sebastian Lotzer and Christoph Schappeler, who gave *The Twelve Articles* its final form, proposed moderate and conciliatory means for resolving property differences between the local community and the claimants to economic resources that the community had alienated.

Although some radical reformers advanced principles of popular sovereignty, republicanism, and civil equality, they were not advocates of democracy in the modern sense. The central social assumption in such programs as Gaismair's or Hergot's was of a male-dominated polity composed of modestly propertied householders – the "common man" as the term was then used. Women and the considerable number of those without property were excluded. Nevertheless, the programs of the Peasants' War implied a transformation of the existing political and social orders so sweeping that they were revolutionary. This is true even of conciliatory programs such as *The Twelve Articles* – or, in an urban context, the influential *Forty-six Frankfurt Articles* – to say nothing of the more radical programs, such as Gaismair's. But the revolutionary goal of sixteenth-century radicals was neither modern democracy nor socialism; their aim was an egalitarian Christian communalism.

III. The radical Reformation after the Peasants' War

In most parts of the empire, the Peasants' War was crushed in a series of battles in May 1525; the Tyrol, where the insurrection continued until 1526, was an exception. Elsewhere the great slaughter of peasant armies at Böblingen (12 May), Frankenhausen (15 May) and Zabern (17 May) was the decisive military turning-point. Except for the few who refused to concede defeat – such as Hans Hut, who continued to preach resistance into the summer of 1525, or Hans Römer, who plotted to seize Erfurt at the end of 1527 – the issue of violence went underground, at least for a time. It resurfaced again briefly among revolutionary Anabaptists at Münster in 1534–35. How did the crushing defeat affect the radical Reformation? In general, the defeat resulted in new divisions. The tenuous unity of a widespread popular movement, based on the hope that Christian society as a whole might be sweepingly transformed in favor of the common man and the local community, collapsed. The radical Reformation, marked from the beginning by internal tensions, broke apart.

Among the issues that radicals now had to confront was one of interpreting the defeat and salvaging what they could. For many, defeat did not alter their fundamental vision. Rather it could be explained in terms of the vision and had lessons to teach. Some, like Hubmaier, accepted Luther's judgment that the military defeat was a confirmation that the commoners' cause was inspired by the devil. But for many radicals the rulers' brutal repression of the commoners was a confirmation that existing authorities were as unchristian as the radicals had maintained. Perhaps typical was the view of Michael Sattler, who referred to the prevailing structure of ecclesiastical and secular power simply as "the abomination." Mystical principles, derived in part from Müntzer, provided Denck and Hut with a vocabulary to explain the defeat. It was due to attachment of the "creaturely" – to greedy, selfish interests – and a failure to cleave to spiritual values. Hut and Hergot evidently took the defeat as confirmation that they were indeed living at the time of the Apocalypse.

Those writing in the immediate aftermath, especially Denck and Hut, returned to the fundamental dissatisfactions with the magisterial reformers, particularly Luther, that had generated the radical Reformation. In different ways both took up the criticism of the magisterial Reformation's moral unproductiveness, its failure to transform individual and social behavior. Denck used the issue of "divine law" – a subject charged with political significance since it had been a basic motto and demand of the Peasants' War – to polemicize against Luther's understanding of justification. For Denck the test of faith was behavior, and without moral improvement there could be no Reformation worthy of the name. He also came to the mystical and antinomian conclusion that once the real, spiritual meaning of divine law as a law of love had been taken to heart, the believer would be freed from all external, written laws and regulations. Love issues, and can revoke, all laws. Such views were subversive – intended to call into question the basis of existing law and to liberate the faith of the commoner from the constraints of an official church.

In Hans Hut's work on baptism the appeal to the religious potential of the common man and the attack on the moral failures of the learned clergy were more explicit. Hut argued for an understanding of the gospel that was independent of Scripture and learning, derivable from nature and from the labor of commoners. For Hut the essential message of his "gospel of all creatures" was a law of suffering: just as nature suffers, as it is transformed through work to suit human aims, mankind must suffer as it is transformed by the action of God to suit divine purpose. Both Denck and Hut were influenced by Müntzer's mysticism, with Hut's gospel of suffering representing the passive converse of the activism of Denck's law of love. In both writers there was more than a moralizing "privatization" of the radical Reformation as dissent was driven inward. Hut's view, that the authentic message of the gospel is one of suffering, offered consolation in the aftermath of the Peasants' War. And his conception of baptism was an admonition to surviving groups of radicals to prepare themselves for the consequences of their refusal to conform. What neither Denck nor Hut provided was a strategy for the survival of the radical Reformation under conditions of persecution. This was the contribution of radicals from southwestern Germany and Switzerland.

By 1527 the authorities' military mop-up and the immediate judicial retribution for the rising were giving way to more systematic efforts to track down leaders and root out surviving pockets of continuing disobedience and radical religiosity. The authorities commonly stigmatized those they were pursuing as "Anabaptists" – practitioners of "rebaptism," a crime punishable by death. Anabaptism, the most cohesive strand of radicalism emerging from the Peasants' War, sprang from diverse sources. As anything like an organized movement, it began during the uprising itself. Even that part of the movement which developed in upper Germany and Switzerland – especially in the city and the canton of Zurich – in the months after January 1525, was marked by internal tensions. Some, especially those from cantonal villages, advocated a communal Reformation and the right of self-defense. Others, especially those from Zurich who were disappointed by Zwingli's version of a communal Reformation, called for nonresistance and for separation from the existing polity. Some early Anabaptists shifted from one position to another. After the Peasants' War, these two views solidified into opposing camps. In addition to differing over the legitimacy of force, each represented an alternative strategy for the survival of the radical Reformation.

The sectarian implications of nonresisting separatism were first clearly formulated by Michael Sattler in *The Schleitheim Articles*. By passing over such divisive issues among Anabaptists as whether Christians were to pay taxes to ungodly authorities, Sattler profiled more sharply the sectarian mentality. True Christians were to separate themselves, insofar as possible, from "the world," the existing polity. They were not to swear oaths, become magistrates, bear arms, or participate in assemblies or religious services that were popish or "neo-popish" (i.e. those of the magisterial reformers). Instead, Christians were to gather themselves into purified communities of true believers committed to the discipleship of Christ. These communities were defined sacramentally through the baptism of mature believers and the administration of the Lord's Supper, "the breaking of the bread," as a ritual celebration of the community of true Christians. The "ban," a combination of exile and excommunication, was used to punish backsliders. The community's pastor was to be chosen and supported by the community. The renunciation of force, taken from Christ's command not to resist evil (Mt. 5:39), was a moral principle that functioned both to sever the bonds with society at large and to define the group internally.

Balthasar Hubmaier's *On the Sword* offered a refutation of the scriptural basis of non-violent separatism and argued for the legitimacy of Christians using instruments of coercion, "the sword." Hubmaier did not grant the powers of coercion to Christian governments reluctantly, aware that moral values are inevitably corrupted by coercion but accepting the necessity of its use. His defense of force was positive. Once one accepted the notion that it is better for a Christian than a non-Christian to judge disputes among Christians (however sinful such contentions may themselves be), it followed for Hubmaier that judges must have the means to enforce their judgment in order to protect the innocent.

However, Hubmaier assigned the right to employ coercion not to the Christian community as a whole but to magistrates whom God has called to perform this function. Hubmaier legitimized the coercive power exercised by such magistrates while simultaneously insisting that the Christian community had no right to take extralegal action against the authorities if they proved to be ungodly or tryannical. There is nothing of the earlier radicals' conditional allegiance to existing authorities. In the end Hubmaier reaffirmed a conception of politics that was conventional for theologians – the existing political authorities are ordained by God; no active resistance against them is justified.

As strategies, the views of Sattler and Hubmaier were both partly successful. Hubmaier's aim was to try to preserve an Anabaptism that was not divorced from the larger polity, by finding a pious protector, a prince who would tolerate reformed communities in his territory, and who would have the power of the sword to protect them. Hubmaier's program for survival was one capable of succeeding in special circumstances, but the key to its success lay not with the radicals but with the magistrates. Princely tolerance could prove reversible, as Hubmaier himself discovered in Moravia. When it did, the most that radicals could count on was permission to go elsewhere in search of another temporary haven. Sattler, the renegade Benedictine influenced by monastic ideals of withdrawal from the world, formulated a survival strategy which was more self-reliant. Nonresisting separatism enabled some concealed groups of radicals to survive persecution and permitted some radical ideals to be retained. But the effort to transform society as a whole was largely sacrificed. Since the use of force even for self-defense was renounced, the ability to survive persecution depended on the extent to which authorities either remained ignorant of a group's existence, or were lax about enforcing laws against dissenters.

In contrast to Sattler or Hubmaier, Hergot's *On the New Transformation of the Christian Life* offered no clear program for survival; there is only the hope of an imminent and divinely produced upheaval that would result in a transformed society. The apocalypticism also contained a revolutionary impulse in Hergot's lack of a clear distinction between the hand of God and the hand of the common man as the agent of this change. Without strategic concerns, Hergot's work nevertheless functioned in another way that was important for the continuation of the radical Reformation – as a reminder of the political and social values for which the Peasants' War had been fought. This reminder took the form of prophecy. Hergot's account of his prophetic vision – of a Christian society oriented exclusively toward the honor of God and the well-being of the commonweal – may in fact have been written during the rebellion. Although Hergot's utopian vision included a hierarchical order of elective world government, the upper levels of his republican political system were abstract, a speculative superstructure without a clear function other than that of delineating a world of peace and unity. Hergot's real interest and the values to which he gave most convincing testimony lay at the local level, that of the *Flur* or agrarian village. He characterized the local community in terms of economic self-sufficiency and liberation from urban exploitation; the absence of privilege and the presence of a publicly financed system of charitable assistance; political autonomy built on the community's choice of its own leader; and the rejection of a system of divided temporal and spiritual overlordship. The work expressed concretely the common man's understanding of the social and political implications of the religious principles which animated the radical Reformation and the Peasants' War.

In the aftermath of the Peasants' War it was inevitable that there would be confusion and division as radicals tried to fathom the meaning of the defeat for their cause, and to devise new ways of continuing their struggle. Hergot's work provided a compass, oriented toward the socio-political values for which the conflict had been fought, and it provided a measure against which to test new strategies. His unusual, prophetic vision of a transformed Christian society was perhaps the most richly detailed statement of the political ideas and values of the radical Reformation.

Chronology 1521–1528

1521

3 January	Luther excommunicated by Pope Leo X.
16 April	Müntzer leaves Zwickau following civil unrest.
16–18 April	Luther appears before the Diet of Worms.
4 May	Luther goes into hiding at Wartburg castle.
8 May	Emperor Charles V signs the Worms Edict declaring Luther and his followers imperial outlaws.
June	Müntzer travels to Bohemia.
November	Müntzer's *Prague Protest*.
December	Death of Pope Leo X, followed by election of Adrian VI.
25 December	Karlstadt at Wittenberg does away with vestments and the notion of the Mass as a sacrifice, distributing communion in both forms.
27 December	The so-called "Zwickau prophets" arrive at Wittenberg and urge more radical change.

1522

January–February	Civil unrest in Wittenberg.
21 January	Imperial governing council issues the Nuremberg Edict prohibiting ecclesiastical innovation.
24 January	A community chest is introduced at Wittenberg.
9–16 March	Luther returns from the Wartburg castle to Wittenberg and preaches "Invocavit Sermons"

	against Karlstadt's reforms.
Lent	Followers of Zwingli at Zurich publicly violate the laws on fasting.
27 August	Imperial knights, led by Franz von Sickingen and Ulrich von Hutten, attack the archbishop of Trier.
Autumn	Preacher Simon Stumpf at Höngg near Zurich calls for a refusal to pay the tithe.

1523

29 January	First Zurich Disputation between Zwingli and a representative of the bishop of Constance begins the official Reformation at Zurich.
February	Karlstadt leaves Wittenberg for Orlamünde.
March	Luther's *On Secular Authority, The Extent to Which it Should be Obeyed.*
March	Müntzer arrives at Allstedt in electoral Saxony, and introduces a German liturgy.
July	Unrest at Mühlhausen leads to adoption of the Mühlhausen Recess.
14 September	Death of Pope Adrian VI, followed by election of Clement VII.
26–28 October	Second Zurich Disputation completes the division between Zwingli and his radical followers led by Grebel and Manz.

1524

24 March	Destruction of the Mallerbach chapel near Allstedt by Müntzer and his followers.
26 May	First peasant uprising in the Black Forest and at Forchheim, Franconia, mark the beginning of the Peasants' War.
June	Luther's *Open Letter to the Princes of Saxony Concerning the Rebellious Spirit* (i.e. Müntzer).
13 July	Müntzer's *Sermon to the Princes* preached at Allstedt castle.
July	Karlstadt's *Letter from the Community of Orlamünde to the People of Allstedt* rejects Müntzer's offer of political alliance.

31 July–1 August	Interrogation of Müntzer and Allstedt councillors at Weimar; Müntzer ordered to close Allstedt press, dissolve his Christian League, and not forestall the prosecution of the Mallerbach culprits.
7 August	Müntzer flees Allstedt, arrives a week later at Mühlhausen in Thuringia.
19 August	Rebellion in Mühlhausen.
September	Karlstadt and Westerburg expelled from electoral Saxony.
5 September	The Zurich radicals around Grebel write their *Letter to Thomas Müntzer*.
22–23 September	*The Eleven Mühlhausen Articles*, influenced by Müntzer and Pfeiffer.
27 September	Müntzer and Pfeiffer expelled from Mühlhausen.
November	Karlstadt's *Whether One Should Proceed Slowly* printed at Basel with the help of Westerburg and Manz, then distributed in Zurich by Manz.
November/December	Müntzer's *Highly Provoked Defense* printed at Nuremberg by Hieronymous Hölzel.
December/January	Manz writes his *Protest and Defense* to the city council of Zurich.

1525

15 January	Disputation at Zurich on infant baptism results in the condemnation of those opposing it.
17–22 January	First adult baptism at Zurich.
21 January	Denck expelled from Nuremberg following his involvement in the heresy trial of three "godless" painters.
6 March	Upper German peasant armies assemble at Memmingen, and form a Christian Union of the Allgäu, Baltringen and Lake Constance armies on the basis of *The Memmingen Federal Constitution*.
19 March	Lotzer's and Schappeler's *The Twelve Articles* published at Memmingen.

13–20 April	*The Forty-six Frankfurt Articles*, influenced by Gerhard Westerburg.
17 April	The peasants of Württemberg and Franconia conclude the Treaty of Weingarten with the Swabian League.
May	*To the Assembly of the Common Peasantry* printed at Nuremberg.
5 May	Death of Saxon elector Frederick the Wise; Luther's *Against the Heavenly Prophets* and *Against the Robbing and Murdering Hordes of the Peasants* printed.
8 May	The peasant army of the Black Forest sends *The Document of Articles*, attached to *The Memmingen Federal Constitution*, to the city of Villingen near Freiburg im Breisgau.
9 May	Peasant uprising in Tyrol.
12 May	Defeat of Württemberg peasant army at the battle of Böblingen.
13 May	Rebellious peasants in Tyrol choose Gaismair as leader.
15 May	Defeat of Thuringian peasant army at Battle of Frankenhausen; Müntzer captured, Hut escapes.
17 May	Defeat of Alsatian peasant army at Battle of Zabern.
27 May	Beheading of Müntzer and Pfeiffer outside the walls of Mühlhausen.
4 June	Defeat of Franconian peasant army at Battle of Ingolstadt.
9 June	Army of the Swabian League occupies Memmingen; Schappeler flees.
Summer	Hut continues to advocate rebellion.
3 September	Peasant uprising in East Prussia.
5 December	Hubmaier flees as Waldshut is conquered by Austrian troops.
1526	
February	Gaismair's *Territorial Constitution for Tyrol*.
7 March	The Zurich council introduces the death

	penalty for the crime of "rebaptism"; Manz, Grebel, Blaurock, and others sentenced to life imprisonment.
March	Renewed peasant uprising in the bishopric of Salzburg.
26 May	Hut baptized by Denck at Augsburg.
May/June	Grebel dies of the plague in the Gray Leagues, Switzerland.
July	Hubmaier arrives at Nikolsburg, Moravia and begins to develop an Anabaptist communal reformation under princely protection.
27 August	The First Diet of Speyer issues a recess interpreted by the evangelical estates as allowing the introduction of the Reformation.
29 August	Battle of Mohács, King Louis II of Hungary and Bohemia killed. Ferdinand of Austria becomes king.

1527	
5 January	Manz executed by drowning at Zurich.
February	Sattler's *The Schleitheim Articles*.
6 May	Sack of Rome by a German imperial army.
May	Debate at Nikolsburg between Hut and Hubmaier leads to Hut's imprisonment, then flight.
20 May	Sattler executed by burning at Rottenburg am Neckar, Hergot by beheading at Leipzig.
June	Hubmaier's *On the Sword* written at Nikolsburg to refute the nonresisting and separatist *Stäbler* group.
16 June	Visitation instructions issued in electoral Saxony to construct an evangelical church on a territorial basis.
August	The so-called "Martyrs' Synod" of Anabaptist leaders at Augsburg.
Autumn	Denck dies of the plague at Basel.
September	Hut arrested in Augsburg.
December	Hut dies in an Augsburg prison.

1528

| 4 January | Imperial governing council at Speyer issues a mandate threatening Anabaptists with the death penalty. |
| 10 March | Hubmaier executed by burning at Vienna. |

Bibliographical note

General works on the radical Reformation

G. Williams, *The Radical Reformation* (Philadelphia, 1962), remains the standard survey, theologically conceived and sweeping in scope, now outdated on some details and inconveniently organized. M. Mullett, *Radical Religious Movements in Early Modern Europe* (London, 1980), is equally broad in scope and uses innovative interpretative categories. H.-J. Goertz, ed., *Profiles of Radical Reformers* (Kitchener, Ont./Scottdale, Pa., 1982), is a valuable collection of biographical sketches. Two collections of important articles are H. Hillerbrand, ed., *Radical Tendencies in the Reformation: Divergent Perspectives* (Kirksville, Mo., 1988), and J. Stayer and W. Packull, eds., *The Anabaptists and Thomas Müntzer* (Dubuque, Iowa, 1980). On the link between mystical theology and radical politics see S. Ozment, *Mysticism and Dissent* (New Haven/London, 1973). A. Friesen, *Reformation and Utopia* (Cologne, 1974) criticizes the Marxist interpretation of the early Reformation and the Peasants' War as an early bourgeois revolution. On Luther's view of the radicals see M. U. Edwards, Jr., *Luther and the False Brethren* (Stanford, 1975), and on Lutheran efforts to stigmatize the radicals see J. S. Oyer, *Lutheran Reformers against Anabaptists* (The Hague, 1964). An older important comparative study of Luther's and Müntzer's political theory is C. Hinrichs, *Luther und Müntzer: Ihre Auseinandersetzung über Obrigkeit und Widerstandsrecht* (Berlin, 1952). The best short introduction to the early Reformation as a social movememt is R. W. Scribner, *The German Reformation* (Atlantic Highlands, N.J., 1986). H.-J. Goertz,

Pfaffenhaß und groß Geschrei (Munich, 1987) examines early Reformation anticlericalism as a key to social history. R. van Dülmen, *Reformation als Revolution* (Munich, 1977) puts the early Reformation in a context of political upheaval. P. Blickle, *Gemeindereformation* (Munich, 1987) deals with the program of the communal Reformation during the early 1520s.

The Peasants' War

F. Engels, *The Peasant War in Germany* (New York, 1966; 1st edn., 1850) is the classic Marxist account. The most important new interpretation is P. Blickle, *The Revolution of 1525* (Baltimore/London, 1981), especially strong on socio-economic causation and political programs. Two important collections of articles are J. Bak, ed., *The German Peasant War of 1525* (London, 1976) and B. Scribner and G. Benecke, eds., *The German Peasant War of 1525 – New Viewpoints* (London, 1979). Two collaborative accounts of the Peasants' War as a whole are the work of West German historians, H. Buzello, P. Blickle, and R. Endres, eds., *Der deutsche Bauernkrieg* (Paderborn/Munich/Vienna/Zurich, 1984), and, for the East German Marxist view of the early Reformation and Peasants' War as an "early bourgeois revolution," A. Laube, M. Steinmetz, and G. Vogler, *Illustrierte Geschichte der deutschen frühbürgerlichen Revolution* (East Berlin, 1974). For evaluations of Blickle's interpretation and other literature which appeared at the time of the 1975 commemoration of the Peasants' War see T. Scott, "The Peasants' War: A Historiographical Review," *Historical Journal* 22 (1979), 693–720 and 953–74, and H. C. E. Midelfort, "The Revolution of 1525? Recent Studies of the Peasants' War," *Central European History* 11 (1978), 189–206. An analysis of the Peasants' War as a political movement is H. Buzello, *Der Deutsche Bauernkrieg als politische Bewegung mit besonderer Berücksichtigung der anonymen Flugschrift "An die Versamlung gemayner Pawerschafft"* (Berlin, 1969). For a systematic overview of the political programs of the Peasants' War see F. Ganseuer, *Der Staat des "gemeinen Mannes." Gattungstypologie und Programmatik des politischen Schrifttums von Reformation und Bauernkrieg* (Frankfurt/Bern/New York, 1985). On the socio-political dimension of the early Reformation and the links between it and social protest see P. Blickle, H.-C. Rublack, and W. Schulze, *Religion, Politics and Social*

Protest (London, 1984), A. Laube, "Social Arguments in early Reformation Pamphlets and their Significance for the German Peasants' War," *Social History* 12 (1987), 361–78, and W. Packull, "The Image of the 'Common Man' in the early Pamphlets of the Reformation (1520-1525)," *Historical Reflections* 12 (1985), 253–77. On the early Reformation pamphlet debate over the use of force see P. Lucke, *Gewalt und Gegengewalt in den Flugschriften der Reformation* (Göppingen, 1974). On the importance of anticlericalism during the Peasants' War see Henry J. Cohn, "Anticlericalism in the German Peasants' War," *Past and Present* 83 (1979), 3–31. J. Maurer, *Prediger im Bauernkrieg* (Stuttgart, 1979) shows the extent to which evangelical clergy supported the Peasants' War. On the connection between emergent Anabaptism and the Peasants' War see W. Packull, "The Origin of Swiss Anabaptism in the Context of the Reformation of the Common Man," *Journal of Mennonite Studies* 3 (1985), 36–59; his "In Search of the 'Common Man' in Early German Anabaptist Ideology," *Sixteenth Century Journal* 17 (1986), 51–67; and J. Stayer, "Anabaptists and Future Anabaptists in the Peasants' War," *Mennonite Quarterly Review* 62 (1988), 99–139. A speculative study of Müntzer's influence in southwestern Germany and of the relationship between three documents central to the Peasants' War there is G. Seebass, *Artikelbrief, Bundesordnung und Verfassungsentwurf* (Heidelberg, 1988).

Anabaptism

H.-J. Goertz, *Die Täufer, Geschichte und Deutung* (2nd edn., Munich, 1988) is a recent survey of the development of the Anabaptist movement, and H.-J. Goertz, ed., *Umstrittenes Täufertum 1525–1975, neue Forschungen* (Göttingen, 1977) is an important collection of articles. J. Stayer, *Anabaptists and the Sword* (2nd edn., Lawrence, Kansas, 1976), examines the theories of secular power expressed by major Anabaptist leaders, and his article "The Anabaptists," in S. Ozment, ed., *Reformation Europe: A Guide to Research* (St. Louis, 1982) is a reliable introduction to current research. H. Hillerbrand, *Die politische Ethik des oberdeutschen Täufertums* (Leiden/Cologne, 1962) examines the political ethics of upper German Anabaptism. C.-P. Clasen, *Anabaptism, A Social History, 1525-1618* (Ithaca, N.Y./London, 1972) is a detailed sociological examination of the various branches of the movement. On Anabaptist economic views see P. J. Klassen, *The Economics of Anabaptism, 1525–1560* (London/ The Hague/Paris, 1964). W. Packull, *Mysticism and the Early South German-Austrian Anabaptist Movement* (Scottdale, Pa. / Kitchener, Ont., 1977) investigates the mystical motif in the theology of Hut and Denck. On the origins of Anabaptism see J. Stayer, W. Packull, and K. Deppermann, "From Monogenesis to Polygenesis: The Historical Discussion of Anabaptist Origins," *Mennonite Quarterly Review* 49 (1979), 83–121. Two articles assessing recent historiographical developments are J. Coggins, "Toward a Definition of 16th Century Anabaptism: 20th Century Historiography of the Radical Reformation," *Journal of Mennonite Studies* 4 (1986), 183–207, and W. Packull, "Some Reflections on the State of Anabaptist History: The Demise of a Normative Vision," *Studies in Religion* 8 (1979), 313–23.

Biographical studies

G. Rupp, *Patterns of Reformation* (London/Philadelphia, 1969), includes studies of Karlstadt and Müntzer. On Müntzer see T. Scott, *Thomas Müntzer, Theology and Revolution in the German Reformation* (London/New York, 1989), which is now the best life in English, and E. Gritsch, *Thomas Müntzer, A Tragedy of Errors* (Minneapolis, 1989), a sympathetic Lutheran account. H.-J. Goertz, *Innere und äußere Ordnung in der Theologie Thomas Müntzers* (Leiden, 1967) stresses the mystical component in Müntzer's thought; and his *Thomas Müntzer: Mystiker, Apokalyptiker, Revolutionär* (Munich, 1989) is a perceptive biography. Of the many other works which appeared in 1989 to commemorate the putative 500th anniversary of Müntzer's birth, U. Bubenheimer, *Thomas Müntzer, Herkunft und Bildung* (Leiden, 1989) is a major study of Müntzer's origins and education, and S. Bräuer and H. Junghans, eds., *Der Theologe Thomas Müntzer* (Göttingen, 1989) a valuable collection of studies on Müntzer's theology. Two new Marxist biographies are G. Vogler, *Thomas Müntzer* (East Berlin, 1989) and G. Brendler, *Thomas Müntzer, Geist und Faust* (East Berlin, 1989). Two important studies of the radicalization of Karlstadt's theology are C. Pater, *Karlstadt as the Father of the Baptist Movement: The Emergence of Lay Protestantism* (Toronto, 1984) and R. Sider, *Andreas Bodenstein von Karlstadt: The Development of His Thought, 1517–1525* (Leiden, 1974). On Grebel see the still useful study by H. Bender, *Conrad Grebel ca. 1498–1526. The Founder of the Swiss Breth-*

ren, Sometimes called Anabaptists (Goshen, Ind., 1950). On Gaismair's religious and political ideas see W. Klaassen, *Michael Gaismair, Revolutionary and Reformer* (Leiden, 1978). On Gaismair's role in the Tyrolean uprising and his political ideas see J. Bücking, *Michael Gaismair, Reformer, Sozialrebell, Revolutionär. Seine Rolle im Tiroler "Bauernkrieg" (1525/32)* (Stuttgart, 1978). T. Bergsten, *Balthasar Hubmaier, Anabaptist Theologian and Martyr*, ed. W. R. Estep, Jr. (Valley Forge, Pa. 1978) is an abridged translation of the German edition. C. Snyder, *The Life and Thought of Michael Sattler* (Scottdale, Pa./Kitchener, Ont., 1984) emphasizes the influence of Sattler's Benedictine background. W. Klaassen, "The Schleitheim Articles and the New Transformation of Christian Living," *Historical Reflections* 14 (1987), 95–111, compares the thought of Sattler and Hergot.

1   Thomas Müntzer, *The Prague Protest*

A protest about the condition of the Bohemians[1]

I, Thomas Müntzer, born in Stolberg and residing in Prague, the city of the precious and holy fighter Jan Hus,[2] think that the loud and moving trumpets [that once sounded in this city] were filled with the praise of the holy spirit. With my whole heart I will testify about my faith and lamentingly complain about present conditions to the whole church of the elect and to the whole world, wherever this document may be received. Christ and all of the elect who have known me from my youth on confirm such a project.

I pledge on my highest honor that I have applied my most concentrated and highest diligence in order that I might have or obtain a higher knowledge than other people of the foundations on which the holy and invincible Christian faith is based. The truth makes me so

---

[1] This work was not published by Müntzer but survived in several different manuscript versions – a Latin version, a shorter German version, a longer German version, which is presented here, and a Czech version, which is a partial translation of the longer German one and which must have been prepared for Müntzer. The sequence of the first three versions cannot be definitively established, but the longer German version, dated 25 November 1521, is the most radical of the three. The translation is based on the text in *MSB*, 495–505.

[2] Jan Hus or John Huss (c.1369–1415) was the Czech leader of a reform movement in the Bohemian church. As a theologian he was influenced by Wyclif, and Hus came to assert the ultimate authority of Scripture over the church, and the right and duty of the state to supervise the church. He was excommunicated and burned at the stake by the Council of Constance. In Bohemia he was viewed as a martyr, and after his death a massive rebellion occurred which was simultaneously a religious struggle against the Roman Catholic church, a Czech national conflict against the Holy Roman Empire, and a social upheaval directed against the power of the landed magnates. The rebellion led to a series of Hussite Wars in the first half of the fifteenth century. In travelling to Prague, Müntzer undoubtedly hoped to make contact with or to rekindle the radicalism that Hus had initially inspired.

bold as to say that no pitch-smeared parson[3] and surely no pseudo-spiritual monk can say anything about the foundation of the faith in even its smallest point. In addition, many people have complained with me that they too, burdened by the unbearable and evident deception of the clergy, were never consoled, and that they have had to direct their desires and works carefully in the faith and to elevate themselves spiritually. The clergy have never been able to discover, nor will they ever, the beneficial tribulations and useful abyss which the providential spirit meets as it empties itself.[4] The spirit of the fear of God has never possessed the clergy, but the elect firmly cling to this spirit as their only goal. The elect are submerged and drowned in an outpouring of this spirit (which the world cannot tolerate). In brief, each person must receive the holy spirit in a sevenfold way,[5] otherwise he neither hears nor understands the living God.

Freely and boldly I declare that I have never heard a single donkey-fart doctor of theology, in the smallest of his divisions and points, even whisper, to say nothing of speaking loudly, about the order (established in God and all his creatures). The most prominent among the Christians (I mean the hell-based parsons) have never had even a whiff of the whole or undivided perfection[6] [God's order], which is a uniform measure superior to all parts, 1 Corinthians 13[:10], Luke 6[:40], Ephesians 4[:3], Acts 2[:27], 15[:18?] and 17[:24–26]. Again and again I hear nothing from the doctors of theology but the mere words of Scripture, which they have knavishly stolen from the Bible like malicious thieves and cruel murderers. They will be damned for this theft by God himself, who spoke thusly through Jeremiah 23[:18], "Behold, I have said to the prophets: I never once spoke to those who steal my words, each from his

---

[3] A reference to the sacrament of ordination.

[4] *dye heilsamen anfechtunge und nutzbarlichen abegrundt des fursehen gemutes in seiner lehrmachung*; here, and elsewhere in his writings, Müntzer used the language of the German mystics to describe a process of purgation through suffering that the soul must undergo before it is prepared to receive divine revelations.

[5] In addition to the traditional theological notion of the seven gifts of the holy spirit that are conferred by sanctifying grace, Müntzer was also drawing on the ideas of Tauler's mysticism.

[6] *das gantze adder unvolkomene*; literally, "the whole or imperfect." The text would appear to be defective at this point. *MSB*, 496, n. 23, suggests that the word *unvolkomene* may have resulted from an unintended contraction and that what Müntzer intended to write was *ungetheylt vokomene* (undivided perfection). This view is supported by the following description of God's order as "a uniform measure superior to all parts."

neighbor, for they deceive my people, and they usurp my words and make them putrid in their stinking lips and whoring throats. For they deny that my spirit speaks to people." So they display their monasticism with flattering, high mockery. And they say that the holy spirit gives them an invincible witness that they are children of God, Romans 8[:16], Psalm 192.[7]

It is certainly not surprising that these damned people, the clergy, in their impudence are opposed to my teachings. For Jeremiah (in the aforementioned chapter 23 [Jer. 23:18] says of their person, "Who has stood in the counsel of the Lord? Who has perceived and heard the speech of God? Who has marked it, or who can say that he has heard God speaking?" At the present time God will pour forth his invincible wrath over such arrogant people, hardened like blocks of oak, callous to all good, Titus 1[:7], in that they deny the basic salvation of faith. For otherwise they would repudiate their lives, and defend the elect like an iron wall from the harm of the blasphemers, as Ezekiel says (in chapter 3, etc.). But, as they are, nothing else comes out of their hearts, brains, and snouts than derision about such revelations. Who among all people can still say that these parsons are the true servants of God, bearing witness to the divine word? And that they are fearless preachers of divine grace? They have been smeared by the Nimrodian papacy[8] with the oil of the sinner, Psalm 141[:5], which flows from the head down to the feet and befouls and poisons the whole Christian church. That is to say, the parsons come from the devil, who has corrupted the foundation and ground of their heart, as it is written in Psalm 5[:10], for they are entirely without the possession of the holy spirit. Therefore, they have been ordained by the consecration of the devil, their rightful father, who with them cannot hear the true living word of God – John [8:38–44], Isaiah 24[:18], and Hosea 4[:6?]. Zechariah 11[:17] also says that such people are scarecrows in the green bean-fields.[9]

And in sum, this much can be said: the parsons are damned people, John 3[:18], who have already been long condemned. And indeed

---

[7] Evidently an error; perhaps Müntzer intended Ps. 89:7.

[8] *vom hunrotussem babst*; the text here is mutilated; the Czech version contains the description of the papacy as Nimrodian. Nimrod in the Old Testament is described as a hunter, but Müntzer evidently saw him as a figure of depredation; see Gen. 10:8 and 2 Chr. 1:10.

[9] The reference to Zechariah seems clearly wrong; Jer. 10:5 speaks of heathen idols, evidently equated by Müntzer with the clergy, being like scarecrows in a cucumber field.

they are not the least, but the most highly placed damned rogues, who have been everywhere in the world from the very beginning, set as a plague on poor people, who as a result are truly coarse. These poor people receive absolutely no justice from either God or men, as Paul adequately showed in Galatians [4:22ff.], where he describes two kinds of people.

Therefore, as long as heaven and earth stand, these villainous and treacherous parsons are of no use to the church in even the slightest matter. For they deny the voice of the bridegroom, which is a truly certain sign that they are a pack of devils. How could they then be God's servants, bearers of his word, which they shamelessly deny with their whore's brazenness? For all true parsons must have revelations, so that they are certain of their cause, 1 Corinthians 14[:30]. But the parsons, with their stubborn hearts, say that this is impossible. Because they are convinced of this – after they presume to have devoured the whole of Scripture – they shall be struck down with the words of St. Paul, 2 Corinthians 3[:3], just like thunder and lightning, for there Paul makes the distinction between the elect and the damned.

The gospel and the whole of Scripture are closed to some people – Isaiah 29[:11] and 22[:22] on the key of David, Revelation 3[:7] on the locked book. Ezekiel unlocked past events.[10] Christ says in Luke 11[:52] that the parsons will steal the key to this book that is locked. They lock up Scripture and say that God must not speak to people in his own person. But where the seed falls on good ground [Mt. 13:5] – that is, in hearts that are full of the fear of God – this is then the paper and parchment on which God does not write with ink, but rather writes the true holy Scripture with his living finger, about which the external Bible truly testifies. And there is no more certain testimony, as the Bible verifies, than the living speech of God, when the father speaks to the son in the hearts of people. All of the elected people can read this Scripture, for they increase their talent.[11] But the damned will surely let God's living voice pass. Their heart is harder than any flint, and it repels the chisel of the master [God] for eternity. There-fore our dear Lord calls them stone, on which the seed falls and fails

---

[10] *Ezechiel hat vorflossen auffgegessen* (evidently a mistake for *aufgescholossen*).

[11] See Lk. 19:12–27 for the parable of the man who gave each of his servants a talent which they were to increase in his absence. Müntzer commonly referred to this parable as a way of talking about spiritual growth or sanctification.

to bring forth fruit [see Mt. 13:5], although they accept the dead word
with joy, great joy, and praise.

Upon my soul, only scholars and priests and monks accept the truth
from books with hearty flattery and pomp. But when God wants to
write in their heart, there is no people under the sun who are a greater
enemy of the living word of God than they. They also suffer no
tribulation of faith in the spirit of the fear of God, so they are on their
way into the fiery lake,[12] where the false prophets will be tormented
with the Antichrist for ever and ever, amen. Moreover, they do not
want to be disturbed by the spirit of the fear of God. So they mock the
tribulation of faith for eternity. They are precisely the people about
whom Jeremiah 8[:8–9] speaks, for they have no experience of holy
Scripture which they have sensed and which they can apply in their
exposition. They have no other manner of writing than that of hypocrites, who throw away the truthful word and all the same need it. So
they will never hear it in an eternity of eternities. For God speaks only
in the suffering of creatures, a suffering which the hearts of the
unbelievers do not have because they become more and more
hardened. Unbelievers can and will not empty themselves. They have
a slippery foundation and loathe their owner [God]. Therefore in a
time of tribulation they collapse. They retreat from the word that
became flesh. In no way does the unbeliever want to become conformed to Christ through suffering; rather he seeks conformity only
with honey-sweet thoughts.

Therefore it is these damned parsons who take away the true key
[to divine truth] and say that such a way [as direct revelations] is
fantastic and fool-headed, and that it is the most impossible thing.
These are the ones already condemned, with skin and hair, to eternal
damnation. Why should I not damn them as well, John 3[:18]? Since
they are not sprinkled with the spirit of the fear of God on the third
day, how can they be cleansed on the seventh day, Numbers 19[:19]?
So they have already been cast into the abyss of the pit [hell].

But I do not doubt the common people.[13] Oh, you righteous, poor,
pitiful little band! How thirsty you still are for the word of God! For
now are the days when none, or only a few, know what they should
hold or which side they should join. They would gladly do the best
thing and yet they do not know what this is. For they do not know how

---

[12] I.e. hell; see Lk. 8:33 and Rev. 21:10.
[13] *volk*; but as *MSB*, 500, n. 97, points out, in the Czech version it was "common people."

to conform to or comply with the testimony that the holy spirit speaks in their hearts. They are so greatly disturbed by the spirit of the fear of God that in them the prophecy of Jeremiah [4:4] has indeed become true, "The children have prayed for bread and there was no one there to break it for them." Oh, oh, no one broke it for them! There have been many money-hungry rogues who have thrown to the poor, poor, poor little people the inexperienced papal text of the Bible, as one usually throws bread to dogs. But they have not broken it with the knowledge of the holy spirit. That is, they have not opened their reason, so that they might recognize the holy spirit in themselves. For the parsons, even if they were all gathered together in one pile, do not have the power to make a single individual sufficiently sure that he has been chosen for eternal life. What more can I say?

The parsons are lords, who only devour, swill, and steal, day and night seeking to contrive how they can feed themselves and get many fiefs, Ezekiel 34[:2,8,10]. They are not like Christ, our beloved lord, who compares himself to a hen that makes her chicks warm.[14] Nor do they give milk to the disconsolate, forsaken people from the fountain of the inexhaustible admonitions of God. For they have not tested their faith. They are like a stork that gobbles up frogs in the fields and ponds and then afterwards spits them out, just as raw, to its young in the nest. So, too, are the profit-seeking and interest-boosting parsons who gobble whole the dead words of Scripture and then spit out the letter and their inexperienced faith (which is not worth a louse) to the righteous, poor, poor people. The result of what they do is that no one is certain of his soul's salvation. For these servants of Beelzebub bring to market only a fragment of holy Scripture. Indeed, no one knows if he is worthy of God's love or hate. This poison comes out of the abyss, for each and every whoremongering priest has the devil as his most deceitful and villainous prince, as the Revelation of John [Rev. 13:4–8] proclaims.

The parsons scatter the sheep of God so widely through this evil that no one looks to the church any more. For no one there separates good people from the new band that is unknown [to God]. There is also no knowledge of the diseased and healthy – that is, no one pays attention to the fact that the church is rotten to its floor and foundations with damned people. For the sheep do not know that they should

---

[14]Mt. 23:37, Lk. 13:34.

hear the living voice of God. That is, they should all have revelations, Joel 2[:28–29] and David in Psalm 87[:7]. The office of the true shepherd is simply that the sheep should all be led to revelations and revived by the living voice of God, for a master should teach the knowledge of God, Matthew 23[:10,26]. This has not happened for a long time, and as a result the elect and the damned are just the same in many respects, and the elect have been almost swallowed up by the damned. Therefore, nearly the whole world also thinks that it is not necessary that Christ himself must preach his own gospel to the elect.

I affirm and swear by the living God: he who has not heard the righteous, living word of God out of the mouth of God, [and can discern] what is Bible and what is Babel, is nothing but a dead thing. However, the word of God penetrates the heart, brain, skin, hair, bones, limbs, marrow, juice, force, and power. It is able to stride in a different way from that in which our foolish, scrotum-like doctors of theology prattle. Otherwise, one can neither be saved nor found. The elect must clash with the damned, and the power of the damned must yield before that of the elect. Otherwise you cannot hear what God is. Whoever has once received the holy spirit as he should, can no longer be damned, Isaiah 55[:3] and 60[:15,21], John 6 [Rev. 6:44–45]. Oh ho, woe, woe to those preachers who proclaim the way of Baal, for they have uttered the words in their snouts, but their hearts are more than a thousand times a thousand miles away from the word.

Thus, the people live without true shepherds. The experience of faith is never preached to them. The Jewish, heretical parsons[15] may well say that such a strong thing is not necessary for salvation. They say that one can indeed flee the wrath of God with good works, with precious virtues. However, from all this the people do not learn what God is in experience, what true faith is, what strong virtue is, and what good works after conversion to God are. Therefore it would not be surprising if God were to destroy us all, the elect with the damned, in a much more severe deluge than that of former times, and break us to dust and rubble in body and life. And it would also be no surprise if he were to damn all the people who have suffered these cursed seductions. For is our faith indeed not oriented more to the

---

[15] In referring to the clergy as Jews and heretics Müntzer intended to call attention to their scriptural literalism and legalism, which he equated with the practices of the Jewish scribes; since this kind of theology also denied the importance of the revelatory experiences Müntzer saw as central to Christianity, he also described the clergy as heretics.

face of Lucifer and Satan than to that of God? And the devil is coarser than wood and stone.

In my view it is not without reason that all other peoples call our faith a monkey-business. For it is evident and cannot be denied that unbelievers have demanded a serious account from us. And we have returned an answer from a chicken-coop – with immense pride we have spattered great books full, saying, "We have written this and that in our laws; for if Christ said this, Paul has written that; the prophets have foretold this and that; holy mother church (a madam in a whore-house) has proclaimed this and that." Indeed, the Nero-like, "holy," most wooden pope and chamber pot at the brothel of Rome has commanded this and that great thing, defending them with the ban of excommunication. And in the opinion of the little straw doctors of theology for the sake of the conscience this ban is not to be despised.

My good reader, let the words [of the Bible] simply be different or arranged differently. Then our theologians could not defend the Christian faith with their inexperienced Bible, no matter how great the twaddle they talk. Oh, alas, alas, woe, woe, woe to the hell-fiery and Asmodaeical[16] parsons who publicly seduce the people.

Yet no one wants to see or hear it when such reasons for our faith, and similar ones, are presented to the unbeliever. Do you not think non-Christians too have a brain in their heads? They may indeed think to themselves, What kind of assurance of faith is this which comes from books? Perhaps [the authors of Scripture] have lied in what they have written? How can one know whether it is true? Without a doubt Turks and Jews would gladly hear our invincible basis for believing, and many of the elect would also like the same thing. But the devil's parsons wrinkle up their noses and damn them forthwith. And yet the parsons cannot judge correctly, since they deny that a person can have revelations. They speak with the mere words of Scripture, "He who believes and is baptized will be saved." Such a firmly grounded account, and no other, they give to our opponents. It cannot be otherwise, nor do I perceive it differently, than that the parsons who thus seek to expound the faith so badly to the enemies are completely mad and foolishly inane. One should call such rascals to account, and those who offer such a lame excuse should be shoved into the abyss of hell. Is not this [defense of the faith] much more

---

[16] Asmodeus, according to Tobit (3:5), was a lascivious prince of the demons.

insane than insanity itself? Who can complain about it and bemoan it enough? Do we lack blood in our body and life that affairs proceed in such a mad and stupid way?

Does one not feel at least a small spark that virtually seeks to expand into tinder?[17] Indeed, one feels it and I feel it too. I have very bitterly pitied the fact that the Christian church has become so badly crushed that God could only do it more damage if he wanted to annihilate it altogether. But God would not want to do this except on account of the diarrhea-makers [the clergy], for they have taught the people to pray to Baal. They are so highly worthy that one may say in the midst of them what Daniel says [Dan. 9:5, 10], that they have not practiced the judgments of God.

I have read here and there in the histories of the ancient fathers of the church. And there I find that, after the death of the pupils of the apostles, the untarnished, virgin church soon became a whore at the hands of the seducing parsons. For the parsons have always wanted to have a ruling position in the church. Hegesippus and Eusebius[18] and others testify to all this. [The downfall of the church came about] because the people neglected to exercise their right to elect their priests. And it has not been possible to hold a true council since the onset of such negligence.[19] Be this as it may, it is still the work of the devil, for matters are only treated in councils or synods as they would be in a child's game. Such things are dealt with as the ringing of bells, chalices, hoods, lamps, and [ecclesiastical titles like] procurators and sextons. But no one has once – no, not once! – opened his snout concerning the true, living word of God. Nor has any thought been given to the proper liturgy.

Such errors had to occur so that the works of all people, the elect

---

[17] A reference to the traditional scholastic theological doctrine of the *synteresis*, which asserted that even after the Fall there remained an uncorrupted "spark" within the human soul that inclined it toward the good.

[18] Müntzer would have read the ecclesiastical history of Eusebius of Caesarea, which contained fragments of the writings of the second-century Christian author Hegesippus, in Rufinus's Latin translation of Eusebius entitled *Historia ecclesiastica*.

[19] Müntzer's condemnation of ecumenical councils except those of the apostolic church would have had special meaning for the Bohemian Hussites because of Hus's condemnation and burning at the Council of Constance. But Müntzer was not engaged in political pandering, since he went on to include the issue of the chalice in his list of childish externals that recent councils had dealt with. More significant is Müntzer's stress on the loss of elective government in the post-apostolic church as the principal cause of its corruption.

and the damned, would be fully manifest.[20] In our time God wants to separate the wheat from the chaff [Mt. 13:26], so that one can grasp, as though it were bright midday, who it is that has seduced the church for such a long time. All the villainy, even in the highest places, must come to light. Oh, how ripe are the rotten apples! Oh ho, how mushy the elect have become! The time of the harvest is at hand! Thus God himself has appointed me for his harvest. I have made my sickle sharp, for my thoughts are zealous for the truth and my lips, skin, hands, hair, soul, body, and my life all damn the unbelievers.

In order that I may do this properly, I have come into your country, my most beloved Bohemians. I desire from you only that which your diligence should demand – you should study the living word of God out of God's own mouth. Through this you will see, hear, and grasp how the whole world has been seduced by deaf parsons. Help me, for the sake of Christ's blood, to fight against such high enemies of the faith. In the spirit of Elias, I want to ruin them in your eyes. For the new apostolic church will arise first in your land, and afterward everywhere. I want to be prepared, if in church the people question me in the pulpit, to do enough to satisfy each and every one. If I cannot demonstrate such a skillful mastery of the truth, then may I be a child of both temporal and eternal death. I have no greater pledge. Whoever despises such warnings as these is already, now, in the hands of the Turks.[21] After this raging conflagration, the true Antichrist will personally reign, the radical opposite of Christ. And shortly after this, Christ will give to his elect the kingdom of this world for all eternity.

Given to Prague on the day of St. Catherine [25 November] in the year of our Lord 1521.

Thomas Müntzer will not pray to a dumb God but rather to one who speaks.

---

[20] Müntzer closes the work by developing the theme of the Apocalypse, only hinted at earlier. One sign of the imminence of apocalyptic upheaval, in Müntzer's view, is that the true character of the actions of both the elect and the damned has become fully evident – a development has reached its point of culmination.

[21] In 1521 Müntzer envisioned an imminent invasion of the Turks as part of the scheme of apocalyptical events. Later he made no further mention of this, just as he no longer referred to the Bohemians in his later writings.

2   Thomas Müntzer, *Sermon to the Princes* (or *An Exposition of the Second Chapter of Daniel*)

An exposition of the second chapter of Daniel the prophet, preached at the castle of Allstedt before the active and dear dukes and rulers of Saxony by Thomas Müntzer, servant of the Word of God.

Allstedt, 1524.[1]

First

The text of the above-mentioned chapter of the prophecy of Daniel the prophet was set forth and translated [from the Vulgate] in its clear literal sense and then the whole sermon, with the correct context, was set down as follows:

It is to be understood that poor, miserable, disintegrating Christendom can neither be counseled nor assisted unless diligent, indefatigable servants of God promote the Bible daily by reciting, reading and preaching. But if this is done, the head of many a pampered cleric must either suffer a continuous rain of hard blows or

---

[1] The sermon was preached on 13 July 1524 at the Allstedt castle before an audience that included Duke John, the crown prince John Frederick, and several officials of the government of electoral Saxony as well as local authorities. Shortly after being delivered orally, an extended version of the sermon was printed in Allstedt. The sermon was not ordered as part of a governmental inquiry into Müntzer's orthodoxy, as was formerly thought. The initiative for the sermon appears to have come from Müntzer. The translation is based on the text in *PSMB*, 49–71.

he will have to give up his profession. How can this be avoided when Christendom is being so terribly devastated by ravaging wolves? – as it is written about the vineyard of God in Isaiah 5[:1ff.] and Psalm 80[:9–14]. And St. Paul teaches in Ephesians 5[:19] how one should train oneself in the recitation of divine praises.

At the time of the beloved prophets Isaiah, Jeremiah, Ezekiel, and the others, the whole community of God's elect had fallen so totally and completely into idolatrous ways that even God himself could not help the people. Instead he had to let them be led away into bondage and suffer long among the heathen until they again acknowledged his holy name, as it is written in Isaiah 29[:17–24], Jeremiah 15[:11–14], Ezekiel 36[:20ff.], and Psalm 89[:31–38]. And just as it was then, it is no less true that in the time of our forefathers and in our own time, poor Christendom has become much more petrified and has only an inexpressibly slight resemblance to its divine name, Luke 21[:5], 2 Timothy 3[:5]. And the devil and his servants finely adorn themselves with this semblance, 2 Corinthians 11[:13ff.]. Indeed, they adorn themselves with it so attractively that the true friends of God are seduced by it; and even with the most practiced zeal they are scarcely able to recognize their error, as Matthew 24[:24] clearly shows.

All this has been brought about by the contrived holiness and hypocritical forgiveness of sins practiced by the godless enemies of God, since they assert that the Christian church cannot err. But, to the contrary, in order to guard against error the church should be constantly built on the word of God and thus kept free from error. Yes, the true church should also acknowledge the sin of its own ignorance, Leviticus 4[:13f.], Hosea 4[:6], Malachi 2[1–7], and Isaiah 1[:10–17]. For it is surely true that Christ, the son of God, and his apostles – indeed, even his holy prophets before him – began a true, pure Christendom, for they cast the seed of pure wheat in the field. That is, they planted the true word of God in the hearts of the elect, as is written in Matthew 12 [see, rather, Mt. 13:3–23], Mark 4[:3–20], Luke 8[:5–15], and Ezekiel 36[:29]. But the lazy, negligent ministers of this same church have not wanted to maintain this work and bring it to fruition through diligent care. Rather, they have pursued their own selfish interests and not those of Jesus Christ, Philippians 2[:21].

Therefore the clergy permitted the damage of the godless – that is,

the tares – to spread in its strength, Psalm 80[:9–14]. For the corner-
stone [Christ and his kingdom] referred to here in the second chapter
of Daniel [Dan. 2:34–44] was still small. Isaiah 28[:16] also speaks of
it. To be sure, it has not yet come to fill the whole world[2] but it will
soon fill it and make it full, ever so full. Thus, in the beginning of the
new Christendom, the established cornerstone was soon rejected by
the masons – that is, by the rulers, Psalm 118[:22f] and Luke
20[:17f]. Therefore I say that the church, begun in this way, has
become dilapidated everywhere, down to the present time of the
divided world,[3] Luke 21[:10], and here Daniel 2[:35] and Ezra 4[:5].
For Hegesippus says, and Eusebius says in the twenty-second chapter
of book IV on the Christian church,[4] that the Christian community
did not remain a virgin any longer than up to the time of the death of
the disciples of the apostles. And soon afterward it became an
adulteress, as had already been prophesied beforehand by the beloved
apostles, 2 Peter 2[:14]. And in the Acts of the Apostles, St. Paul said
to the shepherds of the sheep of God with clear, ringing words, Acts
20[:28–31], "Take heed, therefore, unto yourselves and unto the
whole flock, which the holy spirit has placed you to watch over, that
you should feed the community of God, which he has purchased
through his blood. For I know that after my departure ravaging wolves
which will not spare my flocks will come among you. Also, from
among yourselves men will arise who will promulgate perverted
teachings to attract the younger disciples to themselves. Therefore,
watch out!" The same thing stands written in the letter of the holy
apostle Jude [Jude 4:19], and Revelation 16[:13f.] points to it as well.
Therefore, our lord Christ warned us to guard against false prophets,
Matthew 7[:15].

Now, it is as clear as day – and may God hear our complaint – that
nothing is as badly and as little respected today as the spirit of Christ.

---

[2] Dan. 2:35, "The stone that smote the image became a great mountain and filled the
whole earth."

[3] The present and last epoch of world history (see Dan. 2:33–41), which is characterized
for Müntzer by a division in political power between lay and clerical rulers.

[4] Of Hegesippus's five books on the apostolic church, only a few fragments survived which
were incorporated into Eusebius's work on ecclesiastical history, to which Müntzer is
referring. In his *Prague Protest* Müntzer cited Eusebius as evidence that the apostolic
church was participatory and egalitarian, with the clergy being elected by the laity.

And yet no one may be saved unless this same holy spirit has previously assured him of his salvation, as it is written in Romans 8[:6], Luke 12[:8], John 6[:63] and 17[:2–31]. But how do we poor little worms expect to reach this while we regard the worthiness of the godless with such respect that unfortunately Christ, the gentle son of God, appears before the great titles and lineages of this world like a scarecrow or a painted puppet? And yet he is the true stone that will be cast down from the high mountain [Dan. 2:45] into the sea, Psalm 46[:3], because of the pompous opulence of this world. He is the stone who was torn from the great mountain without human hand, the stone who is called Jesus Christ, 1 Corinthians 10[:4]. He was born just at the time when the evil of slavery prevailed, Luke 1[:52] and 2[:1], at the time of Octavian, when the whole world was in motion and was being counted. Then Octavian, one who was spiritually without any power, a miserable scumbag, wanted to have power over the whole world, which was of no use to him except for his own luxury and arrogance. Indeed, he let himself think that he alone was great. Oh, how very small then was the cornerstone, Jesus Christ, in the eyes of men! He was banished to a stable, like an outcast among men, Psalm 22[:7]. Accordingly, the scribes rejected him, Psalm 118[:22], Matthew 21[:42–46], Mark 12[:10–12], Luke 20[:17–19], as they still do today.[5]

Indeed, since the death of the beloved disciples of the apostles, these scribes have even reenacted the Passion with him. They have turned the spirit of Christ into a laughing-stock and they continue to do so, as is written in Psalm 69[:11ff.]. They have most blatantly stolen him, like thieves and murderers, John 10[:1]. They have robbed Christ's sheep of their true voice and made the true crucified Christ into a completely fantastic idol. How has this come about? My answer is that they have rejected the pure art of knowing God and in its place they have set up a pretty, fine, golden image of God. Before it the poor peasants smack their lips, as Hosea has clearly said in chapter 4[:6–13], and as Jeremiah said in Lamentations 4[:5], "Those who formerly ate fine spiced food have now received instead dirt and filth." Oh, how unfortunate is the pitiful abomination of which Christ

---

[5] Müntzer equates the Jewish scribes who rejected Jesus with the learned clergy of his time, including Luther, who accept the authority of Scripture, base their faith on their interpretation of a written text, and deny continuing revelations from God.

himself spoke, Matthew 24[:15], foreseeing that he would be so wretchedly mocked by the devilish offering of the Mass, the superstitious preaching, the ceremonies and the manner of living. And even so, the whole time, there is nothing there but a mere wooden idol. Indeed, there is only a superstitious, wooden parson and a coarse, loutish and rude people, who cannot grasp the slightest assertion about God. Is this not a pity, a sin, and a scandal? I believe most assuredly that the beasts of the belly, Philippians 3[:19], and the swine written about in Matthew 7[:6] and 2 Peter 2[:22] have trampled underfoot the precious stone, Jesus Christ, as completely and totally as they have been able. He has become a doormat for the whole world. For this reason all the unbelieving peoples, Turks, heathens and Jews, have mocked us in the vilest way and taken us for fools – as one should regard senseless people who do not want to hear the spirit of their faith mentioned. Thus the suffering of Christ is nothing but the baiting at a market festival and the disparaging of rogues, as Psalm 69[:11–12] says, which not even a lowly footsoldier has had to endure.

Therefore, dear brothers, we should come out of this filth and become true pupils of God, taught by God, John 6[:48], Matthew 23[:8–10]. Then we will need God's great powerful strength, which will be granted us from above, in order to punish and annihilate such unspeakable wickedness. This knowledge is the most clear wisdom about God, Proverbs 9[:10], which springs only from a pure, uncontrived fear of God.[6] This same fear alone must arm us with a mighty hand for revenge on the enemies of God and with the highest zeal for God, as stands written in Proverbs 5[:18], John 2[:17], and Psalm 69[:9,18,24]. There is certainly no excusing God's enemies with human or rational considerations, for the appearance of the godless is beautiful and deceptive beyond all measure, like the beautiful cornflower among the golden ears of wheat, Ecclesiastes 8[:14]. But the wisdom of God must recognize such deceit.

---

[6] Fear of God, for Müntzer, was an essential component of an authentic, experienced faith; he also contrasted it in section two with fear of men – specifically, fear of those holding secular political power.

Second

We must examine more closely and correctly the abomination[7] that despises this stone. But so that we correctly recognize the abomination in the godless, we must daily expect God's revelation. Oh, that has become the most precious and rare thing in this corrupt world! For [unless we are expectant] the sly schemes of the clever ones could overcome us at any moment and keep us still more from the pure art of knowing God, Proverbs 4[:12], Psalm 37[:14–32]. Such a thing must be forestalled by the fear of God.

Only if this same fear is completely and purely anchored in us can holy Christendom easily return again to the spirit of wisdom and the revelation of the divine will. All this is encompassed in Scripture, Psalm 145[:18f], Psalm 111[:5–10], Proverbs 1[:7]. But the fear of God must be pure, without any admixture of human or "creaturely" [i.e., materialistic and selfish] fear, Psalm 19[:10], Isaiah 66[:2], Luke 12[:4f.]. Oh, this fear is very necessary for us! For just as one can scarcely serve two masters, Matthew 6[:24], so one can scarcely fear both God and creatures. Nor may God himself have mercy on us (as the mother of Christ our lord says) unless we fear him alone with our whole heart. Therefore, God says, Malachi 1[:6], "If I am your father, where then is the honor due me? If I am your lord, where then is fear of me?"

So, you dear princes, it is necessary in these most dangerous days, 1 Timothy 4[:1f.], that we apply the greatest diligence to combat such underhanded evil, as have all our beloved ancestors who are recorded in the Bible from the beginning of the world. For the time is dangerous and the days are evil, 2 Timothy 3[:1–8], Ephesians 5[:15f.]. Why? Only because the noble power of God has been so miserably disgraced and dishonored that the poor, coarse people are seduced by the great blubbering of the unsaved scribes. The prophet Micah in chapter 3[:11] says about them that this is the nature of nearly all the scribes with very few exceptions: they teach and say that God no longer reveals his divine mysteries to his beloved friends through valid visions, his audible word, or in other ways. Thus the

---

[7] *den grewel (Greuel).* Müntzer sometimes referred to diabolic influence on individuals in positions of power, or existing socio-political conditions – characterized by the intermixture of the godless and the elect, and the rule of the godless over the elect – simply as "the abomination."

scribes remain bogged down in their inexperienced ways, Ecclesiastes 34[:10]. And they have coined a gibe against people who go about with revelations from God, as the godless did to Jeremiah in chapter 20[:7f.]: "Listen, has God spoken to you recently? Or have you directed your questions to the mouth of God lately and taken counsel with him? Do you have the spirit of Christ?" The scribes do this with great scorn and mockery.

Was it not a great thing that took place in the time of Jeremiah? Jeremiah warned [see Jer. 20:4–5] the poor, blind people about the punishment of captivity in Babylon, just as pious Lot warned his sons-in-law, Genesis 19[:14]. But this warning appeared to the people to be most foolish. The blind people said to the beloved prophet, "Yes, yes, God should indeed warn the people in such a paternal way." But what happened then to the mocking crowd during the Babylonian captivity? Nothing, except that they were brought to shame by this heathen king, Nebuchadnezzar. Behold the text [of Dan. 2:47] here! Nebuchadnezzar had received the proclamation of God, and nevertheless he was a powerful tyrant and a rod of chastisement for the people of the elect who had sinned against God. But because of the blindness and stubbornness of the people of God, the most exalted goodness of the world had to be proclaimed in such a way, as St. Paul in Romans 11[:22] and Ezekiel 23[:22–35] say.

Thus, for your instruction here, I too say that the omnipotent God not only revealed to the pagan king those things which were many years in the future – to the unspeakable disgrace of the proud among the people of God who did not want to believe any prophet. The untested people of our time are exactly the same – they are not conscious of the punishment of God, even when they see it right before their eyes. What shall almighty God then do with us? He must withdraw his goodness from us.

Now we come to the biblical text of Daniel 2, "The king Nebuchadnezzar had a dream which vanished from him," etc.

What should we say about this? It is an unspeakable, indeed an abnormal and hateful thing to speak about people's dreams. The reason for this is that the whole world, from the beginning down to the present time, has been deceived by dreamers and interpreters of dreams, as is written in Deuteronomy 13[:2ff.] and Ecclesiastes 34[:7]. So it is shown in this chapter of Daniel that the king did not

17

want to believe the clever fortune-tellers and dream-interpreters. For he said, "Tell me my dream and only then the interpretation. Otherwise you will tell me nothing but mere deception and lies." What happened then? They were not able to do this and could not tell him the dream. And they said, "Oh, beloved king, no man on earth is able to tell you your dream. Only the gods can do this, who have nothing on earth in common with human beings." Yes, to be sure, according to their understanding they spoke correctly and in a reasonable way. But they had no faith in God. Rather, they were godless hypocrites and flatterers, who said then what the rulers gladly wanted to hear, just as the scribes do now in our time, those who gladly want to eat tasty tidbits at court. But opposing them is that which is written in Jeremiah 5[:13–31] and 8[:8f.]. And how much more is written there! The text of Daniel says here [Dan. 2:28] that there must have been people then who had fellowship with God in heaven. Oh, for the clever ones that is a bitter herb to swallow. But St. Paul wants to have it so too, Philippians 3[:20]. And nevertheless such learned ones immediately want to explicate the secrets of God. Oh, the world has now had more than enough of these rogues, who publicly presume to do such things.

And God says in Isaiah 58[:2] about these scribes, "They want to know my ways just as the people do who have fulfilled my righteousness." Such scribes are like fortune-tellers, since they openly deny any revelation from God and hence assault the holy spirit in his handiwork. They want to instruct all the world. And what does not conform to their inexperienced understanding they immediately ascribe to the devil. And yet they are not even assured of their own salvation, although this assurance is necessary, Romans 8[:14ff.]. They can babble beautifully about faith and brew up a drunken faith for the poor, confused consciousness of the people. All this comes from their indecisive judgment and from the abomination. They have derived this view from the contemptible deception of the most damnable, poisonous monks' dreams,[8] through which the devil has effected all his plans. Indeed, this teaching has also irretrievably deceived many pious people among the elect. For, without any instruction from the spirit, they have given themselves over without hesitation to these visions and dreams of their crazy faith. And so from the revelations of

---

[8] The polemic evidently derives from Müntzer's desire to distance the kind of revelations he meant from visions that stem from monastic asceticism.

the devil, monastic rules and sheer idolatry have been written down. St. Paul vigorously warned against this in his letter to the Colossians 2[:8]. But the damnable monkish dreamers have not known how they can become conscious of the power of God. Therefore, their perverted minds have hardened. And they are now shown before the whole world, more clearly from day to day, to be nothing except sin and shame, like do-nothing scoundrels. They are still blind in their stupidity. Nothing else has misled them and nothing else even to the present day seduces them further than this superstition. This is so because, without any experience of the advent of the holy spirit – the master of the fear of God – they despise the knowledge of God and fail to separate good from evil which is concealed under the appearance of good. God cries out about this through Isaiah 5[:20]: "Woe unto you who call good evil and evil good!" Therefore it is not the manner of pious people to reject the good along with the evil. For St. Paul says to the Thessalonians 5 [see, rather, 1 Th. 3:20f.], "You should not despise prophesying. Test all things but hold fast to what is good," etc.

Third

You should also know that God is so completely and totally well disposed toward his elect that, if he could warn them in the smallest matters, Deuteronomy 1[:42] and 36 [see, rather Dt. 32:6,29], Matthew 23[:37], he would most certainly do it, if they could receive this same warning despite the magnitude of their unbelief. For here this text of Daniel agrees with what St. Paul wrote to the Corinthians 2[:9f.] – and is taken from holy Isaiah 64[:3] – saying, "What no eye has seen what no ear has heard, and what has not come into any human heart, this God has prepared for those who love him. But God has revealed this to us through his spirit. For the spirit searches all things, yes also the depth of the godhead," etc.

In brief, it is an earnest conviction of mine that we must know and not only believe in an empty way whether what has been given us is from God or the devil or from nature.[9] If we want to be able to make our natural understanding of these same matters obedient to faith, 2

[9]Müntzer specifies three possible sources for phenomena that present themselves as divine revelations; it is obviously crucial for him to be able to distinguish true from false revelations and in the work's fourth section he sets forth several criteria for doing this.

Corinthians chapter 10[:5], then reason must be led to the ultimate limit of its capacity for judgment, as is shown in Romans 1[:16ff.] and Baruch 3 [see, rather, Jer. 45:3]. But natural reason can in good conscience make no certain judgment without God's revelation. For people will clearly find that they cannot attain heaven with their heads. Rather, they must first become in an interior way complete and utter fools [to the world], Isaiah 29[:13f.] and 33[:18], Obadiah 1[:8], 1 Corinthians 1[:18ff.]. Oh, that is a very alien message to the clever, carnal and sensual world. For when it is received, there immediately follow pains like those of a woman giving birth, Psalm 48[:7], John 16[:21]. For Daniel and every pious person with him find that it is just as impossible for him to acquire by natural reason a knowledge of God as it is for the rest of the common people. This is what the wise prophet means, Ecclesiastes 3[:11], for he says, "He who wants to discover the majesty of God will be crushed by his magnificence." For the more natural reason strives for God, the further the working of the holy spirit distances itself, as Psalm 139[:6] clearly shows. Indeed, if one understood the pretensions of natural reason, without a doubt one would not seek much help from stolen Scriptures, as the scribes do with a scrap or two of text, Isaiah 28[:10], Jeremiah 8[:8]. Rather, he would soon feel how the working of the divine word springs from his heart, John 4[:14]. Indeed, he would not need to carry stagnant water to the well, Jeremiah 2[:13], as our scribes now do. They confuse nature with grace, without drawing any distinction. They obstruct the way of the word, Psalm 119[:110], which arises from the abyss of the soul. As Moses says, Deuteronomy 30[:14], "The word is not far from you. Behold, it is in your heart," etc.

Now, perhaps you ask how it is that the word comes into the heart? The answer is: when the striving for truth is strong, it comes down to us from God above – which I will let stand for now and say more about at another time. And this striving for truth, whether what is called God's word is really God's or not, begins when one is a child of six or seven years of age, as is symbolized in Numbers 19[:19f.]. Therefore St. Paul cites Moses [Dt. 30:14] and Isaiah [65:1] in his letter to the Romans 10[:8]. And he speaks there of the inner word to be heard in the abyss of the soul through the revelation of God. And the person who has not become conscious of and receptive to this inner word, through the living testimony of God, Romans 8[:9], does not know how to say anything essential about God, even though he may have devoured a hundred thousand Bibles.

From this anyone can easily measure how far the world really is from the Christian faith. Still, no one wants to see or hear it. Now if a person should become conscious of the word and receptive to it, God must remove all his carnal desires. And if the impulse from God comes into his heart, so that he wants to kill all the desires of the flesh, it is necessary that the person then give way to God, so that he may receive his action. For a bestial person does not perceive what God speaks in the soul, 1 Corinthians 2[:14]. Rather, the holy spirit must refer him to the serious contemplation of the plain, pure meaning of the law, Psalm 19[:8]. Otherwise, he remains blind in his heart and he fantasizes for himself a wooden Christ and he misleads himself.

Therefore, look how repugnant it became for beloved Daniel [Dan. 2:18] to interpret the vision to the king and how diligently he thus beseeched God and prayed to him! To have revelations from God, therefore, one must cut himself off from all diversions and have a serious desire for truth, 2 Corinthians 6[:17]. And through practicing such a [method of discovering] truth, he must learn to distinguish the undeceived vision from the false one. Thus, beloved Daniel says, in chapter 10,[10] "A person must have the right method of understanding visions in order to know that they are not all to be rejected," etc.

Fourth

You should know that an elected person who wants to know which visions or dreams are from God and which are from nature or the devil must be severed in his mind and heart, and also in his natural understanding, from all temporal reliance on the flesh. And it must happen to him as it happened to beloved Joseph in Egypt, Genesis 39 [rather, Gen. 40:5–20], and also to Daniel here in this second chapter. For a sensual man, Luke 7[:25], will accept nothing but the pleasures of the world, which are thistles and thorns, as the lord says, Mark 4[:7,18], and he will suppress the whole manifestation of the word that God addresses in the soul. For this reason, if God has already spoken his holy word in the soul, the person cannot hear it if

---

[10] Dan. 10:1–12; Müntzer offers a paraphrase of what he took to be the meaning rather than a direct quotation.

he is inexperienced. For he does not look within or see into himself and into the abyss of his soul, Psalm 49[:21]. Such a man does not want to crucify his life, with his lusts and appetites, as Paul the holy apostle teaches [see Gal. 5:24]. Thus, the plowed field of the word of God remains full of thistles and thorns and full of much underbrush. These must all be removed for the work of God to take place, in order that the person is not found to be negligent or lazy, Proverbs 24[:30f.]. And after these hindrances have been removed one sees the fruitfulness of the field and finally the good crop. Only then does the person become aware that he is the dwelling-place of God and the holy spirit for the duration of his days. Indeed, he sees that he has been truly created for one purpose only, that he should seek the testimony of God in his own life, Psalm 93[:4] and 119[:95–125]. He will perceive these testimonies at first only in part, through visual means, and then perfectly in the abyss of his heart, 1 Corinthians 13[:10ff.].

In the second place, he must take note that such visual images and symbols in dreams or visions approximate in every respect those which are testified to in the holy Bible, so that the devil does not intrude next to them and spoil the balm of the holy spirit with his diabolical sweetness, as the wise man says of the flies which die from this sweetness, Ecclesiastes 10[:1].

In the third place, the elected person must pay attention to the manner in which the visions occur. They must not pour forth swiftly through human machinations. Rather, they should simply flow out according to God's irrevocable will. And the elected person must take heed most carefully that not a particle of that which he has seen is lost, so that its effect can be fully reproduced. But when the devil wants to do something, he is betrayed by his lazy posturing, and his lies finally peek out, for he is a liar, John 8[:44].

In this chapter of Daniel the same point is clearly demonstrated by King Nebuchadnezzar, and afterward is shown in fact in the third chapter. For the king quickly forgot the warning of God. Without a doubt this was caused by his carnal desires, which he directed toward pleasures and creaturely things. It must always happen in this way when a person wants constantly to cultivate his own pleasures and yet also have something of God's action and not be in any tribulation. In this condition the power of the word of God cannot overshadow him, Luke 8[:12–14]. God the almighty shows true dreams and visions to his beloved friends most often in their deepest tribulation, as he did to pious Abraham, Genesis 15[:1–6] and 17[:1ff.]. God appeared to him as he shuddered in terrible fear. Similarly, as beloved Jacob fled with great tribulation from his brother Esau, a vision came to him in which he saw a ladder extended up to heaven, with the angels of God climbing up and down on it, Genesis 28[:12]. Afterward, when he came home again, he had a tremendous fear of his brother Esau. Then the lord appeared to him in a vision in which God crushed his hip and struggled with him, Genesis 32[:25f.]. And similarly, pious Joseph was also hated by his brothers and in this tribulation he had two visions of danger, Genesis 37[:5–11]. And afterward in his heartfelt tribulation while imprisoned in Egypt, Joseph was so greatly enlightened by God that he could interpret all visions and dreams, Genesis 39[:21], 40[:12–19] and 41[:25ff.].

More than all these examples, that other Joseph, in Matthew 1[:20–23] and 2[:13,19f.,22], should be held up before the untempted, pleasure-seeking swine who think they are such clever little ones. This Joseph had four dreams when he was terrified by his tribulation, and through the dreams he was reassured. So, also, in their sleep the wise men were instructed by an angel not to return to Herod [Mt. 2:12]. Similarly, the beloved apostles were diligently attentive to visions, as is clearly described in their history, the book of Acts. Indeed, it is a truly apostolic, patriarchal, and prophetic spirit that awaits visions and attains them in painful tribulation.

Therefore it is no wonder that Brother Fattened-swine and Brother Soft-life [Luther] rejects visions, Job 28[:12]. But if a person has not perceived the clear word of God in his soul, then he must have visions. So it was that St. Peter, in the Acts of the Apostles, did not understand the Mosaic Law of Leviticus 11, and had doubts about the cleanliness of food and about whether to have anything to do with heathens, Acts 10[:10f.]. And then in the fullness of his mind God gave him a vision. In it he saw a linen cloth with four corners stretching down from heaven to earth and it was filled with four-footed animals. And he heard a voice saying, "Slaughter and eat." The devout Cornelius had a similar experience when he too did not know what he should do, Acts 10[:3–6]. And when Paul came down to Troas a vision appeared to him in the night. It was a man from Macedonia, who stood before him and greeted him and said, "Come down to Macedonia and help us." After he had seen such a vision, says the text of Acts 16[:8ff.], "Soon thereafter we tried to travel to

Macedonia for we were certain that the lord had called us there." And similarly when Paul was afraid to preach in Corinth, Acts 18[:9f.], the lord said to him through a vision in the night, "You should not be afraid," etc. "No one shall attempt to do you harm for I have many people in this city," etc.

And what need is there to bring forth the many other witnesses of Scripture? In such momentous and dangerous matters as those which true preachers, dukes, and princes have to deal with, it would never be possible for them to guard themselves securely against error on all sides, and to act blamelessly, if they did not rely on revelations from God – as Aaron heard from Moses, Exodus 4[:15], and David from Nathan and Gad, 2 Chronicles 29[:25]. For this reason the beloved apostles were completely and totally accustomed to visions, as the text of Acts 12[:7ff.] proves. There the angel came to Peter and led him out of Herod's prison. And he thought he was having a vision. He did not know that the angel was accomplishing his release by this means. But if Peter was not accustomed to visions, how could it have occurred to him that this was a vision?

From this I now conclude that whoever is inexperienced and an enemy of visions because of a carnal consciousness, and either accepts them all without any discrimination or rejects them all because the false dream-interpreters of the world have done such harm by being greedy and selfish people, this person will not fare well. Rather, he will be in conflict with the holy spirit, Joel 2[:26f.]. For God clearly speaks, as in this text of Daniel, about the transformation of the world.[11] He will bring about this transformation in the Last Days, so that his name will be rightly praised. He will release the elect from their shame and pour forth his spirit over all flesh. And our sons and daughters shall prophesy and shall have dreams and visions, etc. For if Christendom is not to become apostolic, Acts 27 [rather, Acts 2:16ff.] where Joel is cited, why then should one preach? To what purpose then are visions in the Bible?

It is true – and I know it to be true – that the spirit of God now reveals to many elected pious people that a momentous, invincible, future reformation is very necessary and must be brought about. Each one may protect himself against it as he wishes and yet the prophecy

---

[11] At this point Müntzer begins to present his interpretation of the apocalyptic culmination of history, according to which the existing social and political order will be overthrown by the elect, who will then establish a truly Christian society.

of Daniel remains undiminished, though no one believes it, as Paul also says to the Romans 3[:3]. This text of Daniel is thus as clear as the bright sun, and the work of ending the fifth empire of the world is now in full swing.

The first empire was symbolized by the golden head [of the statue in Nebuchadnezzar's dream]. That was the empire of Babylon. And the second empire was represented by the silver breast and arms, which was the empire of the Medes and Persians. The third empire was the empire of the Greeks, which resounded with its cleverness, indicated by the brass. The fourth empire was the Roman empire, which was won with the iron sword and was an empire of coercion. The fifth empire or monarchy is that which we have before our own eyes [i.e. the Holy Roman Empire] and it is also (like the fourth) of iron and would like to be coercive. But, as we see before our very eyes, the iron is intermixed with filth,[12] vain schemes of flattery that slither and squirm over the face of the whole earth. For he who cannot be a cheat [in our empire] must be an idiot. One sees now how prettily the eels and snakes copulate together in a heap. The priests and all the evil clergy are the snakes, as John the Baptist calls them, Matthew 3[:7], and the temporal lords and rulers are the eels, as is symbolized by the fish in Leviticus 11[:10–12]. For the devil's empire has painted its face with clay.[13]

Oh, you beloved lords, how well the Lord will smash down the old pots of clay [ecclesiastical authorities] with his rod of iron, Psalm 2[:9]. Therefore, you most true and beloved regents, learn your knowledge directly from the mouth of God and do not let yourselves be seduced by your flattering priests and restrained by false patience and indulgence. For the stone [Christ's spirit] torn from the mountain without human touch has become great. The poor laity and the peasants see it much more clearly than you do. Yes, God be praised, the stone has become so great that already, if other lords or neighbors wanted to persecute you on account of the gospel, they would be overthrown by their own subjects. This I know to be true. Indeed the

[12] The Holy Roman Empire, like the Roman empire before it, is essentially a coercive apparatus of iron; but now the coercion is blunted and disguised by the intermixture of supposedly Christian spiritual elements. The combination of the two is symbolized for Müntzer by the feet of the statue in Nebuchadnezzar's dream (Dan. 2:41), which were of iron and clay. The clay is intensified by Müntzer to "filth" (*kothe* = *Kot*).

[13] The true nature of the existing political structure has been concealed behind a cosmetic façade of Christianity.

stone is great! The foolish world has long feared it. The stone fell upon the world when it was still small. What then should we do now, after it has grown so great and powerful? And after it has struck the great statue so powerfully and irresistibly that it has smashed down the old pots of clay?

Therefore, you dear rulers of Saxony, stand boldly on the corner-stone, as St. Peter did, Matthew 16[:18], and seek genuine per-severance, granted by the divine will. He will surely temper you on the stone, Psalm 40[:3]. Your path will be the right one. Seek unhesitatingly the righteousness of God at all times and bravely take up the cause of the gospel. For God stands so close to you that you do not believe it. Why do you want to be frightened by the specter of man, Psalm 118[:6]?

Look closely at this text of Daniel! King Nebuchadnezzar wanted to kill the clever ones because they could not interpret the dream for him. This was deserved. For with their cleverness they wanted to rule his whole kingdom, and yet they could not even do what they had been engaged for. So also are our clergy today. And I tell you this truly: if you were able to recognize the harm that has befallen Christendom and rightly reflect on it, then you would win for your-selves as much zeal as Jehu the king, 2 Kings chapters 9 and 10, and as much zeal as the whole book of the Apocalypse [The Revelation of John] shows. And I know for sure that you would hold yourselves back from exercising the power of the sword only with great effort. For the pitiable corruption of holy Christendom has become so great that at present no tongue can fully express it.

Therefore a new Daniel must arise and interpret your revelation for you.[14] And this same new Daniel must go forth, as Moses teaches, Deuteronomy 20[:2], at the head of the troops. He must reconcile the anger of the princes and that of the enraged people. For if you were truly to experience the shame of Christendom and the deception of the false clergy and incorrigible rogues, then no one could imagine how enraged at them you would become. Without a doubt it would gall you and you would fervently take it to heart that you had been so kind to them after they had led you to the most shameful opinions with the sweetest words, Proverbs 6[:1ff.], and against all established truth. For they have made fools of you, so that everyone now swears to

---

[14] Müntzer was obviously thinking of himself as the best candidate for this position.

the saints that princes are heathen people insofar as their office is concerned.[15] Princes, they say, should do nothing but maintain civil unity.

Oh, beloved ones, the great stone will indeed soon fall on and smite this view of your office and smash such rational schemes to the ground. For Christ says, in Matthew 10[:34], "I have not come to bring peace but the sword." But what should one do with these false spiritual leaders? Nothing but what is done with evildoers who obstruct the gospel: put them away and cut them off, if you do not want to be servants of the devil but servants of God, as Paul calls you in Romans 13[:4]. You should not doubt that God will smash to bits all your adversaries who undertake to persecute you. For as Isaiah 59[:1] says, "His hand is not yet hampered." Therefore God is still able to help you and will do so, just as he stood by King Josiah the elect,[16] and the others who defended the name of God. Thus, you rulers are angels when you seek to act justly, as Peter says in 2 Peter 1[:4]. Christ commanded this very earnestly, Luke 10[:27], and said, "Take my enemies and strangle them for me before my eyes." Why? Ah, because they have spoiled Christ's government, and in addition they seek to defend their villainy under the guise of the Christian faith. And with their deceitful infamy they pollute the whole world. Therefore Christ our Lord says, Matthew 18[:6], "Whosoever does evil to one of these little ones, it is better for him that a millstone be hung about his neck and that he be thrown into the depths of the sea." He who wishes, turning [in his evasions] here and there, can gloss over this. But these are the words of Christ. Now, if Christ can say this about someone who does evil to one of the little ones, what should be said about those who do evil to a great multitude in their faith? For this is how arch-villains act, who do evil to the whole world and make it deviate from the true Christian faith, and who say that no one shall know the mysteries of God. Each person should judge them according to their words and not according to their actions, Matthew 23[:3]. They say that it is not necessary for the Christian faith to be tested like gold in the fire, 1 Peter 1[:7], Psalm 140[:11]. But if this were the case, the Christian faith would be worse than the faith of a dog that

---

[15] A reference to Luther's doctrine of two "kingdoms" or "realms," the spiritual and the secular, according to which there is nothing specifically Christian about secular political authority.

[16] 2 Kg. 22–23.

hopes to get a scrap of bread while the table is being set.[17] False scribes present such an image of the faith to the poor blind world. This suits them, for they preach only for the sake of their belly, Philippians 3[:19]. From their hearts they can say nothing else, Matthew 12[:34].

Now, should you want to be true rulers, then you must begin government at the roots, as Christ commanded. Drive his enemies away from the elect, for that is your appointed task. Beloved ones, do not offer us any stale posturing about how the power of God should do it without your application of the sword. Otherwise, may the sword rust away in its scabbard on you. May God grant this!

Let any scribe say whatever he wants to you. Christ's words are sufficient, Matthew 7[:10], John 15[:2–6],: "Every tree that does not bring forth good fruit should be uprooted and cast into the fire." If you now remove the mask from the world, then soon you will recognize it for what it is with a righteous judgment, John 7[:24]. Judge righteously, as God commands! You have sufficient help for the purpose, Proverbs 6[:16–23?], for Christ is your master, Matthew 23[:8]. Therefore do not permit evildoers, who turn us away from God, to live longer, Deuteronomy 13[:6]. For a godless person has no right to life when he hinders the pious. In Exodus 22[:1] God says, "You shall not permit the evildoer to live." Saint Paul also means this, for he says that the sword of rulers is given for the punishment of evildoers and to protect the pious, Romans 13[:1–4].[18] God is your guardian and he will teach you to struggle against his enemies, Psalm 18[:35]. He will make your hands skillful in fighting and he will also sustain you. But in addition you will have to suffer a great cross and temptation, so that the fear of God is made clear to you. This cannot happen without suffering. But it will cost you no more than the danger which is risked for the sake of God's will and the useless prattle of your opponents. Although pious David was driven from his castle by

---

[17] Unless it has been tested in the fire of spiritual anguish and confirmed, faith is nothing more than the expectation of a reward which is arbitrarily bestowed.

[18] Müntzer's interpretation of this passage reverses the usual exposition, including that advanced by Luther, which saw the sense of the passage as an injunction for Christians to be obedient to secular authority since it is ordained by God in order to protect good people and to punish evildoers. Müntzer, however, uses the passage to enjoin positive action by rulers to promote a Christian society, and to legitimize rebellion in the event that rulers fail to fulfill the purpose for which they have been established.

Absalom, nevertheless he finally regained it when Absalom was hanged and stabbed [2 Sam. 15:10–18 and 18:9–15]. Therefore, you dear fathers of Saxony, you must risk it for the sake of the gospel. For God will chastise you in a friendly way, as he does his most beloved sons, Deuteronomy 1[:31], when he is burning with his momentous wrath. Then blessed are all those who rely on God. Say freely with the spirit of Christ: "I will not fear a hundred thousand, even if they have surrounded me."

At this point I imagine that our scribes will hold up to me the kindness of Christ, which they claim for themselves and use hypocritically. But in contrast to this, they should also look at the wrath of Christ, John 2[:15–17], Psalm 69[:10], with which he tore up the roots of idolatry, as Paul says to the Colossians 3[:5–9]. Because of these scribes the wrath of God cannot be removed from the community. If, according to our view, he cast down those guilty of lesser offenses, then without a doubt he would not have spared idols and images if they had been there,[19] as he commanded through Moses in Deuteronomy 7[:5f.], where he says: "You are a holy people. You shall not have pity on the idolatrous. Break up their altars. Smash their images and burn them so that I am not angry with you." Christ has not abrogated these words. Rather, he will help us to fulfill them, Matthew 5[:17]. The visual symbols are all explicated by the prophets, but these are bright clear words that must remain for eternity, Isaiah 40[:8]. God cannot say "yes" today and "no" tomorrow. Rather, he is unchangeable in his words, Malachi 3[:6], I Samuel 15[:10–22], Numbers 22[:6]. But if it is objected that the apostles did not destroy the idols of the heathen, I reply as follows: St. Peter was a timid man, Galatians 2[:11ff.]. He was hypocritical with the heathen. He was also symbolic of all the apostles in this respect, so that Christ said of him in the last chapter of John [Jn. 21:15–19] that he had a very strong fear of death. And it is easy to figure out that Peter acted in this way because he did not want to give the heathen any reason to kill him. But St. Paul spoke out most firmly against idolatry, Acts 17[:16–31]. And if he had been able to carry out his teaching resolutely among the Athenians, without a doubt he would have

---

[19] Müntzer is evidently justifying the destruction of the Mallerbach chapel near Allstedt by his followers as a deed undertaken with the same righteous anger as Christ's expulsion of the money-changers from the temple.

utterly cast out idolatry, as God commanded through Moses, and as also happened afterward through the martyrs, according to trustworthy histories.

Therefore the deficiency or negligence of the saints gives us no reason to allow the godless to continue in their ways. Since they profess God's name with us, they should choose one of two alternatives – either repudiate the Christian faith entirely or put away their idolatry, Matthew 18[:8f.]. But then our scribes come along and, referring to the text of Daniel, say in their godless, stolen way that the Antichrist will be destroyed without a hand being lifted. This is too much! Anyone who says this is already as faint-hearted as the Canaanites were when the elect wanted to enter the promised land, as Joshua [5:1] writes. Joshua nevertheless did not spare them from the sharpness of the sword. Look at Psalm 44[:4] and 1 Chronicles 14[:11]. There you will find the same solution: the elect did not win the promised land with the sword alone but rather through the power of God. Nevertheless, the sword was the means, just as for us eating and drinking are the means for sustaining life. Thus the sword is also necessary as a means to destroy the godless, Romans 13[:1–4].

But for this use of the sword to occur as it should and in the right manner, our dear fathers who confess Christ with us – that is, the princes – should do it. But if they do not do it, then the sword will be taken away from them, Daniel 7[:27].[20] For then they confess Christ with words and deny him in their actions, Titus 1[:16]. Thus the princes should offer peace to the enemy, Deuteronomy 2[:26–30]. But if the princes want to be "spiritual" and not render an account of their art of knowing God, 1 Peter 3[:12–17], they should be gotten rid of, 1 Corinthians 5[:13]. I, together with pious Daniel, bid them not oppose God's revelation. But if they do take the contrary course, may they be strangled without any mercy,[21] as Hezekiah [2 Kg. 18:22], Josiah [2 Kg. 23:5], Cyrus [2 Chr. 36:22f.], Daniel [Dan. 6:27], and Elijah, 1 Kings 18[:40] destroyed the priests of Baal. Otherwise, the

---

[20] Implicit in Müntzer's argument here was a theory of popular sovereignty: as long as the existing rulers perform their proper function of destroying the godless and promoting the well-being of the elect, whom Müntzer associated with the commoners, the rulers may remain in office. But if they fail to do this, the people have the right to take temporal power ("the sword") from them and exercise it themselves.

[21] *Wo sie aber das widderspiel treiben, das man sie erwürge on alle gnade.* Müntzer here lays down an exceedingly bold ultimatum to his princely listeners: either they join his cause and that of the commoners, or they will be subject to the death penalty.

Christian church will not be able to return to its source. The tares must be pulled out of the vineyard of God at the time of the harvest. Then the beautiful golden wheat will gain lasting roots and come up right, Matthew 13[:24–30,39]. The angels who sharpen their sickles for the cutting are the earnest servants of God who fulfill the zeal of divine wisdom, Malachi 3[:1–6].

Nebuchadnezzar perceived this divine wisdom through Daniel.[22] He fell down before him after the mighty truth had overpowered him. He was blown like a straw in the wind, as chapter 3[:26–30] proves. Similarly, there are now innumerable people who accept the gospel with great joy as long as everything is going well for them and in a pleasing way, Luke 8[:48]. But when God wants to put such people in the crucible or when he puts them into the fire of a crucial test, 1 Peter 1[:7], oh, then they are angered by the smallest word of the gospel, as Christ proclaimed in Mark 4[:17]. By the same token, without a doubt many untested people will be angered by this booklet, because I say with Christ, Luke 18 [see, rather, Lk. 19:27], Matthew 18[:6], with Paul, 1 Corinthians 5[:7,13], and with the instruction of the whole of divine law, that godless rulers, especially the priests and monks, should be killed. They tell us the holy gospel is a heresy, and at the same time they want to be the best Christians. Just as their hypocritical, false goodness will turn to rage and become infinitely bitter, it will also defend the godless and say that Christ killed no one, etc. And because the friends of God, most lamentably, are without effective power, the prophecy of Paul is fulfilled, 2 Timothy 3[:1ff.]. In the Last Days the lovers of pleasure will indeed have the appearance of virtue but they will deny its power. Nothing on earth has a better form and mask than false goodness. Thus, all the corners of the earth are full of absolute hypocrites, among whom none is so bold as to be able to proclaim the real truth.

In order that the truth may really be brought to light, you rulers – God grant that you do not willingly do otherwise – must act according to the conclusion of this chapter of Daniel [see Dan. 2:48]. That is, Nebuchadnezzar elevated holy Daniel to office so that the king might carry out good, correct decisions, inspired by the holy spirit, Psalm 58[:11f.]. For the godless have no right to life except that which the elect decide to grant them, as is written in the book of Exodus 23[:29–

---

[22] Dan. 2:46f.

31

33]. Rejoice, you true friends of God, that the enemies of the cross have crapped their courage into their pants. They act righteously, even though they never once dreamed of doing so. If we now fear only God, why should we recoil before vacillating, incapable men, Numbers 14[:8f.], Joshua 11[:6]? Only be bold! He to whom is given all power in heaven and on earth [Christ] wants to lead the government, Matthew 28[:18]. To you, most beloved, may God grant eternal protection. Amen.

3   Andreas Karlstadt, *Letter from the Community of Orlamünde to the People of Allstedt*

A letter from the community of Orlamünde to the people of Allstedt concerning how one should fight in a Christian way.[1]

Divine peace through Christ, our lord. Dear brothers, we have read carefully the letter which you sent us,[2] and we have perceived the reason why you wrote it, which is the violent persecution of Christians in your surroundings. With this letter we are complying with your request to write you a reply to what you wrote. In brotherly fidelity we do not want to conceal from you that we cannot help you with armed resistance (if we have understood your letter correctly). We have not been commanded to do this, for Christ ordered Peter to sheath his

---

[1] Printed at Wittenberg by Hans Luft in July 1524. Although it was written in the name of the community and congregation of Orlamünde, Karlstadt was the author of the letter. In the spring of 1523 Karlstadt became pastor of the small town of Orlamünde on the Saale river, a benefice which he had held previously as archdeacon of the theology faculty at the university of Wittenberg and for which he had engaged the services of a vicar. Karlstadt's decision to leave Wittenberg for Orlamünde was the result of his growing differences with Luther, the university's decision to censor his publications, which Luther concurred with and probably influenced, and Karlstadt's own resulting dissatisfaction with university life. Despite Karlstadt's quarrels with Luther, they were capable of reuniting to oppose Müntzer; this letter could have been printed in Wittenberg only with Luther's approval. The translation is based on the text in Adolf Laube, Annerose Schneider, and Sigrid Looß, eds., *Flugschriften der frühen Reformationsbewegung*, 2 vols. (East Berlin, 1983), I, 443–45.

[2] This letter from Müntzer and the Allstedters must have requested a political alliance in which both parties would be pledged to defend the gospel, including the use of armed force if necessary.

sword [Mt. 26:52] and would not permit him to fight for him, because the time and the hour of his suffering were near. Thus, when the time and the hour arrive that we must suffer for the sake of divine justice, let us not reach for knives and spears and drive out the eternal will of the father with our own violence, for daily we pray [Mt. 6:10], "Thy will be done." If you want to be armed against your enemies, dress yourself in the strong, steel-like and unconquerable armor of faith, about which St. Paul writes to the Ephesians in chapter 6[:13–17]. Then you will conquer your enemies vigorously and destroy them, so that they will not harm even a single hair on your head.

But you write that we should associate ourselves with you and make a covenant or alliance with you, for which you cite from Scripture 2 Kings 24 [rather, 23:1–3], how Josiah made a covenant with God and the people. We find in the same passage that when Josiah received the book of the law, he made a covenant with God to walk in the ways of the Lord, to keep in his heart and with all his strength the Lord's law, commandments and ceremonies, and to fulfill the letter of the covenant which was written in this same book of the law. And the people obeyed this covenant. That is, the king and the people made a covenant with God in like manner. For if Josiah had made a covenant with both God and the people [i.e. if there had been two covenants], then his heart would have been divided in his effort to please both the divine and the human will, whereas Christ says about this [Mt. 6:24], "No one can serve two masters."

Thus, dear brothers, if we were to make a covenant with you, we would no longer be free Christians but bound to men. This would then bring forth a truly prolonged outrage against the gospel. The tyrants would then be happy and would say, "These people boast about one God, and now they make a covenant with one another. Their God is not strong enough to defend them." They would say further, "They want to produce their own sects and rebellion and insurrection. Let them be strangled and killed before they grow stronger than we are." Then we would have to die for these crimes, and not on account of the strict justice of God. What would God say about this? Would not such a thing greatly befoul and betray divine truth?

Therefore, dear brothers, no! Trust in God alone, as King Abijah did in 2 Chronicles 13[:13–18] when he was surrounded by his enemies, and as the children of Israel did when they were pursued by

34

Pharaoh to the Red Sea, and yet, trusting in God, were miraculously delivered and preserved [Ex. 14:13–31]. Thus, hear and receive only the true speech of God, each according to the number of his talents [Lk. 19:11–18], and do not take heed if tyrannical power is raised against you. For the apostles, all the saints, and even Christ himself were not spared this.

For the rest, we will gladly testify to the truth of your teaching insofar as it is from God, and, withholding nothing, we will give the testimony of the holy spirit, which has been communicated to us through the kind gifts of God. And if an account of our faith is demanded of us, we will step forward joyfully to give it, regardless of whether every form of tyrannical rage may rise against us and pursue us to our death.

But may everything take place with the help and strength of God. Therefore, dear brothers, learn to do only the eternal will of God, our heavenly father, which he has revealed to us through his only-begotten son, Christ, in the holy spirit. Then your hearts will be at peace in God and freed from all tribulations. May God help us in this. Amen.

The congregation of Christ at Orlamünde.

4 Conrad Grebel, *Letter to Thomas Müntzer* Zurich, 5 September 1524.[1]

To the truthful and faithful proclaimer of the gospel, Thomas Müntzer at Allstedt near the Harz mountains, our true and dear fellow brother in Christ, etc.

May peace, grace, and mercy from God our father and Jesus Christ our Lord be with us all. Amen. Dear brother Thomas, for the sake of God do not be surprised that we address you without title and as a brother, because we want you to correspond with us. And do not be surprised that, without being asked and being unknown to you, we have presumed to establish a mutual correspondence. God's son, Jesus Christ, who appears to all who are to be saved as the sole master and head, and who calls us brothers – "his" through the one common word for all brothers and believers – has compelled us to create friendship and brotherhood, and to point out the following articles.[2] In addition, your two pamphlets on contrived faith have caused us to write.[3] Therefore, if you receive this letter with good intentions for

---

[1] It is not clear that Müntzer received this unpublished letter. An autograph copy survives in the correspondence of Vadian, the reformer of St. Gall, who was Grebel's brother-in-law. Although written by Grebel, the letter was written in the name of a circle of radicals in Zurich, led by Grebel, Andreas Castelberger, and Felix Manz, who were dissatisfied with the course that the reform movement there had taken under the leadership of Ulrich Zwingli. The translation is based on the text in *MSB*, 437–47.

[2] A reference to the theses presented below, on which the Zurich radicals wished to have Müntzer's views. The first nine articles concerned liturgical singing and the abolition of the Mass; articles 10–25 dealt with the Lord's Supper.

[3] Evidently a reference to Müntzer's two short works of late 1523 and early 1524, *On Contrived Faith* (*Von dem gedichteten Glauben*) and *Protest or Offering* (*Protestation oder Erbietung*). See *MSB*, 217–24 and 225–40.

the sake of Christ our saviour, and if God wills it, this letter will serve what is good, and will produce results.

In the past our ancestors fell away from the true God; from a knowledge of Jesus Christ and true faith in him; from the true, single, common, divine word; and from divine customs and Christian love and ways. And they lived without God, law, and the gospel in human, useless, unchristian practices and ceremonies. And they thought they could attain salvation in this way but they failed miserably, as the evangelical preachers have shown and still show at times. So too, in the same way, everyone now wants to be saved in showy faith, without the fruits of faith, without the baptism of temptation and testing, without love and hope, and without true Christian practices.[4] And everyone wants to remain in their own vices and in all the old ways of these common, ceremonial, and antichristian practices about baptism and the Lord's Supper. They despise the divine word and pay attention to the papal word, or to the word of the antipapal preachers, which is also not in conformity with the divine word. With respect to people's behavior today and the number of the temptations that exist, there is more grievous and harmful error now than has ever been true since the beginning of the world.

We too have been in this total error, because we were only the listeners and the readers of the evangelical preachers, who were responsible for all this. This was the result of our sins. But after we also took up Scripture and examined it on a great many issues, we became better informed, and we discovered the pastors' great and damaging deficiencies, and ours as well. We discovered that we do not ask God every day, seriously and with constant sighs, to lead us from the destruction of every godly way and out of human abominations, and to the true faith and practices of God. The reason for all this is that the evangelical preachers are silent about the divine word and mix it with the human. Yes, we say that it needs no explanation to know that this is what brings about all the damage and the neglect of all divine things.

As we were noticing all this and complaining about it, your writing

---

[4] The radical circle around Grebel accepted the evangelical criticisms of traditional Roman Catholic practices, but they also felt that the Reformation's reliance on "faith alone" had brought neither moral improvement nor the establishment of a Christian liturgy based on Scripture alone.

against false faith and baptism was brought to us.[5] After reading it we were better informed, strengthened, and quite pleased that we had found someone who had a Christian understanding like us, and who was able to point out the deficiencies of the evangelical preachers – how on all the main issues they falsely spare themselves, act falsely, and set their own arbitrary opinions – yes, even those of Antichrist – above and against God. And they do not act and preach as those sent by God should. Therefore we bid and admonish you as a brother – by the name, power, word, spirit, and salvation which all Christians find in Jesus Christ, our master and savior – that you earnestly strive to preach fearlessly only God's word, to establish and protect only divine practices, and to treasure only the good and right which can be clearly found in Scripture alone. And may you reject, hate, and condemn every scheme, word, practice, and arbitrary opinion of all men, even your own.

We understand that you have translated the Mass into German and composed new German hymns.[6] This cannot be good, because [in the first place] we find in the New Testament no teaching or example about singing. Paul scolds the Corinthian scholars more than he praises them for murmuring in the congregation, as though they were singing, just as Jews and Italians pronounce their liturgy in the manner of songs.

Second, because singing in the Latin language arose without divine teaching and apostolic example, and has not brought about anything good, it will edify still less in German and will create an external, specious faith. Third, Paul most clearly forbids singing in the fifth chapter of his letter to the Ephesians and in the third chapter of his letter to the Colossians. He does this by saying that people should talk and instruct one another with psalms and spiritual songs; and if one wants to sing, one should sing and give thanks in one's heart. Fourth, what we are not taught with clear [scriptural] sayings and examples should be as forbidden to us as if it were written, "Do not do that; do not sing." Fifth, Christ tells his messengers to preach only the word that is in the Old and New Testaments. Paul also says that the speech

---

[5] The full title of Müntzer's *Protest or Offering* ends with the phrase ". . . and about true Christian faith and baptism."

[6] Grebel and the other Zurich radicals were clearly familiar with Müntzer's liturgical reforms, the Reformation's first attempt to develop a comprehensive vernacular liturgy. But precisely which of his liturgical writings they may have read is not clear.

of Christ, not song, should dwell among us. Whoever sings poorly is frustrated; whoever sings well is arrogant. Sixth, we should not add to the word what we think is good, nor should we subtract from it. Seventh, if you want to abolish the Mass, this cannot be done with German singing. This counsel of yours perhaps derives from Luther. Eighth, the Mass must be rooted out with the word and command of Christ. Ninth, for it has not been planted by God.

Tenth, Christ established and planted the supper of the covenant [the Lord's Supper]. [Eleventh,] only the words of Matthew 26[:26ff.], Mark 14[:22ff.], Luke 22[:14ff.], and 1 Corinthians 11[:23ff.] should be used in the Lord's Supper, neither less nor more. Twelfth, the servant from the community [i.e. the minister] should recite these words from one of the evangelists or from Paul. Thirteenth, these are the established words of the meal of the covenant, not of a consecration. Fourteenth, ordinary bread should be used, without idols and additions. Fifteenth, for such idols and additions create a showy service, an adoration of the bread, and a distraction from inwardness. There should also be an ordinary cup. Sixteenth, this would reduce adoration and bring about right knowledge and understanding of the Lord's Supper, because the bread is nothing but bread. But in faith it is the body of Christ and an incorporation with Christ and the brothers. For one must eat and drink in the spirit and in love, as John shows in chapter 6 and in the other chapters, Paul in 1 Corinthians 10 and 11, and as is clearly taught in Acts 2. Seventeenth, although it is only bread, if faith and brotherly love precede, it should be taken with joy. If the Lord's Supper is practiced in this way in the community, it should show us that we are truly one bread and one body, and true brothers of one another, and that we are God's, etc. Eighteenth, but if someone is found who is not able to eat it in a brotherly way, he eats to his damnation if he eats without distinguishing the Lord's Supper from any other meal, and he dishonors love – the inner bond – and the bread – the external bond. Nineteenth, for it does not remind him of the body and blood of Christ, or of the testament on the cross, or that he is to live and suffer for the sake of Christ and the brothers, the head and the members. Twentieth, the Lord's Supper should also not be administered by you alone. The Mass degenerated because only one ate. For the Lord's Supper is a sign of the covenant, not a Mass and a sacrament. Therefore no one should use it alone, either at the deathbed or elsewhere.

The bread should also not be broken by one person. For no one should take for himself alone the bread of unity, unless he is divided within himself, which no one is. Twenty-first, the Lord's Supper should also not be administered in temples [churches], according to all Scripture and history, if this produces a false devotion.[7] Twenty-second, the Lord's Supper should be used often. Twenty-third, it should not be used without the rule of Christ in Matthew 18[:15–18].[8] But if it is, it is never the Lord's Supper. For without this rule, everyone pursues what is external and gives up the internal, love. This happens if brothers and false brothers come together and eat. If the Lord's Supper is to be administered, we want it to take place without priestly vestments, without singing, and without additions. Twenty-fifth, with respect to the time for the Lord's Supper, we know that Christ gave it to the apostles at the evening meal, and that the Corinthians also used it then. But they do not determine for us a definite time, etc.[9]

Since you are much better informed about the Lord's Supper and we have only indicated our understanding of it, if we are not right about it, then teach us what is better. And we hope that you want to give up singing and the Mass, and that you want to do everything only according to the word, and to preach and to establish what the apostles practiced. If this cannot be done, it would be better to let everything stay in Latin, unchanged and untranslated. If this cannot be correctly established, then do not administer the Lord's Supper according to either your, or the Antichrist's priestly practices. And at least teach how the Mass should be, as Christ acted and taught in John 6 – how one must eat his flesh and drink his blood not paying attention to the corruption or sparing the people of Antichrist, like the most learned, first evangelical preachers who established genuine idolatry and planted it all over the world. It is much better that a few are correctly informed through the word of God, and that a few

[7] On the basis of this article it has been held that already in the fall of 1524 the Zurich radicals were practicing a commemorative Communion in private homes; no church in the city yet observed an evangelical Communion.

[8] I.e. that a member of the community who has sinned first be admonished in private, then in the presence of two or three witnesses, then before the community as a whole; finally, if he does not listen, he should be expelled from the community.

[9] At this point the Zurich radicals were not consistent with their own biblicist principle, set forth in the fourth article, that anything not clearly found in Scripture should be repudiated.

believe correctly and have virtuous conduct, than that many believe falsely because of an adulterated teaching.

Although we admonish and ask you, nevertheless we hope that you will do it yourself. And we admonish you also, most dearly beloved, because you have given a friendly hearing to our brother Karlstadt, and have admitted that you too have made mistakes. And we hold you, together with Karlstadt, as the purest proclaimers and preachers of the purest divine word. And since you both justly rebuke those who mix human words and practices with divine, you should free yourselves from the priesthood, benefices, all kinds of new and old practices, and your own and traditional opinions, and you should become totally uncorrupted. If your benefices are funded by interest payments and tithes, both are usury, just as they are with us. And if the whole community does not sustain you, you should lay down your benefices. You know well how a pastor should be sustained.

We also very much approve of Jacob Strauss[10] and some others who are held in little regard by the negligent scribes and doctors of theology at Wittenberg. We are also similarly in conflict with our learned pastors.[11] Everybody clings to them. They have generated this by preaching a sinful, sweet Christ; and they lack a good analysis, as you show in your booklets, which have taught and strengthened us who are poor in spirit almost beyond measure. And thus we agree with you in all matters – but it was still painful for us to hear that you have set up tablets,[12] for which we find no scriptural passage or example in the New Testament. In the Old Testament there certainly had to be external writing, but now in the New it should be written in the bodily tablets of the heart. A comparison of both Testaments demonstrates this, as we are informed by Paul in 2 Corinthians 3[:3], by Jeremiah 31[:33], in Hebrews 8[:6ff.], and by Ezekiel 36[:26]. If we are not in error, which we do not believe, you should destroy these tablets. They have arisen from your personal opinion, a useless

---

[10] Born in Basel, in 1522 this preacher was expelled from Tyrol on account of reform activities and by early 1523 had assumed a benefice in Eisenach. Here he composed a series of theses attacking usury which was published in Erfurt in the spring or early summer of 1523.

[11] Especially the Zurich reformers Ulrich Zwingli and Leo Jud.

[12] It is not clear to what these "tablets" (*taflen* = *Tafeln*) refer. *MSB*, p. 441, n. 23a, suggests altar images; but from the context of the letter it is more likely that the Zurich radicals had heard that Müntzer had set up tablets with the ten commandments written on them in St. John's church in Allstedt.

nourishment, and they might grow and become utterly idolatrous and implant themselves in the whole world, as took place with idols. It also creates suspicion, as if something external had to be established to replace the idols, about which the unlearned could teach. Only the external word[13] should be used according to every scriptural example and commandment, especially as we are shown in 1 Corinthians 14 and Colossians 3[:16]. In time all learning from the single word might become somewhat old-fashioned, and even if it never produces harm, I [Grebel] would never think up and introduce something new. I do not want to be the same as the negligent, falsely sparing, and seductive learned ones. I do not want to contrive, teach or establish a single thing on the basis of personal opinion.

Strive with the word and create a Christian community with the help of Christ and his rule [about the Lord's Supper], as we find it set forth in Matthew 18 and applied in the [Pauline] epistles. If you practice earnestness, common prayer, and aversion to evil, following faith and love, without commandments and without being forced, then God will help you and your lambs to full purity, and the songs and the tablets will fall. There is more than enough wisdom and counsel in Scripture about how a person should teach and govern all estates and all people, and make them wise and pious. Whoever does not want to improve and believe, and whoever opposes the word and action of God, and thus remains as he is, should not be put to death; but after Christ and his word – his rule – have been preached to him, and he has been admonished by three witnesses and the community, then – we speak informed by God's word – he should be regarded as a heathen and a tax collector and be left to himself.[14]

Also, one should not protect the gospel and those who accept it with the sword, nor should they protect themselves, as we have learned from our brother[15] that you believe and that you subscribe to. Truly believing Christians are sheep in the midst of wolves, sheep for slaughtering. They must be baptized in fear, need, grief, persecution, suffering, and dying. They must be tested in the fire, and they must not find the haven of eternal rest by killing their bodily enemies; rather they must attain it by killing their spiritual enemies. Also, true

[13] I.e. the preaching of the pure gospel.
[14] I.e. placed under the ban and excluded from the community.
[15] Evidently the goldsmith Hans Hujuff the Younger, who had come to Zurich from Halle, and with whose family Müntzer had contacts.

Christians use neither the worldly sword nor war, for among them killing has been totally abolished. Indeed, believers practiced these things at the time of the old law [Old Testament], during which time (so far as we know) after they had conquered the promised land, war became a plague. No more about this.

With respect to baptism, your writings please us well and we want you to teach us further. We are told that without the rule of Christ about binding and loosening [Mt. 18:15–18], not even an adult should be baptized. Scripture says that baptism washes away sins through faith and the blood of Christ (completely transforming the mind of the baptized person and believer). It means that a person should be dead to sin and should walk in a newness of life and spirit, and that one is certainly saved if through inner baptism one realizes the inner meaning of faith. So, it is not that the water confirms and increases faith, as the learned ones at Wittenberg say, nor that it is a great consolation and the last refuge on a death bed. In the same way, baptism does not save, a doctrine which Augustine, Tertullian, Theophylactus,[16] and Cyprian have taught, and which denies the faith and suffering of Christ for older adults, and denies the suffering of Christ for unbaptized infants. We stand by the following passages of Scripture – Genesis 8[:21], Deuteronomy 1[:39], 30[:6], 31[:13]; and 1 Corinthians 14[:20], Wisdom 12[:1f, 18f.]; again, 1 Peter 2[:2], Romans 1, 2, 7, and 10, Matthew 18[:1–6] and 19[:13–15], Mark 9[:33–47] and 10[:13–16], and Luke 18[:15–17], etc. [And we hold to what these passages teach:] that all children who have not yet attained the knowledge to distinguish between good and evil, and who have not yet eaten from the tree of knowledge, are certainly saved through the suffering of Christ, the new Adam, who returned to them the life that was cursed, because they would only have been subject to death and damnation if Christ had not suffered. Christ died for innocent children who are not yet capable of harming the world. [We will continue to hold this] unless someone can prove to us that Christ did not suffer for children.

But if someone maintains that faith is demanded of all who are to be saved, we exclude children [from this]; and we hold that they will be saved without faith though they do not believe, on the basis of the passages of Scripture mentioned above. And instead, we conclude

---

[16] An eleventh-century Byzantine ecclesiastical teacher.

from the description of baptism, from the biblical accounts (according to which no child was baptized), and from the scriptural passages mentioned above (which are the only ones in all Scripture which say how children are to be dealt with, and the whole of the rest of Scripture does not concern children) that the baptism of children is a senseless, blasphemous abomination, contrary to all Scripture. It is also contrary to the papacy; for from Cyprian and Augustine we find that for many years after the time of the apostles, for six hundred years, believers and unbelievers were baptized together, etc.[17]

Since you [Müntzer] affirm this view ten times better and have published your protests against the baptism of children, we hope that you do not act contrary to the eternal word, wisdom, and commandment of God, according to which only believers should be baptized, and we hope that you baptize no child.[18] If you or Karlstadt will not write against the baptism of children and all that goes with it – how and why one should baptize, etc. – then I (Conrad Grebel) will step forward and write out fully what I have begun to write against all who, up to now, (you excepted) have written enticingly and presumptuously about baptism, defending in German the senseless, blasphemous baptism of children, like Luther, Leo [Jud], Osiander and the Strasbourgers,[19] and also some who have acted in a still more shameful way. If God does not avert it, I and the rest of us will be more certain of persecution from the learned ones than from other people. We bid you not to use the old customs of the Antichrist, such as the sacrament, the Mass, the signs, etc., and to stick to the word alone. And we bid you conduct yourself as is appropriate to all who are sent by God, you and Karlstadt especially. And we hope that the two of you will do more against all the preachers of all nations.

Regard us as your brothers, understand that this our writing comes from great pleasure and hope in you for the sake of God, and admonish, console and strengthen us, as you certainly are able. Bid God the Lord for us that he come to assist our faith, for we would gladly believe. And if God also permits us to pray, we will pray too for

[17] I.e. adults from believing homes and converts from among the heathen were alike baptized on confession of faith.

[18] Grebel and his friends may have heard that, despite his written criticisms of infant baptism, Müntzer continued to baptize children at Allstedt.

[19] Leo Jud (d. 1542) was Zwingli's colleague in Zurich and Osiander a reformer at Nuremberg who supported Luther; the "Strasbourgers" were undoubtedly Martin Bucer and Wolfgang Capito, perhaps also Jacob Sturm.

you and everybody, that we all may live according to our calling and estate. May God grant us this through Jesus Christ our savior. Amen. Greet all the brothers from us, the pastors and the lambs, so that they accept the word of faith and salvation with desire and hunger, etc.

One thing more. We desire your written reply; and if you are publishing anything, send it to us by this messenger or another. If you and Karlstadt are of one mind, we would also like to be informed. We hope and believe it. We commend to you this messenger, who has also brought a letter to our dear brother Karlstadt. And if you visit Karlstadt, so that you answer us together, it would be a sincere pleasure for us. The messenger is to return to us. If we have not paid him enough, the balance will be paid on his return.

God be with us.

If we have not understood correctly, inform and teach us. Zurich, on the fifth day of the month of fall in the year 1523. [Signed:] Conrad Grebel, Andreas Castelberger, Felix Manz, Hans Oggenfuss, Bartholomew Pur, Heinrich Aberli, and your other brothers in Christ, if God wills it, who have written this to you. We wish you, us all, and all your lambs, until another letter, the true word of God, true faith, love, and hope, with all peace and grace of God through Jesus Christ. Amen.

I, Conrad Grebel, wanted to write Luther in the name of us all and admonish him to give up sparing the weak,[20] which he practices without scriptural basis and which he and his followers have started in the world. But the rough circumstances and lack of time have not allowed me to do it. You do it, according to your duty, etc.

This letter is intended for Thomas Müntzer at Allstedt near the Harz mountains.

Most sincerely loved brother Thomas. I wrote hurriedly in the name of us all, and I thought that this messenger would not delay so that we could also write Luther. But due to rain he has waited and delayed. So I have also written to Luther on my behalf and that of my and your brothers.[21] And I admonished him to desist from falsely protecting the weak, which is what he and his followers themselves

---

[20] Grebel and his associates agreed with Karlstadt and Müntzer that Luther was guilty of temporizing about Reformation changes on the false assumption that one should not offend the "weak."

[21] This letter to Luther has not survived.

are. Andreas Castelberger has written to Karlstadt. In addition, Hans Hujuff of Halle, our fellow citizen and fellow brother, who was recently with you, has received a letter here and a shameful pamphlet of Luther's,[22] which no one who wants to be as important as the apostles should have written. Paul teaches differently: "but the servant of the lord," etc.[23] I see that he wants to declare you an outlaw and hand you over to the princes to whom he has made his gospel subservient, just as Aaron worshipped Moses.

With respect to your pamphlet and protest,[24] I find you blameless, unless you totally reject baptism, which I cannot conclude from it. Rather, you damn the baptism of children and the lack of understanding about baptism. We want to study better in your writings and in the Bible what the water means in John 3[:5]. The brother of Hujuff writes that you have preached against the princes, [and] that one should attack them with the fist [i.e. use physical violence]. If this is true, or if you want to defend war, feasting, and singing, or other things which you do not find in the clear word – for you do not find these enumerated points there – then I admonish you by the common salvation of us all. If you end these and all other human opinions, now and hereafter, you will become completely blameless. In other respects you please us better than anyone in Germany or in any other country. If you fall into the hands of Luther and the dukes, set aside the points about which I have taken issue with you and stand by the others like a hero and warrior of God. Be strong. You have the Bible (from which Luther makes bible, bubel, babel[25]) as a protection against the idolatrous Lutheran sparing of the weak, which he and the learned pastors here have planted in the whole world. [The Bible is also protection] against their deceitful, negligent faith, and against their preaching, in which they do not teach Christ as they should, and in which they have just opened the gospel to the whole world, so that everyone reads it or should have it read to him. But they did not open it to many, for everyone clings to the words of the learned. Among us

---

[22] I.e. Luther's attack on Müntzer, *Letter to the Princes of Saxony Concerning the Rebellious Spirit* (*Eyn brieff an die Fürsten zu Sachsen von dem auffrurischen geyst*) (June 1524), *WA* XV, 210–21. Müntzer's *A Highly Provoked Defense* was his reply to Luther.

[23] *porro servum Domini etc.* The reference is unclear; perhaps it was a misquoted reference to 2 Tim. 2:24.

[24] Müntzer's *Protest or Offering.*

[25] Luther used this expression in charging that for Müntzer the Bible was meaningless. Grebel was leveling the same charge against Luther.

there are not twenty who believe the word of God; they believe only in personalities – Zwingli, Leo [Jud], and others who are regarded elsewhere as learned. And if you must suffer on this account, you know well that it cannot be otherwise. Christ must suffer still more in his members. But he will strengthen the members and keep them firm to the end. May God give you and us grace, no matter how much our pastors are furious with us, and from the public pulpit call us rogues and Satans disguised as angels of light. In time we will also see persecution which is caused by them come over us. So pray to God for us on this account.

Once more we admonish you, and we do this in writing, because we love you for the clarity of your message and view you with respect and in solidarity. Do not do, teach, or establish anything based on human opinion, your own or another's. Whatever has been so established, tear it down again. And may you establish and teach only God's clear word and customs, including the rule of Christ, an uncontrived baptism, and an uncontrived Lord's Supper (as we have touched on in the first letter and about which you are better informed than a hundred of us). If you and Karlstadt, Jacob Strauss and Michael Stiefel[26] do not strive purely and stainlessly with all your power (as I and my brothers, however, hope that you will do), then a miserable gospel indeed has come into the world. But you are much purer than our clergy here in Zurich and those at Wittenberg, who lurch every day from one perversion of Scripture to another, and from one blindness to others that are more serious. I believe and maintain that they want to become true papists and popes. No more for now. May the God of hosts with his son Jesus Christ, our savior, and his spirit and word be with you and us all.

Conrad Grebel, Andreas Castelberger, Felix Manz, Heinrich Aberli, Hans Brötli,[27] Hans Oggenfuss, and Hans Hujuff your fellow countryman from Halle – your brothers and, for Luther, seven new young Müntzers.

If you are left free to preach further and nothing happens to you, we will send you a copy of our writing to Luther and his answer, if he replies to us. We have admonished him, and our clergy here too. If God does not hinder it, we will show their failings through this [letter], and we will not fear what may happen to us as a result.

---

[26] Court preacher to Count Albrecht of Mansfeld.
[27] Also known by the Latinized version of his name, Johannes Panicellus.

Otherwise, we have kept no other copies of the letters we have written, except the one to Martin [Luther], your opponent. For this reason, accept with good intentions our unlearned, unformed writing and rest assured that we have written it out of true love. For we are equal in our message, our tribulations, and our opponents, even though you are more learned and stronger in spirit. For the sake of this equality we have spoken or written to you so fully. If God wants it so, and if you are willing to greet us as your Christians and to reply to us all together in a long letter, you will awaken in us great pleasure and increased love for you.

5 Andreas Karlstadt, *Whether One Should Proceed Slowly*

Whether one should proceed slowly, and avoid offending the weak in matters that concern God's will

Andreas Karlstadt 1524[1]

I, Andreas Karlstadt, wish my especially beloved brother in Christ, Bartel Bach, city secretary of Joachimstal,[2] the art of knowing God through our lord Jesus Christ.

Dear brother, in reply to my description of some changes that have taken place here [i.e. Orlamünde], you wrote me that, as far as you are

---

[1] The work, printed at Basel in mid-November 1524, is a reply to Luther's eight "Invocavit Sermons" of March 1522, which were preached following Luther's return to Wittenberg in early 1522; *WA* X/3, 1–64. Luther's sermons were delivered in an effort to moderate the pace of change at Wittenberg and to reassert his leadership over the reform movement there, which Karlstadt had largely assumed while Luther was in hiding at Wartburg castle. Luther's position in these sermons was that Karlstadt's insistence on immediate changes, binding on all, was a new form of legalism; instead Luther urged delay for the sake of the weak (i.e. those who had not yet been won over by preaching) and the princes, who had not approved of the changes. In this reply, Karlstadt calls for the right of every local congregation to implement changes, regardless of those who might be offended and irrespective of the approval of superior political authorities. In preparing the translation, Karlstadt's marginal references to Scripture and marginal comments have been transposed to the body of the text and enclosed within parentheses; editorial material is enclosed within square brackets. The translation is based on the text in E. Hertzsch, ed., *Karlstadts Schriften aus den Jahren 1523–25*, 2 vols. (Neudrucke deutscher Literaturwerke des 16. und 17. Jahrhunderts, 325) (Halle/Saale, 1956), I, 73–97.

[2] Joachimstal was an important mining center in the Erzgebirge region of Bohemia. Karlstadt had been on friendly terms for several years with Bartel Bach, the city secretary (*Stadtschreiber*), who held an influential position in the community. Karlstadt's effort to win Bach's support for himself rather than Luther was unsuccessful.

concerned, you would like to proceed slowly. And through this writing you gave me to understand, without saying it, that one should not proceed quickly or suddenly but slowly in order to avoid offending the weak. You are simply doing what the whole world does now, which is to cry, "The weak, the weak! The sick, the sick! Not so fast! Slowly, slowly!" For this reason I am not angry with you. Nevertheless in this matter you are saying, "Slowly! The sick!," with a great many people. Only you are saying it more politely and with greater sophistication. Accordingly I must tell you that neither in this case nor in other matters concerning God should you regard how the great masses speak or judge. Rather, you should look straight at God's word [i.e. Scripture]. For it has long been clear that the princes, for whom the scribes write, and the great mass of the people have erred formerly and are capable of error. On account of this, God has also ordained what the princes and the whole crowd or ecclesiastical councils should sacrifice because of their ignorance or error (Leviticus 4[:1ff.]). Through this ordinance God clearly shows for all time that all the learned, the princes, and the masses can err and stumble. Therefore God alone has also let it be proclaimed in general and in particular that each one should hasten to righteousness for himself (Exodus 23[:2]) and that no one must follow the masses in deviating from what is right.

God also calls it prostitution and whoring eyes when people look at things other than his rule of conduct – that is, God's word. God has forbidden us to follow our own thoughts. All our good opinions have been chopped down and altogether eradicated: acting or speaking as other people act or speak, or as we believe to be good (Luke 15[:1f.], Isaiah [29:14], Matthew 16[:4, 13ff.], Deuteronomy 12[:8]). The wisdom of all wise men must be destroyed to its foundations if divine wisdom is to arise. Not only your own wisdom, dear brother, must become nothing but foolishness, but also the wisdom of all other people. This must happen so that you do not let yourself be moved by either learned or unlearned people, and so that without mediation you hit upon the naked truth, which frees you and will not let you be harmed for eternity. Look here! Just as you are a reed – something which you should avoid – so too all learned people should become weak reeds to you.[3] The naked truth alone, however, should be your

---

[3] Karlstadt describes Bach's moderate, compromising position as that of a weak reed;

foundation and your rock. If you have this truth, then you will remain untroubled and unwavering, even though all learned people were to change and the apostles to fall away – if that were possible. Accordingly, Paul says, "If I or an angel taught differently, he should be banned" (Galatians 1:[8]). He who understands and grasps the truth in its essentials keeps it, even if Paul preaches against it. Therefore, everyone who wants to withstand the winds and the waves should be eager to experience the true foundations of God. This is the reason why God let it be commanded through Moses that all Jews should hang tassels, small flaps, and yellow cords on their clothes, so that they would be reminded to think of God's commandments as often as were aware of these small flaps, which they had to look at daily (Numbers 15[:37ff.]).

It follows from this that we are bound to Scripture, that no one may judge according to the arbitrary opinion of his heart (Numbers 15[:40], Jeremiah 23[:16ff.]), and also that those who long for things other than God's word are pursuing prostitution. And in truth it is real prostitution and spiritual adultery, no matter how small or insignificant such looking around and desiring seems to the flesh and to reason. For God, the husband of the created spirit,[4] is despised or disregarded and forgotten as soon as the soul looks at things other than his word in divine matters. Since it must always be the case that no one can serve two masters, a servant of two lords must abandon the one to the extent that he clings to the other. Now, spiritual adultery is always a devilish, great vice. All men fall into this blasphemy who have more regard for the princes of the highly learned[5] or for a great assembly, such as an ecclesiastical council, than for God's word. They also fall into it who are looking for something other than God's true message.

For this reason, dear brother, you, no less than the most lowly, are obligated at once, constantly, earnestly, and industriously to consider God's judgments, which are just and true in themselves, and not to pay attention to the strong or the weak. The great crowd can err and

---

instead, Karlstadt urges resolute firmness, so that it is the opponents of change who will be forced to waver and compromise.

[4] God, the uncreated spirit, is the natural partner of the soul, the spirit which he has created.

[5] Karlstadt views the learned theologians as the agents of the princes. Undoubtedly he is thinking of Luther and the theologians at Wittenberg. Here he condemns as blasphemy having more regard for secular authority than for the injunctions of Scripture.

lead one into error. The anointed ones [the clergy] always write about their anointing, for they have been smeared outwardly; but they also fall into error, which displeases God. Now, since this is the case, you must come to the experience of divine righteousness and truth, and you must always pay attention to God's words. All those "wise" in Scripture should be nothing to you, and no one must wait for someone to follow him.

In acting one should not have regard for others.

Now, as I have just proven through scriptural testimony that no one should look around for the other person or wait until others follow him in the knowledge of the truth (John 5[:39–41]), so too when it concerns action, we should obey all of God's commands according to our capacity and not wait until those without understanding, or the weak, follow. For God has always commanded all of us to teach his covenant and to act accordingly. It is always written, "Learn it and keep it so that you act according to it" (Deuteronomy 4[:2], 5[:1]). Action has been commanded of all of us, and each one should do what God commands, even if the whole world hesitates and does not want to follow.

Look, I am asking you whether a son should wait to honor his parents until the weak follow, understand, and want to honor their parents? You would have to reply, "Certainly, those who understand should not rob their parents of their honor, nor wait until all young people follow with understanding and desire." I am asking whether one should wait to stop coveting the goods of other people until others do so? May one steal until the thieves stop stealing? And thus I ask, again and again, in the case of all the commandments, whether it is proper that we wait until others have learned, and have the will to follow us and to do what God wants.

Now, just as I have asked this with respect to the commandments which concern the love of one's neighbor, I also ask it about the works and deeds which directly concern God's honor. Namely, I ask whether I should let the idols stand, which God commands me to remove, until all the weak follow in removing them? Again, may I blaspheme God as long as the others do not stop blaspheming? If you say yes, then the enemies of Christ and God can also say, with the same right, that murderers may murder, thieves may steal, adulterers may commit adultery, and similar rogues may practice every kind of vice until all rogues become pious. For there is one reason and one basis in all commandments.

I shall never say that rogues may sin, for I know that it is the same whether one sins out of ignorance or intentionally violates God's commandment, and they must suffer their punishment for it (Leviticus 5[:17]). How much more, then, must they be punished who participate in adultery, theft, murder, and blasphemy? (Psalm 50[:16ff.].) They shall always be punished in the same measure as those who do such things privately. The Lord says, "The servant who knows his master's will and acts against it shall be beaten severely" (Luke 12[:47]). God will beat him who sins out of ignorance. But how much more seriously and strictly will God punish him who sins against his commandment in order to please a rogue! Paul says, "You shall have no fellowship with the servants of idols, adulterers, and the like" [2 Cor. 6:14ff.]. And you think that one must proceed slowly and gradually abandon evil! But I know that St. Peter will gradually turn the key which he is supposed to have for heaven, and he will get it stuck in the lock or turn it the wrong way for them. And he will always unlock as slowly for them as they were slow in coming [to act rightly].

What should I say? Should we teach God's commandments slowly? Should we wait for the masses? Should one look at the others and wait to see who wants to be first? Oh, how well would it please the great princes if people were no more ready for tithes, payments, and labor services than they are for divine services? They throw the disobedient into prison towers and stocks, and they punish them until their subjects become obedient. And through their rage the princes pronounce the judgment against themselves which God will show them, and which they show to others on account of their disobedience.[6] What lord can tolerate it if he commands his servants to do something, and they all remain silent, no one wanting to be first or to begin?

God will punish them all together when he summons those who failed to obey, even if they offer golden excuses and bring out the best intentions of brotherly love. For there should always be a great and special love between married people. Nevertheless Christ says that he who excused himself because of his wife was unworthy of his meal,

---

[6] God will proceed against the princes with the same severity as they do against their disobedient subjects.

etc. [see Lk. 14:20]. Each person who understands correctly should act correctly, without timidity and without looking around.

If one says, "You should preserve brotherly love," this means absolutely nothing, because it is not yet clear whether their brotherly love is not a cloak of Antichrist, which is certainly as wicked and harmful as any invention of the pope. But for now I will leave that undetermined and say that Christ has removed and cut off all brotherly love if it is against his commandment, or diverts the least person away from God. For love fulfills God's commandments, and it is impossible for someone to love Christ and to act against his commandment, or not to do what Christ commanded. That follows from this saying: "If you love me, then keep my commandments" (John 14[:21]). "He who is not with me is against me" (Matthew 12[:30]). "He who does not hate his father and mother, wife and children, cannot be my disciple," etc. Now, it is also true that it is impossible for one to love Christ and not live according to his commandments, or to hesitate, looking at someone else and waiting to see whether he also wants to do what is pleasing to God or not. Accordingly they will not tie a blindfold over my eyes, so that I omit something which God wants, or do something which God forbids, even though they preach and write to me for a thousand years about offending the weak and about brotherly love.

The Truth [Christ] says, "He who puts his hand to the plough and looks back is not fit for the kingdom of God" (Luke 9[:62]). But Christ says this about the one whom he called to follow him. And that person gave the following answer: "Lord, I want to follow you, but permit me to bless or take care of my family." Now if that person who has regard for others whom he should certainly take care of otherwise is not fit for the kingdom of God, how fit will those be who overlook God's commandments and who hold back for the sake of those who do not want to begin? (Luke 17). Lot's wife looked back and became a pillar of salt (Genesis 19[:26]). What may become of those who now look back at their idle and lazy brothers who intentionally remain blind and lazy?

When Christ said to Peter, "Follow me," and Peter said, "What does this person want?" Christ answered, "If I want him to remain thus until I return, what does it concern you?" (John 21[:19ff.]) See here! Even if God allows it to happen that some are lazy or unwilling to learn to act in the right way, and you do understand it, has he not called you sufficiently? Do you want to ask what others should do or when they will become pious? No! "Follow," it says. Do not stand still and do not consider whether others are also following.

What did Peter ask about the brotherly love of the Christians who were upset that he had baptized Cornelius, a heathen? (Acts 9–10) He did what he understood was God's will and did not ask anyone. But when his brothers wanted to speak to him about his act, he gave the answer that God wanted. Nevertheless there was in Peter's action something that one might reject or rebuke in terms of Christ's language, for he said, "You shall not take up heathen ways" [Mt. 10:5]. Thus Peter could have regarded their offense as justified. But Peter did not pay attention to their offense. What should we do in matters which God commands, or forbids with explicit language? Should we avoid giving offense? Now, if someone were to say, "Peter is not an example for us, but Christ; so give me an example about Christ," then I would say that Christ spoke with a woman of Samaria – and yet the Jews were not accustomed to speak with the Samaritans – and this also amazed his followers (John 4[:27]). Christ did not pay attention to their offense, but freely did that which his Father wanted done. I will demonstrate this in what follows with other examples, such as the sabbath, the temple, sacrifices, fasting, prayer, and the like.

In the matter of offending and in similar matters they[7] introduce Paul so vigorously because they want to prove and conclude that one should go slowly in matters that concern God. The whole day they cry, "The weak! The weak!" etc. But I know well how to quiet them. And I may freely say that Paul did not proceed slowly in more important matters than in our affairs here. And he did not consider that some were offended, or that some were sick, uncomprehending, and weak. We read that many thousands of Jews in Jerusalem had become believers (Acts 21[:20ff.]). They were greatly displeased that Paul taught and preached a departure from Moses, namely that one should not circumcise children or live according to tradition, etc. Therein you see that Paul did not consider that he was offending so many thousand uncomprehending Jews, but freely preached and did not spare the weak.

Here you may want to answer, "It seems to me that preaching and

---

[7] The Wittenberg theologians, especially Luther.

acting are two different things." To this I say that preaching is a work like other works – it is not done in vain, etc. Moreover, Paul prevented circumcision through his actions. How can one then say that we should be Paulinists and not undertake anything which contradicts brotherly love? Paul subsequently did something through which he quieted the outcry against him. This, however, does not force me to say that Paul did not prevent circumcision by his actions. For his Epistle to the Galatians is too evident for anyone to be able to conceal it. And one may conclude from this same Epistle that Paul did not regard the weak, but drew them away from Moses with compelling words when he said, "You foolish people, do you let yourselves be circumcised?"

Thus you have a sincere explanation why we here [in Orlamünde] are not obliged in either teaching or acting to refrain from carrying out God's commandment until our neighbors and the gourmets at Wittenberg follow.

Each community, large or small, should see for itself that it acts righteously and well, and it should wait for no one.

God has given a general law that all believing people – each congregation or community and each person – should hold to, and according to which they should judge. And this same law, which God also calls a covenant, was rightly proclaimed or read to all people. Not so that the whole assembly or community should be the kind of dead body which blind jurists fantasize as the body of the community when they say that this body in itself can neither hear nor see nor do anything. Rather, the covenant was proclaimed so that the people would have ears ready to hear, eyes ready to see, and limbs ready to act justly in everything that pleases God (Deuteronomy 29[:4ff.]). For this reason God also complained about lazy people and threatened to punish such negligent people if they had ears and yet did not hear, had eyes which did not see, and had limbs which did not act. Accordingly it is ever true that Moses summoned the whole multitude of the Jews, and that he explained God's commandments to the whole Jewish assembly. But he also always said that they should do what he taught them (Deuteronomy 4 throughout, 5, 6, 8, 11). And he said that they should be satisfied with his teaching and also with his actions, so that in this way they would add nothing to the teaching nor take away anything from it (Deuteronomy 12[:29–32]). Likewise, they would not consider performing any other action in God's service than what he taught them to do (Leviticus 16[:1ff.]). Moses bound his people so firmly to God's teaching, customs, laws, and the works of the law that they were forbidden to teach or do otherwise than what they had heard. And on account of the bond Moses called the law a covenant, although there were also other reasons.

But God's covenant concerns every individual community, and every household. So no community or household should wait until the others become wise and active. This is shown so often in Deuteronomy alone that I consider it unnecessary to supply evidence. How often it is written! "Within your gates you should keep the laws and customs of God" (Deuteronomy 17[:8–13]). "You should choose and ordain for yourselves judges who shall punish the violators of the covenant" (Deuteronomy 26 [see, rather, Dt. 16:18]). Did God say the following words only to the masses or to the community as a whole? "The lord your God commands you to act according to the whole of this law – customs and rights – from your whole heart and whole soul, as you have promised this to your lord" (Deuteronomy 5[:27ff.]). Who may say that one must keep the commandments of God only in some places, and that in other places we may break God's commandments? If you want to say that God commanded the Jews to set up stones in some places, then I will also say that God commanded that we should write his covenant (the covenant of his ten words[8]) not only in some cities but on the doorposts of houses as a reminder (Deuteronomy 4, 6[:5–9]). And also on the gates, so that they sway before and are evident to the eyes of the household servants and each community, so that in this way all are reminded to safeguard God's commandments (Deuteronomy 26, 27, 28). Not only some commandments, but all the commandments. Not only the Jews who heard Moses at that time, but their descendants. For Moses says, "your children and children's children" (Deuteronomy 6 [see, rather, Dt. 4:9]). Not for one day, but every day. "Your whole life," says Moses.

Each community should have its Levite who proclaims to it the covenant of peace and truth. And the father of each household should enjoin, repeat, and explain God's word to his children. From this it

---

[8] I.e. the Ten Commandments.

follows always that each community and household should pay attention, so that it understands God's commandment and acts accordingly. And God wants us so little to wait until others follow and
become pious that he has commanded that the godless be punished
just as other vices are punished (Deuteronomy 13 and 17). And in
addition he has commanded that whole cities that cultivate their
idolatry or do not want to turn to the right path be killed and
destroyed.

It is astonishing that our scripturally wise and our rulers punish
carnal adultery and allow spiritual adultery to go unpunished. They
want to defeat spiritual adultery with their breath and to stave off
carnal adultery with swords, iron, fire, and the executioner's wheel.
But is this not miserable conduct among Christians? Is it not a
devilish thing that they have more regard for, and punish more
severely, the dishonoring of man than the dishonoring of God? Moses
orders that idolatrous people or spiritual adulterers be killed no less
than carnal adulterers. If they looked at their Paul correctly, they
would certainly find that Paul did not punish the servants of idols less
than the servants of whores. Nor does it have to be true because they
want to have it thus, to defend their honor and their beautiful
reputation.

Action should promptly and always follow understanding.

Gracious God has produced some external works [miracles], and
through them has shown his paternal love. One of these is that God
has given our forefathers divine wisdom and understanding
(Deuteronomy 4[:3–6]) in miraculous visions and stories through his
high, noble word, and has given it to us through our ancestors. For
this reason, all people should rightly say, "What excellent people is
this, having such a high art of knowing God, and such just customs
and laws?" And God has presented to us his covenant, which holds
our wisdom and understanding, so that in all actions that we do and
omit, we act, live, and judge wisely and with understanding
(Deuteronomy 29[:9]). For in everything God wants to have understanding servants who know what they do or omit, why they do or omit
it, and for whose honor. And what God sends and why he sends it
should be understood in sweetness and bitterness, in an active and in

a passive way. As Moses said, "So keep now the word of this covenant and act according to it, so that you are wise in all that you do" (Deuteronomy 29[:9]). And Paul said, "Take heed that you walk prudently, not as the unwise do but as the wise. Therefore do not become ignorant but understand whatever may be the will of the lord" (Ephesians 5[:15–17]). Therefore, God complains through Isaiah that they do not consider his works (Isaiah 5[:1–7]). And Christ often rebuked his apostles because they did not understand his work or teaching. But they – that is, wisdom and understanding – should be followed not only when you do something, but also when you suffer something, so that you know what you are suffering, and why, and for whose honor, and for whose benefit. For that is the characteristic of suffering. As Isaiah says, "Tribulation or worry gives understanding" (Isaiah 28[:11–12?]). And Moses says, "God gives you tribulations so that you are ashamed on account of your sins" (Leviticus 26[:40ff.]). And Paul says, "Affliction gives birth to patience, but patience brings understanding or experience" (Romans 5[:3–5]). For experience is understanding and the perfect work, of which James writes (James 1[:4–5]). Without understanding, no work of God is perfect. Without understanding we are like a muzzled horse in which there is no reason. Accordingly, God's word has been revealed to us out of great grace, so that through it we become intelligent, wise, and understanding, especially through resignation.[9] But it is a great and highly treasured thing that God's secret has been revealed to us. Those who are clever in the ways of the world regard it as a great treasure to be a counsellor of a mortal prince. And everyone holds in high regard such a person, who is beloved by this same prince, etc. How much more highly is a person to be regarded, and how highly and preciously should he treasure the fact that God has revealed his secret to him? Especially since he has a new, divine, and superhuman wisdom? (Deuteronomy 4) That is one reason why God has revealed his secret to us.

The second reason why we should have an eternal and unshakable memory of all his words and stories is so that for all our lives, and at all times, we do not forget any of his words – so that we always fear God and cling to him. But the remembrance should be passionate, industrious, and powerful. It does not hesitate but breaks forth with

---

[9] *Gelassenheit*, a term used by the German mystics to describe a condition of indifference to worldly pleasures.

passion and is active. For this is a common rule: he is damned who performs the lord's work negligently, or who performs it deceptively (Jeremiah 48[:10]). Although the vengeance of God is spoken about in the passage, "May he be damned whose sword spares blood" (Jeremiah 48[:10]), this is much truer in works where blood is not shed. For if it is true that God, who is merciful in forgiving, wants prompt punishment, how much more true is it that he who is lazy in producing works which occur for the betterment of his neighbor is damned, and is an abomination before God. God wants a person to be a free, enthusiastic giver, who gives quickly and willingly. A ready and willing mind, inclined to action, pleases God (2 Corinthians 9[:7]).

All this flows from the eternal and fervent memory of divine words. Whoever reflects on divine teaching rightly and well cannot stand still, nor be idle or lazy, if God's speech obligates and impels him to act. If he remains silent in a case where he can and should act, then this is a certain sign that he has forgotten or does not have the kind of memory he should have, namely from his whole heart (Deuteronomy 29).

Someone could question this as follows: "You want to obligate a servant of God always to act, etc. (Deuteronomy 4 and 11[:1]). There is good reason for this in that it is written, 'You shall always, your whole life long, act according to the law of God' (Tobit 4[:20]). You should always praise God: 'I will always praise God' (Psalm 34[:1]). 'Whoever is a friend always loves his friend' (Proverbs 17[:17]). A friend always shows his love by action, in the manner that Christ says, 'In this they will recognize that you are my disciples, that you love one another' (John 13[:35]). But on the other hand, I also see that it is written, 'Every action has its time' (Ecclesiastes 9[10]). No action can go on forever; it occurs for a time and then stops for a time. Also, God so ordained some commandments that we must keep them at certain times, and not our whole life long or every day, as the Hebrew understanding and you [Karlstadt] want to have it. Namely, God established the Sabbath on the seventh day, the seventh week, the seventh year, the fifteenth year, which came from the number seven. He also established for one time in the year the feast of Passover (Leviticus 25), for one time the feast of the Tabernacles, and the like. They must occur only at one time in the year and not every day."

My answer is that even if such figurative language bound us

---

[10] Perhaps an error for Ec. 3:1ff.

according to the letter, just as it formerly bound the Jews, nevertheless God's word would endure – namely this: "You should keep
God's commandments every day" (Deuteronomy 11[:13]). For these
words "every day" means that each person should keep God's commandments according to the time, place, and occasion that God has
commanded. There is a time when we should awaken and be busy.
There is a time for sleeping. If there are poor people, we should help.
If we do not have needy people, our hand may rest. Nonetheless, we
must act every day according to God's commandments. We must
celebrate every seventh day, etc. We must always come to the
assistance of the poor, the destitute, the imprisoned, the naked, and
the like. We must forgive the debt of the impoverished if we have such
debtors; if we do not have any, then God's law does not bind us. In
the same way, the poor [among the Jews] were not obligated to make
more expensive sacrifices than the rich. But nevertheless this
endures: you should fulfill God's commandments every day. Every
day you should actively show your neighbor your love of God and
neighbor.

The same is true with respect to the abolition of blasphemous and
Christ-blaspheming images [statues and pictures] or Masses. Where
we who believe in God rule, and where we find images, we should
remove them and deal with them as God commanded. We should also
do this for our whole life, or every day. Yes, if we find images in our
community – every community in every city – each community is in
the same way responsible for distancing itself from images
(Deuteronomy 14, 15). This principle must always be right and
endure well: You should act every day according to God's commandments, and it is right and good when his commandments are correctly
understood.

Figurative commandments concern and oblige only the weak. And
on account of the weak it is good that the figurative commandments
were kept and are still kept. As Paul says, "Everything is proper but
everything does not edify" (1 Corinthians 11 [see, rather, 1 Cor.
10:23]). And again, "Although you have true knowledge or understanding, you do not have it in everything. Nor do you know what you
should know" (1 Corinthians 8[:2]). Because the understanding of
many Jews then was small and their blindness large, they were unfree
and bound, and obligated to keep God's figurative language, although
God intended something other than the literal meaning of his words.

And the weak ones erred about the eternal will of God. Thus, they had to keep the sabbath and other celebrations, and fleshly duties such as bathing in water, etc., according to the literal sense of God's language and according to God's implied will, until they recognized more deeply God's true justice and just truth. But whoever broke and violated such a figurative commandment of God had to make a sincere apology, as Christ did, and David, when he made no outward sacrifice to God, Psalm 40[:6–9]. This issue does not belong here, but I have mentioned it so that one knows in what measure the divine commandments must be kept.

"Every day" means, figuratively, at the proper and designated time. But fundamentally it means that one must keep God's commandments every day as far as the occasion requires. There are some commandments which require a particular time, location, or occasion. These had to be kept every day – that is, according to the circumstances. And no one was allowed to look around at another. Whoever was idle merited punishment. But some commandments encompass no particular occasion, time, or location. These commandments must be followed constantly and at no time omitted or violated. These commandments are of this kind: you shall not make, possess, or tolerate images; you shall not steal, murder, commit adultery, bear false witness, covet another's goods, and the like. Such commandments bind us at all times and at all places. Whoever breaks one of these commandments once, anywhere, is a transgressing, disobedient, unjust despiser of God. Nor should a person look around for any assembly or ecclesiastical council, for he already has his commandment which he should not break. Accordingly, he should not make any image, or tolerate them in places where [the people of God] rule, whether they represent God, Christ or the saints. Also he should not blaspheme God, nor do anything similar that God's covenant forbids (Moses expounds this and the prophets interpret Moses' explanation further). He can only do such things if he has received from God a certain and infallible command to break a commandment. As Moses received a command from God to make images of birds over the chair of mercy [judges' chair], and the image of twelve oxen which should hold back the sea, and to set up the image of a snake in the wilderness.[11]

---

[11] Karlstadt is replying here to Luther's Third Sermon of 11 March 1522.

He who does not have such a command from God knows that he sins and disobeys God's voice, which has commanded that we should make no images, nor tolerate those already made, in those places where alleged believers rule. In the same way, no one should steal, murder, commit adultery, or covet another's goods. If he breaks any of these commandments he is disobedient, unjust and sinful. Nor can he be excused because of any group of weak or sick people.

But if God orders someone to steal, rob, murder, commit adultery, or covet another's goods, and if he were certain that this was the divine intention, then he should steal – as the children of Israel stole from the Egyptians (Exodus 12[:35–36]) – and then he should murder – as Moses murdered the kings of Sihon and Heshbron, etc. (Acts 7[:24], Deuteronomy 2[:26–36] and 29[:6–7][12]). But without God's order we must do everything that God included in his Ten Commandments. And we must pay attention to no one, but only to God's commandment and to ourselves, so that we do or omit only what is truly pleasing to God.

God always speaks according to the capacity of the Hebrew tongue.[13] But some oppose God's commandment and word with this escape clause: "not every day." "One should," they say, "delay and not go further for sake of the weak." But what does this mean, except to say that we should let an ecclesiastical council decide beforehand what we do, and in what measure we should serve God? It is always the same thing with this talk that for the sake of the weak one should not promptly fulfill God's commandment but delay until the weak become bright and strong.

Nevertheless, this view could make sense if it were stated properly, as Paul taught. It is odd too that some people want to elevate the weak by delaying and by neglecting clear divine commandments. They actually set the weak back further with their horns and shoulders [i.e. delay and neglect], as Ezekiel prophesied about the horns of oxen.[14] They have absolutely no teaching about that. Thus Paul, whom they improperly and nonsensically introduce as a model, is entirely opposed to their position about sparing the weak. What should I say? I say that this outcry – "Not too fast! Not too soon! Spare them! The

---

[12] Sihon was king of Heshbron.
[13] Karlstadt evidently viewed Hebrew as the natural language of theology.
[14] Ezek. 34:21, "Because you push with side and shoulder, and thrust at all the weak with your horns, till you have scattered them abroad."

weak, the weak! The sick, the sick!" – is an evident addition to God's word and contrary to this command: "You should not add" (Deuteronomy 4[:2]).

This delay – "I restrain myself, I spare the weak and excuse them until they come" – is also the abrupt end of divine works and contrary to this commandment: "You should neither add nor subtract." And contrary to this one: "You should do just what God commanded and always do this" (Deuteronomy 11[:8, 18ff.]).

Offense and love of neighbor are a devilish cloak for every evil.

It is unjust to use the pretext of not offending the weak and of brotherly love, and, under the appearance of not offending and of brotherly love, to practice idolatry. And to allow the Mass and other blasphemies to sprout and bloom. And I will deal with the significance of this issue in a little book that I am writing about giving offense.[15] But on this occasion I want to say that our images are laid out or erected in order to trap and entangle people, and for their ruination, as God has said through Moses and his prophets. In addition, idols are more dangerous in Christendom than whorehouses, and more suitable for committing spiritual adultery than any whore or rogue. Therefore, people do not practice brotherly love who, under the appearance of brotherly love, say that we should maintain idols (which the laity call saints) in the churches, on hills, in valleys, and at crossroads until the weak become strong. For they preach brotherly harm and not brotherly service or love. Such a pretext is nothing but a villain's cloak and a hidden snare for the destruction of poor souls – if God speaks truthfully and Paul teaches correctly. They speak and teach the contrary position in this matter of offending the weak.

We should take such harmful things from the weak, tear them out of their hands, and not pay attention if they cry, scream, or curse about it. The time will come when they who now curse and damn us will thank us. Through an analogy I will show you that he who would break the will of fools with violence would demonstrate toward them the true and best brotherly love. Isaiah says that fools who maintain idols do not understand their foolishness, and they do not know that

---

[15] This work was not published.

they maintain a harmful, foolish thing.[16] I want to say this first. Then I ask this: if I see that a small child has a pointed, sharp knife in his hand and wants to keep it, would I show him brotherly love if I were to allow him to have the harmful knife and have his own way, so that he wounds or kills himself? Or would I show brotherly love when I break his will and take the knife? You must always say that if you take from a child that which would harm him, then you perform a fatherly or brotherly Christian act. For Christ depicted for us genuine Christian and brotherly love in the scriptural passages where he says, "If your hand offends you, cut it off and throw it away" (Matthew 18[:8]). Christ said this in order to point out genuine brotherly love. And Paul agrees with Christ when he speaks about offending.

But if it is true that I am responsible, and that each one is obligated, if he loves God and his neighbor, to take from the foolish their harmful and offensive things without regard for their anger, howls, and curses, then why is there all this talk about brotherly love – that out of brotherly love we should allow idols and other offenses to remain until the weak follow? What they call brotherly love is actually brotherly harm and offense. Their love is like the love of a crazy mother who allows her children to go their own way – and to end on the gallows. Christ never said that we should proceed slowly with offenses if we want to remove them and cast them aside. He says, "Cut it off, chop it down, and throw it away, so that it does not offend you." Moses also says, "Your eye should not spare him, and you should not pity him or conceal him. Instead you should strangle him. Your hand should fall over him first" (Deuteronomy 13[:8–9] and 33[:9], Micah 7[:10]). Moses says this about people who offend. How much more, then, does this language compel the abolition of the offenses through which ignorant souls fall? Such souls have neither flesh nor spirit, neither blood nor breath, and no one may hope for their improvement. About them Moses will always say and cry out, "Spare them not! Kill them! Your hand should be the first!"

Now, whoever wants to add to these words and say that one should proceed slowly, not promptly, and that one should spare the weak and not begin suddenly, this person abuses the words of Christ and Moses. And he adds his own words in opposition to God, and he turns himself into a false Christian and false prophet. Christ says, "If

---

[16] Is. 44:1ff.

65

your eye offends you" – that is, if you understand that your eye offends you – "tear it out and throw it away." When does he say, "Go slowly. Do not be too quick" or "Spare the weak"?

Oh, what great and pernicious blindness! If the world knew what harm comes to simple souls from idols and other offenses it would bite its fingers before it tolerated such fraud. But is it not a villain's cloak to preach and promise hellish brotherly harm under the appearance of brotherly love? Oh, devourers of the world! Christ says that it is better for you to chop your hand off, to tear your eye out, and to throw them away than for you to be thrown into the fires of hell with offensive things (Matthew 18[:8]). I have written in great detail about the damage that comes from maintaining devilish saints – i.e., those which our neighbors call saints and we call idols – against the miserable and wretched goat, Emser, but this writing was suppressed on account of the new papists.[17] But those who now read and understand the Bible note well how I have been oppressed by violence, contrary to God.

The devil has thought up this villain's cloak, just as he also invented the lie that "images are the laity's books."[18] For by this means the devil has thievishly robbed God's word of its honor. And he has given this honor to horrible, miserable, blaspheming creatures. And he has compared God's word to idolatrous filth, which God hates and wants us to hate and flee from. It cannot be expressed to what degree God is disgraced by idols and the weak person is destroyed by them. May a patron of idols step up and tell me why the servants of idols have a root that bears gall and wormwood (Exodus 23[:24], Deuteronomy 29[:16ff.]). If they knew that, they would spit on themselves. (This is said as an aside.) Shame on you, you devastators of Scripture and head-hunters of souls! If as little danger and slight harm arose from idols as you assert, God would not have forbidden them so often through Moses and the prophets. Nor would he have said, "You will destroy yourselves if you make images or any representation," etc. (Deuteronomy 4[:15ff.]). God calls papal sophistry our destruction. But the servants of idols, contrary to God, call it an act of brotherly

---

[17] In April 1522 the Catholic theologian Jerome Emser wrote a rebuttal to Karlstadt's work *On the Abolition of Images* (*Vom Abtuhung der Bilder . . .*). Karlstadt's reply to Emser could not be published because of the censorship that had been imposed on his writings by the university of Wittenberg. Hence, those in Luther's circle at Wittenberg were "the new papists."

[18] A common justification for the use of ecclesiastical images in the Middle Ages.

love. Look there! This is how they understand Paul, who says that the weak – that is, the unwise – perish as food for the idols (1 Corinthians 8[:10–11]).

God ordered the Jews to root out the heathen, their enemies, not in haste or quickly but at a leisurely pace, with measured time. Because of this, it does not follow that therefore Christians should also proceed at a slow, leisurely pace when they abolish offenses.

I should indeed have held back a good arrow for a pigheaded, rutting enemy. But then I would fear that I would meet no learned one, or that I might not be able to fight cleanly with God's word or sword if I took pleasure in mocking my enemy. For it soon happens that the pure word of God is used dishonorably. Therefore I will now anticipate the enemies of divine justice and show them what they could say if they opened their eyes. And then I will quickly knock down their reasoning. And I ask this: Do not the servants of idols and the protectors of images have good reason to preserve and protect their idols, which they will not defend forever, from the fire for a certain time? Because God speaks thus: "I will not expel them in one year, so that the land does not become a wilderness and the wild animals multiply against you. At a leisurely pace or gradually, with delay or time, I will drive them out before you, until you increase and occupy the land" (Exodus 23[:29–30]).

God said this about the heathen, whose land the Jews should take. And he said, "I will not expel them in one year. Leisurely and slowly I will drive them out." This analogy is appropriate and offers a comparison for proceeding with the abolition of images. For if the Jews were to root out their enemies, who were able to do them great harm, in leisurely fashion or over time, then should they not take even longer in driving out idols, which were not able to harm them? It is appropriate that we should also proceed slowly and not devastate the idols in one year. This follows from the text that says, "You should not obligate yourselves to them, and do not associate with their gods. Rather, do not let them remain in your land, so that they do not make you sin against me." God says, "For if you serve their gods, your downfall will take place."

Now look at whether we too should not proceed slowly if we want to drive out idols. We should make no covenant with false gods, just as we should not obligate ourselves to heathens. Furthermore, we should not allow idols to remain in the land. Indeed, with time and at a leisurely pace, on account of the weak, we should expel the idols and also the heathens. Therefore one should not proceed suddenly or noisily or act in haste. Is this not a good, firm and strong reason? Who wants to demolish this wall of steel?

My answer.

Oh, you miserable blind ones! You careless evildoers! How you mend your coat with peculiar patches! You cannot help yourself with such tricks. We wanted to confront you on account of the truth, even though you had more firmly grounded reasons for continuing to practice your craft and for making your countenance more glorious. For the passages of Scripture you have presented sound just as though the abbot at Pegau[19] had sung them, who can also color his arguments in this way.

Now let us see how this text agrees with what you say. If patrons of idols say that, from the beginning, God did not want to expel the heathen in one year, etc., and that God forbade the Jews to proceed hastily and suddenly, this is true. But if you say that for this reason one should also proceed leisurely and negligently with the abolition of images, this is your little invention. I am not talking to you[20] as a dear brother but as a patron of idols. It is your "wisdom" and your addition, and not God's addition, when you say, "on account of the weak." I ask: Where is it written that the Jews were to drive out their enemies slowly for the sake of the weak? God gave his reason. But if God is wise and patient enough, then his reason is also good, upright and sufficient. But God does not say, "You should act slowly on account of the weak." Yes, on account of the weak God would have killed all the heathens at once. Therefore God forbade the Jews to have friendship and fellowship with heathens, so that the Jews would not fall away from him, and so that the heathens would not become a pitfall, a snare and a trap for them (Deuteronomy 7). God has given a reason to which one should cling more firmly than to a wall, and no one should rebuke God's reason by adding human additions (Joshua 23[:6ff.]). God says, "You should not kill them hastily and suddenly for this

---

[19] The monastery of Pegau, a Saxon town on the Elster southwest of Leipzig, was founded in the early eleventh century and dissolved in 1539.
[20] I.e. Bartel Bach, to whom the work is dedicated.

reason: so that the land does not become wilderness, and the animals multiply against you" (Exodus 23[:29]). There you see the reason which is divine, upright, and sufficient, and which Moses also set forth at another place without new addition (Deuteronomy 7[:22]). I have never seen that he said anything other than this: "God will root out these people, one after the other, so that the animals . . .," etc. A patron of idols could say that the enemies also had hands and could strike, harm, and greatly offend them, as Moses and Joshua say, and this is evident. And he could say that the heathen could offend through false teaching and that idols cannot do this, etc.

To this I reply that, since the Israelite people could work side by side with heathens and gain experience, therefore God also, all the more gladly, let them remain, so that the Israelites would learn to fight against their enemies, and so that they would understand through external battle how the spirit conquers the flesh and subdues the flesh, and how it must defend itself against the animals of the field, and conquer false language with truth and salutary teaching (Judges 3, Joshua 1–3). If idols could defend themselves, they would not be so dangerous – and such an unfurled net that can be drawn in – as they are. It is also good if a person knows how to give the reasons for a divine law. If he does not have a divine reason to do that, it would be sufficient if he said about it that God wants to have it thus. The master of the idols sees there that he has put the helmet [of faith] on his feet and has regarded Scripture through a shoe of sheet metal.[21] I would have let him erect an argument on a comparison if Scripture were not damaged, and if simple people were not disadvantaged. But because his language publicly contravenes God's just language and lures the uncomprehending person to his fall and ruination, I am unwilling to do this, and I say that it is contrary to God.

But if he says, "The Jews should not allow the idols of the heathen to remain in their land," this is spoken correctly. But if he adds his view to this and says, "The Jews also had to proceed slowly and not be in a hurry, but expel idols gradually and over time," this is an addition. God says that they should not let idols remain in their land, as heathen do, perhaps because the Jews could not kill a worm or animal and were prepared only for sin and ruination. Therefore Jews should

---

[21] Because those who defend idolatry are confused about the armor of faith – and mix up helmets and footwear – they are incapable of understanding Scripture. It is undoubtedly Luther that Karlstadt is thinking of.

destroy the heathen idols where they could and where they ruled, and they should not allow them to remain.

God ordered the Jews to engage in a twofold expulsion. On the one hand, they should expel their enemies; on the other, they should abolish the heathen gods, and idols or images. The one had to take place gradually, the other promptly and immediately. Thus the text says, "Do not let idols remain in your land" (Exodus 23[:24]). That is, you should not proceed gradually and slowly, as with the heathen, but promptly. That this is the actual and true meaning and sense is shown by the historical circumstances of these passages of Scripture. Above, this is written: "You should not perform heathen works, rather you should destroy them because they are destructive. And you should lay waste their titles or monuments because they lay waste." God does not say that the Jews should break the idols gradually, in the way they should ruin their enemies, but immediately. Because God speaks of heathen people and idols and said that the Jews were to kill the hostile people neither in one year nor rapidly, it follows on the other hand that they must have had to abolish the idols as soon as they were able to do so. But I would prefer to prove this with Scripture rather than with human rules, and I refer the reader to chapter 7 of Deuteronomy, where Moses repeats the above-cited text, confirms it and says the following: "You can or will not devour them totally or hurriedly so that . . ." etc. (Deuteronomy 7[:22f.]). This sentence is complete and finished and has its purpose, and in this purpose we are of one mind.

A special clause follows which refers to the removal of offenses, and it reads thus: "You shall burn images of their gods with fire . . ." etc. (Deuteronomy 7[:25]). It is not written that one should proceed slowly, as asserted above. Rather, you shall ruin them immediately. It is written still more clearly earlier in the above-mentioned seventh chapter, namely, "You shall tear down their altars, destroy their pillars, chop down their leafy trees, and burn their idols" (Deuteronomy 7[:5]). When? Right away, at the time they are to destroy the heathen. Why? So that they do not learn to serve other gods. Or so that the idols do not make them "sin against me," says God (thus Exodus 23[:33]). For it would have contributed to their ruination if they let idols stand.

Now do you see why one should proceed quickly in throwing aside things that offend? And why Jeremiah says, "Israel, if you would remove the offending things from you, you would not fall" (Jeremiah 4[:1–3])? Heathens could not offend others if they did those things through which they destroy themselves. Namely, they have something in their right hand; and they do not say, "This is foolishness in my right hand, whose whole basis rests on what is offensive" (Isaiah 44[:20]). Therefore one should quickly remove that which has been established to offend and ruin one's neighbors. Thus God sent an angel to the Jews and had him utter this view: "I brought you out of Egypt to this land, which I have promised to your fathers, so that you keep my covenant strictly and do not do useless things. And I have charged you to make no alliance with heathens, but rather to tear down their altars. But you have not obeyed my voice," etc.[22] These biblical accounts show clearly that the Jews were neither to make alliances with heathens, nor to proceed slowly in overturning their altars. And they show that God persecuted them because they were negligent.

Now, since God is sufficiently intelligent and adds to his words when and where one should proceed slowly and not suddenly, it is always a great sacrilege of Antichrist to rebuke God's intelligence and to add something to his words. This is especially true when the addition opposes the will of God and damages the soul of one's neighbor. It is a sacrilege to say, "Occasionally one should delay on account of the weak, and proceed slowly," when God has not said that we should proceed slowly or gradually. It is especially sacrilegious when through delay one brings the weak further from the way of truth and into greater error. It is written, "Cursed be he who makes a blind person stray from the path" (Deuteronomy 27[:18]). How much more is he cursed who makes a blind soul err about God's path or word? But each person does this who permits an offense, a mousetrap, or the bait of the devil, to stand in his brother's way. But blessed is he who tears away from his brother what causes his ruination, even against his will, and who grieves for him whom he wishes well, so that he benefits him. Just as a father angers his child, whom he loves, when he takes a sharp knife away from him.

In the case of offenses against faith, he who has a strong spirit and can stand pressure is able to tear out, cast down, and destroy before he preaches – as could Gideon, although he was fearful and destroyed the altar of Baal at night (Judges 6[:25–27]). Nevertheless, I say that it

---

[22] Karlstadt at this point is evidently summarizing several Old Testament passages including Ex. 23:24, Dt. 7:5, 25ff., and Jer. 4:1.

is unnecessary for one to attack public offenses with preaching before committing the deed. Gideon's action shows this, and that of Asa, who swept out the abominations of the idols and deposed his mother,[23] and the actions of Jehoshaphat, Jehu, Hezekiah, and Zedekiah (2 Chronicles 12; 2 Kings 15[24]). Or one may promise [to act against offenses before taking action] as did Shadrach, Meshach, Abednego[25] and many others. For although Paul and Barnabas preached briefly, nevertheless we are not bound by their example, even if they intended to preach a great deal. For Christ's example is always as strong as their example, and he drove the money-changers out of the temple at the same time as he said, "Why do you make of my father's house a den of murderers? A house of commerce?"[26]

Seek God's commandment and teaching and you will find this: "Destroy every place where the heathens (whom you will capture) have served their gods, be they on high hills or mountains or under green trees; and break them down, devastate them, and remove them," etc.[27] God did not command the Jews to preach to the heathen before doing away with their idols. But what are our idolatrous Christians except heathens twice over? Thus, it is not necessary that one teach them before taking their ruination away from them. If they get angry, they will surely laugh later. God did not command the Jews to do this throughout the whole world, but in those places they would conquer and where they would rule. Accordingly the conclusion is that where Christians rule, they should not have regard for any temporal authority. Rather, freely and on their own, they should strike and overthrow what is contrary to God, without preaching beforehand.

There are many such offenses – namely, the Mass, images, the idol's flesh which the parsons now devour,[28] and similar things. But if something is based on God's figurative language, then one should preach beforehand and reveal the hidden, constant will of God before one acts contrary to any part of Scripture. Or one should always preach at the same time as one acts or soon afterward, if there are

---

[23] 1 Kg. 15:8ff.
[24] Karlstadt's intended references would appear to be: 2 Chr. 17:6ff. for Jehoshaphat and 2 Kg. 10:18 for Jehu. For Hezekiah, see 2 Chr. 29:1ff.; for Zedekiah, 2 Kg. 24:17–20.
[25] Dan. 3:8ff. and 3:16.
[26] Mt. 21:12–13, Jn. 2:14–22.
[27] Dt. 12:2–3.
[28] I.e. the Eucharist as traditionally conceived.

people present who might be offended by a practice that is contrary to Scripture. And one should announce the basis for a new practice, just as Christ did when his disciples broke the Sabbath, according to the letter and apparent meaning of Scripture. And as Stephen did when he declared the temple to be superfluous, Peter when he baptized Cornelius, and Paul when he spoke and acted against circumcision. And as all those did who expounded the law of God in the manner of the prophets. Therefore, in this case,[29] Paul wants one to spare the weak, that is, the ignorant.

But here I want to ask why Paul did not let the Galatians practice circumcision until they and the others were strong or intelligent enough to end it. One may certainly break with human traditions when they are not rooted in divine truth, even if they are not suppressed with anything but the word of Christ. "Every plant which my father has not planted will be rooted out."[30] Human laws are the excrement which the Jews had to carry outside their tents and bury in the dirt. What God forbids, and what makes one sin against him and ruins one's neighbor, should be removed quickly – the sooner the better. For in this way one serves God and does good for one's neighbor, even if he complains and scolds. One brings him to strive for what is best for him. May God help us in this. Amen.

I want to write a small separate book on the diversity of the offenses, because I see that this is necessary. And in this book I will show clearly that those who cry daily, "Spare the offense on account of the weak," lie down in the midst of offense and offend the sick most of all.

[29] I.e. where one acts contrary to the figurative sense of Scripture.
[30] Mt. 15:13.

73

6 Thomas Müntzer, *a Highly Provoked Defense*

A highly provoked defense and answer to the spiritless, soft-living flesh at Wittenberg, [Luther] who has most lamentably befouled pitiable Christianity in a perverted way by his theft of holy Scripture.[1]

By Thomas Müntzer, Allstedter.[2]

From the caverns of Elijah, whose zeal spares no one, 3 Kings 18 [see 1 Kg. 19:19ff.], Matthew 17[:1ff.], Luke 1 [:11, 26f.], and Revelations 11[:3].

Written in the year 1524.

Oh God, save me from the false accusations of men so that I may keep your commandments. And so that I may proclaim the truth that was born in your son, lest the stratagems of the evildoers endure longer.[3]

To the most illustrious, first-born prince and all–powerful lord, Jesus Christ, the gracious king of all kings, the brave duke of all believers,

---

[1] Müntzer probably began the composition of his last major tract while he was still at Allstedt, but it was not completed until late September 1524, after he was expelled from Mühlhausen. The work is a direct reply to Luther's *Letter to the Princes of Saxony Concerning the Rebellious Spirit* (*Eyn brieff an die Fürsten zu Sachsen von dem auffrurischen geyst*) published in June 1524; *WA* XV, 210–21. Müntzer's rebuttal was surreptitiously printed at Nuremberg in late November or early December 1524 by the radical printer Hieronymous Hölzel. Müntzer himself visited Nuremberg in late 1524 after his departure from Mühlhausen. Nuremberg officials searching for tracts by Karlstadt discovered Müntzer's *A Highly Provoked Defense* and the entire press-run was confiscated. The translation is based on the text in *PSMB*, 140–62.

[2] I.e. a member of the community of Allstedt.

[3] The source of this Latin quotation is not known; the first line is reminiscent of Ps. 119:134.

my most gracious lord and faithful protector – and to his troubled, only bride, poor Christendom.[4] All praise, name, honor and dignity, title and all glory are yours alone, you eternal son of God, Philippians 2[:9–11], because your holy spirit has constantly had the fate of seeming to those graceless lions, the scribes, to be a most enraged devil, John 8[:48], even though you possessed this spirit beyond measure from the beginning, John 3 [:14]. And all of the elect have received this spirit from your bounty, John 1[:16], and thus it lives in them, 1 Corinthians 3[:16] and 6[:19], 2 Corinthians 1[:21f.], Ephesians 1[:13], and Psalm 5[:12f.]. You give the spirit to all who approach you, according to the measure of their faith, Ephesians 4[:7], Psalm 68[:10–12]. And he who does not have Christ's spirit, so that he can give an unmistakable testimony of it from his own spirit, does not belong to you, Christ, Romans 8[:9]. You have the invincible testimony, Psalm 93[:3–5].

So it is scarcely a great surprise that the most ambitious scribe of all, Doctor Liar,[5] increasingly as time passes becomes an arrogant fool and clothes himself in your holy Scripture, without his own name and comfort withering away at all. And Luther uses Scripture in a most deceptive way and actually wants to have nothing to do with you, Isaiah 58[:1ff.], as if through you he had attained the gates of truth to knowledge of you. And thus he is insolent in your presence and fundamentally he despises your true spirit. For he betrays himself clearly and irrevocably in that, out of raging envy and in the bitterest hatred, he mocks me, a member of the community that is integrated to you. He does this without sincere and true cause before his flattering, mocking, and most ferocious associates. And before the simple people he describes me in uncalled-for anger as a Satan or devil. And he slanders and mocks me with his perverted, vicious judgment.

But in you, Christ, I am blissful and through your mild comfort I am totally satisfied, just as you also most sweetly told your dearest friends, saying in Matthew 10[:24], "The disciple does not have it better than the master." Oh, innocent duke and comforting savior, since they have blasphemously called you Beelzebub, how much more will they insult me, your untiring footsoldier, after I expressed my

---

[4] The salutation is a deliberate parody of Luther's *Letter to the Princes*, which opened with a recitation of their titles and traditional attributes; Müntzer counters by declaring his allegiance to Christ and ascribing to him the titles of secular power. The implication is that while Müntzer serves Christ and the cause of Christian government, Luther serves the princes.

[5] *doctor lügner*, a word play on "Doctor Luther."

views about the flattering rogue at Wittenberg and followed your voice? John 10[:4f.]. Indeed, this will always happen if one does not want to let these soft-living people who follow their own arbitrary opinions get away with their contrived faith and pharisaical tricks, but instead wishes to see their fame and pompousness collapse. In the same way you, Christ, were not accorded recognition by the scribes. The scribes also had the illusion that they were more learned than you and your disciples. Indeed, with their literalistic pigheadedness they were probably more learned than Doctor Mockery[6] could ever be. Even though they had reputation and fame enough throughout the whole world, it was still not right that they proceeded against you rationalistically and sought to prove you wrong with clear Scripture, as they previously rejected Nicodemus, John 7[:50ff.], and spoke of the Sabbath, John 5[:9f.] and 9[:16]. They cited the whole of Scripture against you in the most extreme manner, arguing that you should and must die because you freely confessed yourself to be the son of God, born of the eternal father, just as we confess ourselves to be born of your spirit. Thus the scribes said, "We have a law according to which he must die." And they misapplied to you the text of Deuteronomy 13[:1–6] and 18[:20] and did not wish carefully to explore this text any further, just as the cunning scriptural thief [Luther] now does to me. There, where Scripture reveals itself most clearly, he mocks with fervent envy and calls the spirit of God a devil.

The whole of holy Scripture (as all creatures also prove) speaks only of the crucified son of God. Because Christ himself began to explain his mission or office [in the succession] beginning with Moses and extending on through all the prophets, therefore he had to suffer in such a way [i.e. by crucifixion] in order to enter into the glory of his father. This is clearly described in the last chapter of Luke.[7] And Paul also says that he can only preach the crucified Christ, 1 Corinthians 1[:23]. After Paul searched the law of God more deeply than all his contemporaries, Galatians 1[:11–16], he could find in it only the suffering son of God, who said, Matthew 5[:17], that he did not come to revoke the law or to destroy the covenant of God, but much more to perfect, explain, and fulfill it.

The spiteful scribes were not able to acknowledge all this for they had not searched Scripture with their whole heart and spirit as they

---

[6] *doctor ludibrii*, again a play on Luther's name; *ludibrii* is ambiguous, meaning both idle play and mockery.　　　　[7] Lk. 24:25ff. and 24: 44–47.

should have done, Psalm 119[:2], and as Christ commanded them, John 5[:39]. They were learned in Scripture like apes who want to imitate a cobbler making shoes and only ruin the leather. Oh, why is this? They want to receive the consolation of the holy spirit, and yet in their whole life they have never, as they should, come to the foundation of their existence through sadness of heart. For only in this way can the true light illuminate the darkness and so give us the power to become children of God, as is clearly written, Psalms 55[:2–9] and 63[:1ff.], John 1[:4f.].

If then Christ is merely accepted through the testimony of the old and new covenant of God and is preached without the enlightenment of the spirit, a far more badly confused monkey-business results than there was among the Jews and heathen. For everyone can clearly see that present-day scribes act no differently than the Pharisees previously did, insofar as they too build their reputation with holy Scripture, scribble and spatter all their books full, and they always babble more and more, "Believe! Believe!" And yet they deny the source of faith, mock the spirit of God, and in general believe nothing, as you plainly see. None of them will preach unless he is paid forty or fifty gulden. Indeed, the best of them want more than one hundred or two hundred gulden. And thus in them the prophecy of Micah 3[:11] is fulfilled: "The priests preach for the sake of rewards." And they want comfort, pleasant leisure, and the greatest prestige on earth. And still they boast that they understand the origin of faith! Yet they are driven into the greatest contradiction, for under the cloak of holy Scripture they upbraid the true spirit as a false spirit and a Satan. Christ also experienced this, as in his innocence he proclaimed the will of the father, which was much too exalted and irksome for the scribes, John 5[:16–18] and 6[:41f.].

You will find that things have not changed down to the present. When the godless are trapped by the divine law they say with great lightness, "Well, now it has been set aside."

But when it is explained to them how the law is written in the heart, 2 Corinthians 3[:3], and how one must be attentive to its teachings in order to see the right paths to the source of faith, Psalm 37[:32], then the godless one [Luther] attacks the righteous and drags Paul around with such an idiotic comprehension that even to a child it becomes as ridiculous as a puppet show, Psalm 64[:8]. Nevertheless Luther wants to be the cleverest fellow on earth and he boasts that he has no equal.

Beyond this, he also calls all the poor in spirit "fanatics" and he does not want to hear the word "spirit" spoken or even whispered. He has to shake his clever head. The devil does not like to hear it either, Proverbs 18[:2]. If anyone tells Luther about the source of faith, he is rejected. Thus Luther employs deception, 2 Corinthians 11[:13–15]. He sings in the highest register what he takes out of Paul, Romans 12[:16], "One must not concern himself with such high things, but rather make them equal to trivial things." The pap tastes good to Luther mixed in this way and not otherwise – but he dreads clear broth for breakfast.[8] He says that one should simply believe but he does not say what is necessary for this. Thus Solomon says of such a man that he is utterly foolish, as it stands written in Proverbs 24[:7], "To the fool the wisdom of God is much too remote."

Christ began, like Moses, with the source of faith and explained the law from beginning to end. Thus, he said, "I am the light of the world" [Jn. 8:12]. His preaching was so true and so perfectly composed that he captivated the human reason of even the godless, as the evangelist Matthew describes in chapter 13[:54f.], and as Luke also gives us to understand in chapter 2[:47]. But since the teaching of Christ was too elevated for the scribes, and the person and life of Christ were too lowly, they became angered with him and his teaching. They openly said that he was a Samaritan and possessed by the devil. For their judgment was made according to the flesh. As this false judgment pleases the devil in such circumstances, it must reveal itself as diabolic, for the scribes did not displease the worldly powers, who appreciate a Brother Soft-life [Luther], Job 28 [see, rather, Job 27:13–20]. The scribes did all they could to please the world, Matthew 6[:1–5] and 23[:5–7].

The godless flesh at Wittenberg does the same to me, now that I strive for the clear purity of the divine law, Psalm 19[:8–11], through the right approach to the Bible and the right ordering of its first part [i.e. the Pentateuch]. And I explain through all the pronouncements of the Bible the fulfillment of the spirit of the fear of God, Isaiah 11[:1ff.]. Nor will I allow Luther in his perverted way to treat the new covenant of God without declaring the divine commandment[9] and the

---

[8] I.e. Luther enjoys an opaque "pap" (*prey* = *Brei*) derived from mixing together scriptural texts and confusing profound and trivial truths, but he finds distasteful a clear broth (*suppe*) composed of passages of Scripture whose meaning is plain.

[9] Müntzer protests what he regards as Luther's one-sided elevation of the New Testa-

onset of faith, which is only experienced after the chastisement of the holy spirit, John 16[:8]. For the spirit punishes unbelief only after there is a knowledge of the law, an unbelief no one knows unless he has previously acknowledged it in his heart passionately, like the most unbelieving heathen. Thus, from the beginning all of the elect have recognized their unbelief through the exercise of the law, Romans 2[:12] and 7[:6f.]. I affirm Christ, with all his members [i.e. the true church], as the fulfiller of the law, Psalm 19[:7]. For the will of God and his work must be fundamentally fulfilled through the observation of the law, Psalm 1[:1f.], Romans 12[:2]. Otherwise, no one could distinguish faith from unbelief unless he did so in a false way, as did the Jews with their Sabbath and Scripture, without once perceiving the foundation of their souls.

I have done nothing to the malicious black raven [Luther] (which Noah symbolically released from the ark [see Gen. 8:6ff.]) except that, like an innocent dove, I have spread my wings, covered them with silver, purified them in a sevenfold manner, and let the feathers on the back become golden, Psalm 68[:14], and I have flown over and despised the carcass on which the raven gladly sits. For I want the whole world to know that, as you see in his pamphlet against me, he flatters the godless rogues [the Saxon princes] and he wants to defend everything about them. It is clearly evident from all this, then, that Doctor Liar does not dwell in the house of God, Psalm 15[:4], for the godless are not despised by him. Rather, for the sake of the godless, many God-fearing people are insulted as devils and rebellious spirits. The black raven knows this well. In order to get the carcass, he picks out the eyes of the swine's head. He blinds the pleasure-seeking rulers to their obligations because he is so docile, and so that he will be as full as they of honors, goods, and especially the highest titles.

The Jews continually wanted to slander and discredit Christ, just as Luther now does me. He rebukes me mightily and after I have preached the rigor of the law, he throws before me the kindness of the son of God and his dear friends. I preached that the punishment of the law has not been removed for godless transgressors (even though they be rulers). I preached that the law should, rather, be enforced with the greatest strictness, as Paul instructs his disciple Timothy, and through him all pastors of souls, 1 Timothy 1[:9–11], to preach

ment, which has resulted in an understanding of justification that has set aside the works of the law as also necessary for salvation.

79

the strictness of the law to people. Paul clearly says that the law's rigor should visit those who struggle and fight against sound teaching, as no one can deny. This simple clear judgment is contained in Deuteronomy 13[:9–12], and Paul also renders it on the unchaste transgressors, 1 Corinthians 5[:1–5].

I have let this message go forth in print, just as I have preached it before the princes of Saxony,[10] without any reservations. I have demonstrated to the princes out of Scripture that they should employ the sword [to punish evildoers] so that no insurrection may develop. In short, transgression of divine law must be punished. And neither the mighty nor the lowly can escape it, Numbers 25[:4].

Then, right away, along comes Father Pussyfoot [Luther], oh that docile fellow! And he says that I want to make a rebellion, which he supposedly interpreted from my letter to the journeyman miners.[11] He talks about one part of the letter and he stays silent about the most decisive part, namely how I proclaimed before the princes that the entire community has the power of the sword,[12] just as it also has the keys of remitting sin. Citing from the text of Daniel 7[:27], Revelations 6[:15–17], Romans 13[:1], and 1 Kings 8[:7], I said that the princes are not lords but servants of the sword. They should not simply do what pleases them, Deuteronomy 17[:18–20], they should do what is right. So, according to good old customary law, the people must also be present if one of them is to be rightfully judged according to the law of God, Numbers 15[:35]. And why? If the authorities seek to render a perverted judgment, Isaiah 10[:1f.], the Christians present should deny this judgment as wrong and not tolerate it, for God demands an account of innocent blood, Psalm 79[:10]. It is the greatest monstrosity on earth that no one wants to defend the plight of the needy. The mighty ones do as they please, as Job 41[:24ff.] describes [the Leviathans].

Luther, the poor flatterer, wants to conceal himself beneath a false kindness of Christ that is contrary to the text of Paul, 1 Timothy 1[:7].

---

[10] See Müntzer's *Sermon to the Princes*, the central point of which he summarizes here. ✓

[11] This writing has not survived.

[12] Müntzer asserts that secular political power, the power of the sword or of coercion, rests with the community as a whole (*ein gantze gemayn*). It is to this same social source that, in what immediately follows, he also gives the traditional spiritual power of the keys (*den schlüssel der auflösung*). The result, in effect, is to formulate a view of authority in which the community (*Gemeinde*) emerges as sovereign in both temporal and ecclesiastical matters.

He says in his booklet on commerce[13] that the princes should make common cause with thieves and robbers. But in this same writing he is silent about the source of all theft. He is a herald who wants to earn thanks through the shedding of the people's blood for the sake of temporal goods – which God has certainly not intended. Behold, the basic source of usury, theft, and robbery is our lords and princes, who take all creatures for their private property. The fish in the water, the birds in the air, the animals of the earth must all be their property, Isaiah 5[:8]. And then they let God's commandment go forth among the poor and they say, "God has commanded, 'Thou shalt not steal.' " But this commandment does not apply to them since they oppress all men. The poor peasant, the artisan, and all who live are flayed and sheared, Micah 3[:2f.]. But as soon as anyone steals the smallest thing, he must hang. And to this Doctor Liar says, "Amen." The lords themselves are responsible for making the poor people their enemy. They do not want to remove the cause of insurrection, so how, in the long run, can things improve? I say this openly, so Luther asserts I must be rebellious. So be it!

Luther is totally incapable of shame, like the Jews, John 8[:3ff.], who brought to Christ the woman taken in adultery. They tested him. If he had transgressed the strictness of the father's law, then they would have easily called him an evildoer. But had he allowed the woman to go free without a decision, they would have said that he was a defender of injustice. In the gospel Christ revealed through his kindness the strictness of the father. The kindness of God extends over all the works of his hands, Psalm 145[:9]. This kindness is not diminished by the rigor of the law, which the elect do not attempt to flee. As Jeremiah [in Lam. 3:31–40] and Psalm 7[:9] say, the elect want to be punished with righteousness but not with wrath, which from eternity God has never possessed. Rather, a wrathful God springs from a perverted fear of God on men's part. Men are horrified by the rigor of the law and do not understand how God, after all the rigor, leads them through the deceptions of fear and to his eternity. All those who through original sin have become evildoers within common Christendom must be justified through the law, as Paul said,[14] in order that the rigor of the father can clear out of the

---

[13] I.e. Luther's work *On Commerce and Usury* (*Von Kaufshandlung und Wucher*), *WA* XV, 293–322.
[14] Rom. 2:12.

way those godless Christians who struggle against the saving doctrine of Christ. In this way the just may have the time and space to learn the will of God. It is not possible that a single Christian can devote himself to contemplation in such a tyranny [as the prevailing political order], where the evil that should be punished by the law goes free, and where the innocent must let themselves suffer. That is how godless tyrants justify themselves to pious people. They say, "I must make martyrs of you. Christ also suffered. You should not resist me," Matthew 5[:39]. This is an enormous depravity. Why the persecutors want to be the best Christians must be carefully analyzed.

The devil slyly strives to attack Christ and those who belong to him, 2 Corinthians 6[:14] and 11[:14], sometimes with flattering mildness, as Luther presently does when he defends godless rulers with the words of Christ. And sometimes the devil does it with terrifying strictness, in order to show his corrupted sense of justice concerning temporal goods. Nevertheless, the finger of Christ, the holy spirit, 2 Corinthians 3[:3], does not imprint this kind of rigor on the friendly strictness of the law nor on the crucified son of God, who sought to reveal God's will through the strictest mildness, insofar as both kindness and strictness harmonize when brought into their proper relationship, 1 Corinthians 2[:6]. Luther despises the law of the father and plays the hypocrite with the most precious treasure of Christ's kindness. And he scandalizes the father with his interpretation of the strictness of the law by invoking the patience of the son, John 15[:10] and 16[:15]. Thus Luther despises the distinction of the holy spirit between law and grace. And he uses the one to corrupt the other to such an extent that there is scarcely any true understanding of them left on earth, Jeremiah 5[:31]. He hopes that Christ will only be patient, so that godless Christians can truly torment their brothers.

Christ was called a devil when he pointed out the work of Abraham to the Jews [see Jn. 8:39–52] and gave them the best criteria for punishing and forgiving – namely, to punish according to the proper rigor of the law. Therefore he did not abolish the law, since he said in John 7[:24], just before going on to chapter eight, "You should render a righteous judgment, and not according to appearances." They had no other basis for judgment than to hold as valid that which was written in the law and to judge according to the spirit of the law. Even so, with the gospel, transgression is to be forgiven in the spirit of Christ, for the promotion and not the hindering of the gospel, 2

Corinthians 3[:6] and 13[:10]. But then through such a false distinction Doctor Liar, with his scribes, wants to make me a devil. Luther and his scribes say, "Have I not taught rightly with my writings and dictations? But you have brought forth no other fruit than insurrection. You are a satan, and indeed an evil satan, etc. Behold, you are a Samaritan and possessed by the devil."

Oh Christ, I consider myself unworthy to bear such precious suffering in the same cause as you, however much the judgment of the enemy finds favorable, perverted support. I say with you, Christ, to the proud, sly, puffed-up dragon, "Do you hear? I am not possessed by the devil. Through my office I seek to proclaim the name of God, to bring consolation to the troubled, and to bring corruption and sickness to the healthy,"[15] Isaiah 6[:8], Matthew 9[:12] and 13[:18–23], Luke 8[:11–15] and 4[:18f.]. And if I were to say that I would cease from this because of the bad name with which I am tarnished by lies, then I would be like you, Doctor Liar, with your perverted slander and viciousness. Indeed, at first you could not do otherwise than quarrel with the godless. But now that you have succeeded in this, you have set yourself up in place of the scoundrels whom you have so skillfully attacked. Since you now realize that things might go too far, you want to saddle your name, since it is so bad, on another who is already an enemy to the world; and you want to burn yourself pure, as the devil does,[16] so that no one becomes openly aware of your evil. For this reason the prophet, Psalm 91[:13], calls you a basilisk, a dragon, a viper, and a lion, because first you flatter with your poison and then you rage and howl, as is your manner.

The guiltless son of God rightfully compared the ambitious scribes to the devil. And he left us, through the gospel, the criteria to judge them – by using his immaculate law, Psalm 19[:8]. The desire of the scribes was simply to kill him, for they said, John 11[:48], "If we let him have his way, the people will all believe in him and cling to him. Behold, they already run to him in great crowds. If we allow him to complete his task, we will have lost, and then we will become poor people." Then Caiaphas came also, Doctor Liar, and gave good

---

[15] I.e. to destroy the false confidence and pride of those who imagine themselves to be spiritually healthy.

[16] After defeating the papists and setting himself up in place of the pope, Luther now fears an unwanted revolution; therefore he seeks to blame Müntzer for the mounting social upheaval; his "fiery" attack on Müntzer also purifies Luther with respect to the princes, whose favor he is attempting to curry.

counsel to his princes. He had things well in hand and was worried about his countrymen near Allstedt. But in truth it is simply that, as the whole territory bears witness, the poor thirsty people so eagerly sought the truth that the streets were all crowded with people from every place who had come to hear how the service, the reciting and the preaching of the Bible, were conducted in Allstedt.

Even if Luther racked his brains he could not have done this at Wittenberg. It is evident in his German Mass[17] how jealous he was of my liturgy. Luther was so irked that first of all he persuaded his princes that my liturgy should not be published. When the command of the pope of Wittenberg was ignored, he thought, "Wait! I can still salvage things by breaking this pilgrimage to pieces." The godless one has a subtle head for devising such things, Psalm 36[:4]. For his plans were, as you can see, to promote his teachings through the laity's hatred of the clergy. If he had a true desire to punish the clergy, he would not now have set himself up in place of the pope. Nor would he flatter the princes, as you see clearly written, in Psalm 10[:7–11]. He has interpreted this Psalm very nicely, so that it applies to him too and not only to the pope.[18] He wants to make carrion renderers out of St. Peter and St. Paul in order to defend his princely executioners of thieves.

Doctor Liar is a simple man – because he writes that I should not be prohibited from preaching. But he says to the rulers, "You should see to it that the spirit of Allstedt keeps his fists still." Can we not see, dear brothers in Christ, that he is truly learned? Yes, obviously he is learned. In two or three years the world will not yet have seen what a murderous, deceitful scandal he has caused. But he also writes, innocently, that he wants to wash his hands of the matter, so that no one will notice that he is a persecutor of truth. For he boasts that his preaching is the true word of God since it calls forth great persecution. It astonishes one how this shameless monk can claim to be terribly persecuted, there [at Wittenberg] with his good Malvasian wine and his whores' banquets. He can do nothing but act like a scribe, John 10[:33], "On account of your good works we do not want

---

[17] Evidently a reference to Luther's *Formula Missae et Communionis pro ecclesia Vuittembergensi* (1523), *WA* XII, 205–26. Luther's own German Mass was first published in 1526, after Müntzer's death.

[18] In Luther's interpretation of the Tenth Psalm, which he translated and published in 1524 (*WA* XXXI/1, 194), he referred to the papacy as Antichrist.

to do anything against you, but on account of your blasphemy, we want to stone you to death." Thus the scribes spoke to Christ as this fellow speaks against me: "You should be driven out not on account of your preaching, but because of your rebellion."

Dearest brothers, you believe it is truly not a bad thing that is going on now. Anyhow, you have no special knowledge of the matter. You imagine that since you no longer obey the priests everything is straightened out. But you do not realize that you are now a hundred, a thousand times worse off than before. From now on you will be bombarded with a new logic deceptively called the word of God. But against it you have the commandment of Christ, Matthew 7[:15f.]. Consider this commandment with your whole heart and no one will deceive you, even though he may say or write whatever he wants. You must equally pay attention to what Paul warned his Corinthians, saying in 2 Corinthians 11[:3], "Take heed that your senses are not confused by the simplicity of Christ." The scribes have applied this simplicity to the full treasure of divine wisdom, Colossians 2[:3], in violation of the text of Genesis 3[:3], where God warned Adam with a single commandment against falling into sin in the future, in order that he not be led astray by the multiplicity of material desires, but rather that he find his pleasure in God alone, as it is written, "Delight yourself in God" [Ps. 37:4].

Doctor Liar wants to advance a powerful argument against me: how sincere his teaching is. And he maintains that this sincerity will lay everything open. Yet in the last analysis he puts no weight on preaching, for he thinks there must be sects. And he bids the princes not to prevent me from preaching. I hoped for nothing else than that he would act according to the word, give me a hearing before the world, and abide by his decision to act according to nothing but the word. Now he turns it around and seeks to involve the princes. It was a prearranged scenario, so that no one could say, "Wait, do those at Wittenberg now want to persecute the gospel?" The princes should let me preach and not forbid it, but I should restrain my hands and refrain from putting anything in print. That is indeed a fine thing! Saying, just like the Jews, "We do not want to do anything to you because of your good works, but because of your blasphemy" [Jn. 10:33]. And truly pious people have always said, "Even if he swears an oath, unless he swears by the sacrament of the altar it does not count for anything." This same trick the scribes used very often,

Matthew 23[:18], Luke 11[:39]. Nevertheless, they were "pious" people. Indeed, they did no harm – if you only believe that the weak must be spared being troubled.

Blasphemy could make no impact on the hearts of the Jews, as you can gather from the gospel. Likewise, good works did not concern them much at all, as is also true of Luther. Therefore God held up to the Jews the work of Abraham, John 8[:39]. But there was a cruel hatred in those Jews who wanted to have a good reputation with the people, just as Virgin Martin does now. Oh, the chaste Babylonian woman! Revelations 18[:2].

Luther wants to deal with everything for the sake of the word. But he does not want to begin to justify or condemn my case with the word. He only wants to make a bad case for me among the mighty, so that no one follows my teaching because it is rebellious. Whoever wants to have a clear judgment here must not love insurrection, but equally he must not oppose a justified rebellion. He must hold to a very reasonable middle way. Otherwise he will either hate my teaching too much or love it too much, according to his own convenience. I never want this to happen.

If I were to instruct the poor with good teaching, it would be more useful than to get myself involved in a dispute with this blasphemous monk. He wants to be a new Christ who has gained much good for Christendom with his blood. And what is more, he did this for the sake of a fine thing – that priests might take wives. What should I answer to this? Perhaps I will find nothing to answer, for you have anticipated and defended yourself against everything (or at least you allow yourself to think so). Behold, how elegantly you have sacrificed poor parsons on the butcher's block in your first explanation of the imperial mandate.[19] There you said that the mandate should apply to the priests, etc.,[20] so that your initial teaching would not be brought to

---

[19] I.e. Luther's work of 1523, *Against the Perverted and False Imperial Mandate (Wider die Verkehrere und Fälscher Kaiserlichs Mandats)*, WA XII, 62–67, which Müntzer referred to as the first explanation, in contradistinction to Luther's work of 1524, *Two Contradictory and Opposed Imperial Commands Concerning Luther (Zwei kaiserliche uneinige und widerwärtige Gebot den Luther betreffend)*, WA XV, 254–78. The Nuremberg mandate, issued by the imperial governing council in January 1522, forbade ecclesiastical innovations.

[20] The fourth article of the imperial mandate specified that members of the clergy who married should be tried and punished according to canon law and that secular authorities should not hinder this punishment. Luther expressed a reluctant willingness to

86

trial. Then, hypocritically, you were perfectly willing to allow the priests always to be driven out. Thus you would always have produced new martyrs and you would have sung a little hymn or two about them.[21] Then you would really become an authentic savior! Naturally you would sing in your true manner, *Nunc dimittis*, etc. [see Jn. 8:54]. And they would all sing in imitation of you, "Monk, if you want to dance, the whole world will pay court to you."

But if you are a savior, you must truly be a peculiar one. Christ gives his father the glory, John 8[:54], and says, "If I seek my own honor, then it is nothing." But you want to have a grand title from those at Orlamünde.[22] You seize and steal (in the manner of a black raven) the name of the son of God and you want to earn the gratitude of your princes. Have you not read, you overlearned scoundrel, what God says through Isaiah 42[:8]? "I will not give my glory to another." Can you not call the good people [i.e. the rulers] what Paul calls Festus in Acts 25[:1]?[23] Why do you call them most illustrious highnesses? Does not the title belong, not to them, but to Christ, Hebrews 1[:3f.], John 1[:11] and 8[:12]? I thought you were a Christian but you are an arch-heathen. You make Jupiters and Minervas out of the princes. Perhaps [you think they were] not born of the loins of women, as is written in Proverbs 7[:2] but sprang from the forehead of the gods. Oh, what is too much is too much!

Shame on you, you arch-scoundrel! With your hypocrisy you want to flatter an erring world, Luke 9[:25], and you have sought to justify all mankind. But you know well whom you can abuse. Poor monks

accept this article if all the others were enforced, asserting that those affected, while innocent, should suffer for the sake of the gospel.

[21] A reference to Luther's hymn *About Two Martyrs of Christ at Brussels, burned by the Sophists of Louvain* (*Von den zwei Märtrern Christi zu Brüssel von den sophisten zu Löwen verbrannt*), *WA* XXXV, 411–15. This hymn was composed to commemorate two members of the Augustinian order who were burned for heresy in Brussels in July 1523 as followers of Luther. In Luther's view, their execution was a manifestation that the reform movement had finally begun to bear fruit.

[22] In 1524 Luther conducted a visitation trip to Orlamünde, where his former colleague Karlstadt had established himself after breaking with Luther in 1521. The radicalized evangelicalism of Karlstadt and his followers rejected traditional titles and honors; Luther protested against this and complained to the elector that the "fanatics" (*Rottengeister*) at Orlamünde had refused him his title of doctor of theology. See his *The Treatment of Doctor Martin Luther by the Council and Community of the Town of Orlamünde* (*Die Handlung Doctor Martini Luthers mit dem Rat und Gemeinde der Stadt Orlamünde*), *WA* XV, 345.

[23] Paul gave Festus no title.

and priests and merchants cannot defend themselves, so you can easily slander them. But [you say that] no one should judge godless rulers, even if they trample Christ underfoot. In order to satisfy the peasants, however, you write that the princes will be overthrown through the word of God. And you say in your most recent commentary on the imperial mandate, "The princes will be toppled from their thrones."[24] Yet you still look on them as superior to merchants. You should tweak the noses of your princes. They have deserved it much more perhaps than any others. What reductions have they made in their rents and their extortions, etc.? Even though you have scolded the princes, you still gladden their hearts again, you new pope. You give them monasteries and churches and they are delighted with you. I warn you that the peasants may soon strike out.

But you always talk about faith, and write that I fight against you under your protection.[25] In this claim one can see my integrity and your foolishness. Under your protection I have been like a sheep among wolves, Matthew 10[:16]. Have you not had greater power over me here in Allstedt than anywhere else? Could you not anticipate what would develop out of this? I was in your principality so that you would have no excuse [for failing to show your true colors]. You say: under "our" protection. Oh, how easily you betray yourself! I mean, are you a prince too? What do you mean boasting about this protection? In all my writings I have never sought the elector's protection. I have taken care to prevent him from picking a quarrel with his own people on account of the goat-stall and the Marian idolatry at Mallerbach.[26] He wanted to make incursions into villages and towns without considering that poor people have to live in danger day and night for the sake of the gospel. Do you think that a whole territory does not

---

[24] Müntzer is referring to Luther's 1524 commentary on the imperial mandate, in which Luther warned the princes that the text of Lk. 1:52, *Deposuit potentes de sede . . .*, could apply to them too. See *WA* XV, 255. Müntzer dismisses this upbraiding remark as insignificant within the larger context of Luther's social and political views.

[25] In his *Letter to the Princes* Luther had written that Müntzer was using "our peace and protection" (*unserm fride, schirm und schutz*), *WA* XV, 211. By this Luther did not mean his personal protection but that of the elector of Saxony. It is this discrepancy that Müntzer seizes on in what follows.

[26] The Mallerbach chapel, located near Allstedt and belonging to the convent of Cistercian nuns at Naundorf, possessed an image of the Virgin that was credited with miraculous powers. On 24 March 1524 a small group of citizens from Allstedt burned the chapel to the ground. According to Müntzer's confession, he was personally present during the action; afterward, as Saxon authorities attempted to discover and punish the responsible parties, he used his influence to defend the action and thwart the investigation.

know how to defend and protect itself? May God have mercy on Christendom if it does not have as a protector him who created it, Psalm 111[:6].

You say that three years ago I was expelled from Zwickau and wandered about. And you say that I complained about much suffering. But look what is actually the case. With your pen you have slandered and shamed me before many honest people. This I can prove against you. With your vicious mouth you have publicly called me a devil. Indeed, you do the same to all your opponents. You can do nothing but act like a raven, cawing out your own name. You also know well, together with your unroasted Lawrence of Nordhausen,[27] that evildoers have already been paid to kill me, etc. You are not a murderous or rebellious spirit, but like a hellhound you incite and encourage Duke George of Saxony to invade the territory of Prince Frederick[28] and thus disrupt the common peace. But no, you make no rebellion. You are the clever snake that slithers over the rocks, Proverbs 30[:18f.]. Christ says, Matthew 10[:23] and 23[:34], "If they persecute you in one city, flee to another." But Luther, this ambassador of the devil, certainly his arch-chancellor, says that since I have been driven out [of Zwickau] I am a devil, and he has obtained this understanding of Matthew contrary to the holy spirit, which he mocks and about which he flaps his cheeks, Psalm 27[:12].

Luther makes a mockery and an utterly useless babble out of the divine word. And then he says that I call it a heavenly voice and that the angels talk with me, etc. My answer is that what almighty God does with me or says to me is something about which I cannot boast. I proclaim to the people out of holy Scripture only what I have experienced through the testimony of God. And if God wills it, I seek not to preach my own cleverness from my own ignorance. But if I do preach improperly, I will gladly allow myself to be punished by God and his dear friends and I am ready to assume responsibility. But I

---

[27] I.e. the opposite type of St. Lawrence, who was martyred by being roasted alive. Since Müntzer often spoke of the need to test one's faith "like gold in the fire," he is suggesting that Lawrence of Nordhausen is one whose faith has not been tested and confirmed through suffering. The reference is apparently to Lawrence Süße, a follower of Luther and the first evangelical preacher of Nordhausen. The basis, if any, of Müntzer's accusation that Luther and Lawrence of Nordhausen knew of a plot to kill him with paid assassins remains unclarified.

[28] Duke George, the ruler of ducal or Albertine Saxony, was a cousin of Frederick the Wise, ruler of electoral or Ernestine Saxony. Again, the basis of this charge remains unclear.

owe nothing to this mocker, Proverbs 9[:7f.]. I will not eat the jay, an unclean bird, Leviticus 11 [see, rather, Lev. 1:19], nor swallow the filth of the godless mocker. I am only curious about your true colors. Since you are from the region of the Harz mountains, why do you not call the secret of God's word a heavenly bagpipe?[29] Then the devil, your angel, would pipe your little song for you. Monk, if you want to dance, all the godless will pay court to you.

I speak of the divine word with its manifold treasures, Colossians 2[:3], which Moses offers to teach in Deuteronomy 30[:11–14] and Paul in Romans 10[:8]. Psalm 85[:9] says that the word of God shall be heard by those who are converted with their whole heart and who strive to find in the teaching of the spirit all knowledge about the mercy and, equally, the justice of God. But you deny the true word and hold before the world only an outward appearance of it. You turn yourself most powerfully into an arch-devil since, from the text of Isaiah [see Is. 40:2,6], and contrary to reason, you make God the cause of evil. Is this not the most terrible punishment of God on you? You are deluded and nevertheless you want to be a leader of the blind for the world. You want to make God responsible for the fact that you are a poor sinner and a venomous little worm with your shitty humility. You have done this with your fantastic reasoning, which you have concocted out of your Augustine. It is truly a blasphemy impudently to despise mankind, [which you do in your teaching] concerning the freedom of the will.[30]

You say that I want my teaching believed right away and forced on others, and that I do not want to give anyone time to reflect. I say, with Christ [Jn. 8:47], "He who is of God hears his word." Are you of God? Why do you not hear it? Why do you mock it and condemn what you have not experienced? Are you still trying to work out what you should teach to others? You should much more truly be called a crook than a judge. It will become evident to poor Christendom how your carnal reason has indeed acted against the undeceivable spirit of God. Let Paul render judgment on you, 2 Corinthians 11[:13–15]. You have always treated everything with simplicity – like an onion with nine skins, like a fox. Behold, you have become a rabid, burning fox that

---

[29] The bagpipe was a traditional instrument of folk music in the Harz region.

[30] The papal bull excommunicating Luther, *Exsurge Domine*, of June 1520, accused him of a heretical denial of the freedom of the will. Luther responded, setting forth his position on the bondage of the will, in his *Assertio omnium articulorum* . . ., *WA* VII, 91ff.

barks hoarsely before dawn. And, now that the right truth is proclaimed, you want to upbraid the lowly and not the mighty. You do just as we Germans say [in the legend of "Reynard the Fox"]: you climb into the well, just like the fox who stepped into the bucket, lowered himself, and ate the fish. Afterward he lured the stupid wolf into the well in another bucket, which carried him out while the wolf remained below. So the princes who follow you will be defeated, as well as the noble highwaymen whom you set upon the merchants. Ezekiel renders his judgment on the fox, at 12[:4], and on the beasts and wild animals, at 34[:25], that Christ called wolves, John 10[:12]. They will all share the fate of the trapped fox, Psalm 73[:18ff.]. When the people first begin to await the light of dawn, then the little dogs, Matthew 15[:27], will run the foxes to their dens. The little dogs will not be able to do more than snap at the fox. But the rested dog will shake the fox by the pelt until he must leave his den. He has eaten enough chickens. Look, Martin, have you not smelled this roasted fox that is given instead of hare to inexperienced hunters at the lords' courts?[31] You, Esau, Jacob has deservedly thrust aside. Why have you sold your birthright for a mess of pottage? [Gen. 25:28–43].

Ezekiel 13[:3–9] gives you the answer, and Micah 3[:5–8]. You have confused Christendom with a false faith. And now that distress grows, you cannot correct it. Therefore you flatter the princes. But you believe that all will be well so long as you attain a great reputation. And you go on and on about how, at Leipzig, you stood before the most dangerous assembly.[32] Why do you want to blind the people? You were comfortable at Leipzig, leaving the city gate with a wreath of carnations and drinking good wine at the house of Melchior Lother. And although you were [interviewed by Cardinal Cajetan] at Augsburg, you were in no real danger, for Staupitz the Oracle[33] stood by you, although he has now forsaken you and become an abbot. I am certainly worried that you will follow him. Truly, the devil does not

---

[31] Luther is compared to a fox that is used by the nobility to deceive inexperienced hunters, the commoners who are searching for the truth.

[32] A reference to Luther's and Karlstadt's theological debate with Dr. Johann Eck of Ingolstadt before the ducal court at Leipzig in June and July 1519. In all likelihood Müntzer, who was at Wittenberg in the period 1517–19, attended this debate. Here Müntzer refers to a passage in Luther's *Letter to the Princes* (*WA* XV, 214) in which he speaks of the danger of his appearance at the Leipzig disputation.

[33] Johannes von Staupitz, Vicar-General of the Saxon Province of the Augustinian order, and Luther's friend and adviser.

stand for truth and cannot give up his tricks. Yet in Luther's pamphlet on rebellion[34] he fears the prophecy of his downfall. Therefore he speaks about the new prophets as the scribes did against hrist, John 8[:52]. So I have used nearly the whole chapter [of John 8] for my present condemnation of Luther. Paul says about the prophets, 1 Corinthians 14[:1–5], "A true preacher must indeed be a prophet even if he appears to the world as a mockery." How can you judge people when, in your writing about the monk-calf,[35] you renounce the office of prophet?

When you tell how you punched me in the snout, you do not speak the truth; indeed you are lying from the bottom of your throat. For I have not been with you for six or seven years. But if you made fools of the good brothers[36] who were with you, this will come out. In any case, your story does not make sense. And you should not despise the little ones, Matthew 18[:10]. As for your boasting, one could be put to sleep by your senseless foolishness. It is thanks to the German nobility, whose snouts you have petted and given honey, that you stood before the Holy Roman Empire at Worms.[37] For the nobility thinks only that with your preaching you will give them "Bohemian gifts,"[38] cloisters and foundations, which you now promise the princes. If you had wavered at Worms, you would have been stabbed by the nobility rather than set free. Indeed, everyone knows this. Surely you cannot take credit unless you want once again to risk your noble blood, about which you boast. You, together with your followers, employed wild trickery and deception at Worms. At your own suggestion you let yourself be taken captive and you presented your-

---

[34] Luther's pamphlet of 1522, *A True Warning to All Christians to Guard Themselves Against Insurrection and Rebellion (Eine treue Vermahnung Martin Luther zu allen Christen, sich zu verhüten vor Aufruhr und Empörung), WA* VIII, 676ff., especially 683, where Luther spoke of diabolically inspired rumors and prophecies of his downfall and death.

[35] In 1523 Luther published his *An Explanation of Two Horrible Figures Found in Meissen, the Pope-ass of Rome and the Monk-calf of Freiberg (Deutung der zwo geulichen Figuren, Papstesels zu Rom und Mönchkalbs zu Freiberg in Meissen gefunden), WA* XI, 369ff. In this work, which dealt with two prodigies, Luther declined to offer a prophetic interpretation of the figure of the monk-calf because, he asserted, "I am not a prophet"; *WA* XI, 380.

[36] Perhaps Nicholas Storch and Markus Thomae (or Stübner), two associates of Müntzer from Zwickau, who visited Luther at Wittenberg.

[37] In Luther's *Letter to the Princes* he also described (*WA* XV, 214) his appearance before the imperial diet at Worms in April 1521 as a time of danger.

[38] Ecclesiastical property that has been secularized, on the pattern of the Hussite movement in Bohemia.

self as unwilling.[39] Those who did not understand your deceit swore to the saints that you were pious Martin. Sleep softly, dear flesh. I would rather smell you roasted in your own stubbornness by the wrath of God in a pot over the fire, Jeremiah 1[:13]. Then, cooked in your own suet, the devil should devour you, Ezekiel 23[:46]. Your flesh is like that of an ass and you would have to be cooked slowly. You would make a tough dish for your milk-sop friends.

Most dearly beloved brothers in Christ, from the beginning of the quarrel I have been wearied by the unavoidable trouble it would give to the poor masses. But if Doctor Liar had let me preach, or defeated me before the people, or let his princes judge me when I was before them at Weimar,[40] where they interrogated me at the request of this monk, then I would not have had this problem.

It was finally decided that the prince [Duke John] would leave the matter to the decision of the strict judge [God] at the Last Judgment. The prince did not want to resist the other tyrants, who wanted, for the sake of the gospel, to let the case remain in his sphere of competence.[41] It would be a fine thing if the matter were remanded to this eschatological jurisdiction. The peasants would gladly see this happen. It would be a fine thing if everything were postponed to the Last Judgment. Then the peasants would also have a good precedent, when they were supposed to do the right thing. When it came to their judgment, they could say, "I am saving it for the divine judge." But

---

[39] A reference to Luther's sudden disappearance after the Diet of Worms, where he was declared an imperial outlaw and a heretic. After leaving Worms a fake kidnapping was arranged, so that Luther could surreptitiously be brought into the elector of Saxony's protective custody.

[40] On 1 August 1524 Müntzer and several officials of Allstedt were interrogated at a hearing before chancellery officers of Duke John of Saxony at Weimar. Müntzer saw this interrogation as the fruit of Luther's pressure on the Saxon court. The results of the hearing were inconclusive in that a final judgment on Müntzer's teachings was postponed.

[41] After the Weimar hearing, the local Saxon official in Allstedt, Hans Zeiss, ordered the disbanding of the organization that Müntzer had created in Allstedt, his "Christian League" (*Christliche Verbündnisse*), as well as the closing of Müntzer's press in Allstedt; he also forbade Müntzer to preach politically inflammatory sermons or to block the prosecution of those who had burned the chapel at Mallerbach. Müntzer had justified the existence of the Christian League on the grounds that its purpose was to defend followers of the gospel from persecution by nearby Catholic lords who had prevented their subjects from coming to Allstedt for Müntzer's services. Thus Müntzer saw the prohibition of the League by Duke John as an instance of one tyrant helping others; he is clearly being ironical in saying that the other lords let Duke John have competence in the matter "for the sake of the gospel."

in the meantime the rod of the godless is their chief hindrance.

When I returned home from the hearing at Weimar, I intended to preach the strict word of God. Then members of the Allstedt city council[42] came and wanted to hand me over to the worst enemies of the gospel. When I learned this, I could remain in Allstedt no longer. I wiped their dust from my shoes.[43] For I saw with open eyes that they paid much more attention to their temporal oaths and duties than to the word of God. They assumed that they could serve two masters, one against the other. They did this even though God most clearly stood behind them. And God, who had saved them from the powerful clutches of the bears and lions, would also have saved them from the hands of Goliath, 1 Kings 17[:36f.]. Although Goliath relied on his armor and sword, David taught him a thing or two. Saul also began something well, but David[44] had to carry it out after a long delay. David is a symbol of you, oh Christ, in your dear friends, whom you will diligently protect for eternity. Amen.

In the year 1524.

"Sly fox, with your lies you have saddened the hearts of the righteous, whom the lord has not deceived. And you have strengthened the hands of your wicked ones, so that they do not turn from their evil life. Because of this you will be destroyed and the people of God will be freed from your tyranny. You will see that God is lord," Ezekiel 13[:22f.].

This should be translated: oh Doctor Liar, you sly fox. Through your lies you have made sad the hearts of the righteous, whom God has not deceived. Thereby you have strengthened the power of the evildoers, so that they remain set in their old ways. Thus your fate will be that of a trapped fox. The people will be free. And God alone will be lord over them.

---

[42] Perhaps a reference to certain members of the city council over whom Müntzer had previously exercised some influence but who now, after the Weimar hearing, distanced themselves from his cause.

[43] During the night of 7–8 August 1524, Müntzer climbed over the city wall and fled Allstedt.

[44] Presumably Müntzer meant by "Saul" Luther, who began the Reformation, and by "David" himself, who intended to carry it to its appropriate conclusion.

7 Felix Manz, *Protest and Defense*

Zurich, before 17 January 1525[1]

Wise, prudent, merciful, dear lords and brothers.[2]

In your wisdom you certainly know how much strange talk is going around. Some maintain that a newborn child, as soon as it comes from the mother's womb, is to be baptized, and that this can be proved from holy Scripture. Others believe on the basis of the divine word that infant baptism is bad, false, and that (rather than being true) it was contrived by and grew out of the Antichrist, the pope, and his followers. Among those holding the latter belief, I too have been charged by some people with being a rebel and inhuman. But I have been accused too quickly and unjustly, and the accusation cannot be shown to have any truth. All those with whom I have had anything to do will testify that I have nowhere engaged in any rebellion, nor

---

[1] This work, without title or date and heavily corrected, was not published until the modern period. It was written between December 1524 and mid-January 1525. The work was formerly thought to be by Conrad Grebel, but it has now been established that Felix Manz wrote it. The work is a petition to the Zurich city council that they examine written arguments, based on Scripture alone, for and against the practice of infant baptism. Manz's opposition to infant baptism may have been influenced by Karlstadt's views on the subject; in the fall of 1524 Manz facilitated the publication in Basel of writings by Karlstadt, including one on baptism. On 10 and 17 January the Zurich council listened to arguments by both Zwingli and the radical circle around Grebel and Manz; it decided to retain infant baptism and to punish with exile those who refused to have their children baptized. A few days later, on 21 January 1525, at the home of Manz, the Zurich radicals acted out the converse and positive side of their baptismal views: the layman Grebel baptized the former priest George Blaurock, an event that is traditionally viewed as the start of the Anabaptist movement. The translation is based on the text in *QGTS*, I, 23–28.

[2] Unlike some of the other Zurich radicals, Manz was a citizen of the city; hence he addressed the members of the council both as his superiors and as fellow citizens.

anywhere, in any way, taught or told them anything that has brought or can bring rebellion.[3] For this reason I am accused unfairly. Since I am thus charged – even though untruthfully – I have thought it necessary that I now deliver to you, my merciful, dear lords a justification and explanation of my faith.

I would certainly have thought that, should you be presented with the truth, you would respect it. Your shepherds [the Zurich clergy] have repeatedly maintained [their interest in a disputation], and they have always negotiated with me on the following basis, namely that one should let Scripture speak, and that we should neither add to it nor delete anything from it. This has never been fulfilled.[4] They have certainly presented their opinion, but have not based it on passages of Scripture. We have not been able to come to speak, and Scripture could not be heard. In addition, if the clergy think that someone wants to say something about the truth, they choke the speech in his throat and attack him, demanding scriptural citations, which they themselves should have presented to support the truth. This is what they do; God knows this well. They also know, much better than anyone could expound from Scripture, that Christ never taught the baptism of children, and that it was not the custom of the apostles. Rather Christ and the apostles taught and practiced as the meaning of baptism that only those should be baptized who are improving, who are taking on a new life, who are dying to vices, and who are buried with Christ and resurrected with him in the renewal of life out of baptism.

From now on, for God's sake and the sake of the common name which we bear together,[5] I want to bid you wise lords to be willing to set aside personal interests, to analyze seriously, industriously, and fairly the pure, clear truth as it has been revealed to us through the word, and to consider well what we are dealing with. You should not let yourselves be angered by the short time [it requires to study this question], because it is no small matter – although some present it differently – that the two actual ceremonies[6] which Christ left us are practiced differently from the way that Christ commanded.

First, the eternal wisdom of God provided for one who would be a

---

[3] Zwingli charged the Zurich radicals with advocating the right actively to resist laws that they viewed as unjust, which conflicted with their understanding of the gospel.

[4] I.e. no disputation under this condition had taken place. Hence the scriptural truth about baptism had never been presented to the council.

[5] I.e. the common citizenship which Manz shared with the members of the council.

[6] The Lord's Supper and baptism.

forerunner of his own son [i.e. John the Baptist], who should prepare his way, should show his people their vices, and should admonish them so that they desist from their vices and improve themselves. For when the ax is laid to the tree, each person who does not bear good fruit will be chopped down and thrown into the fire. And thus the forerunner showed to those who desired improvement the lamb of God, who would then take away the sins of the world [John 1:29]. And he baptized them so that their sins were forgiven in the future suffering of Jesus Christ, if they would change their lives and henceforth produce rightly created fruit. You find this in Matthew 3[:10], Mark 1[:9ff.], Luke 3[:9], and John 1[:29] and 4[:29]. Just as John baptized only those, as is clearly shown, who improved themselves, fled the evil fruits, and did good, in the same way the apostles, after the ascension of Christ, received a command from Christ. For he said, "All power in heaven and on earth has been given to me. Therefore go and teach all peoples and baptize them" [Mt. 28:19]. And in Mark [16:16], "Who believes and is baptized will be saved." And the same is true of Peter, for we are told in the tenth chapter of the Acts of the Apostles that when he was sent for by Cornelius and was asked why he had been sent for, Peter told Cornelius how Christ came, taught, healed the sick, was killed, and rose again [Acts 10:36–42]. The text goes on to say [Acts 10:40ff.] that God raised him up on the third day and let him be revealed – not to all people but only to the witnesses whom God had previously chosen, like us, who were to eat and drink with him after he was resurrected from the dead. He commanded that we preach to people and testify that he has been ordained by God to be a judge of the living and the dead. All the prophets testify that every one who believes in him will attain forgiveness of sin through his name. And as Peter was still saying these words, the holy spirit descended on all who were listening to this speech. And they of the circumcision [Jews] were astonished, and all those who were with Peter believed that the gift of the holy spirit was also given to the heathen, etc. [Acts 10:44ff.].

From these words a person can see very clearly that the apostles understood the command of Christ, which was cited above from Matthew [28:19]: namely that they should go forth and teach all peoples that Christ has been given all power in heaven and on earth, and that in his name forgiveness of sin is given to everyone who believes in him and does righteous works from a changed spirit. And after receiving this teaching and the descent of the holy spirit, which was proved by those who had heard the words of Peter speaking in tongues, water was then poured over them [Acts 10:48]. Just as they were purified internally by the descent of the holy spirit, so too water was also poured over them externally as a symbol of their inner cleansing and dying to sin.

And as evidence that this is the meaning of baptism, we also have the twenty-second chapter of the Acts of the Apostles [Acts 22:14–16], in which Paul tells what happened to him on the road to Damascus. When Ananias came and spoke these words, "The lord God prepared you, so that you would understand his will, see what is right, and hear the voice from his mouth. For you will be his witness to all men of the things which you have seen and heard. And now why do you delay? Stand up and be baptized and wash the sin from you, for you have called the name of the Lord. And what do you lack now, other than to be baptized and cleansed of your sins after the name of the Lord is called?"

We see very clearly from these words what baptism is and when baptism should be practiced. That is, a person should be baptized if he has been converted through God's word, if he has changed his mind and wants to live henceforth a renewed life, as Paul clearly shows in chapter 6 of his Epistle to the Romans [see Rom. 6:4], if he is dead to his old life and his heart has been circumcised, and if he has died to sin with Christ. Then he should be buried with Christ in baptism and be resurrected with him to a new life, etc.

To ascribe such things, as they [the clergy] now do, to children is without any foundation in Scripture and against all of Scripture. The whole of the New Testament is full of such sayings [as I have cited] and similar ones. I have now learned clearly from the New Testament and know for sure that baptism is nothing but the dying of the old man and the putting on of the new, that Christ ordered the baptism of those who have been instructed, that the apostles baptized only those who had been instructed about Christ, and that they baptized no one without external evidence and a certain knowledge or desire. And whoever says or teaches otherwise does what he cannot prove with any passage of Scripture. Also I would gladly like to hear someone who can show me from authentic, clear Scripture that John, Christ or the apostles baptized children or taught that they should be baptized. If this cannot be shown, no one should talk about it any more. For the baptism of children is contrary to God, an insult to Christ, and a trampling under foot of his own true, eternal word. It is also contrary to the example of Christ, who was baptized when he was thirty years old but circumcised on the eighth day.

Now Christ has presented us with an example, and as he has done, so we should do as well. Therefore I want to request in a friendly way, but most urgently, that you wise lords accept my letter with the best intentions. For, truthfully, I am not concerned about honor, name, and reputation. Nor am I writing out of envy or hate, as I will show you. Rather [I write] only because this is the eternal truth of God, which no one may conquer. Furthermore, no angel from heaven is able to teach differently from what has been presented above. The eternally true word of God will sing in the heart of each person that this is the truth, whether he opposes it or not.

I also want to admonish you wise lords that you should be aware of idol worship which is bound to certain times and is sometimes right and sometimes wrong. For which reason one person was killed.[7]

I am certain that Master Ulrich [Zwingli] understands this view of baptism, and much better than we do. But I do not know why he will not publicly express it. I do know certainly, however, that if one presents the one word freely and simply, no one can oppose it, and that God will destroy the counsel of the godless. If the word has found its way in other matters and abominations, it will also find its way in this one – that is, if one lets God's word be free and lets the truth be the truth. But if someone says that it is of no importance how baptism is practiced, he will not prove it with Scripture. Rather, Scripture proves that God wants us to keep his commandments and ceremonies as he has given them to us. We also have many examples of how God has severely punished the violation of external commandments, as when the two sons of Aaron were burned, and innumerable other examples which would be too long to recount here.

I also want to warn you wise lords that civil and state laws are neither to be strengthened nor improved through baptism.[8] There-

---

[7] Apparently a reference to Klaus Hottinger, who toppled a crucifix at Stadelhofen near Zurich in September 1523 and was exiled from the city for two years. He was then arrested in Baden and finally executed at Lucerne in March 1524.

[8] This assertion would have been a matter of gravest concern for the city council. In rejecting infant baptism, Manz was also repudiating the sacrament which made the polity coterminous with the Christian community. In Zurich, as elsewhere, laws were enacted and enforced on the ground that such measures were necessary to the spiritual well-

fore I have bid you most urgently not to stain your hands with innocent blood, thinking that you do God a service if you put to death or
exile some people. [Do not do this] so that all this innocent blood is
not also demanded from your hands.[9]

I also bid you, wise lords, the following: Master Ulrich thinks that
he can prove such baptism of children with holy Scripture, although
this baptism was contrived by the pope, even contrary to the first
popes and their laws, as we know from written history; it has been
established and contrived by men. But I do not believe [that infant
baptism can be proved from Scripture]. Therefore I would like to bid
you, wise lords, most urgently that he [Zwingli] put this [his justification for infant baptism] in writing, as he has always done for all those
with whom he has dealt. I will read him sympathetically and answer. I
am not a good speaker. And I could not [reply to him earlier], because
either he attacked me often with so much talk that I could not answer
him, or I could not answer on account of his long speeches. Much
quarreling and strife will also be avoided by this kind of discussion
[i.e., if Zwingli puts his position in writing], and I would be very
pleased by it.

Therefore I appeal to you, my gracious, dear lords and brothers, as
a citizen. And with this letter I also insist that this is my view and
understanding [of baptism] and it is not without its specific basis in
holy and divine Scripture. Now if anyone, whoever he may be, thinks
that he can show from divine Scripture that young, newborn babies
should be baptized, and that he can demonstrate this to you, my lords,
in writing and from Scripture, I will answer each one [who thinks
this]. I cannot dispute about many issues and do not want to. Rather I
want to deal only on the basis of holy Scripture and with the question
whether the baptism of pure, young, newborn children, who have no
notion of baptism, was practiced by the apostles on the command of
Christ. I believe, and know it too, that no man on earth can prove it.

being of the community. Each year residents of Zurich, and of many other cities, took
oaths as Christians to uphold and obey the law.
[9] Manz's hope that the Zurich council not stain its hands with blood was to be disappointed. In a mandate of 7 March 1526 the Zurich council attached the death penalty to
acts of "rebaptism." This was supplemented on 19 November by a new law which also
made those who attended Anabaptist sermons subject to the death penalty.

8 Anonymous, *To the Assembly of the Common Peasantry* May 1525[1]

To the Assembly of the Common Peasantry which has come together in revolt and insurrection in the high German nation and many other places. Concerning whether their rebellion takes place justly or unjustly, and what they owe or do not owe the authorities etc., based on holy divine Scripture. Issued and discussed with good intention by your brothers in upper Germany, etc.

Now is the hour and time of the wheel of fortune. God knows who will remain on top.[2]
"What increases the Swiss? The greed of the lords."

Grace be with you and the eternal peace of God, from the father and our lord, Jesus Christ, who gave himself for our sins to save us from

---

[1] The work was printed at Nuremberg by Hieronymous Hölzel, the publisher of Müntzer's *A Highly Provoked Defense*, but thus far attempts to identify the author have not proved successful. It has been argued that Karlstadt wrote the piece, but this has now been disproved. Certainly the argument of the tract is much closer to the thought of Müntzer than that of Karlstadt. The translation is based on the text in S. Hoyer and B. Rüdiger, eds., *An die Versammlung Gemeiner Bauernschaft* (Leipzig, 1975).

[2] This line, as well as the following caption, relates to the illustration on the pamphlet's title page, which depicted in the center the pope bound to a wheel of fortune, on the left an infantry formation of commoners, and on the right a cavalry unit of princes and prelates.

this present evil age according to the will of God, our lord. May he be praised for ever and ever. Amen.

Dear brothers in Christ, you know that the Lord says, "Render unto Caesar that which is Caesar's," etc. Cling to this saying in Matthew chapter 23 [rather, Mt. 22:21], just as Christ himself also gave the tax money to the emperor, Matthew 17 [:24–27]. Look now, my dear brothers, the lord of heaven and earth, the true God, subjected himself to worldly authority, and voluntarily made himself liable to taxation, to give us an example to imitate. "The servant should never be above his lord." Because of this commandment, we cannot excuse ourselves from the terrible punishment, as St. Paul said to the Romans in chapter 13[:2–6], "He who resists the authorities opposes the order of God . . . and he will incur judgment . . . For the authorities do not bear the sword in vain. They are servants of God. Therefore one should pay taxes and other dues," etc.

In this respect, dear brothers, it is a shocking sacrilege to oppose the authorities and not to be obedient to them.

For as St. Paul says in this passage, "There is no authority but from God" [Rom. 13:1]. In truth, if there were no authority, the human race would perish in a shorter time than through the tortures of godless tyrants. For the hairy worm[3] would tear itself apart like a poisonous viper or a mad dog. The human race is most evilly inclined from childhood on, Genesis 6 [:5] and 8 [:21]. Again, Isaiah 59 [:7], "Their feet run swiftly to shed desolation, and they do not know the path of peace."

Thus you can see how necessary the authorities are for us, and how God ordained them because of our great need. Thus both great need and divine commandment compel us to be obedient to authorities, "and even if they are rogues," as some translate St. Peter into German, 1 Peter 2 [:18].

But now a mighty, heavy curse descends upon you as disobedient people, who do not want to give your lords payments, taxes, customs, heriot dues, entry fines, and similar fees which you were obliged to pay in the past. And the complaints and curses against you are not few.

A great crowd of very destructive people is angry with you and, like

---

[3] *das zottet* (= *zottig*) *gewürme*; i.e. human nature unrestrained by authority of any kind. See Job 25:6.

the heathen and Turks, they will not change their attitude because of your pain.

However, merciful God will graciously enlighten you with his truth and lead you along the path of resolute faith in him, in order to escape this malicious curse. Otherwise, your innocent wives and young children will need heartfelt mercy. This moves me to write you out of brotherly loyalty and divine duty. If a way can be found to prevent this terrible misery, it would be a special joy for me in God. So raise your hands and cry from your heart to God, and help me to beseech him so that I may accomplish this according to his divine will.

In truth, disobedience is hated by God to the highest degree. He never lets the disobedient go unpunished. For example, Adam, Lucifer, etc. Scripture is full of such examples. I do not doubt that without my efforts you have already been sufficiently informed of these examples by the blabbering scribes with their Clementine and Codex[4] – indeed, dementia and camouflage[5] – which clearly belong to the crimson whore of Babylon, above all the "praiseworthy" Pope Pelagius II [578–590], who so strictly enjoined obedience.

But in truth there is a very different meaning [from the one the scribes give these texts about obedience]. They overextend the meaning of obedience, making a painted idol out of it and, thus far, making a fool of the world with it, finely decking out obedience, and setting it up, making a great wail on the pan pipes with it, and making their cause appear wholly correct. But if one investigates the essence of this shining knight of obedience, it turns out to be nothing but a disguised straw doll, with which the lords have long played their carnival games. Yes, they have certainly done much blustering and blowing about their majesty and power on the basis of the passages of Scripture and law which have been mentioned above. But so far God has never enlightened them with his grace so that they recognize what authority really is. This ignorance would be tolerable, if they did not turn authority into a raving madness.[6]

So listen now to the password! A real battle will begin about whether the above-mentioned curse has been put on you justly or not. The time of grace is indeed here for the truth to be revealed. The

---

[4] I.e. the Constitutions of Pope Clement V (1305–14), which were added to canon law in 1314, and the Codex of Justinian, embodying Roman civil law.

[5] *ja, dementin und lodex*, which rhymes with the preceding *Clementin und codex*.

[6] Again, a rhyme is involved: authority (*oberkayt*) is turned into raving madness (*tobickayt*).

preachers who tickle people's ears with what they want to hear, and the priests of Baal, and those from the city that Columbanus deserted,[7] must duck down and learn something more unpleasant. And even if the stones must speak [Lk. 19:40], the truth must come out. May God, the heavenly father, help us, through the merit of his son, our savior Jesus Christ. May he be praised everlastingly for all eternity. Amen.

Chapter one
True Christian faith needs no human authority.

As a basic proof of this, we have taken from divine law and Scripture three mighty and irrefutable sayings, which the gates of hell with their entire knighthood are not able to destroy. First, Matthew 7 [:12], "Everything that you wish people to do to you, do the same to them," etc. Second, Matthew 22 [:39, 37], "Yes, God equates brotherly love with his love [for mankind] . . . which should come from the whole mind, the whole heart and soul." Third, St. Paul wrote to the Galatians 3 [:28], "Here is neither lord nor servant . . . We are all one in Christ, thus indeed one," and to the Ephesians, 4 [:15–16], "One shall be a limb of the other, to make one body from us all, under the head, Jesus Christ."

But then it is certainly true that the death of any single member is the ruin of the others. In truth, as soon as death ensnares one limb, there is no remission for the whole, until it spoils the other members as well. Therefore all the limbs bear an implanted capacity to love and suffer with one another; but above all, they have been created not for suffering but for salvation and love. This is the intention of St. Paul in Romans chapter 13 [:8], on taxes, customs, etc., where he says, "You do not owe anything to anyone, except that you should love one another, for love is the fulfillment of the law." But how all the commandments of God are fulfilled with love will follow quite clearly in the third chapter.

---

[7] The early Irish missionary St. Columban or Columbanus (c. 540–615) attempted to reestablish Christianity in the city of Bregenz and in Switzerland; the hostile reaction of the impious forced him to move to Italy. As in the preceding reference to the "priests of Baal," the author is describing clerics who fail to preach the authentic message of Christ.

Chapter two
Only the unchristian way of life requires human authority.

The carnal, unchristian, lustful life and its power rule so strongly in us and damn the Christian spirit in us so completely that from our youth on we are inclined to evil, as was heard above from Genesis 8 [:21]. We are inclined to pride, avarice, sensual pleasure, etc. and what flows from these same evils. And we are so drowned in an unchristian essence that all love and fear of God, and also brotherly loyalty, are extinguished in us. And so true Christian faith has been torn from our hearts. Each considers how he can take advantage of the other with all disloyalty. Thus, we are not unjustly called fake Christians, for in our hearts Christ is completely denied.

The torturing punishments of hell are never so terrible that they would drive us from evil if there were no temporal fear and punishment. Thus it follows – but not from the nature of the Christian faith – that authority must be maintained, so that the unchristians are condemned by it and the pious are protected. In sum, as St. Paul says in 1 Timothy 1 [:9], "I know that no law has been ordained for the pious but only for the wicked." And again, in Romans 13 [:3], "The powers that be are not to be feared by the good, but by the wicked."

Chapter three
The obligations of a Christian official, be he prince, pope, or emperor.

Each pious person, illuminated with true Christian faith and love, considers justly and takes to heart that God is no respecter of persons – so Paul in Romans 3.[8] It is the same for all – shepherd, pope, emperor, or bath-house keeper.[9] Where there is no Christian brotherly heart, someone's crown, shield, or helmet will not ennoble him before God.

Second, each authority shall be established to rule with God himself (for God is the lord), and each authority holds office as a steward

---

[8] An incorrect reference; the actual citation is Eph. 6:9.
[9] The first and last occupations represent the lowest strata of society in the countryside and the cities, the middle two titles, the pinnacles of society in spiritual and temporal affairs.

of God. Oh, would to God that such a person were worthy of the office to which God has ordained him! About which Paul says to the Ephesians [Eph. 6:9], "Consider, you lords, that your Lord is also in heaven." The divine King David considered this deeply and said, "Not us, Lord; not us, Lord; it is your name that brings honor" [Ps. 115:1].

In sum, we all belong to God in body and soul. And each authority, be it spiritual or temporal, has been established only to tend God's lambs. Their Latin title shows this, namely *dominus terre*, which is translated into German as "a householder." For the word *dominus* is derived from the little word *domus*, which means "a house." Thus whoever proves to be worthy of his title is a true patriarch of a household in his lands. The one who administers his office truly – truly protects brotherly love, zealously serves God, his lord, and paternally tends the flock of Christ – is justly called an authority. For he is an upright and honorable person who watches over the flock. And therefore Scripture calls him an angel, yes, an earthly god [Gal. 4:4].

But now it is certain that each territory or city must have a common fund with which to build roads and bridges, to protect the territory and always to protect the common good, which we presently have a great need for. And what Christian would oppose this? And who would not give, out of brotherly love, the required part of his wealth in order to protect himself and to maintain his wife and children? Whoever was not driven by brotherly love to make his contribution for this cause would have to be a coarse kind of person. In this sense Christ also gave his tax money into the common fund of Rome, Matthew 22 [: 15ff.], and certainly he did not give it to Tiberius for making war, for gambling, or for whistling and singing, or committing fornication and other vices, on which the whole wage of the poor harvester, earned in sweat and blood, is usually squandered.

In sum, each authority should collect taxes, customs fees, etc., in no other capacity than as a loyal, dear foster-parent, who uses his budget for the benefit of the poor and the orphans. It is thus clear that the subject is obliged to pay taxes, customs, etc., out of brotherly love. In the same way, the authorities or powers should take taxes and customs from their brother Christians only out of brotherly love, and in order to use them in the interests of their subjects. This is the view that Paul confirms in Romans 13 [:8], about obedience, also about taxes and customs, etc., "You owe no one anything except to love one another. Love is the fulfillment of the law," etc. On these grounds and none other, we are obliged to pay taxes, customs, etc., and certainly not, as the scribes and lawyers jabber, because of their own ancient laws or rights.

But whoever is against this, and does not offer his Christian authorities every honor, indeed does not entrust his body and honor to them, if common brotherly need requires it – as now among you fellow brothers of the common peasantry – then, as Paul says, he will be justly judged. And immediately! Put away these opponents! Put them far away from the good lambs!

And if you now set up a tailor, shoemaker or peasant as your authority, to lead you faithfully in all brotherly loyalty and to maintain Christian brotherhood, that person should be regarded as a king or emperor and given all obedience. In sum and in conclusion, as St. Paul says, 2 Corinthians 10 [:8], "Every authority has been established to improve the territory and not to corrupt it."

In truth, offices, whether of prince or lord, are an unbearably heavy burden from which a true Christian derives little joy, and which he endures with a quaking heart, in constant worry about how he can justify his office. Therefore every official, be he of high or low estate, should rightly bid almighty God with a Christian spirit and fervent heart to grant him wisdom and understanding through divine grace, so that he can perform his office completely and properly and can give an account of it before God and the world. Just as Solomon too prayed to almighty God for wisdom and right understanding, saying, "Oh lord, I beseech you, give your servant an understanding heart, and give him a knowledge of good and evil, so that he is able to judge and rule your people. For who could judge and rule your great people without your divine grace and wisdom?," as is clearly stated in 1 Kings 3 [:9].

Chapter four
On false and unlimited power, which one is not obliged to obey.

All the popes, emperors, kings, etc. who puff themselves up in their own estimation above other pious poor Christians, claiming to be a better kind of human – as if their lordship and authority to rule others were innate – do not want to recognize that they are God's stewards and officials. And they do not govern according to his commandment to maintain the common good and brotherly unity among us. God has established and ordained authority for this reason alone, and no other. But rulers who want to be lords for their own sake are all false rulers, and not worthy of the lowest office among Christians. For God alone wants to be lord and he says in Deuteronomy 12 [:1], "You shall keep my commandment in your hand like a measuring rod according to which you shall judge – straight ahead, not deviating either to the left or to the right." The same point is made in Job 5 [:8].

Therefore whichever prince or lord invents and sets up his own self-serving burdens and commands, rules falsely, and he dares impudently to deceive God, his own lord. Where are you, you werewolves, you band of Behemoths,[10] with your financial tricks which impose one burden after another on the poor people? This year a labor service is voluntary, next year it becomes compulsory. In most cases this is how your old customary law has grown. In what "dementia" or "camouflage"[11] did God, your lord, give you such power that we poor people have to cultivate your lands with labor services? But only in good weather, for on rainy days we poor people see the fruits of our sweat rot in the fields. May God, in his justice, not tolerate the terrible Babylonian captivity in which we poor people are driven to mow the lords' meadows, to make hay, to cultivate the fields, to sow flax in them, to cut it, comb it, heat it, wash it, pound it, and spin it – yes, even to sew their underpants on their arses. We also have to pick peas and harvest carrots and asparagus.

Help us, God! Where has such misery ever been heard of! They tax and tear out the marrow of the poor people's bones, and we have to pay interest on that! Where are they, with their hired murderers and horsemen, the gamblers and whoremasters, who are stuffed fuller than puking dogs? In addition, we poor people have to give them taxes, payments, and interest. And at home [they assume that] the poor should have neither bread, salt nor lard for their wives and small children. Where are they, with their entry fines and heriot dues? Yes, damn their disgraceful fines and robber's dues! Where are the tyrants and raging ones, who appropriate taxes, customs, and user fees, and

---

[10] A term repeatedly used by the author to describe the mighty in society; see Job 40:15–24.

[11] Mentioned above in the opening section, p. 103.

waste them so shamefully and wantonly, and lose what should go into the common chest or purse to serve the needs of the territory.

And nevertheless no one can turn up his nose at them, or he is immediately treated like a treacherous rogue – put in the stocks, beheaded, quartered! He is shown less pity than a mad dog.

Did God give them such power? On the peak of what monk's cowl is it written? Indeed, their authority is from God. But so remotely that they have become the devil's soldiers and satan is their captain. Yes, they have been truly rejected, being enemies in their own territory. And what about their serfdom? Damn their unchristian, heathen nature. How they torture us poor people! We are the spiritual serfs of the clergy and the bodily serfs of the secular powers. Help us, eternal God! What great unchristian misery and murder is being done to your property, which your only-begotten son, lord of heaven and earth – and lord of this band of Behemoths – purchased at such a high price with his bitter death! Put these Moabites[12] and this band of Behemoths as far behind you and as far away [as you can]. This is God's greatest pleasure. And how little they will be prayed for! If one of their village officials wanted to impose anything on the poor in his own self-interest, they would depose him with a harsh punishment. The princes and lords themselves deserve nothing less for making self-serving commandments, which are outside the common good and unserviceable for brotherly unity.

Do not let yourselves be led astray and blinded to any degree because every day the authorities endlessly repeat what the apostle Peter says in 1 Peter 2 [:18]: "You should be submissive to your lords, even if they are rogues," etc. In truth, the sword [of Scripture] cuts sharply on both sides, and until now they have fought masterfully with it. But we want to see how Tileman [a foolish man] so strangely confuses divine Scripture again, and the wolf so cleverly puts on sheep's clothing. Truly, truly, St. Peter's view means something very different; for according to their interpretation, we would have to deliver our pious wives and children to them, so that they could satisfy their lust with them.

The basic cause and source of the whole confederation of the Swiss was the unlimited, tyrannical power of the nobility and of other authorities. For daily, with their unchristian, tyrannical rape, they did

---

[12] I.e. domineering and unjust political rulers. Judges 3:12–30 recounts how, after years of domination by the king of Moab, the people of Israel revolt against the Moabites.

not spare the common man, but forced and compelled him contrary to all equity. And this grew out of their pride, blasphemous power, and enterprise. Their rule had to be abolished and rooted out through great war, bloodshed, and use of the sword, as is indicated in the Swiss chronicles and in many other reliable histories and writings. The conclusion of this pamphlet talks a bit about this. The lords were also allowed to murder pious and upright people for hunting a hare; and they did similar things because of their perverted minds. Indeed, such a Babylonian captivity has tightly confined us.

But the primary responsibility for it rests with the authority which saw itself as, and boasted of being, "spiritual." Indeed, it was lustful! The bishops were sheep-biters.[13] The sheepdogs of the parish themselves tore apart the good lambs, which they were supposed faithfully to tend and protect. In this way the werewolves [tyrannical secular authorities] joined them in falling violently on the good sheep. For a long time now they have tended the sheep according to their pleasure and to their heart's content, and – I should surely say it – have made monkeys of the sheep.

God can and will no longer tolerate this great misery and wantonness, which is now found everywhere. May God enlighten his poor lambs through divine grace and with true Christian faith, and protect them against these ravaging wolves. And he will not enlighten the lambs in the form in which the pernicious and cursed vermin copulate with each other – "If you help me, I will help you." Look, is it not a lamentable plague that they market divine Scripture in such a miserable and shameful way, [insisting] so strictly and without any foundation on obedience to their roguish commands? In truth, there is a great remedy [for what they do], namely none other than divine Scripture – according to which they should judge and administer, strictly adhering to justice and without deviation.

In sum, the Latin word *discolus* in this passage of St. Peter's letter [i.e. 1 Pet. 2:18] can in no way be translated as "rogues," as they jabber; rather it means "a coarse, uncouth or angry person, who may also be very pious at the same time." For David says in Psalm 4 [:5], "Be angry, but sin not."[14]

---

[13] A pun on the word for "bishop" (*bischoff*), which becomes "bite-sheep" (*beyß-schoff*). In the preceding sentence there is a similar word play between "spiritual" (*gaystlich*) and "lustful" (*gayßlich*).

[14] The author presents philological and scriptural arguments against an overly broad

And St. Peter mentions here only servants. They should faithfully serve their lords. Even if their lord is upset and angry with them, they should serve him no less faithfully despite this. If they do not, they cannot excuse themselves for taking their wage without earning it. They should leave his service instead. That would be the Christian way to live. And even if this text of Peter had the meaning which they blabber about, that "rogues" should be obeyed, it is still in the sense of divine commandments.[15]

In sum, the basis of St. Peter's whole epistle is directed only to God's honor, brotherly fidelity, and unity. The selfish rogues boast that they follow these commandments. Indeed, they follow them as werewolves do good lambs!

Chapter five
Which form of authority, hereditary or elective, should be chosen to replace the present authority?

This subject is much debated on both sides. And a great many insist on the first [form of government, i.e. hereditary or monarchical rule], in the opinion that the natural father takes care of his children much more faithfully than the stepfather. This argument has obvious support; one sees it it very clearly in the case of such Christian princes as Frederick of Saxony and Philip, Margrave of Baden, etc.[16]

But, on the other hand, if one looks through Scripture and considers the matter precisely, one finds in truth that immeasurable, unspeakable, and terrible misery and grief have arisen from hereditary authorities. And why should we think of ancient tyrannical deeds? What is still more terrible is that now in our age, because of greed and pomp, the pure word of God is completely and blasphemously suppressed with the use of prison, torture, and similarly arrogant actions, and violence. And what may the godless, blasphemous, hereditary

interpretation of 1 Pet. 2:18. Obedience to an angry, chastising – but pious – ruler is accepted, but not to a sinful one who violates God's commandments.

[15] Another argument against the scribes' interpretation of 1 Pet. 2:18 is that the injunction to obedience refers only to those commands of authority which conform to divine commandments.

[16] The Elector Frederick the Wise of Saxony (d. 5 May 1525) was the protector of Luther; Margrave Philip of Baden acted as a mediator between rebellious peasants and princes in the southwestern part of the Empire. Since the work speaks of Frederick the Wise as though he were living, it must have been written before mid-May, when knowledge of his death would have become general.

authorities not do to their subjects! When the Romans ruled with guild masters and a council in a communal government [i.e. a republic], the might of their great authority over the whole world increased daily. But when lust enticed and led them to fall away from communal government, and they began to set up kings as their own lords, then all their misfortune soon began and the destruction of their empire as well. This resulted from the dirty greed, pomp and pride of the emperors whom they themselves set up. Thus their first emperor, Julius Caesar, whom they set up with great joy and jubilation, was stabbed in the Senate because he wanted to act criminally against their freedom. Here one should consider that a sole ruler is insatiable until he brings everything under his power and is the only free person; and no one else is free, and everybody else belongs to him, body and goods.

After the above-mentioned Julius Caesar, his stepson Octavian became emperor, under whom Christ was born. He ruled well, and the Roman Empire increased mightily, for which reason he was called Augustus – which means "an augmenter of the empire."[17] The emperors today still receive this title. May God grant that they deserve it, not just *pro forma* but in their hearts. After Augustus, his stepson as well, called Tiberius, was accepted as emperor, under whom Christ was tortured. Tiberius was a prosperous man in his time. But great power brought forth what earlier lay hidden in him: his great tyranny. He killed many of his sons, and did the same to his legal wife. He committed many other acts of murder. And truly the saying of Boethius [in *The Consolation of Philosophy*,] book two, was fulfilled in him, "A man is often placed in office or dignity because of his virtue, but virtue seldom arises from power," etc. And the name of this emperor Tiberius was changed, and he was called "Biberius," which translated means "a drunkard," because he committed his tyrannies while drunk.

Now, in our age, whoever does not gorge, guzzle, or feast, and is not always fuller than a full, puking dog, is not held to be a man. But their rule is held to be so Christian that in justice it should produce happiness. What should I say about this? It is best that I say nothing.

In the end the Romans gave this emperor Biberius a Venetian soup [i.e. poison], for they did not know a better way to get rid of him. After

---

[17] In fact *augustus* meant "elevated," "honored."

him, Gaius Caesar [Caligula] became emperor, a unique and absolute rascal. He debauched three of his sisters. Here one sees what lechery is hidden in power gained by force! He was also killed. After him, Claudius became emperor. He was stoned to death by the common people in the streets, where he could not get away, because of his treachery as emperor during a famine.

But if we were to stone to death all those who pursue dishonest practices during famines, and who orphan the poor, oh, how few of the powerful would remain alive! Especially the insolent mendicants, the bishops – yes, the sheep-biters – and the prelates, who from year to year receive and take in grain but never give out a single grain or small measure until, in a few years, they have caused a famine again with their abuse. This is nothing but the chest of usury about which St. Paul commanded the Thessalonians [1 Th. 2:9] that they should burden or harm no one. But who in all Christendom is more burdensome to the poor than, first of all, the spiritual estate [i.e. the clergy], with their rents, dues, right to best-head – yes, right to rob[18] – right to fatted swine, etc.?

After Claudius, Emperor Nero began to tyrannize. In the beginning he was virtuous. Afterward, he killed his tutor Seneca, a very famous and pious man, because he virtuously punished him for his vices. Here can be seen clearly how the lords want to go entirely unpunished, as though they were possessed by the evil enemy [i.e. the devil]. Nero let Rome be set alight and burn for seven days because of his desire to see a great fire. He had his living mother cut open for the sake of a shameful desire, to see where he had lain in his mother's body. Does not this terrible deed suffice to show that the lords spare neither God nor the world? Their lustful hearts must be wanton, and nothing else. Nero was condemned to be scourged with rods and then thrown to his death from a high tower. But he fell to his death while trying to escape. And on his grave a tree grew, in which devils congregated and instituted great misery and murder. A great deal could be written about this, but it will be omitted in order to shorten the tedium.

After Nero, Galba was elected emperor. He was beheaded. Next, Emperor Otho committed suicide. After him Vitellius became

---

[18] Again a pun: right to best-head (*hauptrecht*) and right to rob (*raubrecht*). The right to best-head was commonly part of the heriot, or death-duty, paid by a serf's family; the lord received the best animal belonging to the family.

emperor, and he was dragged naked through the streets and killed.

How much more should I tell about these preeminent sinners? In short, from the first emperor, Julius Caesar, to Charlemagne, there were seventy-six emperors. Thirty-four emperors were shamefully and miserably killed, all on account of their tyranny; some were drowned, some beheaded, and some burned. I will remain silent about others, such as Maximian, Domitian, Diocletian, etc., whose tyranny and persecution of pious Christians is unspeakable.

In sum, as soon as the Romans fell from a communal [i.e. republican] government to emperors, all their miseries began and remained among them until they became poor serfs, they whose power had previously ruled mightily over all the world. I am showing all this here only because all the great lords usually pride themselves on their ancient, preeminent descent from Rome. Yes, they pride themselves on an ancient, heathen descent. And they do not consider that we are all descended from God, and that nobody is a minute older in his lineage than anyone else, be he king or shepherd, etc. This [concern about descent] is only a poisonous puffing up of a clod of earth [from which Adam was created]. Adam is the father of us all, and we will all certainly, in one part of us [i.e. the body], fall apart again into rotten pieces of earth. The other part, the soul, will be the booty of either the devil or God. Look, what will you now make of yourself?[19]

Here one also sees how often the powerful commit great rape and murder against the poor. Scripture is full of the band of Behemoth. And what could be more terrible than that a whole community should be entirely subject to the pleasure of a single head, no matter how wild and tyrannical he might be?

In sum, [hereditary rule] is not Christian. The fundamental and true root of all idolatry is the unlimited power of hereditary rulers, which had its origins in Babylon under the first established king, Ninus or Nimrod.[20] He built the high tower [of Babel] with the aim of surpassing God, and also set his father's image on a column and issued a command that it be honoured as a god. Then God sent a plague on the unfeeling people; the devil began to speak through this

---

[19] Perhaps an allusion to Gen. 1:26, "Then God said, let us make man in our image and likeness . . . ."

[20] The author mistakenly identifies Ninus with Nimrod; Ninus was the legendary founder of the Assyrian empire, which extended from Egypt to India, and the spouse of Semiramis, who had him murdered around 2000 B.C. For Nimrod, see Gen. 10:8–12.

image. And the image was believed and thus the first idol was set up, and it was named Baal. And in this way the foolish people were deceptively seduced away from their creator and true God and drawn to damnable idolatry, and so they established the first idolatry as well as the first powerful lordship in Babylon. Not only did God destroy this empire down to its foundations; he also surrounded it with snakes, dragons, and innumerable other poisonous reptiles, so that no one within a radius of a hundred miles wanted to live there. He who has eyes to see, let him see; he who has ears to hear, let him hear! [Mt. 11:15].

Furthermore, when that elect race, the children of God, the Israelites, had a communal [or republican] government and no king, then God dwelled cordially among them, and they ruled in a praiseworthy way and lived blessedly. But then heathen desire also enticed and charmed them to establish a powerful king among them, and they bade the prophet Samuel to obtain a king for them from God, as is clearly shown in 1 Samuel 8. God was greatly displeased by this and he foretold great misery and grief, with serfdom and other things which would bind their hands as a result of the power of hereditary kings. These things they then repeatedly experienced through the godless kings Achab, Moab, Agag, etc. [see 1 Kg. 16:29–31, Num. 25:1–5, 1 Sam. 15:8 and Ex. 17:8–16]. And before that King Jerobam also established heathen idolatry among them [see 1 Kg. 11]. And although God punished Jeroboam at his altar by laming and withering his arm, and also by splitting the altar [so that ashes poured out: 1 Kg. 13:4–5], and although his plea was mercifully heard by God and his arm was healed again, nevertheless his hardened heart did not appreciate all this, and he persisted in devilish idolatry.

And who has thrown the elect race of God, the children of Abraham, into this fourth fearful captivity, Amos 2 [:1],[21] that will have no end? Nothing but the power of the rulers and, prior to it, the unchristian greed of the bishops. For even the true and divine warning did not help; the hardened people wanted to have a king – as the frogs in Aesop wanted to have a stork![22] (He who has ears to hear, let

---

[21] See also Amos 1:3. The author is referring to the repeated phrase, "For the third and fourth transgressions . . . I will not revoke the punishment . . . says the Lord," and then goes on to ask who is responsible for the fourth, present-day transgression, which has called forth the punishment of God.

[22] In one version of Aesop's fable, the frogs petition Zeus for a king and he gives them a

him hear!) So God gave them Saul as a king, under whom they came to repent greatly their desire [to have a king]; indeed they repented with misery and every grief. And although Saul was rejected by God, he still wanted to remain king, and his children after him. Although David was ordained king by God, Saul nevertheless did not want to be robbed of his kingship; instead he wanted to be an even mightier king, whether God wanted it or not. He put his trust in his bloody gang, who clung to him in great numbers. And so great and mighty wars often arose between these two kings.

Thus a basic divine truth is not to be doubted and is now as clear as the light of day: the godless now constitute a great number. Even if they actually knew that the devil himself was the ruler of a territory, if they could benefit from him, they would still adhere to him, support him, and not desert him.

In short, hereditary and powerful lordship commonly turns into true idolatry. Indeed, one must even fear a [lord's] forester more than the commandments of God – to say nothing of the rulers themselves – even if, in so doing, Christian brotherhood and the divine commandments were to be destroyed one day. Yes, brotherhood and God's commandments already count for less than the decision of the poor juror Conrad [the common man].

Chapter six
Whether game belongs to the common man or not.

Look and observe what arbitrary power is able to get away with! How has Christendom permitted the great misery of this cruel tyranny to spread? It would not be surprising if the earth [opened and] swallowed us all because we looked on and tolerated the making of so very many poor, innocent widows and orphans. Because of [hunting] harmful game animals, their fathers and husbands have had their eyes gouged out so piteously, thus are robbed of their sight, and are rotting in prison towers. And now, most briefly to the issue!

Christian faith cannot tolerate the godless, unprincely system and government in which a lord appropriates game for himself. In short, he is robbing the poor of what is theirs. For game is free to everyone who catches it on his property. Indeed, another thing is still more

log; they complain about the log's lack of power and Zeus sends them a devouring stork and remarks that since they rejected a good king, they should experience a bad one.

important. Every Christian who sees game damaging his neighbor's land is obligated out of Christian brotherly love to drive out the animal which is damaging the community, in order to protect his neighbor from harm, be this by spearing or shooting it, as he can and may. For a harmful animal is good for nothing and should be killed immediately!

Is it not a constant cause of pity that the poor man is so violently robbed and, since this is not enough, he is also murderously tortured and robbed of his life? Rot! Damn this tyranny! In sum, note this well and if you can crack this nut for me, without a doubt you have a strong wolf's jaw. If game belongs to the lords, then in justice they would bring the poor people to court and tell them what is right and let what is right be done in the name of God, and not obfuscate matters. But the lord has masterfully characterized these godless ones in John 3[:20]: "The evildoer hates the light, and does not come into the light, so that his deeds are not punished." Oh, how else would they have been able to put on such an open carnival play with innocent blood?

Here one sees, as in many other acts, how much justice or fear of God lies in this limitless insolent power! Yes, but they want to cover up their powerless, rotten evil, their unchristian deeds, with a wordy cloak, and they dare to say that they are not punishing anyone on account of his having hunted game but because he is a disobedient transgressor and a despiser of their commandments. Look here! Look here, dear tightened *Bundschuh* [politically organized peasants],[23] at what a heavy charge is leveled against you! Now you should explode [in anger].

Why is that such a powerless excuse and apology? What devil thought up this gloss, and what is it except wanting to be a lord, whether it pleases God or not? Indeed, it is to set oneself up as an idol, a painted puppet, as was mentioned above in chapter 5, my dear tightened *Bundschuh*.

---

[23] In contrast to the boot of the nobility, the common footwear of the peasantry was a shoe with a cloth wrapping or binding; this "Bundschuh" became the symbol of peasant revolution in a series of failed rebellions in 1493, 1502, 1513, and 1517 which were led by Joss Fritz.

Chapter seven
Whether a community may depose its authorities or not?

Now to the heart of the matter! God wants it! Now the storm bells will be sounded! Now the truth must come out, in this time of grace, Luke 19[:11], even if the cliffs should speak [see Lk. 19:40]. May the almighty lord and God, and also your pleas, protect me from the intentions of the lords, to say nothing of their desire to do me in. Did not that blasphemous animal, the ass, punish the false prophet Baal for his godlessness? Numbers 24 [rather, Num. 22:25–33]. Was not godless Cain shot by blind Lamech without any danger to himself? [Gen. 4:23–24]. Here God's miracles can be seen clearly, in that he brings such hard punishment on the godless! But how else will arbitrary power (our harsh Babylonian captivity by the unchristian nature of the criminal authorities) reach its end?

I will speak only briefly about this. All the lords who issue selfish commands stemming from the desires of their hearts and their willful, unjust heads, and who appropriate for themselves – I will remain silent about their plunder – taxes, customs, payments, and what similarly serves the common fund for the protection and maintenance of the common territory, these lords are in truth the real robbers and the declared enemies of their own territory.

Now, to knock people such as Moab, Agag, Ahab, and Nero from their thrones is God's highest pleasure. Scripture does not call them servants of God, but instead snakes, dragons, and wolves. Go to it! Perhaps the grievous lamenting calls of the harvesters and the cries of the workers have come to the ears of the Lord of Sabaoth. Perhaps he has graciously granted their plea, and the day of slaughter will begin for the fatted stock, who have grazed pleasurably and to their hearts' content on the poverty of the common man, James 5[:4]. For this reason it must be discussed on whom God has visited his wrath. This is even more clearly evident where the blasphemers and murderers of God have strangled an evangelical Christian. There 20,000 will spring from the silenced member, so that the Gospel of John 12[:24] will be confirmed, "If a small sown grain of wheat does not die, it remains unfruitful. But when it dies, it brings forth fruit a hundred-fold." But the blind and hardened fools still do not want to recognize the miraculous work of God. The devil has possessed them.

I will prove that a territory or community has the power to depose its pernicious lords, by introducing thirteen sayings drawn from divine law, which the gates of hell with all their knights cannot destroy. Whoever wants to, can attempt to dispute with me. I expect this. But he should tell lies in private, so that he does not betray himself as do the papists. What would they not give now to have followed Luther in his first true admonition in the *Booklet on the Papacy*?[24] Then they could have rested. Many thoughts would have stayed in their pens which now no one will allow to be scraped or scratched away. But when the goat lowers his horns, it is ready to charge. The thorns they are fed so upset them that they do not want anyone to comb them.

And the first saying from divine law is this. Joshua 1[:7f.] commands the principle that no lord has the power to act according to his own will, but only on the basis of divine law. If he does not, simply get rid of him and leave him far behind. This is most pleasing to God. St. Paul provides us the second saying from divine law in 2 Corinthians 10[:8], where he says, "Power is given to build up and not to destroy." And what does St. Paul intend with his punishing and mocking words other than that a harmful ruler should not be tolerated? For he says in 2 Corinthians 11[:19], "You suffer fools gladly because you are clever. You suffer it gladly if someone makes slaves of you, if someone cheats you, if someone robs you, if someone sets himself above you, if someone strikes you in the face," etc. Look at how St. Paul here describes the criminal rulers and lords as fools! Why should fools be tolerated as rulers over the lambs of Christ? Indeed, in many other places he depicts them as unchristian, e.g. in 1 Timothy 5[:8] he says, "But if anyone does not provide for his own people, and especially for his household, he has denied the faith and is worse than an unbeliever," etc.

Behold! Should a condemned Antichrist then rule the people of Christ, whom the lord of heaven and earth purchased so dearly with his bitter death? What a great need there is to reflect seriously on these words of the divine spirit!

Therefore it is not wholly out of place to consider whether it would now be desirable for the Turks to be lords over us, in the hope that

---

[24] I.e. Luther's *On the Papacy of Rome, against the Famous Romanists of Leipzig* (*Von den Papstum zu Rome widder den hochberumpten Romanisten zu Leiptzek*) (1520), *WA* VI, 285ff. The author's claim here is that the papists now regret that they did not reach an agreement with Luther on the basis of the principles set forth in this work.

they would allow the gospel to be preached to us freely and without hindrance. For now we are so violently robbed of it by the most powerful ones and their henchmen, because of their greed and pomp, that we poor people are not only ruined in body and goods, which would be tolerable, but indeed, our souls would be lost if we now followed and obeyed them.

Thus, in any case, we Christians have sufficiently sound and sincere reasons [to depose our lords], and we are also obliged to redeem ourselves from these godless lords out of this Babylonian captivity, as St. Peter says, Acts 5[:29], "We must obey God rather than men." And earlier the divine chancellor, Paul, says in 1 Corinthians 7[:21], "If you are a slave, you can make yourself free, so take the chance." The fourth divine jurist, Matthew, writes in chapter 7[:6], "Do not give what is holy to dogs, nor cast pearls before swine, so that they do not trample these things underfoot, and lest they turn on you and attack you," etc.

Although this divine teaching is twisted in many ways, it is nevertheless based on the true meaning of the [biblical] texts about judges and about the powerful. This teaching makes it evident that neither the law nor the authority of the divine order is a true, holy sanction to evil people. It should be commanded that those whom Christ upbraided here as dogs and swine should be thrown from their thrones! This would be most pleasing to God. The rotten tree cannot bring forth good fruit; so it should be cut down and thrown into the fire, Matthew 18 [rather, Mt. 7:18]. It is not becoming that someone should want to remove a speck from the eye of another, and have a log in his own eye [Mt. 7:3f.]. The third divine jurist, St. Luke, also writes to us in chapter 13[:6–9] about the barren tree which should be cut down so that the whole land is not ruined – the tree which earlier was cultivated for a year or two, and yet it would not sprout, etc. From this it follows that – and there is no other meaning – if a common territory has suffered its lord's arbitrariness and ruination for a long time without hope that he will improve himself, then the common territory should arm itself boldly with the sword, Luke 17[:1f], and say, "We no longer owe anything to this untrue steward and evil lord." Luke also presents us with this view in chapter 12[:41–48?].

Also, the fourth divine jurist, St. Mark, writes most clearly for us in chapter 9[:43–47], "If your eye, hand, or foot offends you, cut it off," etc. Both kinds of authority are indicated here, the clerical with the eye and the temporal with the hand. And although some say that this refers to spiritual things, as does Matthew 5[:29f.], I shall say, "No!" For here he deals quite obviously with external, proud, and useless authorities, who rule with frivolous wrath and who give an example of every vice, such as inordinate drunkenness, vomiting, whoring, blasphemy, torturing, making a show of their power and might, etc. It is their "Christian tongue" which daily prays, "Holy be your name," etc. Therefore St. Mark affirms here[25] that it would be better to hang a millstone around the necks of such authorities and throw them into the depths of the sea!

But are not all these clear divine sayings directed against godless authority, which is not to be tolerated but to be deposed without any timidity? Some lip-service Christians may still maintain, "The gospel does not refer to the worldly sword." But their hearts are false, and nothing is more damnable, for they boast that they are servants of God on the basis of Romans chapter 13. Yet the princes of this world want to have Beelezebub as their captain. Is this not the greatest blasphemy, to use God as a pretext for concealing their own vices?

In sum, let them prattle and gossip about whatever they want. Their power derives ultimately either from the spirit or from the flesh. If it derives from the spirit, it is just and most pleasing to God, says Paul to the Romans in chapter 8[:1–8]. But if their authority is derived from the flesh, it is devilish and a most openly declared enemy of God. May God pity us that such fleshly authority should rule over Christian people. And unceasingly they may talk about two kinds of commandments, namely the divine, which concerns the salvation of the soul, and the political, which concerns the common good. Oh God, these commandments cannot be separated from each other. For the political commandments are also divine: truly to further the common good is nothing except truly to maintain brotherly love, which is of the highest merit for blessedness. The fifth divine jurist, Solomon says, "Just people stand together most bravely against their rulers, who tear away from them what they produce by the sweat of their brow."[26]

And, to silence their snouts a sixth time – from their own secular laws – the pope and emperor do not hold hereditary lordships but elective ones. And they may be deposed, as they often have been,

---

[25] The reference to Mark is mistaken; the intended references would appear to be Mt. 18:6 and Lk. 17:12.

[26] The biblical reference here is unclear, perhaps Prov. 2:21.

because of their misdeeds. Look! Pope and emperor are also the highest authorities. And should their representatives or lawyers, the princes, and other lords, not be deposed on account of their evil rule? And yet they want to hold their power, together with the emperors, on the basis of the gospel, Matthew 23 [rather, Mt. 20:25]. In addition, the servant should not be higher than the master, Luke 6[:40]. But if they say that such a deposing of the powerful properly belongs to the emperor and not to the subjects of princes and lords, these claims are lies and fairy tales. Why, what if the emperor and kings were also useless?

Have there not been in human memory kings and emperors of this kind, who have been driven from office by their subjects? In sum, no partisan judge should be established [to judge their case]. For nothing will come of it except "If you help me, I will help you."

Chapter eight
In what form a community may depose its lords.

Although deposing in its strict form is sometimes indicated against certain [lords], as in Deuteronomy 13[:1–4] and 18[:20], I think it best to omit this, so that I will not be regarded as an instigator of disturbances. It is my zealous wish that God may always protect me from this. It is much more important to write about the common peace. Dear brothers, this is your highest goal! What you can do is to throw the rotten tree into the fire. God will certainly ordain this, regardless of what you are thinking.

But if the lords always want to be lords and to treat you poor people in the most arbitrary way, contrary to the divine laws which I have discussed above, then follow Solomon and bravely assemble now! Arm yourselves in the spirit of the bold oxen and steers, who gather together staunchly in a ring with their horns outward, not with the intention of rebelling, but only to defend themselves against the ravaging wolves. In truth, if a wolf is attacking them, he does not get away without cracked ribs, even if he escapes with his life. Thus, you dear brothers, do not engage in this insurrection in order to get rich with other people's property, or your hearts will turn false. Victory will bring you nothing good. You should hate greed as the devil hates the cross! Come together only for the sake of the common peace of the land and to practice Christian freedom! Be united in your goal! Your enemies howl and call miserably for justice. They maintain that they are nonpartisan judges and lovers of God, above all the evangelical preachers. After you have assembled, if your opponents still want to have a war, and they pursue this crazy idea of disputing the gospel with lances, halberds, guns, and armor, then it is God's will. Then let happen what cannot happen differently. Their sacrilegious attacks are hated by God. But you trust in God! Be firm in faith! You are not your own but God's warriors to uphold the gospel and to tear down the Babylonian prison! Each of you should make every effort to deal with the others in all fidelity and love! Do not quarrel among yourselves and be strict with one another! Let each tolerate the others with the greatest discipline and goodness; maintain the fear of God; and do not tolerate any drinkers! In no case allow blasphemers with their damned tongues among you! Then God will surely be your general.

Chapter nine
Who should be blamed for being a rebel?

Some, along with their bloody band, blame you and cry out that you are deviant, treacherous rogues [who have betrayed] your hereditary and natural lords. But do not let yourselves be led astray and do not worry about what they jabber. This breed cannot do anything else. Accept as your defense counsel the godly prophet Elijah, who also elevated a poor lower official to be king against his godless king, Ahab [see 1 Kg. 19:16 and 2 Kg. 9:10]. And when he was summoned before the king to justify himself and charged with being an instigator of rebellion among the common people, the prophet said, "Not I, but you, king, with your godless breed from your father, the devil, are causing the insurrection" [1 Kg. 18:18]. Indeed, should the poor man not have the full right to keep for himself and his children the fruits of the blood and sweat of his toil? And did divine King Solomon, mentioned above, lie? And, on the other hand, should tyrants be allowed violently to rip from the poor people what belongs to them, and then to waste it so shamefully on jousts, races, games, and gorging, as we have heard above? What devil on his kingly throne will justify this kind of thing? It is bullshit.

On this account, Christ himself must also be a rebel. Yes, indeed he is – he drove the money-changers out of the temple, Matthew 19 [actually Mt. 21:12ff.], and said, "My house is not a den of thieves but

123

a house of prayer." Thus each authority has not been established to rob its subjects, but faithfully to protect them from the wolves.

In sum, they can say whatever they want. No rebellion has ever taken place among the subjects of a Christian lord who rules well. It has only occurred under wastrels and godless tyrants. Scripture is full of testimony about this, and especially Moses. Although he was to be a king of Egypt, nevertheless he took pity on the poor people under the mighty tyrant Pharaoh, and elevated against him, too, a minor official [i.e. Aaron; Ex. 7:1f.], and repudiated his royal honor. And it is ineffable in what unspeakable fear, need, and misery he united himself with the poor people, until he released them from the tyrants [see Ex. 3:7–12].

Yes, they scream, rant, and curse rebellion so violently, seeking to damn it completely. And in doing this they never think about the cause of the disturbance, which is themselves and their godless nature. Be proud, my dear Sibyl, of your peasants' bound shoe.[27] And even if the lords say more and more, and bring up their ancient lineage, and politely promote their cause, do not be fooled. Old lineage here and old lineage there! The issue is not "ancient lineage" but "rightful lineage"! A thousand years of injustice do not make a single hour just. Truly, truly, they will try arguments and tricks, with flattering words and all kinds of cleverness, whatever they can think up, to make you desert one another. In truth, in truth, "guard yourselves against those who come to you in sheep's clothing but inwardly are ravaging wolves," Matthew 7[:15]; and again David in 5 [see Ps. 146:3], "You should not trust the princes of men, nor the children of the world, in whom there is no salvation."

Chapter ten
What misery and grief would befall the common peasantry if they betrayed themselves.

Listen, dear brothers. You have embittered the hearts of your lords with overflowing gall so grievously that they can never be sweetened.

---

[27] *Rüem dich, mein liebe Sibilla, mit deinem preißschüch.* The Sibyls were prophetesses of the ancient world, to whom were attributed the Sibylline Prophecies of the late Roman period. The so-called Tiburtine Sibyl, or Thirteenth Sibyl, was a prophecy added to the collection in the Middle Ages, one which prophesied the end of the world and the coming of a kingdom of peace and social justice.

All thought of mollifying them is in vain. The lords want to be unappeased. They want to be lords, indeed idols, whether this pleases or pains God. And nevertheless you are commanded! Their power is drunk with pleasure and not justice, Luke 19[:43–47]. It has been prophesied about them that they will oppose God and his son, Psalm 2[:2], "The kings of the earth have come together and the princes of nations have assembled against God and his Christ," etc.

See, this time they will spare you even less. If you do not see through their game, then woe, forever woe, and terrible murder will befall you and the whole peasantry! Oh, woe forever to your children! How can you leave behind such a stepfather's inheritance for them? Look, you must perform labor services with spades, hoes, and horses. Later your children will have to draw the harrow themselves. Up till now you have been able to fence off your holdings against game; from now on you will have to let them stand open. And if up till now your eyes have been gouged out [for poaching], in future you will be impaled. Up till now, if you have paid the heriot, then you are serfs. Henceforth you will become true slaves, with nothing more of your own, neither in body nor in goods. You will be sold completely in the Turkish manner, like cattle, horses, and oxen.

If one of you even turns up his nose against this, then only torture, coercion, and repression will follow from the lords. And there will be no limit to their persecution and slander. Then you "treacherous rogues" will be immediately thrown into the nearest prison tower, and one torture after another will be imposed! And there will be no relief until a person confesses what he has never even thought of. Afterward, one will be scourged with rods, another will be burned through his cheeks, his fingers will be chopped off, his tongue torn out, and he will be quartered and beheaded! The same absence of pity will be shown to you as to evildoers and murderers. And so, woe! Always woe, on account of the eternal murder of the whole peasantry! It would be better if you had never been born. You will never find peace. And what Christian person would not weep for the miserable grief which you will bring upon yourselves if you are faithless and dishonorable to one another, if you desert one another, and if you do not persevere bravely and brotherly with one another, and stand like Solomon? Since you have been truly warned, do not be foolish! Pay attention and take to heart the kind of murderous misery that occurred nine years ago in Hungary and in the Wendish lands,[28] indeed, before your own door in the "Poor Conrad" [revolt in Württemberg in 1514]. And who scattered these peasant troops and brought about this grievous misery? In truth, not by the great number of their enemies but only through their own equivocating disloyalty were the peasants betrayed, taken captive, thrown into the severe Babylonian prison, and given over to sword and axe.

In sum, they would have overcome all this, if they had kept brotherly fidelity with one another, and had not deserted one another. Thus, untruthfulness strikes those who are untruthful.

Chapter eleven
An appropriate warning to the aforesaid Christian brothers.

You, dear brothers, guard yourselves against such grief, so that among one another you are not deceived, etc. And if one among you in the army has already set himself up as a great hero, he could certainly be the first to take flight, as I have already warned you most sufficiently above, in chapter eight. And I truly admonish you once again about this: watch out and make sure that no disloyalty arises among you and that no one among you misuses his office. Look what great harm can grow from such cases, of which Scripture is full, although they are unbelievable. Maintain good order in brotherly unity to prevent such things.

In truth, necessity requires good order. Always establish a platoon-leader over every ten men and a centurion over every ten platoon-leaders. Also establish a captain over every ten centurions, and over every ten captains a general, and so forth. In truth, such an order often brings good fruits to a common band.

Choose all these leaders from your own ranks. For in truth it certainly will not do to let a wolf in sheep's clothing creep in among you. Their inborn natures never allow the crow and the dove to unite. Just as is the case with nature, people's inborn qualities cannot be changed. If you wanted to judge the external person and not his Christian piety, your heart would be basically false. God certainly does not dwell in this kind of pride.

---

[28] I.e. the Hungarian peasant revolt of 1514 under György Dózca, and the 1515 revolt in the Slavic areas of Carniola.

Again, everyone should be diligent and obedient to his authority [in the peasant army]. Hold general assemblies among yourselves often, for nothing strengthens and holds together the common band more heartily.

In the name of Christian order, offer to submit yourselves to the emperor directly and completely, like the other pious imperial cities.

Do not soil your hands with the property of other people unless there is compelling need. Keep all your own goods in moderation, as discussed above and in chapter eight.

But if someone ever wants to exert arbitrary power over you, and will not leave you alone, then the matter must be commended to God [through military conflict]. And let happen what cannot be avoided. If someone is so eager for the innocent blood of Abel, may he indeed be confronted with it – and drowned in it. Furthermore, did not the two brothers, Adrammelech and Sharezer, on God's command, have to slay King Sennacharib, their own father, the drinker of blood, with his own sword? [2 Kg. 19:37].

Be sincerely consoled and thankful to God; your great, compelling need, as well as your good reputation and honor have resounded clearly up the Rhine and across the Etsch and Danube. And wherever I travel, far and wide, the prayers of the commoners are heaped on you. On the other hand and without a doubt, the curse of the commoners is heaped with equal vigor on your opponents. The cause will bear fruit, dear brothers, so walk with dignity in this praiseworthy calling.

Hold yourselves solidly together in all fear of God, and brotherly loyalty and love, so that you all become a unified body under the head, Jesus Christ. Then Christ, the true God, will certainly be your general. Therefore be manly, courageous and fearless, even if the godless band comes rushing against you, large and strong as it may be. Their own conscience will defeat them and put them to flight. As Solomon says in Proverbs 28[:1], "The godless one flees when no one pursues him. But the pious believer will stand like a bold lion." In truth, as Maccabees 22 [rather, 1 Mac. 3:18] says, "It will be no problem, for you few will defeat a great army. Victory in this war is not due to the size of the army but due to the strength that comes from heaven." Again, in 2 Chronicles 21 [rather, 25:7f.], the prophet says to King Amaziah, "If you think that war is decided by the strength of the army, God will let you be conquered by your enemies.

For conquest and putting to flight is the work of God." Again, Hosea 10[:14], "Because you trusted in the ways of your own might, rebellion will arise among your own people, and all your fortresses will be destroyed." For God is not pleased by great cavalry and cuirassiers, but by a trusting heart. Did not the whole fainthearted army of Gideon flee, Judges 8 [rather, Jg. 7:3–8], so that from 10,000 only 300 remained by him in firm faith? With these, he defeated his enemy, who numbered 120,000.

And I will remain silent about what is in the old histories: how often great, ineffable deeds have been performed by that poor little band of peasants, your neighbors, the Swiss. How often their enemies have defeated them by boisterous bragging while drinking wine! Then each and every one wants to overcome three Swiss, or wants to defeat them with shepherds and chantry priests. But in most cases their enemies have been put to flight everywhere. And king, emperor, princes, and lords have turned themselves into laughingstocks, no matter how mighty and how well armed was the great force they sent into the field against them. And as often as these aforesaid Swiss fought for themselves, for their country, wives, and children, and had to protect themselves from proud power, in most cases they always triumphed and gained great honor. Without a doubt all this has occurred through the power and providence of God. Otherwise, how could the Swiss Confederation, which still increases daily, have grown constantly from only three simple peasants?[29]

And because there is no end to their limitless personal power, and because all the authorities refuse to give us a rest, perhaps the prophecy and the old saying will be fulfilled: "A cow will stand on Schwanberg mountain in the land of Franconia and low or bellow so loudly that it is heard in the middle of Switzerland."[30] In truth, this is not without irony; and in this sense another saying may be fulfilled: "What increases the Swiss but the greed of the lords?"

But is this not the work of God? Did not God plant these three peasants, with their branches, as a rod of chastisement over the godless, criminal powers? But the present-day Swiss, on the contrary,

---

[29] An allusion to the legend of the Oath of Ruetli, a secret association of the first three Swiss "confederates," who on the Wednesday before St. Martin's day 1307 swore to expel the administrative bailiffs on the coming New Year's Day.

[30] The lords of Franconia have generated a rebellion that will be heard about even among the Swiss.

have won very few victories since they left the paths of their forefathers. Rather, they have become a mockery, for they have marched
out of their land and into the armies of other lords for money. Thus,
he who does not want to recognize that both the victory and the defeat
of the Swiss are God's work, is blind with seeing eyes and deaf with
open ears. But God stands most faithfully with the poor little band if
someone arbitrarily tries to coerce them to get the sweat of their labor.

Thus, you dear brothers, put the greedy desire to get rich with
other people's property far from your hearts, or your hearts will have a
false foundation. God will not dwell with you. Fight only for what is
yours, as the prophet Nehemiah 4[:8] shows you, saying, "You shall
not be afraid before their faces; think of the wrath of the Lord [over
them], and fight for your houses, wives and children." Base your
hearts and minds on these things and be fearless with David, who says
in Psalm 23[:4], "Even if I walk in the midst of the shadow of death,
nevertheless I will not fear, for the Lord is with me." Again, he says in
Psalm 25[:12], "The Lord will strengthen all you who acknowledge
and fear him." And again, in Psalm 125[:1], "All who put their hope
and faith in God will stand as firmly as Mount Zion."

But may God, the lord of consolation and patience, grant that you
be of one mind among one another, following Jesus Christ in a firm
faith, so that unanimously and with one voice you praise God, the
father of our lord Jesus Christ. So support one another, just as Christ
has supported you, in order to praise God and to gain the protection
of his grace, to gain peace here on earth, and to praise his majesty in
heaven, so that you may say joyfully with David, Psalm 115[:1], "Not
to us, Lord, not to us, but to your name give honor." Amen.

> So mobilize yourselves, and do it quickly.
> You must do the job, e'en you whose sight is sickly.

9   Hans Denck, *On the Law of God*
On the law of God. How the law must be removed, and yet must be fulfilled.[1]

Preface[2]

No time has ever been so evil that God has not done something for mankind for which he cannot be thanked enough. Again, there has never been such prosperity in this world that some evil has not had to be feared. Not that God himself is so inconstant or takes pleasure in such unrest. Rather, everything carnal is so perverted that it always misuses what is at its disposal, even the very best things that God shares with it. Therefore the Lord always mixes his sweetness with salt for all his friends, as long as they stay in this world, so that the sweetness stays fresh, and his friends do not get lazy and dull.

Some people, even the majority, complain that the world is now

---

[1] The work was first printed in Augsburg by Philip Ulhart. Denck was in Augsburg from September 1525 to October 1526 and *On the Law of God* was the second of three tracts that he wrote during this period; it was probably printed in the first half of 1526. It was formerly thought that Balthasar Hubmaier converted Denck in Augsburg from a mystical and spiritual theology deeply influenced by Thomas Müntzer to Swiss Anabaptism, and that *On the Law of God* was Denck's first treatise following his baptism by Hubmaier. But there is little evidence that such a conversion or baptism took place, and – whether or not stemming from Müntzer – the work itself develops an essentially mystical conception of divine law. The translation is based on the text in Georg Baring and Walter Fellmann, eds., *Hans Denck, Schriften*. Vol. I, Part 2, *Religiöse Schriften* (Gütersloh, 1956), 48–66.

[2] Much in Denck's prefatory remarks can be read as a reflection on the religious meaning of the defeat of the commoners in the Peasants' War.

filled with evil. This is indeed true. For although the world has always been an evil tree, it has never borne so much evil fruit as in our time. All history books and chronicles show the truth of this. But still, however much there is to complain about, there is much more that God should be thanked for if one does not look at things with a jaundiced eye. For, to say nothing of the secret work of God, if God has awakened the whole world only to ask what is the truth and to worry about error, all the treasures and values of the whole world cannot be compared to this. Whoever is unable to thank God for this shows that he loves worldly peace more than truth, and that he cannot stand human division for the sake of divine unity.

There are nearly as many, however, who are of the opposite opinion, and even delight that God has been so merciful to people. And their delight is not unreasonable, for God cannot be other than merciful, even when he is most wrathful. But though there is much to be happy about, there is as much, in turn, to fear – perhaps even more. For in a time of affliction, those who are careful and joyful have it much worse than those who are mournful and expect nothing but affliction. For as Scripture also says, it is better to go into a house where people mourn than one where they feast (Ecclesiastes 7[:2]).[3] May he who so delights in God that he surrenders himself, and is willing to drink from God's chalice, be happy as long as he is able; he will succeed in everything. It would be better for him who says he delights in truth – but does not conduct himself as the truth teaches – if he were unable to tell the truth.

Thus, the majority of those who now are happy are, unfortunately, happy without being improved – just as the majority of those who complain are also not improved. And these two groups always despise one another, each thinking that it is better, even though neither is a bit better than the other, as their fruits [actions] demonstrate. Some want to do God's will here and there, yet they can neither hear not proclaim it. Some say that they know God's will completely, but they do not act on it. Some would like to conduct themselves according to God's commandments, so they say. But they do not really want to, and thus they show they are useless. The latter say that they would gladly do God's will but are unable to do it, that God does not give them

---

[3] Scriptural citations enclosed in parentheses appear as marginal references in the original; the work's few marginal comments have also been transposed to the body of the text as parenthetical remarks.

enough grace to do it. In this way they excuse themselves and openly put the blame on God. In short, they do not want to be the ones about whom the Lord says that he often wanted to gather them in as a hen gathers her chicks (Matthew 23[:37]); but they do not want to be gathered. This is the evil of which now, unfortunately, there is much too much in the world, and more appears daily. And every other evil that can be mentioned – flood, fire, war, hunger, and plague – is no evil compared to this.

Rather, God sincerely and paternally intends to do good for us when he brings about such evil things, and he wants to save those who love him, if only this unique evil did not exist in his people.[4] Oh, God, the lord our God, wishes we had the courage to fear him and to keep his commandments faithfully (Deuteronomy 5[:26]). Is there anyone who would say it was not God's intention to grant this? But truly he only bestows it as he always has – namely to the hungry. Because there are now so few who are truly hungry for his teaching (but many who are always curious), he persists, everywhere and in every way, in making us hungry. That child is well off who does not despise his father's rod; he who despises it is not worthy of being punished by his father.

In truth, time passes in this way: He who is careful will have plenty to worry about; he who is secure and without worries should pay attention to what he is relying on, so that he does not stand naked when his time comes. Let each who can, get along with his enemy – and the sooner the better (Matthew 5[:25]). Woe to them who wait until the divine judge appears. Oh, most dearly beloved, no one should quarrel with another person, for it is necessary not to quarrel. Each should suffer as much injustice as he can without harming himself for the kingdom of God. In this way we will stand well before the wrath of God. For I fear indeed that a grievous sin is committed when so many words on both sides are uttered in vain. Of what use is it if you now suddenly despise all external things? But of what use is it, equally, if you get all external things?

If you see your brother valuing something that he should not, teach him beforehand to know God, and then he will value him alone. If he

---

[4] I.e. the absence of morally good conduct. The treatise uses the concept of divine law, which provided the religious justification for the socio-political demands raised by the common man in 1525, to raise one of the radical reformers' central criticisms of the magisterial Reformation – its failure to bring about positive moral change.

does not, leave him alone and do not try to convince him. Otherwise, if you forbid him everything, and he follows you, he will soon replace what you have forbidden him with something else just as bad or worse. But you, if you hear your brother saying something that sounds wrong to you, do not contradict him immediately. Rather, listen to see if it might be right, so that you also accept it. If you are unable to understand it, then you should not judge him. And if he seems to you to be erring, you should consider whether you might be erring at a still higher level. Nobody should respect those at the top in this world – be it in terms of power, learning or riches. Rather, if someone's heart is directed to heaven, he should direct his eyes downward, to the despised and the small of this world, whose lord and master is Jesus Christ, who was the most despised among all people and was therefore elevated by God the father to rule all creatures who can be named or conceived.

Woe to him who looks anywhere but at this end. For whoever thinks that he is a Christian must travel the path which Christ traveled (John 8[:51] and 10[:27f.]). In this way the eternal abode of God is reached. He who does not travel this path errs eternally. He who travels along, or points out, another path is a thief and a murderer (John 10[:1]). These are all those who love God and his son for the sake of their own benefit. The whole world acts in this way. God knows who is not of this world, and he to whom God has revealed it may rejoice that his name is written in the book of life.

If I can point out someone's error and show him the right path, I will do it most gladly. That I can teach him is not something of my own doing. Rather, God has given me this kind of heart. If it is able to bring forth fruit, God too has granted this. Though I would like to do so, I do not wish to compel the sinner, even if I could command him. And although this wish of mine is already in vain, nevertheless I am content with God.

This is the reason I have written this pamphlet about the law of God. For I see that both sides err, not only the people but also the shepherds. Whoever does not err does not need my hints. But whoever says that I err should prove it to me as soon as he can. Thereby I will perceive that he loves truth. If someone is to convince me that I have made a mistake and that I do not admit it – as is appropriate for someone who made a mistake – that person should recognize him who has ordered me to speak. If someone has another way of testing the spirit, I will await it in the name of God. But I request all who read this pamphlet – for God's sake – not to judge it too hastily. And I entreat those who would be quick to judge – I will swear it to them by the future [coming] of Jesus Christ – to judge it as they would like to be judged by the Lord. If they truly hope for God's mercy, then I can bear their righteousness. If they avoid the justice of God, then at least I can expect mercy from them. If someone violates my rights, it is not I who suffer but my Lord, when one uses sacrilege or force in his affairs. And therefore no one can save me but he alone, in his – that is, at the right – time.

I know for sure that some brothers will think my language sophistry and that it poses odd questions. And I do not ask them not to call it this. For the slightest wisdom that truly comes from God is so profound that the reasoning of the most learned cannot comprehend it, unless they have previously become fools to the world. For this reason I ask them, as mentioned above, not to despise it [Denck's writing] too hastily, and not to call it foolishness before they have understood its message and judged it reasonably. Real intelligence remains in the world. A true friend of God should refute with the truth any wisdom that is not from God, and demolish it. God in heaven would be sorry if much intelligence needed to be used; and in truth it would not be needed if the world were not so perverted. Because we are now so perverted, God uses perverted means to deal with mankind. If you are going to please the whole world, God is pleased and his heavenly choir also, for eternity. The person who weeps in his heart about the evil world will truly be happy with God.

The one whom the whole world affirms with its mouth and denies with its deeds [Christ] says, "I did not come to abolish the law but to fulfill it!" (Matthew 5[:17]). The carnal wisdom of the world, which always presents itself as the light of divine knowledge, tears this saying out of context and says that Christ has fulfilled the law, so we do not need to.[5] And if we had to fulfill it as well, it would follow that Christ had not fulfilled it sufficiently. The saying is interpreted in this way for carnal people thus serve perverted nature, for which everything that comes from God is pus and poison. All human life proves this. If this understanding of the saying were true, its meaning would be the way most people live after being converted. The whole world is full of

---

[5] A reference to Luther's doctrine of justification by faith alone.

such people, whose conduct and life were better before they boasted of their faith than afterwards. And these are supposed to be the people through whose good works the heathen should be moved to praise God the father in heaven (Deuteronomy 4[:6], Matthew 5[:16]). Indeed, heathens do praise God, just like the works of these people do – namely by saying contemptuously to us, "What kind of God is yours?" As if they wanted to say, "Either he is not merciful, as you maintain, since he lets you err so much; or he is not just, because he can only watch your evil; or he is not omnipotent, since he is unable to assist or punish you." Lord, mighty God, act for your name's sake, so that you do not permit what the perverted permit, which is what they should not do. Amen.

You say,[6] "But is it not true that Christ has fulfilled the law?" My answer is: No matter how high a law is – either understood or written – it must be fulfilled in the body of Christ [i.e. in the Christian community] (Romans 12[:4ff.], Ephesians 4[:1ff.], Corinthians 12[:4ff], and Romans 8[:1ff.]). Whoever wants to be a member of this body and does not fulfill the law as perfectly, according to his measure, as the head, Christ, fulfilled it, this person should take care that he does not deceive himself. For if the members do not accept what the head accepts, things are not going well. The member who does not feel joy or compassion with the happiness or suffering of his head, Christ, is certainly a useless and dead member, who is deprived of all the good works of the body, as if he were not part of it.

You say, "Did not the head do enough and fulfill everything that had to be fulfilled for the members?" I reply, yes, he did enough for the whole world, and he blazed the path that no person before was able to find, so that one turns to this path and comes to life (John 14[:6]). Those who do not walk it do not come to life; for them the path was found in vain. He fulfilled the law, but not to abolish it for us; rather, he set us an example, so that we might follow him (John 13[:15]).

You say, "If he did no more than make a path, and one can follow him or not, then he would not be greater than Moses. And the path would remain untraveled, for we are all twisted and lame." I reply that, although Moses was only a servant in the house of God, his son did not belittle Moses' function, namely the interpretation of the law

---

[6] From this point on, the work takes the form of a dialogue with an evangelical opponent who seeks to defend a Lutheran theological position.

(Matthew 5, 6, and 7). And Moses not only interpreted the law, but also made it possible to follow it, through the power of the word which was written in the hearts of the Jews (Deuteronomy 30 [:14]). Nevertheless, Christ did much more, just as the son counts for more in the household than the servant (Hebrews 3[:3ff.]). Christ not only proclaimed or wrote the law of God externally for his followers, as did Moses. Rather, he speaks and writes it to them in their hearts from the beginning of the world to the end (Hebrews 8[:10], Jeremiah 31[:3]). Whoever has the law in his heart lacks neither path nor feet, neither light nor eyes, nor anything that is necessary to fulfill the will of God. Whoever does not have it in his heart finds neither path nor foot of any use, however well off he may be. But everyone should try not to deny that he has [the law in his heart], so that he may not get what he wants to do without [i.e. misfortune], and so that he may get rid of what he wants to be rid of.

You say, "Oh, it is not possible for any man to fulfill the law." I reply that, indeed, it is not possible for any man as a man [to fulfill it]. But for the faithful, all things are possible (Mark 9[:23]) – not as men, but as those who are one with God and who are independent of everything creaturely, and in part independent of themselves. For people who live according to the flesh, good conduct is impossible. But such people should realize that they are living lies and not the truth. In the truth all creaturely reason, will, and power are God's own, and one with him. Whoever wants to have a different reason, will, or power – one that is opposed to God's will – could indeed imagine that he has what he does not really have. And it seems to him that he lacks what all creatures are filled with (Jeremiah 23[:24]). And on account of this lie alone, the holy spirit testifies truly through his followers that something in people is contrary to God, whether reason, will, power, or whatever it is. Those who want to understand this will see clearly that in truth they are nothing in comparison to God. Yes, even this madness of which I speak is nothing. But someone who is living this madness is not any more successful. For the more he wants to be something that he is not, the more God is opposed to him – God who in truth was never opposed to anything (Ezekiel 18 and 33, 2 Peter 2). That is the reason that something which actually is easy is impossible for someone. And again, what is actually impossible (for it does not exist) is nevertheless the believer's essential characteristic.

You say, "The apostles conducted themselves according to the spirit, and nevertheless called customs or ceremonies a yoke which neither they nor the father have been able to bear (Acts 15[:10]). How then can the highest commandments be made easy?" I reply that ceremonies are external arrangements; they were instituted to improve the coarse people of Israel, to whom all spiritual talk was alien. [They have been instituted] namely, so that through ceremony people may remember the simple heart of all commandments, which was revealed to Adam from the beginning in paradise – that one must love God alone and hate everything that can hinder this love. For the apple which God forbade Adam and all mankind with him – every single creature – is this: whatever one loves more than God (Genesis 2[:17]). Whoever really has this simple essence [of all the commandments] in his heart is independent and free of all ceremonies. If it were necessary to give others an external image of this love, one should carry out the ceremonies. But if the perfumed ceremonies were a hindrance, one should relinquish them.

Thus, the highest commandments of love are not difficult for the apostles and all enlightened people, as John says (1 John 5[:3]). And the same is true of ceremonies, insofar as they are useful, as has been said. But when they hinder the higher divine service, then it is true that they are an unbearable burden to all enlightened people. This is the reason that all true followers of Christ have been freed from all ceremonies – because of their improvement. Those who do not really follow Christ, if they are Jews, remain under the law; if they are heathens, they remain such and may boast of neither the gospel nor the law. Whoever has really fulfilled the law of love has fulfilled all ceremonies (Romans 13[:8]), even if he never thinks about them. Whoever has enough gulden does not bother about small change; it would be hard for him to keep track of it. Not that he despises small change, but he does not want to miss the larger coins. Whoever has enough gulden, has hellers[7] left over, even if he does not have a single one.

You say, "He who has faith fulfills the commandment of God in spirit." I reply that whoever fulfills God's commandment finds his law pleasing and enjoys hearing people talk about it. Whoever does not like to hear about the curse of the law has certainly not yet escaped it.

---

[7] A coin of small denomination, named after the city of Schwäbisch Hall, where it was minted.

But he who finds it a curse does not have faith. Where faith is absent, there certainly a fulfillment [of divine law] never occurs. One perceives in this the disbelief of all false Christians, who create for themselves their own law and a rootless faith, for they do not like to hear about God's commandments.

You say, "No one lives without committing sin. Thus no one is able to fulfill the law. So if we say that we are without sin, we are deceiving ourselves, and the truth is not with us, as John says (1 John 1[:8])." I reply that because of sin we have all fallen. The less one confesses this, the more he sins. The more one bewails it, the less he sins. Whoever has actually bewailed it once is born from God and sins no more. Everyone who sins has neither seen nor known God. John testifies about all this (1 John 3[:6]), and truth itself is not concealed to those who have ears and eyes.

You say, "Why then does Paul say (Romans 7[:19]), 'The good that I want to do I do not, and the evil I do not want to do I do'?" I reply that in the gospel Paul was both a man under the law, and a new man. Accordingly, he had temptations to sin, just as he did before, and even more so. But he did not sin. For the elect, temptation cannot be so strong that their resistance and triumph over it is not stronger still. However holy one is, he still finds nothing good in his flesh. That is, he notices that to the extent that there is flesh in him, all laws and the order of God transcend his power. Therefore he wails and complains on account of his flesh, not because it has conquered him (for whoever is his lord has also conquered him), but because he would rather be rid of the conflict (Romans 6[:11]). But according to the spirit, he is happy and triumphant beyond measure. For there [in the spirit] he perceives a conquering and a salvation which is higher than he can ever express, and he is completely satisfied no matter how long he still must struggle. Yes, the more conflict there is in the flesh, the more peace there is in God. Therefore after long and heartfelt lament, St. Paul said, "I thank God, through Jesus Christ, our lord!" (Romans 7[:25]). What did he thank God for? For the fact that he gave him much more than he can ever request.

You say, "He thanks God that God never counted his sins against him, for although he still sins, he does not do it, but rather the sin that resides in him does it." I answer: if someone committed adultery and excused himself with this reply, would it be adequate? Yes, his answer is granted gladly, but he has no part in the kingdom of God

(Ephesians 5[:5]). And the law commands him to be stoned (Leviticus 20[:9ff.], Deuteronomy 22). Whoever takes advantage of his brother[8] does not love him. For how can you lay down your life for your brother if you do not grant him small concessions, and if you take from him? How could someone whom the world is unable to punish in the right way be excused before God? And who will justify what the world regards as good?

No one should deceive himself. Whoever does not love his brother certainly does not love God either, for he does not keep his commandments (proven from its obverse in 1 John 5[:2]). Whoever loves God always has his heart with God, and he is sorry if he says a single idle word or does a single idle thing – to say nothing of when he sins. Whoever seeks amusement in idle words proves that God bores him. Whoever is galled by God has never tasted how sweet he is. A friend of God regards the slightest thing he thinks, says or does transgressing God's will as a sin, as has been said. Thus, Paul also lamented his sins (Ephesians 5[:17]), but he had nothing in common with the works of darkness.

You say, "But, as is well known, David in the Old Testament and the Corinthians in the New Testament committed adultery (2 Samuel 11, 1 Corinthians 5[:1ff.]), and yet they were again accepted by God, even though for a time they were rejected." I reply that the whole world indulges in mortal sins but is not better off, because it does not know with certainty when God will afflict or reward it according to merit. If the servant who does not know his master's will must nevertheless expect such wrath, the servant who knows it must expect it much more. Yes, such a person belongs to death, and lies in death, and God does not owe him anything more.

Now, whoever is dead can never live from his own strength nor improve his life (God alone knows and can give him these things). Therefore Scripture says, terrifyingly, "Whoever has once tasted future things and falls away from them is not able to turn back" (Hebrews 6[:4ff.] and 10[:26], 2 Peter 2[:20], Matthew 12, and Luke 11[:24ff.]). But unfortunately there are few people who have experienced this anticipation, as life itself proves. Whoever has had this experience follows it. Whoever recognizes the kingdom of God in himself also lets it rule. Woe to him who knows God and is a servant

---

[8] Literally, "Whoever makes a heller's profit on his brother . . ."

of the flesh. God is indeed merciful, and one reads that he has forgiven many great sinners. But however merciful he is, one seldom reads about people who sin after knowing the truth and who are again forgiven. Therefore these sinners are a warning for us to fear God's anger and not to despise it – to praise his mercy and not to sin. Whoever truly fears God remains secure before his wrath, but even God's mercy serves to damn a blasphemer (Luke 1[:67ff.], Romans 3[:8]).

You say, "The Lord says through his prophet (Ezekiel 18[:23, 31] and 33[:11]), 'If a sinner repents, I promise that I will no longer think about his sin'." I answer: the Lord is truthful and merciful, more so than any man or angel can express. But one certainly sees every day how people repent – namely, the more they repent the more violent they become! Or improvement is assumed for the sake of appearances only. The tree with foliage looks pretty indeed, but it only bears crab apples. We repent our sins in the manner of someone who strikes his brother on the cheek and says, "Excuse me, I did not enjoy doing that!" Oh, much, much is still remiss, dear brothers.

Conversion must take place from the roots if one is to come before God in such a way that a hypocrite surpassing all sinners does not emerge from a sinner. Those who want to be new men and do not want to give up their old life are like sows that have been washed and then wallow in the mud again (2 Peter 2[:22]). Those who talk about a future conversion, and console themselves with this, will see how they appear to God with their plotting. The reason is that those who love God do not think of moving away from him. But those who have never been near him and sincerely desire to approach him would not talk about a future conversion. For those who postpone the good prove that they do not miss it (Proverbs 24[:12ff.]). Those who want to buy oil only when the bride arrives, will miss the wedding (Matthew 25[:8ff.]).

You say, "What good does it do to repent, however much? For if everyone has violated the law at least once, then according to what you say no one will be blessed." I reply that if someone breaks what God has created, God can still restore it. But if God does not want to restore it, then it remains broken forever. That which he has restored is not damaged because it was once broken. A damage that is repaired is no damage. God, lord of heaven and earth, established a plan for salvation in which the whole damage was repented (Romans 5[:1]). This penance must be difficult for the flesh, no matter how small the violation of the law may be. And it must be equally difficult for the spirit, to the degree that the flesh opposes the law (Ephesians 1). And to the same degree that something was taken from the law and from God, it must be restored to them [the law and God] through penance (Colossians 1[21ff.]). Happy is he who has such repentance in him and has a place in his life for it. To him who does not desire repentance, nothing is nearer and better than perdition itself. If God could give such a person anything better, God would gladly do it. Yes, he might gladly give it if we were able to receive it. For no one is able to receive anything from God unless he is ready to oppose his own desires if that pleases God. Those who ask God for wisdom and do not want to tolerate falling into foolishness, do not ask for what God wants, but for what they themselves want. As long as the person does not want his salvation taken out of his own hands, salvation cannot come to him. As long as a person rejects damnation, damnation is not removed from around his neck. A perverted person [who truly repents] may certainly say, "I will gladly do without salvation for the sake of God and gladly accept damnation for the sake of God." Then God cannot show himself to him in anything other than in his very essence, namely good, and God would have to give him the best and most noble thing he has, which is himself.   .

You say, "If the law has to be fulfilled so completely, then Christ has lived in vain. Then merit is set up [as the basis of salvation] and grace is rejected." I answer that no one is able to fulfill the law sufficiently who does not truly know and love Christ. Whoever fulfills the law through him certainly has merit (Luke 18[:13ff.]). But no one has glory before God, for all praise belongs to God, through whose mercy a path has been blazed which was impossible for the whole world [to find]. For this reason also merit does not belong to the person but to Christ, through whom everything that the person has is given to him by God. Whoever seeks glory by virtue of his merits, as though these merits came from him, certainly destroys the grace that comes through Christ. But whoever says that a man does not need to keep the law turns God into a liar. God gave the law in order that it be kept, as all of Scripture testifies (Deuteronomy 32[:46]). All those [turn God into a liar] who say that the law was not given for man to fulfill, but only so that through it man recognize himself [as sinful]. As though it were sufficient that man recognize himself as evil, regardless of whether he remain so or not.

On the other hand, those who say that they are not able to keep the law have a spirit that is not from God, for they do not confess that Jesus Christ has become flesh (1 John 4[:10]). They say in their hearts that Christ is 10,000 miles away from them (contrary to Paul, Romans 10[:8]). All those who do not know God talk like this, and they are everywhere. Those who say that they know God, and also talk as if they do, are surely blind, for they do not want to see the truth, which nevertheless they must see (Deuteronomy 30[:8]). It is a plain lie to say that it is impossible to keep the commandments of God, because Scripture explicitly says that these commandments are easy and not difficult (1 John 5[:3]). And the lie can be seen when a person does not want to hear the truth, for lies cannot be defended against it. Those who accept carnal truth and try to overlook the truth of the spirit are those who cannot put two contradictory assertions in Scripture on the same scale. Whatever they gather from the two, they still have only a half-truth. And a half-truth is more evil than a lie because it seeks to sell itself as the truth (Proverbs 24[:21]). Those who are true pupils of Christ keep the whole Mosaic Law, even if they have never read it. Those who do not keep it, and those who do not want to hear about it, listen to a much lesser extent to God (Matthew 25[:41ff.]). Those who are not able to see God will have their eyes blinded as a result, for they do not speak their own words, but the word of God, which can never be neglected without harm. Yes, everything that God said through Moses must be truly fulfilled – and to the degree that God expressed it through Christ and the apostles (Matthew 5[:17ff.]). Therefore the bellies of all these carnal Christians must explode, as they fear.

You say, "Why then does one say – and it is written – that the law has been abolished (Hebrews 7), that it is too weak for justification (Romans 8[:3]), and that no law has been given to the just (1 Timothy 1[:9])?" I reply that whoever has received the new covenant of God – that is, whoever has the law written in his heart by the holy spirit – is truly just (Romans 5; Paul treats this throughout his letter to the Romans on the topic of the law). Whoever thinks he can bring this about by reading the Bible and by keeping the law, ascribes to the dead letter what belongs to the living spirit. Whoever does not have the spirit and presumes to find it in Scripture seeks light and finds darkness, seeks life and finds death, and this is true not only of the Old Testament but also of the New (Ephesians 1, Colossians 1).

This is the reason that the most learned ones always get the most angry at the truth. For they think that they could not lack understanding, which they have derived so cleverly and tenderly from holy Scripture. If a carpenter's son who had not gone to school had to come to them and charge them with lies, where would he have learned to do it (John 7[:15])? Therefore they thought that he rejected the law, because he did not want to make concessions to their literalistic unreason. Oh, brothers, this is still happening today! Blessed is he who does not get angry with Christ. Those who actually have the truth [in their hearts] can recognize it without any Scriptures. The scribes can never do this, because they have not received the truth from the Truth [Christ]; they steal the truth from the witnesses to the truth [Scripture] (Jeremiah 23[:30]). But it is said of those who have the truth in their hearts, that for them the written law has been completely abolished. Not that they reject the law. But if they do not yet understand the testimony [of Scripture] in every aspect, they still have truth and justice itself in their hearts, which do not mislead them. Scripture gives them abundant testimony of this, even if they do not know about it.

But to the degree that anyone does not know God, love him, and keep his commandments, to this degree that person must remain subject to all the laws which show him his lack of justice and which can punish him. The more the laws are held up to him, the more hostile he is toward them. For they are not able to make him just, regardless of who has written them – a prophet or an apostle. First he must recognize the root of his evil, namely that he hates the God whom he [thinks he] loves in his consciousness. Only then does the power of the most high work in his heart, and without any means (for God himself is the true means, the beginning, and the end of all good). As a result he fears God, and recognizes, loves, and believes in him; these are all things which no creature nor creaturely thing in heaven or on earth ever was able to give a person. Where this has not taken place, no written testimony can help. Rather, either it establishes hypocrisy, when the testimony is weak; or the better the testimony, the more God is hated through it. This is what Paul says (Romans 5[:20]): "The law was introduced so that sin prevails."

You say, "If this were true, it would be better if there were no law and no one preaching it." My answer is this: Whoever is not in God and wants to come to him must first recognize that he is not in God (Romans 7[:7]). The more strongly and truly all creatures or creaturely things give testimony against such a person, the more his enmity to God grows, until it can grow no more. This happens so that God alone and no creature, however holy and good it may be, is given all praise. Not that God is pleased by the enmity, but that everyone carnal has no other way of getting rid of sin than to become tired of it.

Now, the person who can show the world and all false Christians that everything they do and fail to do, even the most attractive thing, is darkness, that person is a witness known to God and sent by him, regardless of how much anger against God he arouses. For God alone knows the purpose of this. The person who tells the world what it wants to hear, and cannot address the hearts of false Christians to the point where they collapse, is a servant of God who has not been called and ordained (Jeremiah 23). A true messenger of Christ can propagate the best message of his Lord so that it is hateful to everything carnal as long as the message is not truly accepted. Those who propagate the message so that it pleases dogs and swine are stewards who do not regard the treasure of their Lord as precious, and who have not thought to increase their talent, although they think that they will finally emerge unharmed (Ezekiel 3[:17ff.] and 33[:1ff.]). Those who truly proclaim God's wrath are also able to proclaim his grace fruitfully. Those who are silent about, or abbreviate, the one [God's law] are not able to speak about or to realize the other [God's grace]. Where the aforementioned enmity to God is overcome in a single human heart through the power of God, the law and the gospel have been heard with righteous ears (Psalm 40). The law and the gospel will be experienced and received in the heart, even though they were never heard externally [through preaching]. Then the prophecy will be fulfilled which God promised through Jeremiah (Jeremiah 31[:33]), that one will no longer say, "Recognize the Lord, for this is the highest and best knowledge." To the degree that such a person knows God, to this degree the person is sincerely happy about all testimonies, no matter how small, which come from a truthful heart and a solid foundation. All the punishments [of the divine law] which are written and spoken truly please him. He submits himself day and night to the law of God, with and without testimonies. Yes, all creatures must give testimony about God, who dwells in their hearts and who has also created all creatures to proclaim God's majesty (Psalm 1[:2], Psalm 19[:1ff.]). Not that one seeks, loves, and praises creatures, and abandons, hates and blasphemes God. Also, for this reason, such a person cannot keep the holy Scripture in a higher way than by doing what it teaches – that is, that he should love God alone with his whole heart. Whoever honors Scripture and is cold toward divine love should take heed that he does not make an idol of Scripture. All the scribes who are not learned enough for the kingdom of God do this.

You ask, "If someone does not yet know God, is it wrong for him to elevate Scripture, so that through it he is able to come to knowledge?" My answer is that if someone gives you a document assuring you that it contains much good, and you do not know whether he is pious and rich or not, it would be foolish to rely on the document. If he is as true as the documents maintain, you still cannot rely or build on the documents until you have in part experienced whether he is such. (He who has not experienced the attraction of the father has a faith that is as uncertain as a straw in the wind, Matthew 11[:17]). If you find that he is indeed pious and rich, then you say: "Hey, lord, let me be your servant. I do not ask about your documents, for I do not wish any other payment than to be your servant and you to be my lord."

The document is of no use to those who do not dwell in God's house. Those who dwell in God's house know without the document how pious the Lord is. Those who dwell in God's house and are not willing to do without the document prove that they do not want to trust the Lord without the document. That is, the document means more to them than the Lord – an attitude which the document itself has forbidden on pain of losing what is promised in the document. Therefore, you cannot dispense with the document, no matter how faithfully you always serve the Lord, for it has also been instituted as testimony against you, in case you fall from God one day (Deuteronomy 31; Revelations 22[:18f.]). If you do not keep the terms of the document, you will not be able to console yourself with it. If one could recognize God only from his documents, and not from the actions he carries out every hour and moment, then God would remain unknown for a long time indeed. Those who do not learn to recognize God from God himself have never known him. The person who seeks God with the greatest diligence and does not perceive through God that God was with him before he began to seek him, that person has not yet found him and is still far from him (Jeremiah 23).

Oh, who will give me a voice enabling me to cry so loudly that the whole world hears me? To cry that God, the Lord, the highest one, is in the deepest abyss of the earth, and that he waits for the moment when those who should repent are willing to do so. Lord, my God, in this miserable, perverted world how is it possible that you are so great and still no one finds you? That you speak so loudly and no one hears you? That you are so close to everyone and yet no one sees you? That you let each one see you and yet no one knows your name? But praise be to you, Lord, for you are merciful and just, and all the perverted must be destroyed, for they flee you and say that they are unable to find you (Jeremiah 2 and 32). They turn their backs to you and say that you will not let yourself be seen. They have closed their ears so that they do not have to hear your voice. For they, the perverted, say that they would die if they heard your voice, although through it one should and must come to life (Isaiah 55, Zechariah 7, Psalm 94, Exodus 20, and 1 Samuel 12). They have sealed their hearts with the padlock of an unknown idol, and they say that you [God] do not want to let yourself be seen. The world does not want to hear a single word about this, and proves it undeniably with its works. Therefore the time will also come that God, the Lord, has predicted through his servants and his son. The time when, although they seek him, they will not be able to find him; although they flee him, they will not be able to escape him. For as you trusted God in the lie, so he will deal with you in the truth. (To the perverted, God is also perverted, Psalm 18.) So that in this way God proves to all who fear him that he is the truth, which you are not able to believe on account of the lie.

The person who willingly suffers for the truth is blessed because he has escaped the lie. To such a person even this suffering becomes easy, precious and good. But to the world it is difficult, painful and evil. And again, what the world thinks easy, precious and good will be for that person only difficult, painful and evil. Those who find God's commandments difficult to keep do not love God and do not know how good he is. And in turn, those who do not know God are not able to love him. Those who do not love him do not keep his commandments, and do not have life. The covenant of God and the yoke of his son are not difficult for anyone, except someone who has never borne them (Matthew 11[:30]). The more one of the elect works in God's vineyard, the less tired he becomes. Rather, for him even work is repose in God.

You say, "If all laws were commanded equally by God, then it would follow that one must also accept customary law. And it is not true that one should be bound so completely by externals." I answer that there are three forms of law, which Scripture calls commandments, customs, and laws. The commandments are those things which follow directly from love of God and one's neighbor, and which can never be omitted without sinning, as the conscience of all reasonable people testifies (Romans 2). Those who do not love God always sin. They may do whatever they want, yet they become more guilty the more they transgress the commandments. Customs are an external ordering,[9] directed to the natural daily uses of people, so that they may be reminded of those things which are divine and eternal[10] (Colossians 2). For all customs are sacraments or symbols, and whoever understands their meaning may certainly omit the symbol (Hebrews 10). When the meaning is absent, then the symbol is a mockery and an abomination before God, and therefore to be rejected as if it had never been commanded, as Jeremiah says (Jeremiah 7). True laws are those decisions which one makes between brother and brother, to protect the innocent and to punish the unjust (Matthew 5). All these forms of law are equally pleasing to him who truly seeks the kingdom of God. That is, he is able to accept all laws between himself and his neighbor, and he must not go to court in his own interests, though the greatest injustice happened to him. He may resist no judge if that man judges correctly. He himself cannot judge and punish further than is necessary for the kingdom of heaven (Matthew 18).

All commandments, customs, and laws, insofar as they are written in the Old and New Testaments, have been abolished for a true follower of Christ (1 Timothy 1[:9]). That is, the true follower has the word written in his heart; he loves God alone. Accordingly, he knows how to judge all that he does and omits, even though he has nothing that is written. If there is a part of Scripture that he cannot understand from the context of the whole, then he certainly does not despise the testimony of Scripture. Rather, he seeks its meaning with all diligence and compares [all parts of Scripture] with one another. But he surely does not accept them until they have been interpreted

---

[9] I.e. concerned with matters of public behavior.
[10] In Denck's view, customary law has a religious function and purpose.

for him by the anointing of the spirit (2 Peter 1). What he does not understand, he reserves judgment about, and expects revelation from God (1 John 2). For a belief or a judgment that has not been unlocked with the key of David cannot be accepted without great error. This is so because [such a belief or judgment] does not want to be disbelief, but it is worse than disbelief because it thinks it is the same as true faith.

Those who so love God that nothing is able to hinder or help them in their love truly need no other law. But if something is able to hinder or help them, then their love of God orders them to do not only what has been written but also what never could be written. Everything that has been written is directed to this goal; happy is the person who can use it correctly. For the whole of Scripture has been given in order to punish, to teach, and to console (Romans 15[:4]). But as long as the person is perverted, he cannot use it for the purpose for which it was given (1 Corinthians 10[:11]). Scripture and the law are in themselves holy and good (Romans 7[:12]). But to a perverted heart all things are perverted, and so nothing is able to help it except God himself. God willingly lets those who think they can come to their own imagined goals through the written law do so. But because it is not possible for this to happen, he sets a fiery sword, that is a burning, cutting word, between [the law and the goal] (Genesis 3[:24], Hebrews 4[:12]). This sword points to the life of Jesus Christ, which is bitter to human nature. Those who want to risk this sword will eat from the true tree of life (Revelations 2[:7]). The meaning of life that someone seeks from creaturely things is of no use to one who does not want to accept the sword from God and to suffer – even if God allowed him to seek this life for all eternity. Whoever knows the true goal has no need of such means [as laws and Scripture]. To the extent that anyone needs such means, he lacks knowledge about the goal. Whoever does not know this goal has neither the means to, nor the beginning of, the truth. For these three things [goal, means, and beginning] are one (1 John 5[:8]). Whoever does not have one thing, does not have any of the three. This one thing is love. Love is God himself. No creature can help him who does not have God, even though he may be the lord of all creatures. But whoever has God has all creatures, even if he has none.

If the people of Israel had had a true love of God, then they would have had little need for the many commandments and especially the customary law. Without commandments and customary law they would have used properly all physical things in God's name. All heathens are accustomed to wash themselves if they have touched a carcass or something unclean. Again, they are accustomed to exclude lepers, and demented women, and not to eat the blood, slime, and entrails of any animal. Again, nearly all peoples (although they have never heard God's commandments) are reluctant to eat most of the unclean animals that are forbidden in the Mosaic Law. Why then, did God forbid his people to do these things? For precisely the reason that they were not able to keep a natural order which everyone knows and praises. How then could they have accepted of God spiritual and divine laws, which no one wanted to know? With the Mosaic Law, God also wanted to show that all human ordinances were certainly in harmony with him, in that they were for, and not against, true love (1 Peter 2 [:2ff.]). But whoever acts against love cannot excuse himself with either divine or human law, for all laws should yield to love. They are there for the sake of love, and love is not there for the sake of laws. If laws are not able to bestow love, they should at least not hinder it. But love issues all laws, and therefore may also revoke them, each according to its circumstances. To the extent that love is lacking, so much must always be remembered today in all that is done or left undone.

Therefore, a person once washed of the uncleanliness of this world will not eat a bite of bread without reflecting on how God loves him, and on how he should love God – namely, so that God in his way breaks like bread for the person's benefit, and so that the person should break like bread to honor God. God sets aside his divinity, and the person should set aside his humanity, so that the sacrifice may be perfect and the [divine and human] love become one, as happened in Jesus Christ, the only-begotten son of God – and as should still happen in all the elect. Insofar as one is united with God, he is free of all time and space, and released from all human laws. But he is no longer able to enjoy such freedom. For to the same extent he gladly wants to be subject to all laws. Whoever is not the servant of all creatures for the sake of God may never inherit the kingdom of God with his son.

You say, "Why was this distinction [between laws and love] not explained to the Jews in the desert? Did God withhold it from Moses, or Moses from the people?" My answer is that God is not ashamed of his actions, and he performs them before all people (Amos 3[:7]). So it is not necessary for him to withhold what he will do in the future. Thus, he let Noah proclaim the flood; Isaiah, Jeremiah and the other prophets the destruction of Israel and Judea; and Christ and all the apostles the great day of the Lord – so that no one might complain that he was deceived. And not only these things. God also revealed beforehand the greatest works of his mercy, but often either with ambiguous words or to very few people. The reason for this is that the flesh is not able to understand what God is saying unless it has been previously humbled (Matthew 13, Mark 4, Luke 8[:4ff.]). If the whole world could understand these messages without getting angry, God would soon address the whole world.

Moses knew from God that after him a prophet would arise in Israel who would equal him in signs and miracles, who would explain the law to the people in a much better way, and who would lead them out of Egypt differently than he did. But he could not clearly reveal such things to the people with any good outcome. For if carnal people had perceived that the law was going to be explained in a better way, they would have swiftly consoled themselves with this, accepted it, and they certainly would not have despised the customary law (as some did without this happening) (Leviticus 10, Numbers 16). They would have done this, not on account of the truth, but because of their own selfish interests. Therefore God commanded that the law be kept for eternity (Deuteronomy 29), even though it was not to be for an eternity, as they thought.

They could have understood [what was to come], for Moses said to them that God would awaken among them a prophet equal to him, whom they should heed (Deuteronomy 18[:15]). If he was to be Moses' equal, then he would have to be his equal in miracles and in the power of God, which was never conceded to any other prophet in Israel, as Scripture testifies (Deuteronomy 34[:10]). If they heeded him, and this was a sign of who he was, his speech would seem to contradict Moses; and yet in truth it would not contradict him. Therefore Moses also established a test through which one could recognize a true prophet. Namely, he would not lead them to foreign gods but to the one God of Israel, no matter how alien his speech might appear (Deuteronomy 13[:2ff.] and 18[:15ff.]). For all who show the way to the one God surely have one truth and one message, no matter now far away from one another they seem.

But two prophets who do not agree with each other may both be false prophets, for they cannot both be servants of God. The prophet God has sent knows God, and his word is God's word. Therefore he also knows how to make sure that what he says agrees with the writings of all the prophets and apostles. Whoever says a single word that cannot be reconciled with the truth could say anything, however true it may be, without any truth. For he who has the truth has a well which he can never empty, and he does not find it necessary to recount the fantasies and dreams of his heart (Isaiah 58[:11], Proverbs 18[:4]). Woe to him who does not allow himself the time to draw [water from the well of truth].

This is the goal to which one must come if the law is to be abolished, a goal which was always far from all carnal Jews and Christians, although it is everywhere. Therefore it was not fitting for those under Moses to hear much about the coming alteration of the law – or for [carnal Christians] now to boast about something that they have never received. To the degree that one possesses the law [in his heart], the written law has been abolished. To the extent that one lacks it, one should be subject to it.

The truth told me to write this, and the lie will be able to do nothing against it. Whoever is born of God will bear witness to the truth. Whoever despises truth, God will also despise. Let him be damned who does not truly love God and who does not keep his commandments. Let him be damned who proudly violates the smallest commandment of God. To those unable to say "amen" to this, God himself will nonetheless show the truth with his deeds. Fortunate is he who says in truth – that is, from his heart – that he will gladly suffer all the curses of the law so that God's will alone be done, so that God alone may rule, so that his name alone may be holy and our will be broken, so that the power of sin be destroyed, and so that all false praise be eliminated, always and forever, amen. This may, must, and will occur.

10 Hans Hut, "*On the Mystery of Baptism*"

On the mystery of Baptism, both the symbol and the essence, a beginning of a right, true Christian life.[1]

John 5[:39], "Search Scripture, for you think you have life in it,
and it is Scripture that testifies about me."

I wish the pure fear of God, the beginning of divine wisdom, to all brothers and sisters in the Lord, who make up genuine Christendom, the community of God, the only spouse and bride of Christ, united by the movement of the holy spirit in the bond of love. And I wish grace and peace in the holy spirit to all who yearn for the rigorous justice of the crucified son of God with saddened hearts and depressed spirits, and to all those who wish to be fed by this justice. Amen.

Since the last and most dangerous age of this world is now upon us,[2] we see – and realize with seeing eyes – how everything that the prophets, patriarchs, and apostles prophesied from the beginning and proclaimed for the future, is now coming about again and will be

---

[1] Although this work was not published until the modern period, it circulated earlier in manuscript form; slightly differing manuscript versions of it have been found in Budapest and Bern. The tract contains no internal evidence of authorship but has been reliably ascribed to Hans Hut. Hut was with Müntzer during the Thuringian stage of the Peasants' War but escaped the slaughter of the commoners at Frankenhausen. After the Peasants' War he continued to preach radical ideas in a variety of places until his arrest in Augsburg in September 1527. This work, the fullest expression of his thought to have survived, perhaps largely grew out of his preaching. The translation is based on the text in Lydia Müller, ed., *Glaubenszeugnisse oberdeutscher Taufgesinnter*, vol. I (Quellen und Forschungen zur Reformationsgeschichte, 30) (Leipzig, 1938), 12–28.

[2] Here, and occasionally elsewhere in the work, Hut expresses a belief that the Apocalypse is imminent.

restored, as Peter prophesied to us in the Acts of the Apostles (Acts 3[:17–26]).[3] The whole world – God have mercy on us – shows absolutely no judgment concerning this prophecy, especially those who teach other people and understand less about it than apes, although they want to be masters and teachers of Scripture. However, Scripture is sealed seven times over to them (Revelation 5[:1ff.]), and they cannot tolerate that it be opened to them through God's action, to which they are enemies, as St. Paul says (Philippians 2[:13–16]). Therefore everything that they teach and read has a perverted order and false judgment, and [scriptural truth] is completely concealed and hidden from them. By all that they do poor men are misled, deceived, and brought to every kind of pernicious damage, a fact which no one is able to believe, although it has been foretold. No worldly, pleasure-seeking scribe can know the judgments of the Lord. For, since they are perverted, to them all things are perverted, and they mislead both the poor and the rich with their flowery words. So be it. Those who want to be misled will always be misled.

Therefore I warn all believing people who love justice to guard themselves zealously against all the profit-seeking, pleasure-loving, ambitious, hypocritical scribes who preach for money. For they do not want your well-being but the benefit of their bellies. Among them one sees conduct no different from that of other worldly people, and whoever relies on them will be deceived. For their teaching, as anyone may hear, is nothing but "believe!" and it goes no further.[4] They do not explain through what means one should come to faith. Thus the world is horrified by them. For where the order of the divine mystery [the sacraments] is not rightly kept, there is nothing but vain error, and nothing can endure. One recognizes their error in all things.

Therefore, my dearest brothers in the Lord, you must learn God's judgments[5] concerning his commandments and message by your-selves, and be informed about them by God. Otherwise you will be deceived along with the rest of the world. For the scribes do not know a single judgment. Still worse, they do not know what judgment is.

---

[3] Scriptural citations enclosed here in parentheses appear as marginal references in the original.

[4] A reference to Luther's doctrine of justification by faith alone.

[5] *die urtl* [= *Urteil*] *Gottes*; the notion of divine judgment was central to Hut, as it was to Müntzer. On the one hand, he meant by it God's real intention in issuing revelation or law; on the other hand, the notion also had apocalyptic associations – the future judgment of God on those who fail to accept and act according to divine will.

For this reason they say that one should not know the judgments of God – that they are inconceivable to us. In this they insincerely cite St. Paul (Romans 11[:33f.]), and forget what he says in the First Epistle to the Corinthians. And Solomon says the same thing (Wisdom 9). And David also very zealously asks the Lord to teach him his judgments (Psalm 11). God called them with a solemn commandment to learn and to carry out his judgments (Deuteronomy 4[:1ff.]). If we are to do them, then we must also know them. Oh, how very miserably the scribes now deceive the whole world under the cloak of holy Scripture with a false and contrived faith, from which absolutely no improvement results. Each may judge this for himself; and each may recognize it from the fact that when two or three of them preach on the same passage of scripture, no exegesis agrees with another.

Therefore, my dearest brothers in the Lord, if you truly want to learn correctly the judgments of God, the testimony of the holy Scriptures about the truth, then do not listen to the cries of those who preach for money. Rather, look upon the poor, who are despised by the world and charged with being fanatics and devils, as were Christ and the apostles. Listen to these poor folk. For no one may attain the truth unless he follows in the footsteps of Christ and his elect in the school of every grief, or at least has consented partly to this, according to the will of God and in the justification of the cross of Christ. For no one can learn the mystery of divine wisdom in the underworld hangouts of every villainy, as is believed at Wittenberg or at Paris.[6] Nor is it learned at the courts of the lords or in magnificent prebends. For God's wisdom does not dwell where Brother Soft-life[7] is. Our new evangelicals, the tender scribes, have thrown the pope, the monks, and the parsons from their thrones. Having successfully done this, they are now whoring anew with the Babylonian whore [the papacy], in every pleasure, pomp, honor, greed, envy, and hate – to the outrage of the whole world. And they establish – God have mercy on us – a worse popery than before over the poor man. They will not listen, and they cannot bear to be convinced by Scripture, for they do not want to be seen as unknowing or unlearned. Thus, all who do not believe as they do must be the worst rogues, devils, false prophets,

---

[6] The theological centers of both the new evangelical faith and traditional Roman Catholicism.

[7] *brueder sanfileben*. Müntzer used this term to refer specifically to Luther; here it has the more general meaning of those clerics who enjoy a life of ease and plenty.

and fanatics – and this also happened to Christ. So be it. Let them cool their spirits with their gods and with the mighty ones, whom they butter up, as long as God allows it. For they still have a little time until everyone will see publicly what a shameful end they come to.

Therefore, moved by Christian love and brotherly fidelity, I will declare the teachings which are necessary for starting a Christian life – to the extent that God's grace permits me – as a testimony to all those brothers and sisters in the Lord who thirst and hunger for justice in their hearts. And I certainly do not do this for the sake of worldly, pleasure-seeking people, for whom such judgments are inconceivable, too subtle, perverted, heretical, despicable, and damned. Thus, I admonish all brothers and sisters who have a love and a desire for truth: if you do not comprehend such judgments when you first read them, do not despise them. For everyone thinks that they are impossible because of the perverted way in which they have been misled and deceived by the new scribes. So, if we are to come to a correct understanding of such judgments in a different way, we must begin by becoming children and fools about them. For it is a difficult, even impossible thing for carnal people to grasp the judgments of God truthfully when these judgments are not set forth and comprehended, in all their aspects, in the right order.

Therefore at the outset we will examine the judgment about baptism, the beginning of a Christian life, and we will note diligently how Christ established and commanded it, and how the apostles maintained it, with proof from the divine witness of holy Scripture, and not according to the arbitrary opinion of human wisdom, as has been held up till now – also by those who boast of being evangelicals. May God pity all people and especially the poor. May the cross of Christ help us. Amen.

If we want to attain a correct understanding of baptism, we must not deal with it according to our own opinion, leaving aside the form and manner prescribed by Christ and his apostles. For God has forbidden us to do as we think fit. Rather, we should do what he commands, hold to this, and not deviate either to the left or to the right (Deuteronomy 12, Joshua 1, Proverbs 4, Deuteronomy 5). Now, if baptism is to be kept in the right way, as commanded by Christ and maintained by the apostles, we must perceive precisely and with all seriousness the commandment of Christ when he institutes an order and gives a rule, so that a correct foundation for the Christian faith may be laid. He who has ears to hear, let him hear. Whoever wants to get angry about this, let him.

First, Christ says, "Go into the whole world and preach the gospel of all creatures."[8] Second, he says, "He who believes," and third, "and is baptized," will be saved (Mark 16[:15f.]). This order must be maintained if a true Christendom is to be established, even if the whole world is destroyed because of it. Where this order is not kept, it is also true that there is no Christian community of God but rather one of the devil, despite what the whole world and all false Christians do, because they alter Christ's order with their perverted order and combat it as unjust.

First, then, Christ says, "Go into the world and preach the gospel of all creatures." Here the Lord shows how man should come to a knowledge of God and himself, namely through the gospel of all creatures. Thus, in the first place we must learn what this gospel of all creatures is. But, God pity us, the whole world still knows nothing of it, and it is never preached in our age. But if it is preached and proclaimed by poor people, whom the world despises – as is right – and to whom it has been revealed, then [this gospel of all creatures] is the greatest foolishness and fanaticism to soft, pleasure-seeking people, especially those who preach for money and who nevertheless boast that they preach the gospel. And they berate those who preach it as the worst sort of false prophets and lying spirits. So be it. Time will reveal the truth. Therefore Paul has said so clearly that the word of the cross is foolishness to those who are lost, but to those who are saved (that is, us) it is a power of God (1 Corinthians 1[:23f.]).

In the gospel of all creatures nothing else is shown and preached but the crucified Christ alone. But not Christ as the head alone, rather the whole Christ with all his members – this is the Christ that all creatures preach and teach. The whole Christ must suffer in all his members, and not as our scribes preach Christ. Nevertheless they want to be the best Christians, as one hears from them every day. They preach that Christ as the head has borne and accomplished everything. But where are the members and the whole body, in which the suffering of Christ must be fulfilled? Paul gives us testimony of this when he says, "I rejoice in my suffering, for I repay with my body

---

[8] *das evangelion aller creaturen.* Hut makes clear in what follows that he does not read Mk. 16:15 as an injunction to preach the gospel to all creation, but to preach a gospel which is manifest in all creatures.

what is lacking in the suffering of Christ" (Colossians 1[:24]). Thus, in a short time – which has already begun – they must be turned into fools with their wisdom. For it is most pleasing to God to save those who believe through what the clever ones call foolish and fanatical preaching, even though they rage so much against it. So in the near future, with all their wisdom and greed, the learned must yield to the poor in spirit, whom they think must be fanatics, as Paul clearly shows (1 Corinthians 1[:18f.]).

Now, my dearest brothers, you must perceive diligently the words that Christ utters here: "the gospel of all creatures." This is not to be understood as though the gospel should be preached to creatures like dogs and cats, cows and calves, leaves and grass. Rather, as Paul says, "the gospel that is preached to you in all creatures." He also shows this, and says that eternal power and divinity will be seen if one perceives it in the creatures or the works produced since the creation of the world (Romans 1[:20]).

Therefore I proclaim that the gospel according to the commandment of Christ, and as Christ and his apostles preached it, [is still valid] for our age. And those who regard themselves as the best Christians do not yet know what the gospel of all creatures is (Mark 16[:15]). It is hidden from them because they do not seek the pure and simple honor of God, but instead their belly or their own honor. If they are told about it, they mock it and say, "Here are fanatics and sophists." So you should note diligently, most dearly beloved brothers, what this gospel of all creatures is, and how Paul described it when he said, "the gospel that is preached to you in all creatures" (Colossians 1[:23, 16]).

Hence, as he expounds it in another place, it is nothing but a power of God which makes blessed all who believe in it (Romans 1[:16]). But if one wants to perceive God's power and divinity, or his invisible essence – and affirm them in the works or creatures of all creation from the beginning of the world – one must reflect on how Christ always showed the kingdom of heaven and the power of the father to the common man: in creatures, through parables, through craftwork, and through all manner of work that people do. He did not direct the poor man to books, as our uncomprehending scribes do now. Rather, he taught them the gospel, and illustrated it, through their work – to the peasants by their fields, seed, thistles, thorns and rocks (Matthew 13, Mark 4, Luke 8[:4–16], John 12[:24]). In the prophets God says that one should not sow among thorns, but instead first clear the ground, hoe it or plough it, and then plant (Jeremiah 4[:3] and 1[:10]). The power of God which is shown here is God's work toward us – God's power must be shown to us in ourselves, as the work of the peasant is shown in the field. Christ shows this with the field, and Paul says, "You are God's husbandry" (1 Corinthians 3[:9]). As the peasant does with the field before he sows it with seed, so too God does with us before he plants in us his word, so that it may grow and bring forth fruit (Matthew 17[:20] and 12[:33]).

Christ teaches the gospel to the gardener from trees, to the fisherman from the catch (Matthew 4 and 1), to the carpenter from the house, to the goldsmith from the testing of gold. He teaches it to women from dough in Matthew 13, Luke 13, 1 Corinthians 5, and Galatians 5; to vintners from the vineyard, vine, and shoots in Isaiah 4, Jeremiah 2, Matthew 20, Luke 20, and John 15; to tailors from the patch on the old garment in Matthew 9; to businessmen from the pearls in Matthew 13; to harvesters from the harvest in Matthew 9, Mark 2, Luke 10, and Joel 3; to foresters from the ax on the tree in Isaiah 10; to shepherds from sheep in Ezekiel 34, Zechariah 11, John 10, Ezekiel 37, and Hebrews 13; to the potter from his pottery in Psalm 2, Isaiah 30, Jeremiah 18, Romans 9, Acts 2, and Ecclesiastes 27, 33, and 38; to the steward and official from accounting in Luke 16; and Acts 12; to threshers from the winnowing shovel in Matthew 3, Isaiah 41, and Luke 3; and to butchers from their slaughtering in Psalm 44, Isaiah 53, and Romans 8. Paul testifies to the body of Christ through a human body in Romans 12, 1 Corinthians 12, Ephesians 4 and 5, and Colossians 1. And Christ always preached the gospel of the kingdom of God in creatures and in parables; without parables he preached nothing. So David, too, says, "I will open my mouth and speak in parables" (Psalm 78[2:2]).

From such parables one should carefully note how all creatures must suffer the actions of mankind,[9] and so come through pain to the purpose for which they have been created. One should also note that no one can come to blessedness other than through the suffering and grief which God works in him (Acts 14[:22], 2 Timothy 3[:12], Judges 8), just as all of Scripture, and every creature also, show nothing but the suffering Christ in all his members. Therefore the whole of

---

[9] Mankind stands above the rest of creation and rules over it, transforming it to serve his purpose; but nature suffers as a result of being thus changed.

Scripture is also described through mere creatures. God thus gave the children of Israel to understand his will through "creaturely" [i.e. physical] and ceremonial actions; God proclaimed, preached, and described this through Moses. God commanded that one should sacrifice to him oxen, sheep, he-goats, rams, and bullocks. But through Isaiah he testified that he does not want such things, since he says, "I have not willed the sacrifice of bulls, the blood of sheep, calves, and he-goats" (Isaiah 1[:11]). And through David he says, "I do not want to take any bullocks from your household or he-goats from your stall" (Psalm 50[:9]).

Thus, God's commandments are not based on the language or speech he uses but on the power of the spirit. The power of such commandments will always influence those people who are in the same relation to God as such sacrifices are in relation to man. Thus, instead of burnt offerings like rams, cattle, and he-goats, David sacrificed himself to God as a calf (Psalm 51[:17]). So, such ceremonial sacrifices are symbols and witnesses that people should give themselves as living sacrifices (Romans 12[:1]). Afterward, God commanded that clean animals be eaten (Leviticus 11[:4], Deuteronomy 14[:3ff.]), the meaning of which refers to such people who so give themselves to God, to suffer the will of God as such animals must suffer our will. And God forbade unclean animals to be eaten, the meaning of which is that I should have nothing to do with unclean people, who are compared with such animals. For it is written (Acts 10[:15] and 11[:9]) that nothing is unclean and everything is good. The ceremonies show only what the will of God is, and they are presented to us as validly as to the children of Israel.

Thus, Christ always speaks in parables, and they consist not in the words spoken but in their power and meaning. All animals are subordinate to man. If man needs one, first he must prepare, cook, and roast it, according to his will, and the animal must suffer. God does likewise with man. If God wants to use or take pleasure in us, first we have to be justified by him and made clean, inside and out (2 Timothy 2[:21]). Inwardly, from desires and lusts, outwardly, from all unjust conduct and misuse of creatures. The peasant sows no seed among thistles, thorns, sticks, and rocks. Rather, first he roots them out and then he sows. So God does with us, not sowing his word in a person who is full of thistles and thorns, or whose desires and lusts are only for things of this world. The concern for sustenance [i.e., physical welfare], which God forbids (Matthew 6[:25ff.]), must first be rooted out. The carpenter does not make a house from whole trees (Jeremiah 31[:4]). Instead, first he cuts them down and hews them according to his pleasure; then he makes a house from them. In the same way we should learn God's work and will toward us, which is comparable to a person making a house before he lives in it, and this house is us (Hebrews 3[:6]). Often in Scripture man is called a tree. If he is to be turned into a house, he must be cut off from the world in all his lusts. Then, just as on a tree one branch sticks out here and another there, so it is with the desires of a person: one branch sticks out to property, another to wife and child, a third to great wealth, a fourth to fields and meadows, and others to pomp and temporal honors.

Therefore, all the actions which we perform on creatures should be our Scripture and should be diligently reflected on. For the whole world with all its creatures is a book in which one sees in actions everything that is to be read in Scripture. And all elected people, from the beginning of the world down to Moses, studied in the book of all creatures and perceived in it the knowledge that was written in their hearts by nature through the spirit of God (Romans 2[:15]), because the whole law has been described with "creaturely" works. And all peoples act thus with creatures (as the law shows), even heathens, who do not have the scriptural law but still do the same thing as those who have the scriptural law. The scriptural law shows how animals must be slaughtered before they are sacrificed to God, and only afterward eaten. So heathens who have only the law of nature do as well. They eat no living animal. So first we have to die to the world and then we can live in God. In the law there is a lamp trimmer beside the lamps, and the heathen do likewise beside their lamps, and the same is true with nearly all ceremonies and commandments. Thus, Moses writes his book with such ceremonies of creatures, so that he reminds and admonishes people to search for and learn God's will in them.

Therefore, just as the law is written and revealed in all creatures, so we read it daily through our work. We deal with this book every day, and the whole world is full, yes full, of the written will of God, about which our own hearts give us testimony (Romans 1[:20]), if we defend[10] them from coarseness, worldly disorder, and lust.

[10] There appears to be an error in Hut's text at this point, which has *warnemen*, "perceive," instead of *wehren*, "defend, preserve."

So man can perceive God's invisible essence and eternal power in the actions of creatures. And he can recognize how God acts through man and prepares him for [the goal of] perfection, since perfection can only occur beneath the cross of suffering according to God's will. Therefore, all creatures are subordinate to man, who rules over them. And as the whole Bible is written in terms of all creatures, so also Christ spoke or preached and showed the gospel in all creatures through parables. And he did this because he preached the gospel to the poor man. So he never directed people to the chapters of a book, as our scribes do, for everything that can be shown through creatures will prove everything in Scripture. Christ needs no Scripture except because of the soft scribes, to show them with it.

If the gospel in all creatures is thus preached according to the commandment of the Lord, man can understand through it that reason is included in a natural and real way in his own actions, which he performs on all creatures. In these actions he recognizes God's will toward him and he surrenders himself – a prisoner in ecstasy – in obedience to Christ. Then he must recognize that man cannot attain blessedness in any other way than by suffering the will of God in body and in pain, as it pleases God. And he says that he believes it must happen thus with him, and with all people who wish to be saved.

From such obedience [to Christ] comes the second part of the divine order, when Christ says, "Who believes . . ." Even though a person may understand the gospel in all things or creatures immediately, and may understand that it must happen as he hears and believes, nevertheless this is still not enough. For all men can prove this. The third part of the divine order must also follow, in which Christ says, ". . . and is baptized, will be saved." Here baptism must be added to the first two parts, in that a person consents to bear everything that will be imposed upon him by the father through Christ. And baptism gives him the task of abiding with the Lord and renouncing the world, and of accepting the sign of baptism as a covenant of his consent before a Christian community which has received the covenant from God, and in the name of God. The community, in turn, has the power and authority to give baptism to all those who desire it from their hearts. For the Lord says here (Matthew 18[:18]), "What you shall bind on earth, shall also be bound in heaven." But no person should be accepted into such a community and united with it unless he has first heard and learned the gospel, believes only what he has heard, and has consented to it. For this covenant is a consenting to obedience to Christ, with a demonstration of divine love toward all brothers and sisters with body, life, goods, and honor, regardless of the evil that the world may speak about him.

Indeed, where are such Christians as these? They are a small band. If now in this community there were only two or three, that does not matter if Christ is among them as a witness. For every testimony is corroborated by the mouths of two or three witnesses. Through such a baptism a man will always be assured that he has been accepted as a child of God, a brother or sister of Christ, and a member of the Christian community and the body of Christ. For he has consented with a true heart to such a unity, according to the will of God. God orders his saints to assemble, those who have more regard for the covenant than for any kind of sacrifice. For God does not want the sacrifice of a he-goat, but the sacrifice of thanks. He wants each to sacrifice his body willingly for justification, as Paul says (Romans 12[:1]). And God wants each to believe that God will not abandon him in need, but save him from every need, when he is led into grief. Even though [at baptism] such a faith is not perfect and is untested, God will impute it to him for justification until he is justified and tested as gold is tested in the fire.

Thus the baptism which follows preaching and faith is not the true essence through which people become pious, but only a symbol, a covenant, a likeness, and a reminder of a person's consent, so that he is reminded daily to expect the real baptism. Christ speaks of real baptism as the water of all grief, through which the lord purifies, washes and justifies all carnal lusts, sins, and impure actions (Matthew 20). Because the person has recognized that without mankind, to which creatures are subordinate, no creature is able to justify itself in order to come to its final goal; and that no man is able to justify himself in order to come to his goal – that is, to come to salvation. Rather, this justification must occur only through the action of God in the baptism of every grief shown to and exercised upon man by God, to whom alone man is subordinate for justification. Therefore, if a person is to be justified by God, the person must always allow God, as his lord, to perform his work in him. Then God will bring it to pass (Psalms 31 and 55). As David says, "Commend your way to the Lord and hope in him, and he will bring it to pass" (Proverbs 16[11]).

---

[11] See, rather, Ps. 37:5.

Thus, the water of every grief is the true essence and meaning of baptism, in which the person sinks in the death of Christ. It was not in Christ's time that this baptism was first established; it has existed from the beginning (Joel 3, Judges 8). All the elect friends of God have been baptized in it, from Adam down to the present, as Paul shows (1 Corinthians 10[:2]). So Christ also accepted this covenant from God in the Jordan river. And with it he testified that he was obedient to the father, in order to show love toward all people unto death, and as an example. For afterward he was richly endowed by the father with the baptism of every grief.

Thus, the symbol and the essence of baptism must be sharply distinguished. The Christian community extends the sign or covenant of baptism through a true servant, as Christ received it from John. True baptism follows afterward. And God gives it through the water of every grief, and also in the consolation of the holy spirit. God allows no one to sink in this baptism. As it is written, "He leads into hell and out again; he kills and revives" (1 Kings 2, Luke 12). The Lord must administer this baptism afterward. Whoever wants to be a disciple of the Lord must be baptized in this manner, and he will be cleansed in spirit through the bond of peace toward the one body [the community of Christians] (Ephesians 4[:4] and 5). God thus makes his own blessed and capable (1 Peter 2), and everything occurs by means of this covenant of the holy spirit's rebirth and renewal in faith. God works this according to his great mercy, so that we are justified alone through this same grace, and in hope we are heirs to eternal life (Titus 3[:5]). In this way one is washed, healed, purified, and born again (Romans 8). And a community not needing punishment is established before God – not as present-day, oath-taking Christians [have tried to establish it] through profit-hungry and greedy scribes. As are the people, so too is the parson (Hosea 4[:9]).

Therefore, dear David asked God to wash and purify him of his sins. And then God mercifully heard him, as we read, when he was in the water of every grief and cried to the Lord for help. And God brought him out of the depths of the abyss again, and thus his sins were killed and he was again made living in Christ. So Paul also admonishes the brothers to suffer, as they have seen him suffer (Ephesians 3). For the kingdom of God does not consist of talk or an exterior thing, but of power. Thus, the gospel is not a speech but a power of God (1 Corinthians 2[:4] and 4[:20]), which is given only by

God and which completely renews the person, from his mouth to his heart, and in all his conduct and behavior.

Therefore, it is a very bad gospel which the world and learned preachers down to our age are involved with, and which does not improve people but only aggravates them. This I leave to all Christian brothers to judge. But blessed are they who hear the word and preserve it. For a lamb of Christ hears the voice of the Lord and is afraid. But whoever hears it and is not afraid is a fool and will never be righteous. But whoever wants to come to God without the justification which is valid before God, throws away the means to justification, which is the suffering or the cross of Christ, indeed Christ-the-crucified himself. This the whole world does now, but it still cannot escape suffering. For without the son, who is given in discipline, no one comes to the father. Whoever wants to rule with God must be ruled by God. Whoever wants to do God's will must set aside his own. Whoever wants to find something in God must lose as much in him.

The whole world now talks about freedom, and yet always remains in carnal servitude. It does not want to lose anything but always wants to have more. Oh, how masterfully the world conceals itself. Thus, everyone says that each should remain in his calling. If this is so, why did Peter not remain a fisherman and Matthew a publican? And why did Christ tell the rich young man to sell what he had and give all to poor people? If it is right that our preachers have so many goods, then the young man was also right to keep his goods. Oh, Zacchaeus, why did you give away your goods so lightly? According to the rules of our preachers, you could have kept them and still been a good Christian! Oh, dear "associates", how openly you let your villainy be noticed! So be it. The Lord who will judge you is there.

A true, genuine friend of God, who daily waits for the lord and in consolation hopes in him, will have his heart strengthened, so that he can bear the will of the Lord under the cross. Everything that such a person suffers is called the suffering of Christ and not ours, for with Christ they who suffer are one body with many members, united and bound together through the bond of love. Therefore Christ takes care of such people as his own body. He testifies to this and says, "Who touches you touches the apple of my eye," and further, "what you do to the least of my followers you have done to me." For the suffering of Christ must be fulfilled in each member until the suffering of Christ is compensated. For as Christ, the lamb, is killed from the beginning of the world, so he will also be crucified to the end of the world – so that the body of Christ is made perfect in the length, breadth, depth, and height of the love of Christ, which surpasses all understanding. This is done so that a person may be filled with the rich fullness of God. Under this suffering and under the cross of rightly produced baptism, a person becomes aware of his faith, is justified, and is tested like gold in the fire. Through this suffering authentic faith will be revealed from God's goodness and mercy, when – after much suffering and grief – a person is consoled again in the holy spirit. Then he will be ready for the Lord and useful for every good work. It cannot happen to a person otherwise; the truth should be revealed without deception.

The faith which one receives from hearing the gospel will be imputed for righteousness, until a person is justified and purified under the cross. For then such a faith is conformed to the faith of God and is one with Christ. The just person then lives from such a faith (Acts 2). So the faith which one has initially must be sharply distinguished [from tested faith]. God's faith is always true, just, and constant in all his promises.

In the beginning our faith is like silver which is still in the ore, full of dross and unproved, but held to be good silver until the testing, in which all the impurities are separated from it. Therefore the apostles say, "We believe. Help our unbelief." Oh, how well may our initial faith be compared to unbelief! – as a person then discovers in the testing of justification, since too often he finds in himself neither faith nor trust (Romans 11). And he is so completely closed in unbelief that he thinks that he has also been rejected in the eyes of the Lord. Then nothing can console him, indeed no creature. As David also says, "My soul will not be comforted" (Psalm 77[:2]). And in another place he says, "I have been rejected in the sight of your eyes" (Psalm 31[:22]). Thus, a person is enclosed in the abyss of hell. Christ calls this the sign of Jonah the prophet (Matthew 1). Then nothing can bring joy except he who led him there. And this he must await, until God comes with his consolation through the holy spirit. And then the person will be so full of joy that he will forget all worldly lusts, pleasures and honors, and will regard everything as dross. Then the person returns from the depths of hell, and he gains joy and courage in the holy spirit. This justification is valid before God, and it does not come from an untested faith. For an untested faith reaches only to where righteousness begins, and there it must be prepared and justified. But the whole world fears justification as it fears the devil. It would gladly pay with a contrived faith – and still it does not want to come to justification.

Such justice is not proclaimed by the world's preachers, for they themselves are enemies of the cross of Christ and of justice. They seek only their own honor and what serves their belly, their god. So God exercises his justice on us through the suffering of the holy cross, which he lays on each one. And the faith of God will be revealed to our faith according to his promise, so that we may believe that God is true, and that he will prove his faith in ours. Here all the lusts to which we have been accustomed in this creaturely life will be rooted out and broken. Thus the world's yoke of total sin will be thrown off, so that the world no longer rules, but Christ. Then the law of the father will be fulfilled in us through Christ, as in his members. Then there is a desire and love to do the will of God in true obedience. His burden is light and his yoke sweet to such people (Matthew 11[:30]), and everything is possible that was not possible before. Then a person might indeed say, "Christ has extinguished my sin."

But whoever does not want to submit to the discipline of the Lord and clings to the pleasures of the world will often be overcome with greater ruination and suffering, and he will die (Deuteronomy 32). And if such people cry out to God in their suffering, God will not hear them; and through their [afflicted] members he will mock them (Proverbs 1[:26–28]). Thus, all those who fear God will look for their consolation in the Lord, and he will save them from all grief. May God help us in this through the bath of rebirth.

Now follows the essence of true baptism

Now we will speak further about the baptism of rebirth, which is not an exterior sign that Christ shows, but a bath of souls that washes and rinses them clean from all lusts and desires of the heart. That is, baptism is an obliteration of all the lusts and disobedience which are in us and which incite us to oppose God. God did this to the ancient world at the time of Noah (Genesis 6), when he washed away all evil from the world through the flood, and it also happened to Pharaoh and his Egyptians in the baptismal bath of the Red Sea, when they sank to the bottom like lead. The whole world – including Noah and his household, Pharaoh, and all his followers, and the whole of Israel

– is baptized in the same way. But all people do not emerge from baptism alike, nor is baptism equally useful to all. The wicked certainly come to it but do not emerge again, because with their lusts they sink to the very bottom in creaturely things. They have not been able to let go of either worldly things or themselves. But they live continually and happily in lust and the love of creaturely things. Thus, they persecute the elect, who do not cling to these things as they do. The elect desire to swim, and they strive unceasingly for the bank or dock, like Peter, so that they come out of the world's violent sea and the water of all grief and adversity. And they reach solid land because they see that God reached out his hand and wants to help them out of the water.

So, to those who live for a renewal of their lives, baptism is not only a submersion and drowning, but a joyous departure from the wavering wishes and impulses of our own desires. We once lived hectically – for these desires and this vehemence are the conflict of the spirit and the flesh which is in a person. In this conflict, if the desires of the flesh, the lusts, the impulses, and the attractions and repulsions are to be stilled and overcome, then the sweet waters – that is, lust and the desires of the flesh – must become, by contrast and to the same degree, acrid and bitter through the movement of divine justice that sweeps out everything. For the desires were sweet in a creaturely way – coming not from God but from the person himeslf, for he was inclined to them. Then the vehement conflict in one's consciousness between spirit and flesh arises. Oh, the way to life gets narrow at this point! Then the person, through the dying-out of the old man, must turn to a new life in God. And this is the rebirth in baptism. Here such fears, trembling, and shuddering attack the person as those of a woman in childbirth. When God directs such waters through one's soul, one must be patient, until he has been taught and understands (Psalms 6 and 143). And peace from the impulses of the flesh is born on this earth. Then, in the patient waiting[12] of his time, in the endurance of God's hand, a person becomes a prepared residence of God. Then, just as the troubled waters become clear, the bitter sweet, and the turbulent calm, the son of God appears on the waters (1 John 3), stretches out his hand, pulls a person from the turbulence, and lets

---

[12] *Langen weil*, a term Hut derived from the late medieval German mystical tradition, and perhaps from Müntzer; it implies detachment from and boredom with the world of created matter.

him see that he unlocks our darkness through his truth – that is, the flow of the living water that is concealed in us. Christ does this in order to prepare us sinful, earthly people for eternal life. The waters which rush into the soul are tribulation, affliction, fear, trembling, and worry. So baptism is suffering. So Christ was also constricted by his baptism before it was perfected in his death. True baptism is nothing but conflict with sin through one's whole life. So the waters of adversity wash from the soul all the lasciviousness and lust which defile and cling to it.

The baptism by John with water[13] is incomplete and can free no one from sin, for it is only a symbol, a preparation, and a pattern of the true baptism in Christ (Acts 19[:4]). Therefore all of [the elect] had to be baptized differently, in Christ. For Christ enters [the soul] symbolically in baptism, in that he destroys his true form in favor of his true essence. Thus, Christ had to be baptized first, as an example for us, that in him everything came true. For in the death of Christ we are all members of one body in the equality of dying, which is consented to under the sign (Mark 15). As Paul says to the Romans, "You are all baptized in the baptism of Christ" (Romans 6[:3]). That is, in Christ's death, so that henceforth we look to Christ and receive true baptism from the father. Christ came to be baptized by John in order to humble himself beyond other men; to retake upon himself our proud nature which had deviated from God; and to make it obedient to God again through the baptism which he shows, and in which each must be baptized into a new creature through the killing of our evil, disobedient, insolent nature, in order to wash away all sin and human weakness. As Paul testifies, "You who are baptized in Christ have put on Christ." So everyone will live in Christ who dies to Adam (1 Peter 3[:21], Romans 5[:14], 1 Corinthians 15[:22]). But who does not want this baptism always remains in the dead Adam. Therefore baptism is a struggle to kill sin throughout one's whole life.

Now, whoever is pursued by Pharaoh – that is, all persecution, grief, fear, and need – and has the sea before him – that is, helplessness in the face of all creaturely things – and thinks that he has been abandoned by God, and finds nothing but death, this person has received real baptism, to which he consented symbolically before God and his community or people. The world absolutely does not desire

---

[13] I.e. the baptismal ceremony itself.

this baptism. Thus, baptism in its present state is a piece of villainy, one with which the whole world deceives itself and denies Christ. People do not want to let Christ work in them, nor allow the abode where he should live to be cleaned. Therefore everything is perverted, and there is no longer on earth a correct judgment about the secret of the divine commandments. Yes, we would all gladly find Christ and boast about it. But no one wants to suffer with him. Yes, if God's spirit were given to the world through pleasure and splendor, the world would be full of Christians. But Christ conceals himself beneath the flesh. And he only allows himself to be seen so that we notice him in the suffering of the greatest resignation, in which he shows himself to all his brothers. Only then does one find for the first time the goodness of God, which is the highest degree of divine justice and the beginning of divine mercy. Then the person becomes conformed to Christ, the crucified son of God – united with him who is totally and completely locked in us in one body. Then the person lives no longer, but Christ.

For this reason Christ says, "Whoever wants to be my disciple and wants to learn the potency and will of God, must let himself be disciplined by the father for his disobedience." And he must put the cross on his neck, as did Christ, and thus fulfill the will of God the father through suffering, as long as he deserves to suffer; and afterward he must realize the will of God through his actions. In no other way will Christ regard a man as his brother and God regard a man as his son. Christ the crucified has many members in this body and still is no member. Nevertheless every member bears the work or suffers, or consents to suffer, according to the model of the head [Christ]. Without this remedy, no one knows Christ; and in another way no one is known by Christ. This is the power of the father which makes us pleasing to him (Matthew 20). He calls this suffering the baptism in which he lets no brother or sister sink or be destroyed. Instead they should be made good in it, cleansed of all blemish, and made ready to receive the goodness of God, so that afterward they may be healed through the recognition of the divine will.

The whole world is repulsed and angered by the weakness of Christ. Yet no one can attain the sweet son of God unless he has previously tasted the bitter Christ in justification. For this reason the life of Christ is so bitter, his teaching so difficult, and his person so simple and dreadful that one may indeed say that he is blessed who is not angry with Christ. If lusts are few, then one does not remain long in the water of grief. Rather, the water becomes pure, clear, joyful, lovely, and translucent, so that one can accept the spirit of God in all its fullness in order to carry out the will of God. But we, like Christ, must be obedient to the father, so that in him and through him we assume the sin that is in us. For sin did not touch him because of his own person; he was most grievously troubled and his soul most terribly afflicted on account of our sin.

Matthew and Luke describe baptism of fire and spirit (Luke 12[:49f.]), and John of water and spirit (John 12). Mark describes it as neither fire nor water. God's spirit, which is called fire in Matthew and Luke, is what John terms the water of the holy spirit; so they all agree with each other. Water and fire in Scripture are tribulations; the sea is the world (1 Corinthians 10[:1f.]). Fire and water purify all things. All things are purified in time, be it through water or fire. What is soft and cannot take fire will be cleansed of impurities through water. But what is hard, like gold, silver, copper, iron, and tin will be melted by the fire and cleansed of additional elements. So the spirit of God appears to us in fire and water in opposite ways. Human reason, which is caught in these opposites, is found to obey, like Christ. Just as water removes what is impure and fire consumes all dross, cleanses and purifies from all extraneous elements, so the power of God does as well, as it works toward truth through the suffering of every grief. And whoever is in the water and does not want to listen to the voice of God must listen to it in the fire (Mark 9).

God pushes us into many kinds of tribulations, so that they sweep lusts out of us and lead us to indifference[14] to all worldly activities. Thus God helps us and uses us for his work, just as impure gold is of no use to a goldsmith until it has passed through fire and all its dross is burned and consumed. And what stands the test of fire becomes pure and good. For this reason God orders all disobedience to be thrown into the fire and its spirit transformed in flames. He tastes like fire, issues his commandments from fire (Exodus 19[:18] and 20[:18]) – and so calls himself a consuming fire which devours all things and in itself gives birth to all things (Deuteronomy 4[:24]). Therefore, he also wants no alien fire in his house as a sacrifice and burnt offering to him (Leviticus 10[1f.]). All living creatures prove this traditional say-

[14] *glassenheit* [= *Gelassenheit*], a mystical term for a state of calm toward the pleasures of the world.

ing about water and spirit. For all creatures on earth are first conceived and born in water. But if they remain in water, they must drown and rot.

Therefore, baptism has its time and goal and age, just as our first birth has its goal and time and also its age. And thus all creatures are born to their essence and perfection through water; and without baptism nothing is able to live fully and be blessed. Infant baptism, the practice of the existing world, is a pure invention of man, without the word and commandment of God. It is a defrauding of simple people, a pernicious trick on all Christendom, and an arch-villain's cloak for all the godless. For not a single verse in all of Scripture can be brought forth to defend it. Infant baptism is so totally without foundation that the godless must all remain silent about it, no matter how eloquent they wax. According to the words of Christ in the context of Scripture, no one should baptize another unless the baptized person is able, in passionate fidelity, to account for his faith and trust. If this sign of baptism is accepted, it points to the true baptism of suffering which follows, about which I have spoken and without which no one is able to be saved. But the contrived baptism of children is not only useless, it is also the greatest hindrance to truth.

11 Michael Sattler, *The Schleitheim Articles*
The brotherly agreement of some children of God concerning seven articles.[1]

Among all who love God and are children of light may there be joy, peace, and mercy from our father, through the atonement of the blood of Jesus Christ, together with the gifts of the spirit, who is sent by the father to all believers for their strength, consolation, and perseverance through every grief until the end, amen. These children of light are dispersed to all the places which God our father has ordained for them, and where they are assembled with one mind in one God and father of us all. May grace and peace exist in all your hearts, amen.

Beloved in the Lord, brothers and sisters,[2] our first and paramount concern is always what brings you consolation and a secure conscience, which has been misled previously. We are concerned about

---

[1] The work was the product of a conference held in February 1527 among Swiss and South German Anabaptists at Schleitheim, a small village northwest of Schaffhausen on the border between Switzerland and Germany; several individuals may have contributed to the document, which was written in the name of all who were in agreement on its contents. But the tradition, going back to the early 1530s, which credits Michael Sattler with being the principal framer of the work, has been confirmed by comparing the text with other writings which are known to be by Sattler. The work initially circulated in manuscript form; Zwingli first published parts of it in August 1527, in a Latin translation he prepared from four manuscript copies in order to refute the work. By 1533 at the latest, a vernacular version was published in a pamphlet containing other writings by and about Sattler. The translation is based on the text in *QGTS*, II, 26–35.

[2] Those addressed in the introductory cover letter to the articles are fellow radicals who have not accepted the strategy of nonresisting separatism which is set forth in the body of the work.

this so that you may not be separated from us forever, like foreigners, and almost completely excluded, as is just. We are concerned that you might turn, rather, to the truly implanted members of Christ, who are armed with patience and self-knowledge, and so that you may again be united with us in the power of one divine, Christian spirit and zeal for God.

It is also evident that the devil has slyly separated us through a thousand tricks, so that he might be able to destroy the work of God which has partly begun in us through God's mercy and grace. But the faithful shepherd of our souls, Christ, who has begun this work in us, will direct it until the end, and he will teach us, to his honor and our salvation, amen.

Dear brothers and sisters, we who are assembled together in the Lord at Schleitheim,[3] are making known through a series of articles to all who love God that, as far as we are concerned, we have agreed that we will abide in the Lord as obedient children of God, sons and daughters, and as those who are separated from the world – and who should be separated in all that they do and do not do.[4] And may God be praised and glorified in unity, without any brother contradicting this, but rather being happy with it. In doing this we have sensed that the unity of the father and our common Christ have been with us in spirit. For the Lord is the lord of peace and not of dissension, as Paul shows [1 Cor. 14:33]. You should note this and comprehend it, so that you understand in which articles this unity has been formulated.

Some false brothers among us have nearly introduced a great offense, causing some to turn away from the faith because they suppose they can lead a free life, using the freedom of the spirit and Christ.[5] But such people lack truth and are given over (to their condemnation) to the lasciviousness and freedom of the flesh. They have thought that faith and love may tolerate everything, and that nothing will damn them because they are such believing people.

Observe, you members of God in Christ Jesus, faith in the heavenly

---

[3] *Schlaten am Randen* – the term in local dialect for Schleitheim, a Swiss village a few miles north of Schaffhausen.

[4] Sattler briefly sets forth at this point the fundamental features of that wing of the radical Reformation of which he was a principal spokesman – the refusal to acknowledge the legitimacy of existing governments and the commitment to have as little as possible to do with the existing polity. This "separatism" entailed the effort to construct an alternative society.

[5] Sattler charged some among the radicals with being antinomians.

father through Jesus Christ does not take this form. It does not result in such things as these false brothers and sisters practice and teach. Protect yourselves and be warned about such people, for they do not serve our father, but their father, the devil.

But you are not this kind of people. For those who belong to Christ have crucified their flesh with all its lusts and desires. You certainly know what I mean and the brothers we are talking about. Separate yourselves from these brothers, for they are perverted. Ask the Lord that they acquire the knowledge to repent, and that we have the steadfastness to proceed along the path we have undertaken, following the honor of God and his son Christ. Amen.

The articles which we have discussed and about which we agree are these: baptism, the ban [excommunication], the breaking of bread [Lord's Supper], separating from the abomination [the existing polity], shepherds in the community [ministers], the sword, the oath, etc.[6]

First, concerning baptism, note this. Baptism should be given to all who have learned repentance, amendment of life, and faith through the truth that their sin has been removed by Christ; to all who want to walk in the resurrection of Jesus Christ and to be buried with him in death so that they can be resurrected with him; and to all who desire baptism in this sense from us and who themselves request it. Accordingly, all infant baptism, the greatest and first abomination of the pope, is excluded. You have the basis for this in the testimony of Scripture and the custom of the apostles. Matthew 28[:19]; Mark 16[:6]; Acts 2[:38], 8[:36]; 16[:31ff.], and 19[:4]. We wish to maintain this position on baptism simply, yet firmly.

Second. We have agreed as follows concerning the ban. The ban should be used against all who have given themselves to the Lord and agreed to follow his commandments, and who have been baptized into the one body of Christ, letting themselves be called brother or sister, and who nevertheless sometimes slip and fall into error and sin, and have been unknowingly overtaken. These people should be admonished twice privately and the third time should be punished or banned publicly, before the whole community, according to the command of Christ, Matthew 18[:15–18]. This banning should take

---

[6] Evidently among the issues where there was not agreement – and which were hence passed over in the work – was that of whether to pay taxes levied by the authorities.

place, according to the ordinance of the spirit [Mt. 5:23], before the breaking of bread, so that we are all of one mind, and in one love may break from one bread and eat and drink from one cup.

Third. We are agreed and united about the breaking of bread as follows. All who wish to break one bread in memory of the broken body of Christ, and all who wish to drink from one cup in memory of the blood that Christ shed, should previously be united in the one body of Christ – that is, God's community, of which Christ is the head – namely, through baptism. For as Paul shows [1 Cor. 10:21], we cannot simultaneously sit at the Lord's table and the devil's table. We cannot simultaneously drink from the Lord's cup and the devil's cup. That is, all who have fellowship with the dead works of darkness do not partake of the light. Thus, all who follow the devil and the world have nothing in common with those who are called out of the world to God. All who reside in evil have no part of what is good. And it must be thus. He who has not been called by one God to one faith, to one baptism, to one spirit, and to one body in the community of all the children of God, may not be made into one bread with them, as must be the case if one wants to break bread truly according to the command of Christ.

Fourth. Concerning separation, we have agreed that a separation should take place from the evil which the devil has planted in the world. We simply will not have fellowship with evil people, nor associate with them, nor participate with them in their abominations. That is, all who have not submitted themselves to the obedience of faith, and have not united themselves to God so that they want to do his will, are a great abomination before God. Since this is so, nothing but abominable things can issue from them. For there has never been anything in the world and among all creatures except good and evil, believing and unbelieving, darkness and light, the world and those who are out of the world, God's temple and idols, Christ and Belial, and neither may have anything to do with the other. And the commandment of the Lord is evident – he tells us to become separated from evil [2 Cor. 6:17]. In this way he wants to be our God, and we will be his sons and daughters. Further, he also admonishes us to withdraw from Babylon and worldly Egypt so that we will not participate in the suffering which the Lord will inflict upon them [Rev. 18:4ff.].

From all this we should learn that everything which is not united with our God and Christ is the abomination which we should flee. By this we mean all popish and neo-popish works and divine services,[7] assemblies, ecclesiastical processions, wine shops, the ties and obligations of lack of faith, and other things of this kind, which the world indeed regards highly but which are done in direct opposition to the commandments of God, as is the great injustice in the world. We should leave all these things and have nothing to do with them, for they are vain abominations which make us hated by our Christ Jesus, who has liberated us from the servitude of the flesh and made us suitable for service to God through the spirit, which he has given us.

Thus, the devilish weapons of force will fall from us, too, such as the sword, armor and the like, and all their uses on behalf of friends or against enemies; [such nonviolence is commanded] by the power of the words of Christ, "You should not resist evil" [Mt. 5:39].

Fifth. We have agreed as follows concerning the shepherds in the community of God [i.e. ministers]. According to Paul's prescription [1 Tim. 3:7], the shepherd in God's community should be one who has a completely good reputation among those who are outside the faith. His duties[8] should be to read, to admonish, to teach, to warn, and to punish or ban in the community; to lead all sisters and brothers in prayer and in breaking bread; and to make sure that in all matters that concern the body of Christ, the community is built up and improved. He should do this so that the name of God is praised and honored among us, and the mouths of blasphemers are stopped.

Should this pastor be in need, he should be provided for by the community that chose him, so that he who serves the gospel should also live from it, as the Lord has ordained [1 Cor. 9:14]. But if a shepherd should do something requiring punishment, he should not be tried except on the testimony of two or three people. If they sin [by testifying falsely], they should be punished in front of everybody so that others are afraid.

But if a shepherd is banished or through the cross [execution] brought to the Lord, another should be ordained in his place immediately so that God's little people are not destroyed, but maintained and consoled by the warning.

Sixth. Concerning the sword[9] we have reached the following agree-

---

[7] I.e. those of both Roman Catholics and magisterial reformers.

[8] *ampt = Amt*, office; i.e. any ordained position with defined functions and responsibilities.

[9] I.e. civil government's power to employ instruments of coercion. Except for the first

ment. The sword is ordained by God outside the perfection of Christ. It punishes and kills evil people and protects and defends the good. In the law the sword is established to punish and to kill the wicked, and secular authorities are established to use it. But in the perfection of Christ the ban alone will be used to admonish and expel him who has sinned, without putting the flesh to death, and only by using the admonition and the command to sin no more.

Now, many who do not recognize what Christ wills for us will ask whether a Christian may also use the sword against evil people for the sake of protecting the good or for the sake of love. Our unanimous answer is as follows: Christ teaches us to learn from him that we should be mild and of humble heart, and in this way we will find rest for our souls. Now, Christ says to the woman taken in adultery [Jn. 8:11], not that she should be stoned according to the law of his father (yet he says, "As the father has commanded me, thus I do" [Jn. 8:22]), but that she should be dealt with in mercy and forgiveness and with a warning to sin no more. And Christ says, "Go and sin no more." We should also hold to this in our laws, according to the rule about the ban.

Secondly, it is asked about the sword, whether a Christian may pass judgment in worldly quarrels and conflicts at law such as unbelievers have with one another. This is the answer: Christ did not want to decide or judge between brother and brother concerning an inheritance, and he refused to do so [Lk. 12:13]. Thus, we should do likewise.

Thirdly, it is asked about the sword, whether a Christian may hold a position of governmental authority if he is chosen for it. This is our reply: Christ should have been made a king, but he rejected this [Jn. 6:15] and did not view it as ordained by his father. We should do likewise and follow him. In this way we will not walk into the snares of darkness. For Christ says, "Whoever wants to follow me should deny himself and take up his cross and follow me" [Mt. 16:24]. Also, Christ himself forbids the violence of the sword and says, "Worldly princes rule," etc., "but not you" [Mt. 20:25]. Further, Paul says, "Those whom God foresaw, he also ordained that they should be equal to the model of his son," etc. [Rom. 8:30]. Also Peter says,

point in the discussion of this article – that God has ordained the sword to punish evildoers – Sattler's treatment of the sword stands in direct contrast to that of Balthasar Hubmaier's *On the Sword*.

"Christ has suffered, not ruled, and he gave us a model, so that you shall follow in his footsteps" [1 Pet. 2:21].

Lastly, it should be pointed out that it is not fitting for a Christian to be a magistrate for these reasons: the authorities' governance is according to the flesh, but the Christian's is according to the spirit. Their houses and dwellings remain in this world, but the Christian's are in heaven. Their citizenship is of this world, but the Christian's is in heaven. Their weapons of conflict and war are carnal and only directed against the flesh, but the Christian's weapons are spiritual and directed against the fortifications of the devil. Worldly people are armed with spikes and iron, but Christians are armed with the armor of God – with truth, with justice, with peace, faith, and salvation, and with the word of God. In sum, what Christ, our head, thought, the members of the body of Christ through him should also think, so that no division of the body [of the faithful] may triumph through which it would be destroyed. Now, as Christ is – as is written about him – so too must the members be, so that his body may remain whole and united for its own benefit and edification.

Seventh. We have reached agreement as follows concerning the oath [i.e. swearing oaths]. The oath is a confirmation among those who are quarreling or making promises. And it has been ordained in the [Mosaic] Law that it should take place truthfully and not falsely, in the name of God alone. Christ, who teaches the perfection of the law, forbids his followers all swearing, either truthfully or falsely, either in the name of heaven or of earth or of Jerusalem or by our own head [Mt. 5:34f.]. And he does this for the reason which he gives afterward: "For you are not able to make a single hair white or black." Notice this! All swearing has been forbidden because we cannot fulfill what is promised in swearing. For we are not able to alter the slightest thing about ourselves.

Now, there are some who do not believe God's simple command. They speak as follows and ask, "Did God not swear to Abraham on his own godhead when he promised that he wished him well and wanted to be his God, if he would keep his commandments? Why should I not swear also when I promise somebody something?"

Our answer is this. Listen to what Scripture says. Because God wanted to prove conclusively to the heirs of the promise that his counsel does not waver, he sealed it with an oath, so that we could rely on the consolation received through two unwavering things [i.e. the promise and the oath; Heb.6:17f.] about which it is impossible for God to lie. Note the meaning of this passage of Scripture: "God has the power to do that which he forbids you. For all things are possible for him" [Mt. 29:26, Mk. 10:27]. God swore an oath to Abraham (Scripture says) in order to prove that his counsel never wavered. That is, no one can resist or hinder his will, and so he was able to keep the oath. But, as has been said above by Christ, we can do nothing to keep or fulfill an oath. Therefore we should not swear at all.

Some now say further, "In the New Testament it is forbidden by God to swear; but it is actually commanded in the Old, and there it is only forbidden to swear by heaven, earth, Jerusalem, and by our head." Our answer is this. Listen to Scripture – "He who swears by the temple of heaven swears by the throne of God and by him who sits on it" [Mt. 23:22]. Notice that it is forbidden to swear by heaven, which is a throne of God. How much more is it forbidden to swear by God himself? You fools and blind people, which is greater, the throne or he who sits on it?

Some say further, "Why is it now unjust to use God as a witness to the truth, when the apostles Peter and Paul have sworn?" Our answer is that Peter and Paul testify only to that which God promised Abraham through the oath. And they themselves promised nothing, as the examples clearly show. For testifying and swearing are two different things. When a person swears, in the first place he makes a promise about future things, as Christ – whom we received a long time later – was promised to Abraham. But when a person testifies, he is testifying about the present, whether it is good or evil, as Simon spoke to Mary about Christ and testified to her, "This child is ordained for the fall and resurrection of many in Israel, and as a sign which will be rejected" [Lk. 2:34]. Christ has also taught us this same thing when he said, "Your speech should be 'yea' or 'nay' for anything else comes from evil" [Mt. 5:37]. Christ says, "Your speech or words should be 'yea' or 'nay'," so that none can understand it in the sense that he has permitted swearing. Christ is simply "yea" and "nay" and all who seek him in simplicity will understand his word. Amen.

Dear brothers and sisters in the lord,

These are the articles about which some brothers have previously been in error and have understood differently from the true understanding. The consciences of many people have been confused through this, as a result of which the name of God has been greatly blasphemed. Therefore it has been necessary for us to reach agreement in the Lord, and this has happened. May God be praised and glorified!

Now, because you have amply understood the will of God, which has now been set forth through us, it will be necessary for you to realize the will of God, which you have recognized, perseveringly and without interruption. For you know well what reward the servant deserves who knowingly sins.

Everything that you have done unknowingly or that you have confessed to having done unjustly is forgiven you through the faithful prayer which is performed by us in our assembly for all our failures and our guilt, through the merciful forgiveness of God and through the blood of Jesus Christ. Amen.

Beware of all who do not walk in the simplicity of the divine truth which is encompassed in this letter from us in our assembly. Do this so that everyone among us may be subject to the rule of the ban, and so that henceforth false brothers and sisters may be prevented from joining us.

Separate yourselves from that which is evil. Then the Lord will be your God, and you will be his sons and daughters.

Dear brothers, keep in mind how Paul admonished Titus. He said this: "The saving grace of God has appeared to all. And it disciplines us so that we shall deny ungodly things and worldly lusts and shall live chastely, justly, and piously in this world. And we shall await our same hope, the appearance of the majesty of the great God and our savior, Jesus Christ, who gave himself to redeem us from all injustice, and to purify a people as his own who would be zealous for good works" [Tit. 2:11–14]. If you think about this and practice it, the lord of peace will be with you.

May the name of God be eternally blessed and highly praised, Amen. May the Lord give you his peace. Amen.

Enacted at Schleitheim on St. Matthew's day [24 February] in the year 1527.

12   Balthasar Hubmaier, *On the Sword*

On the sword. A Christian explanation of the Scriptures which are cited very earnestly by some brothers against government – that is, that Christians should not occupy positions of power or wield the sword.

Dr. Balthasar Hubmaier of Friedberg. 1527[1]

To the noble and Christian lord, Sir Arkleb of Bozkowic and Tzerne-hor at Trebitz, Chancellor of the Margravate of Moravia, my merciful lord.[2] I wish you grace and peace in God.

[1] The work was printed at Nikolsburg in Moravia by Simprecht Sorg (Froschauer) of Basel, who came to Nikolsburg with Hubmaier in the summer of 1526. Hubmaier became pastor of a German congregation at Nikolsburg at the invitation of Leonhard von Liechtenstein, the lord of the city. Hubmaier wrote the work in June 1527 as division arose within the Anabaptist community at Nikolsburg concerning whether Christians could rightfully participate in government and use instruments of force. The translation is based on the text in Gunnar Westin and Torsten Bergsten, eds., *Balthasar Hubmaier, Schriften* (Gütersloh, 1962), 434–57.

[2] With the death of Louis II, king of Hungary and Bohemia, at the battle of Mohács in 1526, the margravate of Moravia and his other possessions passed into the hands of the Habsburg dynasty as a result of the marriage of Louis's sister to Ferdinand of Habsburg (later Emperor Ferdinand I). Hence Arkleb of Bozkovic, to whom the work is dedicated and who had been chancellor of Moravia since 1519, was an important official in the new Habsburg government. Despite Hubmaier's claim in the dedication that he had never advocated sedition, in March 1528 Hubmaier was burned at the stake in Vienna by Ferdinand's government, ostensibly for earlier radical activities against Habsburg rule while he was pastor at Waldshut.

Noble, merciful lord, your grace probably knows well that all those who accept, love and preach the holy gospel in these last and dangerous times must not only be deprived of goods and tortured in body (Matthew 5[:11f.]);³ even their honor, which people regard as the most precious jewel on earth, must also be wounded and violated by the godless. Precisely these things are the weapons of hellish Satan, through which he unceasingly tries to suppress, root out and hinder evangelical teaching and truth. But he will not succeed. His head must be crushed because of that. Especially now, the servants of the devil must call all Christian preachers rebels, demagogues, and heretics on the grounds that they repudiate authority and teach disobedience. But this is not a cause for wonder. The same thing also happened to Christ (Luke 23[:2], Jeremiah 38[:4], 1 Kings 18), although he publicly taught that one should "render to Caesar that which is Caesar's" (Matthew 22[:21]), just as he paid the tax for himself and for Peter (Matthew 17[:24]). Nevertheless he had to suffer a flogging by the blasphemers, for they denounced him as a rebel and charged him with inciting [to rebellion] the people, whom he was supposed to have forbidden to pay tax money to the emperor (Matthew 17[:24]). If such things happen to us now, what difference does it make? For the servant is not greater than the lord, nor the disciple greater than the master (Matthew 10[:25]). If they have blasphemed the father of the household, they will do such things to us to an even greater extent.

I have composed a small booklet in which I am making known my views to your grace and to everybody else, so that your grace may recognize and know what opinions and views I have had, always and everywhere, concerning the authorities, as I preached these views publicly from the pulpit at Waldshut and elsewhere,⁴ wrote about them, and often taught them. And [I have also written] so that you may know how very much I have suffered on account of this (without boasting). Although my detractors put out many different stories about me, their stories lack truth. And in this work I will refute all the

---

³ Scriptural citations enclosed here in parentheses appear as marginal references in the original; marginal comments to the body of the text have also been changed to parenthetical remarks.

⁴ In the spring of 1521 Hubmaier became pastor at Waldshut, near Zurich; during the summer of 1522 he joined the evangelical movement and corresponded with Zwingli in Zurich. Shortly thereafter he introduced a German liturgy in Waldshut, abolished fasting regulations, and married. During the Peasants' War, which began in Upper Germany in the nearby county of Stühlingen, the city of Waldshut made a treaty for mutual assistance and protection with the rebellious peasants.

pamphlets which my opponents up till now have earnestly deployed and used against me in order to reject authority among Christians.

(I have dealt more seriously with Scripture's treatment of pious authority than any preacher for twenty miles around. But I have also shown tyrants their vices, from which arise jealousy, hate, and enmity.)

May your grace graciously accept such a tract from me, and briefly note my sentiments concerning Christian government according to the content of Scripture. And may you note that I desire in this and all my other teachings and deeds what is just and right. If I am mistaken, I will very gladly allow myself to be reprimanded and punished. (A fair offer. 1 Peter 3.) But only if previous testimony of my evil has been found in Scripture. And if I am not mistaken, why then am I beaten? What am I accused of? But if my opponents, of whom I have as many as the old serpent [the devil] has scales, do not concede that I am right, then that is a problem they have with God. If my God and lord can tolerate their crimes and violence to his word, then I must tolerate them too. But not, God be praised, as an evildoer! (1 Peter 4[:15]). Let each one judge here as he would like to be judged by the Lord. So be it! If because of our sins it is the will of God, then it should and must also please my will – even if it be against my will. With this writing I bow down in all submissive service for all time to your grace as my especially gracious lord. May your grace live well in Jesus Christ. Given at Nikolsburg on 24 June 1527.

Your obedient Balthasar Hubmaier of Friedberg.

On the sword

The first passage[5]

Christ said to Pilate, "My kingdom is not of this world. If it were of this world, without a doubt my servants would fight for me, so that I would not be delivered to the Jews," John 18[:36].

---

[5] The work takes the form of an analysis of fifteen passages from Scripture which were cited by some among Hubmaier's fellow radicals to support the view that Christians should not participate in secular government. In part as a result of the influence of Hans Hut, who was in Nikolsburg in the spring of 1527, the radical community at Nikolsburg began to polarize into two camps which were later designated the "people of the staff" (*Stäbler*) – i.e. nonresisting separatists – and the "people of the sword" (*Schwertler*), who approved the use of coercion or the sword by Christians holding civil office. Hubmaier's tract was a defense of the second position. It is not clear that Hubmaier was aware of the development among the Swiss Brethren at this time of a position very similar to that of the *Stäbler*; this position was set forth in Michael Sattler's *The Schleitheim Articles*.

Concerning this passage some brothers say, "If the kingdom of the Christians is not of this world, a Christian may not wield the sword." To this I answer: if such people would really open their eyes, they would have to say something very different, namely that our kingdom should not be of this world. But unfortunately – may we complain about it to God – it is of this world, as we confess in the "Our Father," where we pray, "Father, thy kingdom come" (Matthew 6[:10]). For we are in the kingdom of the world, which is a kingdom of sin, death, and hell (Luke 11[:2]). But, father, help us out of this kingdom. We are immersed in it over our ears and here on earth we can never be independent of it. It clings to us until death. Lord, release us from this evil and help us to come home to your kingdom.

Such brothers now see the truth and must admit that our kingdom is of this world, which should grieve our hearts. But Christ alone could truly say, "My kingdom is not of this world," since he was conceived and born without sin, an innocent lamb, in whom there is no deception and who is without sin or stain. And he alone could also truly say, "The prince of this world, the devil, has come but found no evil in me" (John 14[:30]). We here on earth could never truthfully say this. For as often as the prince comes – the devil – he finds in us evil lusts, evil desires, and evil inclinations. For this reason St. Paul, while filled with the holy spirit, also calls himself unholy (Romans 7[:24]). Thus, the most pious and godly Christians must also confess that they are unsaved until their death. May God help us to make something of our lives.

The second passage

Jesus says to Peter, "Put up your sword, for he who takes up the sword shall die by the sword. Do you think that I could not request my father to send me more than twelve legions of angels? But how then could Scripture be fulfilled? It must take place so," Matthew 26[:53f.].

Pay sharp attention here, pious Christian, to the words of Christ, and then you will already have an answer to the accusation of the brothers. First Christ says, "Put up your sword." It is not proper for you to wield it.[6] You are not in power. You have not been commanded

---

[6] The following remarks are a repudiation of the commoners' use of violence during the Peasants' War.

to use it. You have been neither called upon nor elected to use it. For he who takes up the sword shall die by the sword. They perish by the sword who use it without being elected, who are disorderly, and who use it without rules and in the service of their own arbitrariness. And no one should take up the sword unless he has been elected and thus required to do so. For then he himself does not take up the sword, but it is brought to him and given to him. Then he can say, "I have not taken up the sword. I would rather be without it, for I myself am most deserving of punishment. But since I have been called to use it, I bid God to grant me grace and to lend me wisdom so that I may wield it and govern according to his word and will." So Solomon prayed, and God gave him great wisdom to wield the sword in the right way (1 Kings 3[:6ff.]).

In addition, in this passage you hear that Christ says to Peter, "Put your sword in its sheath." He does not say, "Get rid of it and throw it away." For Christ rebuked him because he drew it, not because he had a sword at his side. Otherwise, if it were wrong to carry it, he would have rebuked him long before. In addition, the following part of the text says that he who takes up the sword shall die by the sword. That is, he has fallen to the judgment of the sword, even if he is not always executed by the sword for just reasons. Notice here how Christ confirms the sword, with which one should punish those who pursue their own arbitrary power and crime. And those who have been elected for it should do this punishing, whoever they may be. Thus it is evident that the more pious rulers are, the better and more justly will they wield the sword according to the will of God, to protect the innocent and to induce fear in evildoers. God has appointed and ordained them for this reason (Romans 13[:1f.]).

Thirdly, there is what Christ said to his disciples when they wanted to prevent him from going to Jerusalem. For the Jews wanted to stone him at once. Christ said, "There are not twelve hours in the day" (John 11[:9]). As if he wanted to say, "They will not kill me until the twelfth hour comes – that is, the hour that God has ordained for my death," which Christ also calls "the hour of darkness" (Luke 22[:55]). But when this same twelfth hour had come, Christ himself said to his disciples on the Mount of Olives, "Arise and let us go down. The hour is here in which I shall be given over to death, so that the Scriptures are fulfilled" (Matthew 26[:46]). Note this! Peter hears that the hour has come which had been determined and ordained by

God, yet he wanted to prevent it, and he drew his sword on his own authority. That was the greatest error. Therefore Christ said, "No protection or defense is of use any longer. The hour decided by God is here, and even if twelve legions of angels were here, they would not be able to help me against the will of God, my heavenly father. So put away your sword. It is useless. I told you before that the hour has come. Scripture shall and must be fulfilled."

Here every Christian learns that a person should not cease protecting and guarding all pious and innocent people, as long as he is not certain that the hour of their death has arrived. But when the hour comes, whether you know it or not, no protection or defense is then able to help. Therefore the authorities are bound, on the salvation of their souls, to protect and defend all innocent and peaceful people until a definite voice comes from God clearly saying, "You should no longer protect this person." Abraham heard such a voice, telling him that he should kill his son, contrary to the commandment, "Thou shalt not kill" (Genesis 22[:2], Exodus 20[:13]). Thus, the authorities are responsible for protecting and liberating all oppressed and coerced people, widows and orphans – whether familiar to them or strangers – without regard to the person, according to the will and earnest commandment of God. Isaiah 1, Jeremiah 21 and 22, Romans 13, and in many other places. They must do this until they are called by God to do something different, for which they must wait a long time. For this reason God has hung the sword at their side and ordered them to be his handmaidens[7] (Romans 13[:4]).

The third passage

"Lord, if you wish it, we will say, 'May fire fall from heaven and consume them,' as Elijah did." But Jesus turned to them and rebuked them and said, "You do not know of what spirit you are. The son of man did not come to destroy men's souls but to save them," Luke 9[:54f.].

About this my brothers make a great outcry, as though Lucifer were there, and they say, "There, Balthasar, you see that Christ did not

---

[7] *dienerin*; i.e. the ordained wielders of the sword are designated as females. This is not consistent with the patriarchal foundation for secular authority that Hubmaier presents below in the seventh passage, where he ascribes the establishment of civil authority to the power which God gave Adam over Eve after their expulsion from the Garden of Eden.

want to punish them with fire. And so we should not do it either. And we should use neither fire nor water, neither sword nor gallows. I answer: Look, dear brothers, at the reason Christ came to earth, and at what office[8] and orders God gave him. As you do so, also think about what the office of a superior is. If you do this, you have already accepted the answer. Christ came, as he himself said, not to judge people, not to condemn or to punish them with fire, water or sword. He did not become man for this. But it was his command and office to make people blessed with the word. This was the office he carried out, and to do so he had become man. Thus he himself says in Luke 12[:14], "Who has elected me to be a judge between you and your brother?" As if he had wanted to say, "Go find another judge. I did not come here to interfere with the office and commands of other people." On the contrary, God has given office and orderly command to the authorities, so that they should protect and guard the pious and punish and kill the wicked (Romans 13[:4]). He hung the sword at their sides for that reason. But why is it there if there is no need to use it? Now, God always punishes the wicked, sometimes with hail, rain, and sickness, and sometimes through special people, who have been ordained and elected for this. Therefore Paul calls the authorities handmaidens of God. For what God can do himself he often prefers to do through his creatures as his tools.

Yes, and although sometimes the devil, Nebuchadnezzar, and other evil people are also called the servants of God in Scripture, it is a very different matter for an orderly governmental authority to punish those who disobey the commandments of God, for the good of the pious and innocent. But the devil and his band do nothing for the good or peace of people and everything to injure and harm them, in a jealous and vengeful spirit. But the authorities feel a special sympathy with all who have committed misdemeanors. They wish from their heart that it had not happened. But the devil and his followers wish that all people were miserable. Here you see, brothers, how far apart from one another these two kinds of service are, that of the devil and that of the ordained authorities, as well as how Christ wanted to do enough on earth through his office. In just this way we should fulfill our duty and calling, be it authority or obedience, for we must give God an account of it on Judgment Day.

[8] *ambt = Amt*, office in the sense of an official or established position, with its own specific functions and responsibilities.

The fourth passage

"One of the people spoke to the Lord, 'Master, tell my brother to divide his inheritance with me.' But he said to him, 'Man, who appointed me to be a judge or executor over you?' " Luke 12[:13f.].

At these words my brothers cry to high heaven, but too loudly, saying, "Do you hear it, Friedberger?[9] Christ too does not want to be a judge or executor. Courts and governing councils are rejected by Christ. Accordingly, Christians should never judge, nor sit in a council, nor wield the sword, for Christ too did not want to issue judgments nor to act as a judge between the two brothers." The answer is this: stop crying, dear brothers. You do not know Scripture; so you err and do not recognize what you are crying about. Christ says, "Man, who has set me as a judge over you?" Thus, he wanted to say, "I have not been elected or appointed a judge. This is not my office. It belongs to others." Notice here that Christ does not reject the office of judge, for it is not to be rejected, as will be shown shortly in what follows. Rather, he shows that no one should set himself up as a judge unless he has been called and elected to be one. The elections of mayors, village mayors, and judges are part of this. Christ permits them all to remain, so that they are able to rule and judge well in temporal and physical matters, with God and according to their best judgment. But he did not want to accept such offices himself. He did not become man for this reason, neither was he appointed for this purpose. In the same way, no one should use the sword unless he has been properly elected to do so (Exodus 2[:12]), or called by God in another way, as was Moses between the Israelites and the Egyptians (Genesis 14[:14ff.]), and Abraham when he saved his brothers Lot and Phineas from the fornicators (Numbers 26[:7–9]).

The fifth passage

"If someone wants to quarrel with you in a court and take your shirt, let him also have your coat," Matthew 5[:40].

---

[9] Hubmaier himself, who was a native of Friedberg, a small community close to Augsburg.

The sixth passage

"That you have lawsuits with one another is already a mistake. Why do you not prefer to suffer injustice? Why do you not prefer to suffer harm and cheating, rather than to inflict injustice and cheating? And this you do to your brothers," 1 Corinthians 6[:7f.].

The brothers cite these two passages in such an exalted and fearful way, as if they believed that they should offer to be burned for them: A Christian cannot be a judge. So be it. Let us search the Scriptures, and then we will find the right orientation. First, we confess that lawsuits, disputes, conflicts, and quarrels before a council or court because of temporal goods which one seeks for himself are not right, as the two passages cited above plainly show. (Quarreling at law is unjust.) But this is not to say that if both parties want a legal judgment, a Christian cannot without sin be a judge and pronounce a decision between them. Therefore let us judge this according to the sixth chapter of Paul's first epistle to the Corinthians. (A Christian can certainly be a judge.) Paul writes thus: "How dare anyone among you, if he has a legal dispute with another, allow himself to be judged by the unjust and not by the saints – that is, by Christians? Do you not know that the saints will judge the world? But if the world is to be judged by you, are you not then good enough to judge lesser matters? Do you not know that you will judge the angels? Should you not then be more capable of judging matters of temporal life? If you now have lawsuits about temporal sustenance, take the most despised people in the community and appoint them to be judges. To your shame I say this. Is there not a wise man among you, or one who is able to judge between brother and brother? Instead a brother who has litigation with another lets himself be judged, and in addition by unbelievers?"

Listen to what Paul says at this point – precisely here – dear brothers, and pay attention. If Christians ever seek to go to court about matters of sustenance – that is, about temporal goods – which is already wrong, then this should take place before a Christian judge and not before an unbeliever. Note this, brothers. You have overlooked this. If Christians ever seek to go to law and are not at peace with one another, they sin still more, indeed they sin doubly if they allow a decision to be pronounced by an unbelieving judge, not a Christian. For this reason Paul mocks the Corinthians and says that, if they ever want to go to court, they should appoint the most despised among them as the judges. He tells them this to shame them. It is as though they had no pious and wise Christians among them who were capable of pronouncing judgment between them, and instead had to go to an unbelieving judge. They should be most ashamed.

Even a blind man can see that a Christian may certainly, and with a good conscience, sit in a court and in a council, and also judge and pronounce judgment in temporal matters. Although the quarrelers and disputers sin, they sin still more if they take their litigation before an unbelieving judge. And if a Christian may thus issue an oral judgment in the power of the divine word, he may also protect him who wins the case, and he may punish the unjust. For what use are laws, courts, and judges if there is no need to carry out punishment on the evildoer? Why do we have shoes, if we dare not put them on? Do you see, dear brothers, that councils, courts, and laws are not unjust? And that the judge may and should be a Christian, even though the quarreling parties sin in not preferring to be cheated? Therefore, according of God's order a Christian certainly may wield the sword, as a representative of God, over the evildoer and punish him. Because there are evildoers, it has thus been ordained by God for the protection and defense of pious people, Romans 13[:3–4]. Scripture really intends this when it states, "You judges, watch what you do! Your office is not from man but from God. You will be judged by your judgments. Therefore, may the fear of God be with you. And you should act diligently, for God cannot see and suffer injustice," 2 Chronicles 19[:6–7]. This passage has been given to us as well as to the ancient Jews, for it concerns brotherly love.

You will answer, "Granted, but one should not judge." My reply is: yes, and one should not wrong another. But if this happens among Christians, then a Christian judge should be employed, who issues just decisions to citizens and foreigners alike. This must happen or Scripture must fall apart, and nobody can ever topple it for me.

The seventh passage

"If your brother sins against you, go and rebuke him alone. If he listens to you, you have won your brother. If he does not listen to you, take one or two others with you, so that everything depends on the oral testimony of two or three. If he does not listen to them, then tell it to the community. If he does not listen to the community, regard him as a heathen and a tax collector," Matthew 18[:15–17].

On the basis of this text my brothers bring a serious charge against me. They say, "If authorities should exist among Christians, the Christian ban[10] would be in vain and destroyed. For where evildoers are punished with the sword, the church cannot use the ban." I reply that the ban and the sword are two different commands which God has given. The first was promised and given to the church by Christ – Matthew 10 and 18, John 20[:23] – for use in admitting the pious into its holy society and excluding the immoral, according to its will. (Banning is the office of the church.) Thus, the sins of people whom the Christian church forgives on earth are already forgiven them in heaven as well. And the sins of those whom the church does not forgive here on earth, they are not forgiven in heaven.

Christ entrusted his power to loosen and to bind – to the full extent that he received it from the father – to his spouse, the Christian church, in his bodily absence,[11] so that in the meantime the Christian church might and should teach people everything that Christ commanded it to teach. And so that the church might have the power to designate with water baptism[12] all people who accept its teachings, believe them, and want to guide and conduct their lives thereafter according to these teachings; and to enroll and accept these people into its holy community. For everything that the church commands here on earth is immediately created and done, permitted and excluded in heaven as well, until Christ, its bridegroom, descends again in physical and visible form, in his glory and majesty, and enters his kingdom in person. Only then will he hand it over to his heavenly father, so that God, as Paul writes, may be all in all (1 Corinthians 15[:28]). Precisely this is the secret in Christ and in his church, according to the content of the epistle to the Ephesians 5[:32].

The other command of God concerns external and temporal power and government, which was initially given by God to Adam after the fall, when God said to Eve, "You shall be under man's authority, and

---

[10] I.e. the ecclesiastical penalty of expulsion from the community of Christians – regarding the evildoer "as a heathen and a tax collector."

[11] I.e. until the Second Coming.

[12] I.e. the baptismal ceremony, as opposed to the internal baptism of the spirit. Hut's *On the Mystery of Baptism* examines the difference between the two.

he will rule over you." (Wielding the sword is the office of the authorities, Genesis 3[:16].) Now, if God set Adam in authority over Eve, he also received power over all flesh and blood that has been borne by Eve in pain. Likewise, God afterward bestowed the sword on, and gave commands to other special and godfearing people, such as Abraham, Moses, Joshua, Gideon, and Samuel. But afterward the evil of people became still more powerful and violent – indeed it became so prevalent that the people then desired a king from Samuel and rejected God (1 Samuel 8[:5]). At God's command Samuel also gave them this king. And thereby they became responsible for bearing all the royal privileges, burdens, and services that they owed the king from that time on, because they despised and rejected God and wanted a king, like other nations, who would be determined by Samuel and not by God. We must and should endure and bear willingly such services and grievances down to the present. And we must also give tribute to whom tribute is due, customs fees to whom customs are due, fear to whom fear is due, and honor to whom honor is due (Romans 13[:7]). For our sins are responsible for this, just as the sin of Eve is responsible for her having to bear children in pain, and as the sin of Adam is for his having to earn his bread by the sweat of his brow (Genesis 3[:16f.]). For if we had remained pious and obedient to God, there would have been no need for us to have either law, sword, fire, stocks, or gallows. But since we have sinned, it must be so, and neither insurrection nor anything else on earth is able to help us. For God's word is "yes" and not "no" (2 Corinthians 1[:19f.]). But if we heap disobedience upon disobedience and multiply sin by sin, God in his wrath will give us kings and children as our princes. Indeed, he will let suffragan bishops rule over us.[13] And if we try to flee Rehoboam, we shall fall into the hands of Jeroboam. All this happens on account of our sins, according to the common and true proverb, "As is the people, so too is the king." A stork ate up the frogs who did not want to acknowledge the harmless wooden block as king, according to Aesop's fable.[14] Accordingly it is highly necessary, oh you pious Christians, to ask almighty God with great diligence and earnest devotion for pious, just, and Christian authorities here on earth, so that we can lead a peaceful and quiet life in all blessedness

---

[13] Perhaps a reference to the many prince-bishops in the Holy Roman Empire who held temporal as well as spiritual power.

[14] The same fable is referred to in *To the Assembly of the Common Peasantry*.

and honesty among one another. When God gives us these authorities, we ought to accept them with special thanksgiving. But if he does not give them to us, then it is obviously and certainly true that we are not worthy of other or better authorities on account of our sins. The Old Testament of the Bible shows us many historical examples and testimonies of this.

Do you see now, dear brothers, that these two offices and commands, the ban and the external sword, are not opposed to one another, since they are both from God? For often the Christian ban has authority, namely in many private sins in which the sword cannot always be used. The punishment should be according to the circumstances of the sin. Christ teaches us this most clearly (John 8[:10f.]) when he asks the adulterous woman, "Woman, has no one condemned you?" She says, "No one, Lord." He says, "Then neither will I condemn you. Go and sin no more."

Notice that Christ asks, "Woman, has no one condemned you?" As though he had said: If you were judged according to the law that God proclaimed for adultery, I would say nothing to the judge, for it is the command of God my father that adulterers be stoned to death. But since no one has condemned you, neither will I condemn you, for this is not my office. I have not been appointed to be a judge but a savior. Therefore, go and sin no more. It is my office to forgive sin, and my command that henceforth people beware of sin. Do you hear this, dear brothers? How Christ executes his office so properly, and nevertheless allows the value of the judicial office to remain? Thus, the church with its ban and the authorities with their sword can proceed side by side, without either infringing on the office of the other.

The eighth passage

"You have heard that it has been said, 'An eye for an eye and a tooth for a tooth.' But I say to you that you should not resist evil. Rather, if someone strikes you on your right cheek, offer him the other one," Matthew 5[:38f.], Luke 6[:27–29].

The brothers cite this passage in such a high-handed way that they mean to unbuckle the sword from authorities who want to be Christians. But proceed slowly, do not be too hasty, dear friends, and listen. We want to deal with the passage correctly. "You have heard that it has been said" – obviously in the Old Testament – "An eye for an eye and a tooth for a tooth" (Leviticus 24[:20], Deuteronomy 19[:21]). Thus, if one were to accuse another before a judge of having knocked out his eye or one of his teeth – when such accusations were allowed the ancient Jews, as you find in Deuteronomy 1 – the judge had to hear the complaint and testimony; then he had to judge [according to the principle of] an eye for an eye and a tooth for a tooth, according to the law of God. But it should not happen in this way according to the New Testament. Rather, if someone strikes you on the right cheek, do not accuse him, do not go to a judge, do not desire revenge as did the ancient Jews, to whom such accusations were permitted. Instead, offer the other cheek as well (Matthew 5[:39]). For to accuse is always forbidden to Christians, as you have heard, 1 Corinthians 6[:1.7]. If you now suffer and do not resist, you act correctly, for Christ has taught each one to act particularly in this way. But this does not mean that the sword of the authorities has been unbuckled. On the contrary, the authorities are commanded – if they become aware of such arbitrariness or crime on their own or through other people – to protect the pious and to punish the wicked with the sword. They have been ordained as handmaidens of God to bring peace to good people and fear to evil ones. In this way they carry out the will of God.

Likewise, although two quarrelers about temporal goods sin in going before a judge, a Christian judge nevertheless does not sin when he judges the quarrel correctly. Thus, even if no one makes an accusation, but if the authorities know that someone has done violence and injustice to another, they should still carry out their ordained office, decide justly, and punish the evildoer. For they do not bear the sword in vain. In this sense there is a higher standard in the New Testament than in the Old: the one who has been insulted and damaged does not complain, and nonetheless the authorities punish the evildoer. In the Old Testament the plaintiff makes the accusation, and the judge punishes. Look, dear brothers, you must let Romans 13[:3–4] remain valid, where stand the above-mentioned words of Christ, for in this way one gear meshes smoothly with another.[15]

***

[15] Secular authority wielding the sword and ecclesiastical authority employing the ban can function together harmoniously.

The ninth passage

"So stand now, your loins girded with the belt of truth and having donned the breastplate of righteousness, and on your feet the armor of the gospel concerning peace. But in all matters grasp the shield of faith, with which you can extinguish all the fiery arrows of the evil one. And put on the helmet of salvation and the sword of the spirit, which is the word of God," Ephesians 6[:14–17].

The tenth passage

"The weapons of our knighthood are not worldly, but mighty before God in destroying fortifications, so that we destroy the schemes and all the pride that raises itself against the knowledge of God," 2 Corinthians 10[:4–5].

But in this matter the brothers raise a great hue and cry, "There you see what the armor and weapons of Christians should be! they are not made of iron or wood. Rather, the gospel, the gospel! Faith, faith! The word of God, the word of God! These should be our sword and weapons. Certainly Paul can polish our armor and properly clean our Christian weapons. All other arming is devilish." My answer is this: stop running, dear brothers, and calmly pay attention to what I want to tell you.

First, I find in Scripture that Paul shows us one sword with these words to the Ephesians, and another with his words to the Romans, chapter 13. Now tell me whether he has written in these two epistles about one sword or two? You cannot truly say, dear brothers, that he has written about one sword. (A twofold sword in Scripture.) For Paul speaks to the Ephesians and Corinthians of a spiritual sword. And he himself says, "With the word of God one destroys that which raises itself against the knowledge of God." But he writes to the Romans of a material sword, worn at the side, which terrifies evildoers, who are not frightened or punished by the word of God. If there are two different swords, one of which concerns the soul and the other the body, dear brothers, you must allow both to remain in force.

Second, I bid you for the love of God, to begin reading eleven lines above the passage from the letter to the Ephesians that you quote [i.e. at Eph. 6:10]. Then you will actually see that Paul describes there the sword and armaments which should be used against the devil to protect souls, and not the sword which is used against evil people here on earth who harm the innocent in goods, body, and life. Now start to read there, and the truth will be revealed to you from that moment on, for the text reads as follows. "Lastly, my brothers," writes Paul, "strengthen yourselves in the lord and in the power of his strength. Put on the armor of God, so that you can resist the clever attacks of the devil. For we are not doing battle with flesh and blood but with princes and powers, and with spirits of evil under heaven," etc. [Eph. 6:10–12].

Pay attention here, dear friends. If your spirit were right, you would say this, "There are two kinds of sword in Scripture. A spiritual one, which is used against the deceptive attacks of the devil, as Christ also used it against Satan, Matthew 4. And this spiritual sword is the word of God. Yes, Paul speaks of this sword here in his letters to the Ephesians and Corinthians. And Christ says of it, "I have not come to bring peace but the sword," Matthew 10[:34]. In addition there is also an external sword, which is wielded to protect the pious and to frighten evil people here on earth. This sword has been given to the authorities so that they can maintain the common peace of the land with it. And this sword is also called a spiritual sword when it is used according to the will of God. These two swords are not contradictory.

Third, since Paul teaches that we should pray for the authorities (1 Timothy 2[:1f.]) so that we can lead a quiet and calm life with each other in all piety and honesty, I ask one question of all you brothers together. Would a believing or an unbelieving government be more effective and skillful in maintaining people in this peaceful, quiet, calm, pious, and honest life? You must, must, must certainly confess that Christian authorities can and would do this much better and more earnestly than unchristian ones, which have at heart neither Christ, God nor blessedness, but only consider how they can maintain their power, pomp, and splendor. You have the examples of David, Hezekiah, and Joshua, and by contrast those of Saul, Jeroboam, and Rehoboam. Therefore, get behind us, Satan, and stop misleading simple people under the appearance of great patience and spirituality. We know you by your old tricks.

The eleventh passage

"You have heard that it has been said, 'You should love your neighbor and hate your enemy.' But I say to you, 'Love your enemy. Speak well of those who speak ill of you; do good to those that hate you; and pray for those who insult and persecute you, so that you may be children of your father in heaven. For he lets his sun shine on the evil and the good, and his rain fall on the unjust and the just. For if you love those who love you, what kind of reward will you have? Do not the publicans do this? And if you act in a friendly way toward your brothers, what is special about it? Do not the publicans do this also? Therefore you should be perfect, just as your father in heaven is perfect,' " Matthew 5[:43–48].

But here the brothers again cry murder against the authorities and say, "See here, the authority that a Christian would be willing to exercise should absolutely not strike with the sword. Rather, it should love its enemies, do them good and pray for them." I answer: so be it. Let us take these words of Christ and weigh them, then we cannot err. Christ says, "You have heard that it has been said, 'You should love your neighbor and hate your enemy.' " Pay attention here to who is an enemy – namely, he whom one hates and envies. But a Christian should hate or envy no one, rather he should love everybody. Therefore a Christian government has no enemy, for it hates and envies no one. For what it does with the sword is not done from hate or envy but because of the commandment of God. Thus, to punish evildoers is not to hate, to envy or to be an enemy. For otherwise God would also be hateful, envious, and an enemy of mankind. But he is none of these. Although he certainly punishes the wicked, he does not do this out of envy or hate, but out of justice. So a just and Christian government does not hate those it punishes. It is deeply sorry that such punishable people have committed offenses. Yes, what it does it does from the ordinance and earnest commandment of God, who appointed it to be a handmaiden and placed a sword at its side to administer justice. For this reason, on Judgment Day it must give a careful account of how it has used the sword. For the sword is nothing but a good rod and scourge of God, which he ordered to be wielded against evildoers. Now, what God calls good is good, and if he ordered you to slaughter your son, it would be a good work. Thus, God wants to do many things through creatures as his tools, which he could easily

197

perform without them. But he wants to use us so that we serve one another and are not idle, and so that each one fulfills the office to which God has called him. One should preach, the second should protect, the third cultivate the fields, the fourth carry out his work in another way, so that we all eat our bread earned by the sweat of our brow. Truly, truly, he who rules in a just and Christian way has plenty to sweat about. He is not idle.

Now we plainly see again how the above-mentioned words of Christ and the sword agree with and support one another in a loving and friendly way. Thus, the sword may not be unbuckled on account of brotherly love! Yes, and if I were a Christian, and were rightly disposed, and were to fall into sin, I would wish and pray that the authorities punish me swiftly, so that I might not pile sin upon sin. It follows from this that the authorities can and should punish an evildoer's sins, not only out of justice but also out of the great love which they have for him; but not for his evil deed. For it is good and useful to the sinner that a millstone be quickly hung around his neck and he be thrown into the water, Matthew 18[:6].

The twelfth passage

"You have heard that it was said to the ancients, 'You shall not kill, and whoever kills shall be liable to judgment,' " Matthew 5[:21].

Dear brothers, what is the matter? Why do you cry out to the heavens and shout more loudly than is necessary, "It is written! Thou shalt not kill! Thou shalt not kill!" Those in the Old Testament also had the commandment, just as we do, and nevertheless they killed. You say, "Yes, God ordered them to kill." And here again I reply as follows: God has also called the authorities to kill those who are not peaceful. He has always given them the sword for this purpose and not in vain, as Paul wrote to the Romans (Romans 13[:4]). But if you, a pious Christian, ask, "How do 'kill' and 'not kill' agree with one another?" I answer, "Almost completely."

As completely as to be chaste and to be married (Matthew 19[:1off.]).

As to take a wife and not to take one (1 Corinthians 7[:9,29]).

As my testimony is true and is not true (John 5[:31–32] and 8[:14]).

As to have all things and to have nothing (2 Corinthians 6[:10]).

As to be rich and to be poor (Matthew 5).

As to preach the gospel to all creatures and yet not to cast pearls before swine (Matthew 16,[16] 7[:6]).

As to love father and mother and to hate them (Exodus 20[:12]; Luke 14[:26]).

As to see God and not to see him (Genesis 32[:30]; John 1[:18]).

As all people will be saved, and those who do not believe will be damned (1 Timothy 2[:4]; Mark 16[:16]).

As to swear in the name of God and not to swear (Deuteronomy 5[:11] and 6[:13]).

As not to sin and yet to be sinful (1 John 1[:8]; 3[:6]).

As to sell everything we have and to give it to the poor, and yet to give them only what we have left over, so that we do not fall into poverty (Matthew 19[:21]; 2 Corinthians 8[:13–15]).

As to be poor, and to be happier in giving than in receiving (Matthew 5[:42]; Acts 20:35]).

As Christ will always be with us until the end of the world, and yet not to have him always among us (Matthew 28[:20]; Matthew 26[:11]).

As God punishes the sons for the evil of the father to the third and fourth generation, and yet the son does not bear the evil of his father (Exodus 20[:5]; Ezekiel 18[:20]).

As we should not perform our good works before people, and yet should do them so that people see our good works (Matthew 5[:16] and 23[:5]).

As we do not know the mind of the Lord, and yet he has revealed to us the secret of his will (Romans 11[:34]; 1 Corinthians 2[:16]; Ephesians 1[:17]).

As we ask God for all things and receive them, and ask and yet do not receive them (Matthew 7[:8]; James 4[:3]).

As to melt swords into ploughshares and to break spears into pruning hooks, and to beat ploughshares into swords and hooks into spears (Isaiah 2[:4]; Joel 3[:10]).

As we should not judge, and yet should appoint judges who judge among us (Luke 6[:37]; 1 Corinthians 6[:2–4]).

As Abraham was justified by his faith, and yet by his works (Romans 4[:5]; James 2[:21]; Hebrews 11[:17]).

As to please our neighbors, and yet not to please people (Romans 15[:2]; Galatians 1[:10]).

---

[16] The actual reference is Mt. 28:19.

As to hate evildoers, and yet to speak well of those that persecute us (Psalm 119[:113]; Romans 12[:14]).

As we should become children, and yet should not be children (Matthew 18[:3] and 19[:14]; 1 Corinthians 14[:20]; Ephesians 4[:14]).

As God wants to save all people, and yet he is merciful to those to whom he wants to be, and he hardens whom he wants (1 Timothy 2[:4]; Romans 9[:18]).

As the yoke of Christ is sweet, and yet is impossible for people (Matthew 11[:30] and 19[:26]).

As the angels desire to see the face of God, and yet if his glory appears they are satisfied (1 Peter 1[:12]; Psalm 17[:15]).

As the law of God is good, and yet God has given a law that is not good (Romans 7[:12]).

As a king should not have many wives, and yet Rehoboam had fourteen, Abijah as many, David also many, and Solomon 700 and 300 concubines (Deuteronomy 17[:17]; 2 Chronicles 11[:21], 13[:21]; 2 Samuel 12[:18]; 1 Kings 11[:3]).

As God will not be angry forever, and yet the damned must go into the eternal fire (Jeremiah 3[:12]; Psalm 103[:9]; Matthew 25[:41]).

As no law is given to the just, and yet Christ has given us a new commandment (1 Timothy 1[:9]; John 13[:34]).

As God does not tempt, and yet he tempted Abraham (James 1[:13]; Genesis 22[:1]).

As the father and Christ are one, and yet the father is more than Christ (John 10[:30], 14[:10]).

And there are many similar passages, which outwardly appear to be as opposed to each other as the wings of cherubim, and yet which all come together in Christ. For this reason the cloven hoofs of Scripture should be split and chewed well before they are swallowed (Leviticus 11[:3]), that is, believed. Otherwise one will eat death with them, and through half-truths and half-judgments one will deviate far, far from the whole truth, and grievously err. Let me give you an illustration. If Christ says, "This is my body" (Matthew 26[:26]), this is a half-truth. But if he says, "This is my body, which is given for you. Do this in memory of me" (Mark 14[:22]; Luke 22[:29]; 1 Corinthians 11[:24]), that is now a whole truth. Now, he who judges on the basis of the half-truth says that the bread is the body of Christ, and he errs. But he who judges on the basis of the whole truth says that the bread is the body of Christ which has been given to us, but not the body itself or the essence. (Oh Christian, learn to judge rightly.) Rather, the Lord's Supper is held in commemoration according to the commandment of Christ at the last supper, and this is the whole truth and nothing else is. Whoever understands this also understands how "not to kill" and "to kill' can be highly compatible in the whole truth, and yet are contradictory.

So be it. Let us accept the words of Christ and see whether the authorities are forbidden to kill. Christ says (Matthew 5[:21ff.]), "You shall not kill," and, what is more, he pulls killing out by the roots and says, "But I say to you, whoever is angry with his brother is liable to judgment. Whoever says to his brother, 'take vengeance,' 'raka,' is liable before the council. And whoever says 'you fool' is liable to the fires of hell." In reading this, dear brothers, you see plainly which killing Christ has forbidden. Namely, killing that occurs out of anger, mockery or contempt. But the authorities – I am speaking of just authorities – do not kill from anger, nor are they moved by mockery or contemptuous words. Rather, they act from the order of God, who has earnestly commanded them to do away with evil people and to maintain the pious in peace.

Now, if the authorities may kill evildoers, and are responsible for doing this according to God's order, and yet they cannot do it by themselves, if they then ordain and call me or another to do it, we are obliged to help them. And whoever resists doing this resists the order to God, and he will receive eternal judgment. (Subjects are obligated to help the authorities in all appropriate matters.) Do not believe me in this, dear brothers, but believe Paul, where you will also certainly find this view. Therefore those whom we now call hangmen were regarded in the Old Testament as pious, honorable, and brave men.[17] And they were called "prefects" – that is, executors of the order and law of God. Since it is honorable for the judge to condemn the guilty out of their own mouths, how can it be unjust to kill them with the sword and fulfill the word of the judge? For the executor of the law strikes or kills with the sword no one unless the judge has ordered him to.

We read that Solomon commanded the honorable Benaiah to kill Shimei, Adonijah, and Joab (1 Kings 2), that Saul ordered his Doeg

---

[17] In the sixteenth century the occupation of executioner was regarded as dishonorable.

to kill the priests (1 Samuel 22[:18]), and that David ordered his servant to kill also the slayer of Saul (2 Samuel 1[:15]). For neither the judge nor the executioner kills the evildoer, but rather the law of God. Therefore, Scripture calls judges, authorities, and executors of the law servants of God and not slayers (2 Chronicles 19; Romans 13). God judges, condemns, and kills through them, and they themselves do not do the killing. It follows from this that those who do not want to kill evildoers but let them live actually violate the commandment "Thou shalt not kill," and they sin. For he who does not protect the pious person kills him and is responsible for his death, just as much as he who does not feed the hungry.

The thirteenth passage

"Worldly kings," says Christ, "rule, and the powerful are called gracious lords. But not so you," Luke 22[:25].

I cannot say enough about the great clamor that my brothers make about this passage, and especially about the little phrase, "But not so you." But I complain to you, as I have above, that you do not want to look at either the preceding or the following words. For if you examined the passage rightly, we would soon reach an agreement. So be it. If we begin this passage three lines above [at Lk. 22:24], the meaning is then clear. The text reads as follows: "A dispute arose among the disciples about which of them should be regarded as the greatest. But Christ said to them, 'Worldly kings rule, and the powerful are called gracious lords. But not so you. Rather, the greatest among you should be like the least, and the most prominent like the servant.' "

First of all, it is essential to know that Christ is speaking here to those who would preach his word. These should not assume alien offices, nor mix themselves in worldly affairs, as up to now our pope and bishops do in all worldly matters. Indeed, even in making war they have been the first and last. If two cocks on a manure pile in France or Italy have pecked at each other, the pope and his cardinals will have sided with one of them. (The pope has forbidden conflict between two people, and yet has led 8,000 into battle and allowed them to be killed. And he has bestowed grace and indulgences for this.) Now Christ cannot tolerate this, and he says that the proclaimers of his holy word should exercise the functions of their calling, and do enough [in this sphere], and that other worldly business must be set aside, as Paul also writes to Timothy (2 Timothy 2[:22–26]).

Second, the passage clearly shows that each one among the disciples wanted authority and would gladly have been preeminent. And they quarreled over which among them should be the greatest. Christ cannot tolerate such a quarrel. And it is not appropriate for any Christian to gain favor with the authorities out of a desire for power. Rather, he should avoid authority as much as he can. For governmental office and temporal rule are as dangerous an estate as one can find on earth – apart from the office of preaching. Christ says of it, "Worldly kings rule and are called gracious lords." But as soon as a Christian is in a position of authority he does not rule. Nor does he desire to be called a gracious lord or aristocratic landlord (*Junker*). Rather, he is aware that he is a servant of God, and he is diligent in acting according to the order of God, so that the pious are protected and the evil are punished. The Christian magistrate does not elevate himself above anyone; rather, he very truly takes to heart the words of Christ that the most preeminent should be like a servant. Brothers, you see that Christ himself shows here how the greatest should recognize and regard himself as the least, and the most preeminent as a servant. For there must always be among Christians the great and the small, the preeminent and the subordinate; otherwise he gave us this rule in vain.

Thus, dear brothers, do not make a patchwork of Scripture; rather, place the preceding and following words together in one whole judgment, for then you will receive a complete understanding of Scripture, and you will see how the little phrase, "But not so you," does not forbid Christians to hold authority. Rather, they teach us that we should not quarrel, make war, or fight, nor conquer lands and peoples with the sword and coercion. This is against God. And we should not want to be gracious lords and *Junker*, like worldly kings, princes, and lords. (With this the honor of the authorities is not abolished; Romans 13[:1].) For authority is not ruling, and the lordships of the *Junker*, but a service according to the order of God.

The fourteenth passage

"Avenge not yourselves, my beloved, but leave it to God's wrath. For it is written, 'Vengeance is mine, I will repay, says the Lord.' So, if your enemy hungers, feed him. If he thirsts, give him to drink," Romans 12[:19f.].

Whoever has paid attention above to the tenth and eleventh passages can now reply easily. For just as Christian authority has no enemy, hates no one, and envies no one, so too it does not desire revenge on anyone. Rather, what it does must be done at the command of God, who wants to punish evil and pernicious people with Christian authority as his tool. It does not act out of anger, but with a sad heart. But revenge results from wrath. So if one desires revenge as a result of one's own anger, that is forbidden here, for vengeance is God's. He will repay evil (Deuteronomy 32[:35f.]; Hebrews 10[:30]; Proverbs 25). For this reason, after this twelfth chapter of Romans, in the thirteenth chapter Paul shows the reason why we should not avenge ourselves: God ordained the authorities as his handmaidens for vengeance, and it is appropriate for them to protect, to punish and to avenge.

The fifteenth passage

"Christ is our head and we are his members," Ephesians 1, 4, and 5; Colossians 1 and 2.

But here I have to be patient. For here they shout at me, "Do you not see that our head, Christ, did not quarrel or fight? Therefore we too should not enter into conflict but go patiently to our death." To begin with, dear brothers, I fear that you do not know what is divine or Christian, and there is a great difference between them. With respect to this, if we consider ourselves as we are by nature, Christ is not our head and we are not his members. If he is just and truthful, we are evil and full of lies. Christ is a child of grace; we are children of wrath. Christ never committed a sin, we are conceived and born in sin. You see how the members agree with the head.

Second, Paul called us members of Christ, but that happens in faith. That means the same as if we confess that we should be members of Christ, and yet are not. We admit this and ask God for pardon through Jesus Christ. On the basis of having asked this, we wholly believe that God has forgiven us our sins. Now in faith we will be members of Christ, but not in essence – that is, not in desire and action as far as the flesh is concerned, which cannot be made subordinate to the law of God. But in faith we have now been given the power to become children of God, according to the spirit and the soul, and to desire and to do good (Isaiah 64[:5]), although according to the flesh all our works are still blameworthy, rotten, worthless, and utterly without righteousness in the sight of God.

Third, since we now know that we are children of God and members of Christ in faith alone, we do not all have one office. Instead, one should take the lead in teaching, another in protecting, a third in cultivating the earth, a fourth in making shoes and clothing. But all these works should flow from faith and be made useful to our neighbors. Indeed, useful in external and physical things, for secular authority has power over the flesh or body and over temporal goods alone, but not over the soul. (Body and goods belong to the emperor, but the soul to God.) Accordingly the sword has been commanded to the authorities through the divine order, and is not for them to use in fighting, making war, quarreling, contending, engaging in conflict, and tyrannizing, and however many other names there are for wrangling. Rather, the sword has been given for them to use in protecting orphans, defending widows, maintaining the pious, and taking care of all those who are coerced and suppressed by violence. This is the office of the authorities, as God himself often shows in Scripture. And this office cannot be performed without bloodshed and death. For this reason God placed a sword and not a foxtail at the side of authority.

The last passage: to sanction government among Christians

"Let each person be subject to authority and power, for there is no power that is not from God. And the power that exists in all places is ordained by God. Thus, he who sets himself against those powers opposes God's order. And those who oppose it will incur judgment. For the powers are not a cause of fear for those who do good, but for those who do evil. If you do not want to be afraid, then do good, and you will be approved by the authorities. But if you do evil, then be afraid. For the authorities do not bear the sword in vain. They are

God's servants, punishing avengers for those who do evil. Thus, of necessity you are subjects, not only to avoid punishment, but also for the sake of conscience. For this reason you must also pay taxes, for the authorities are God's servants who should have the means to provide this protection," Romans 13:[1–7].

This passage alone, dear brothers, is sufficient to sanction the authorities against all the gates of hell. And Paul always plainly concludes that everyone must be obedient to the authorities. Be they believing or unbelieving, one should always be obedient and submissive to them. He points out the reason: because "there is no authority that is not from God." For this reason, the authorities are owed obedience in everything that is not opposed to God, for God did not ordain the authorities against himself. Now, if the authorities want to punish evildoers, as they are bound to, on the salvation of their souls, and if they do not have sufficient means to deal with evil people, and if they then call up their subjects by bells, by firing alarm signals, by letters, or by other means, the subjects are then bound on the salvation of their souls to assist and help their superiors, so that evil people are eliminated according to God's will.

Nevertheless, subjects should first thoroughly test the spirit of their rulers, to see if they are moved and incited more by arrogance, pride, greed, envy, hatred, or their own selfish interests, than by love of the common good and the territorial peace. (One should test whether the authorities order what is opposed to God.) If that is the case, then the sword is not wielded according to God's order. But if you see that the authorities are punishing evildoers only so that the pious can live in peace and without injury, then help, counsel, and stand by them, as often as you are ordered to. In doing this you will fulfill God's order and you are doing his work and not a work of man.

But if an authority is childish or foolish, indeed even unfit to rule, it is always good to get rid of him and accept another ruler. This is good because God has often punished a whole land on account of an evil authority. But if that removal cannot be undertaken legally and peacefully, without great harm and rebellion, then unfit rulers should be tolerated because God has given them to us in his wrath and wants to plague us thus, as being worthy of no better rulers, because of our sins.[18]

---

[18] This assertion effectively precludes any right of rebellion or active resistance.

Now, someone who does not want to help the authorities to save widows, orphans, and other oppressed people, and to punish those who damage the territory and make it needy, opposes God's order and will be judged by him. For he acts contrary to the commandment of God, who wants the pious to be protected and the evil punished. But if you are obedient, truly you should know that you have been obedient, not to the authorities or to man, but to God himself. And you have become a special servant of God, just as the authorities themselves are nothing but handmaidens of God.

Paul plainly testifies that the authorities have the power to kill evil people, since he says, "The authorities do not bear the sword in vain." If the authorities did not have the power to kill, why should they bear the sword? They would bear it in vain, and this Paul cannot stand. He explicitly adds that power is God's servant. Where are they now who say, "A Christian may not wield the sword"? If a Christian could not be a servant of God, if he could not execute the command of God without sinning, then God would not be good. He would have created an order which a Christian could not fulfill without sin – and that is blasphemy.

Accordingly I honestly advise you, dear brothers, to turn back. Acknowledge yourselves for what you are. You have erred badly and, under an appearance of spirituality and a cloak of humility, you have committed much filth everywhere against God and against brotherly love.[19] God knows whom I am talking about. The filth consists of this: if you did not go to war without God having sent you, all matters would now stand in a more peaceful condition. For if one were to see to it that a Christian authority agreed with his subjects in an honest, brotherly, and Christian way, many a tyrant would be taken to court on account of his coercion, which is against God and all justice. And he would be removed from office and his sword taken from him, according to the commandment of God. But if God ever wanted us to suffer tyrants, his will would still not be hindered by our efforts to protect ourselves. In sum, it is the earnest commandment of God that the pious be protected and the evil punished. This will remain until Judgment Day and no one can deny it. Look at Scripture, oh Christian reader – Isaiah 1[:17], Jeremiah 21[:12] and 22[:3], Psalm 62[:11], Micah 6[:8], Nahum 3[:1ff.], Proverbs 3[:27–35], Zechariah

---

[19] A reference to the involvement of some radicals in the Peasants' War.

7[:9ff.], and the whole of Habakkuk. This commandment binds the authorities today just as it did fifteen centuries ago.

Paul writes further, "Thus, you are subjects out of necessity, not only to avoid punishment but also for the sake of conscience" [Rom. 13:5]. What does that mean? A great deal. Secular authority has been ordained by God for the sake of temporal peace. Thus, even if there were no passages of Scripture which called for us to submit to authority, our own consciences would tell us that we should help the authorities protect, defend, punish, and enforce. And that we should provide them with services, labor dues, watch duty, and taxes. This is so that we are able to live in temporal peace with one another, for having temporal peace is not contrary to Christian life. Otherwise Paul would not have taught us correctly in Timothy to pray that our kings, princes, and authorities keep the peace with all people as much as we can. That is correct and Christian. (It is not wrong to have temporal peace, 1 Timothy 2[:2]). But if God sends us adversity, we should patiently accept it (Romans 2). Now do you see, dear brothers, that your own consciences compel you to give counsel and aid, so that evil people are punished and good ones protected? This is called, in good German, "the common territorial peace" (*ein gemeiner Landesfrieden*). Paul says that we must pay taxes, customs and tribute precisely to promote and maintain this peace of the territory.

Pay attention here, dear brothers. If the authorities are so unchristian that a Christian may not wield the sword, why then do we help and support them with our taxes? If we are not responsible to our neighbors as well as ourselves to prevent them from being harmed, why then do we elect authorities? Or, are those in authority not our neighbors? Indeed, if we want to live in peace under a heathen authority, why not more so under a Christian one? For a Christian one is much more concerned about God's order than a heathen one. How do you get out of this, dear brothers?

But Paul continues and says, "Power is a servant of God," who should handle this protection, and this occurs for the benefit of our neighbor and the support of the common territorial peace. Now where is it written that a Christian may not be such a servant of God, one who can fulfill the commandment of God for the benefit of all people? Or that he cannot undertake such a divine work (as Paul himself calls it)? God surely wants to share his grace with us all, so that we in turn come to the true path of his holy word and remain on it until the end, through Jesus Christ our lord. May the peace of God be with us all. Amen.

Truth is immortal. 1527

13 Hans Hergot, *On the new Transformation of the Christian Life*[1]

"Guard yourself, devil – hell will soon collapse."[2]

Three transformations have taken place. God the father brought about the first with the Old Testament. God the son brought about the second transformation for the world in the New Testament. The holy spirit will bring about the third change with a future transformation of the bad situation in which people now find themselves.[3]

In order to promote the honor of God and the common good, I, a poor man, know those things which are in the future: that God will humble all social estates, villages, castles, ecclesiastical foundations and cloisters. And he will institute a new way of life in which no one will say, "That is mine."

The cities[4] will be humbled, their buildings reduced to ruins, and

---

[1] The pamphlet appeared anonymously and Hergot's authorship is likely but not certain. Hergot was a Nuremberg printer and colporteur who was arrested in May 1527 for distributing the work, which was also ascribed to him. It was probably printed earlier that spring. But the work is divided into two parts (see below note 23) and the first part may have been written before the second; some scholars have suggested that the first part, the vision of a new Christian society, may have been written during the Peasants' War. The translation is based on the text in *FB*, 547–57.

[2] The source of this motto is not known.

[3] The opening paragraph shows the influence of a millenarian conception of history developed by Joachim of Fiora and later taken up by many radicals in the Franciscan movement, who gave it much greater currency in society. According to this view, history is divisible into three great ages: that of the father, associated with Judaism and the Old Testament; that of the son, associated with Christianity and the New Testament; and a coming age of the holy spirit, in which people will be enlightened by direct revelations and hence in which God will establish his personal rule over a just and peaceful society.

[4] There appears to be a printing error here. The text of the original has, not "cities" but *secten*, i.e. religious divisions or social groupings as well as "sects." Later in the work, however, the phrase is repeated, and there the word is *stedt*, i.e. cities.

their inhabitants and crafts will abandon them. The villages will become rich in property and people, and all their grievances will be redressed. The nobility of birth will pass away, and the common people will occupy their houses. Cloisters will lose the four mendicant orders and the right to beg,[5] and the other rich cloisters will lose what they possess in payments and rents. All religious divisions will pass away together and be made into a single church. All resources – such as woods, water, meadows, etc. – will be used in common. Each land will have no more than a single lord; spiritual and temporal lords, regardless of their current form, will pass away. Our obedience to spiritual and temporal lords will find an end. Also, the servants of the princes and lords will abandon their service. And if anyone thinks that he can maintain his social estate, it will be in vain.

I have taken the above thesis from the knowledge that I have of the Christian flock[6] (among other scriptural sources, from John 10[:1]). For I have seen the whole sickness of the flock, and I have said, "Oh eternal God, what miserable things are happening to those in your Christian flock." Then I realized that God has discharged from service the two shepherds and all their relatives [i.e. spiritual and temporal rulers] whom he set over the Christian flock. And their mighty efforts [to prevent change] will be in vain.

Then I realized that from now on God has instituted a single shepherd over his flock by bestowing the earth on it. This happened in this way: God bestowed on each agricultural community[7] the churches that stand on its land, and as many people as each community can sustain. And everything that grows on the land belongs to the church and the people who live there. Everything is bestowed for common use, so that people will eat from one pot, drink from one vessel, and obey one man insofar as it is necessary for the honor of

---

[5] The mendicant orders, especially the four most important ones – Dominicans, Franciscans, Augustinians, and Carmelites – will dissolve, since cloisters will lose the right to beg.

[6] *schaffstall*; literally "sheepfold," but the author often uses impersonal objects to refer to groups of people.

[7] *Fluer* (= *Flur*), a term that refers directly to land or soil, but for Hergot embraces both the local agricultural community and the land belonging to it. The politically autonomous and economically self-sufficient *Flur* is for Hergot the building block of a new social order. Economic and social relations in each *Flur* are determined by what is best for the common good. The *Flur* also constitutes the base unit of a hierarchy of administrative levels which Hergot sees as ultimately embracing the whole world. In this "world state" the officials of each ascending geographic level are elected by those directly beneath them.

God and the common good. And they will call this man whom they will obey a "sustainer of the community."[8] And the people will all work in common, each according to his talents and his capacities. And all things will be used in common, so that no one is better off than another. And the community will be completely free, for neither fees nor taxes will be paid, and yet the community will be maintained by the authorities. The transformation of the people will be better than that produced in all the religious orders. The people will believe in God, and prove this with works, prayers, fasting, and by reflecting on God's suffering, divine mercy, and other matters. And when these people have children, they will bring those which are three or four years old into the church and dedicate them to God. And the sustainer of the community will come to them, lift them up, and order the person in the village who has the best conduct to take the children into his house and to raise them as a trusted father, for the honor of God and the common good. Female children will be given over to an honorable pious woman or maiden from the same children's house, who will instruct them until they are marriageable. And their inclinations and talents will be encouraged, for the honor of God and the common good.

It will be the custom of the people to elect every twelfth person to serve God and the common good, so that those who want to be elected are always ready to serve God.[9] All the male and female cloisters and all the ecclesiastical foundations are too few to organize these services, because they must all accept the new transformation. The four mendicant orders are included here – to which charitable "gifts" will no longer be paid. And fees and rents will no longer be paid to the other cloisters and foundations. The nobility will have to

---

[8] *eyn gotshaus ernerer*, lit. a "nourisher of God's house." The term *gotshaus* was used more commonly for a cloister rather than merely a church; again, it is used here as an impersonal metaphor for a community. The notion of a "sustainer of the community" is unique to Hergot. He regards the sustainer as a community's spiritual leader and political representative. Each village or *Flur* constitutes a parish or congregation as well as an economic unit. Although Hergot does not specify how the sustainer of the local community was selected, the subsequent discussion both of those in the village who are especially designated to organize worship services – i.e. "clergy" in the strict sense – and of government above the level of the *Flur*, imply that the nourisher was elected to his office by the village.

[9] *Gots dienst*; i.e. worship services. These people constitute an elected "clergy," in the sense that their lives are especially dedicated to the organization and execution of the village community's religious activities.

endure the same fate.[10] And the beggars too – they will be completely provided for and taken care of like everyone else. In this way mankind will be humbled. The people will be housed next to each other in a community, in the manner of the Carthusians.[11]

The people will also be in constant readiness to be called up for military service when this is necessary for the honor of God and the common good. They will also have a house in which old people will be provided with food and drink, and all their physical needs taken care of, and better than in any poorhouse. There will also be a hospital for those who have physical ailments, and another for those who are mentally ill, such as those who do not conduct themselves in the right way with respect to their souls. They will stay in this house until they repent their sin. And the inhabitants of these houses will also have their crafts, such as that of tailor, shoemaker, wool or linen weaver, blacksmith, miller, baker, and the other crafts that are necessary for each village community. All crafts will also be practiced as they should, and desires for selfish gain will be done away with. And a longing for the common good will prevail over the whole village. Then the "Our Father" will be fulfilled, and the word which the lord often uses in the "Our Father" will be meaningful: our, our, our.

Also each craftsman will take on another person as an apprentice, to teach him his craft for the sake of the commonweal. Their transformation will be good. The people will call on and pray to God, who is the elected and the highest good, and to all of God's saints. For God's sake the people will disregard selfish interests and do what serves the common good. They will wear a garment which they can produce in the village – white, gray, black, blue. And what can be grown on the land will be their food and drink. Everything that lies on the land will be theirs, such as wood and water, and this will be used in common. Whoever has produced something on his land will

---

[10] Without gifts, fees, and payments, the economic basis of the privileges enjoyed by both the cloisters and the nobility will disappear; both estates will have to work.

[11] Of the medieval religious orders, the Carthusians, an order of hermits founded by St. Bruno in 1084, continued in the early Reformation to maintain a good reputation for the strictness of their devotion and the quality of their piety. The appeal of their way of life to Hergot undoubtedly lay in the organization of their cloisters, which features separate and identical "houses" for the members, rather than individual cells in a common building. Their foundations thus served as a model for the equal but distinct households which constituted Hergot's village community or *Flur*.

exchange it with another for other goods.[12] The people will also stop
eating meat during Advent, and from Ascension to Whitsun.

The seven sacraments will be reduced to three,[13] and the other four
regarded as good works performed to produce an indissoluble bond
between God and man. And whoever violates this bond will be
severely punished. And the punishment, administered by those in his
household, will be to bind the culprit's hands and feet and to walk on
him in order to shame him, as often as he does it. The sacrament of
extreme unction will be reserved for the time when the saints are
called on [i.e. the hour of death]. And the sacrament of confirmation
will be reserved until the time when one confesses his faith, which will
be done at thirty years of age.

The sustainers of the community throughout the territory of each
region will elect a captain or lord[14] above them, who will be the lord of
the territory. It will not be permitted to give him payments or rents.
He will travel from one village to another throughout his territory and
supervise all the community sustainers and the whole territory, making sure that the honor of God and the interests of the common good
are maintained. He will also eat and drink with the people, dining as
they do on what they are able to produce in the village community.
And anything more that he merits for his work, he can expect to
receive from God.

If the lord wants to wage war, he will be given every third man in
each village community,[15] if the war accords with the honor of God
and the common good. The troops will follow him and the infantry
and cavalry will be obedient to him. This lord will also [have the right
to] mint coins whose inscription will be the name of Jesus and the
community where the coin was minted in the territory of this lord.
This coin will be of value everywhere in the world. Although the lord
may accept neither salary nor rents, he will still be able to provide for
the needs of the territory by seeing to it, through the sustainers of the

[12] Hergot envisions a simple system of barter as the basis of economic exchanges between
households in the village community.
[13] A common change introduced by the Reformation. By the early 1520s, e.g., Luther
accepted only baptism, communion, and confession as valid sacraments, and confession
was soon thereafter discarded. Hergot's sacramental views, however, were quite unor-
thodox for early Protestantism; he accepted confirmation and extreme unction as sacraments but did not specify the third.
[14] *eyn heubt* (= *Haupt*) *odder eynen herrn.* The "territorial lord" (*Landherr*) is the political
authority immediately above the local village or *Flur*.
[15] This was a common practice among villagers at the time of the Peasants' War.

community, that each village builds paths and roads. The lord will also have his agricultural and scriptural experts. The agricultural experts will understand what the soil is capable of producing and sustaining, and they will be responsible for nourishing people's bodies from the soil. Each village will have one of these agricultural experts. The scriptural experts will be those who teach the word of God for the salvation of the soul, and so nourish the soul with Scripture. And each village will also have one of these.

The territorial lords will also take charge of rebuilding old churches. Worship services will be held in them, and the people will be sustained by the village community. The territorial lord can also permit each sustainer of the community to mint coins for the needs of the common good. The lord will reside in the middle of his territory, and everything in this territory will belong to the people of the village communities who live there. Two or three times a year, or as often as necessary, the territorial lord will call together the community sustainers in a territory to learn what is abundant or beyond their needs with respect to people or goods. He will have special buildings built to store the surplus yield in each village, and it will be used to serve the common good of the territory, or to assist and provide for another territory. The lord will also maintain a university in his territory where the honor of God and the common good will be taught, and all the books which are useful for this will be found there. The ruler will also arrange for the maintenance of worship services in each village community, and they will be more and better than any cloister now has. Every time people dine to satisfy their bodies, they will also feed their souls with the word of God. The territorial lord will have no more than a single territory, and he will use what the territory and the village communities can produce. And everything that is in a territory will belong to him and to the people living in the villages of the territory.

Every twelve territorial lords will elect a captain or lord as their superior. And he will move about among these twelve and make sure that they rule correctly over their twelve territories. He will also mint a coin, which will be as valuable as the sum of the twelve coins which are minted in his jurisdiction, and which will bear the image of God and the name of the territory where they have been minted. This overlord will also eat and drink with the twelve territorial lords, as well as they can provide for him in their houses, and he will be called a "quarter lord" of the Latin empire.[16] And all of the territorial lords will come to him once or twice a year and inform him about the surpluses and deficiencies in their territories. And this quarter lord will also confirm all the territorial lords when they are elected from their territories. He will be a supervisor of the other lords who are under him, to make sure that no one seeks his own selfish interest. And he will also make sure that they instruct their subjects, the masses, so that no one seeks his selfish interest, but instead that of the common good. This quarter lord will also be an agricultural and scriptural expert. And he will mint coins of gold and brass with the image and name of Jesus, and the name of the quarter where they were minted. There will be four of these quarter lords in the Latin empire. All the territories which speak a common language will be united in a quarter. The four quarter lords will have to administer the quarter for which each is responsible.[17]

Each of these four quarter lords will mint a coin of gold and brass, which will be as valuable as the sum of all the other coins which are minted by the other territorial lords subordinate to his quarter. Each of these quarter lords will have a university in his quarter where the three languages – Latin, Greek, and Hebrew – which are needed to establish a single shepherd, will be taught.[18] Each of the quarter rulers will have not more than a single shop for making purchases,[19] which will be large enough for the territory under his control.

There will also be four quarter lords in the lands where the Hebrew and Greek languages are spoken. And each of these lords will also mint coins of gold and brass, which will be identical in form, bearing the name Jesus and the quarter of the territory where the coin

---

[16] *eyn virtels herr der lateynischen zungen.* Literally, "a quarter lord of the Latin tongue." As is evident below, Hergot divided the world into three language groups and polities: Latin (perhaps roughly equivalent politically to the Holy Roman Empire in its claims to universal rule over Latin Christendom), Greek, and Hebrew. It is unclear how the Turks, whom he mentions at the conclusion of the work, fit into this politico-linguistic scheme.

[17] I.e. each quarter lord will only be permitted to rule over one quarter.

[18] I.e. a single governing authority instead of the traditional division between spiritual and temporal authorities, the "two shepherds" whom, Hergot says at the outset, God has discharged from service.

[19] *eynkauff.* In Hergot's economic system, in which most goods are bartered, there is need for only a restricted number of shops. His concern with the details of coinage at various administrative levels is perhaps the product of both the suspicion which many rural people had about money, which they regarded as an instrument of their exploitation, and Hergot's desire to provide an economic foundation for the scheme of world government that he elaborates.

was minted. These twelve men of the three languages will travel among the territorial lords who are under them, each within his quarter, and they will make sure that they rule justly, honoring both God and the common good. And they will arrange for the instruction of those others who are under them, so that they heed in the same way the honor of God and the common good.

These twelve quarter lords will also elect above them a chief lord,[20] who will confirm the twelve when they are elected from their quarters. And he will move about in the areas of the three languages, and he will supervise the quarter lords, making sure that they rule well according to the honor of God and the common good. And if he dies and cannot visit all the lords and lands, then the twelve will elect another to his office, and this replacement will complete the administration which the dead lord has left. And this chief lord will be confirmed in his office by God. He will also mint a coin of gold and brass, which will be worth as much as the sum of those which are minted by the twelve lords directly under him. And it will also bear the image and name of Jesus and the inscription, "One shepherd and one flock."

Thus, the required release from the twofold shepherds [existing spiritual and temporal authorities] and the institution of a single shepherd lie in the future. And from now on all your efforts and work [within the existing order] will be in vain. And your discontent will also continue, until our affairs are constituted in the manner I have described here.

This disposition of the earth and the establishment of a single shepherd will restore to us all the fruits of the earth and the use of them that people need for body and soul. Through this disposition of the earth, the small villages will be able to defend their land from the big cities and [feudal] lords. And what they get from the soil will be theirs. The buildings of the cities will be reduced to ruins, for they will not need them. City people will have enough with the cloisters which they have on their land and which they will own for the honor of God and the common good.

Therefore one must pay attention that no part of these buildings is destroyed in this insurrection of the people.[21] Through this new

---

[20] *eynen heuptherrn*; i.e. a lord who stands at the summit of the political system as a kind of elected world emperor.

[21] *ynn diesem auffrur des menschen.* Why Hergot abruptly introduces this concept is

disposition of the earth, no one will remain in his social estate as he now is, for everybody will be integrated in a single order.

To construct this order, it will be praiseworthy to be of a "nobility of virtue;"[22] the great cities will be instruments of the countryside; and the master of the construction will be God and the common people. Thus, all religious and social divisions will be forged into a single unity.

Through this new disposition of the world the nobility of birth, and reason as it is now defined [will pass away]. For wise and pious people from the common folk will be listened to constantly, and they will determine what reason is. These people will be drawn from every estate where they are to be found. And through this disposition the villages and cities will have all their grievances redressed. And through it as well, a single shepherd and a single flock will be established on earth. And the shepherd will pray correctly: "I believe in the holy spirit and I will prove it with deeds," through which all the foundations will lose their estate, their rents, and their property, and because of this end of their estate they will no longer be able to shame the word of God which says, "Render unto Caesar that which is his" [Mt. 22:21, Mk. 12:17, Lk. 20:25, Rom. 13:7]. For God has ended their estate and the world will do likewise. The truth of [this prediction of] their demise will be proved by miracles and miraculous signs, as many as are needed to believe it. Confronted by these events, the people will be moved by fear and love of God, and they will begin to destroy selfish interests and to elevate the common good.[23]

This pamphlet concerns all the estates of the whole world, clerical and secular, noble and non-noble, kings and princes, middle classes and peasants, and it affects them all equally, city, country, and people. Everything that has ever been proclaimed by God affects everyone equally. No one should be angry about this. God does not ask whether man is angry or not; he will not diminish his punishment. But the world and especially the scribes at the princes' courts and in the big cities think that their reason and their wisdom is so elevated that they can forego God's wisdom. They say, "Yes, all of God's proclamations

---

uncertain, except that he plainly wishes to say that the transformation he has envisioned must be brought about by force.

[22] *der adel der tugent*; i.e. a nobility that is defined by virtuous behavior rather than by blood.
[23] Some scholars hold that the work is a composite of two separate texts and that at this point the first text comes to an end.

which he has revealed through all the prophets are invalid. Yes, all of the miraculous signs which he lets us see every day in the heavens are invalid." And these signs are termed mere fables by the scribes, so that they can reject God's power, and nothing is valid but their wisdom.

Can anyone show me a single legal system on earth, among all who work in them and pronounce decisions, judgments, and laws, which is like that which the holy spirit shows me? All laws should be applied so that things are judged according to truth and justice, not from affection or favoritism. For this reason the holy spirit placed twelve men together, as God did the apostles. He did it for this reason: if five men fail to produce the right decision and let themselves be guided by their own spirit, the other seven are still in a majority, and the law should be what the seven judge it to be. And if this happens, the law will gain approval. But God, who is almighty and has instituted law in favor of the poor people, will appropriately punish the judges and proclaimers of law when the end of time arrives, and everyone, big and small, is full of fear. Nevertheless [under existing laws] no one improves his conduct, as is indeed evident in all legal systems.

Is anyone, from the most highly placed to the lowest man on earth, able to tell us where there is a law that is interpreted differently than the scribes want? Whomever they want to favor in the law, they proclaim to be in the right, whether he is or not. The Bible teaches them that they are always in the right. The holy spirit does not teach this. He teaches nothing but truth and justice, and so he is the enemy of all scribes, who in turn are enemies of the holy spirit. And all who want to judge according to the spirit and according to truth regard the scribes as fools. At present the holy spirit has no power to issue judgments. The truth of the holy spirit is as worthless to the scribes as a felt hat; but before God's truth it is eternally valid.

The twelve [person system discussed in this work] sit and judge the two [i.e. the clergy and nobles] who [think they] are worth more than all others. They must say "yes," but God knows their hearts [see Mt. 19:28–30; Lk. 22:25–30]. Do you think that the holy spirit will always remain dumb and allow himself to be buried as though he may no longer speak? His voice and his truth arrive and resound like a trumpet in every human heart. And his voice and truth reveal all the injustice of the scribes.

You mighty rulers, as you are called, from the most high to the most lowly, do you think that conditions would be so bad on earth if you had let the old, unlearned ones judge and proclaim the law down to the present? Do you think that evil can stand on earth? I believe that the holy spirit gives more wisdom to an old, unlearned man than to a young, learned one. For the old man speaks the truth and says, "If the young one knew what I know, he would be without despair."[24] But now the wisdom of old people is no longer valid; the holy spirit no longer has a place in their wisdom. The scribes have monopolized wisdom and they share it with no one. He who prides himself in the Lord must everywhere suffer, unless he is one of the scribes.

But I believe that God does not want to have anything to do with the scribes. For when he was on earth he did not have much to do with them. He feared them, for he knew for sure that they would transform all his justice and truth into injustice and lies.

For this reason he accepted merely simple fishermen and customs officials, who did not think they were clever. If God alone is clever, he only needs those who hold that through God's holy spirit they are wise and clever. The scribes do not assert this; they boast of the books and Scripture which make them wise and learned, indeed cleverer than they would make God. And so they issue judgments according to the Bible and do not ask about God's judgment, as is evident. Even those who have the holy spirit are not allowed to talk differently from what pleases the scribes.

But now the fact of the matter is that the holy spirit will and does teach differently than what pleases the scribes. And he shows the whole truth. The scribes cannot stand this.

Therefore the scribes cry to the princes and kings that publishers should be done away with, and that it should not be permitted to bring [bad] people into disgrace and every evil to light.[25] For the devil tells them how their crimes will be revealed. But if someone tells the truth to princes and kings, knights and counts, noble and non-noble, and if he writes about all their injustice, and publishes it, letting it go forth into the world for all to hear what kind of people they are, this will be right and it will please the scribes well that the injustice of the nobility comes to light.

[24] I.e. inexperienced youth, aware only of how contingencies or unforeseen events can disrupt the fabric of life, is fearful and despairing about the future.

[25] The following discussion of publishing and censorship may reflect Hergot's experiences as a printer in Nuremberg.

But now that their own injustice is also about to be proclaimed and come to light, the scribes cry murder and try to forbid all publishers so that publishing does not take place.[26] But all God's proclamations must be made public to the whole world, and not just once but often, often – just as formerly Noah proclaimed to the world repeatedly, for a century, how God would eradicate it [Gen. 6:5–13]. But if one announces to the scribes now that God will not suffer injustice any longer, they become enraged and do not consider the great miracles that are occurring in the sky and on earth.

The whole nobility, including all the princes, has seen God's force and power.[27] No building, castle, or city can be relied on. When God's wrath arrives, nothing is of any use, if men leave house and castle and flee them, and if God's fear pursues everyone, as has been seen. Who would dispute this: if the emperor were to come with all the princes [and attack the nobility], he would not make the nobility as fearful in a year as God made them in ten weeks. Nothing is of any use. People say that the peasants are responsible for the upheaval, but I reply "no." Peasants armed with flails certainly do not destroy walls. It simply takes honor away from God to say, "The peasants did it," and to incite the nobility by saying, "Kill the peasants. They are enraged. They are destroying your castles." This is the wisdom of the scribes. In this way, one blind man leads another and both fall into the ditch, as God himself says [see Mt. 15:14]. But if the scribes taught correctly, according to the gospel, there would not be as much disunity and discord on earth as there is now.

In the gospel the Lord says, "Your hairs are numbered and none will be touched without the will of my father" [Mt. 10:30]. If God's will is to be done, an event must have always been going to occur. If it is less good that the peasants did it rather than other people, it still must have had to take place. But if God did not make it take place, truly I would rather say that the scribes were more responsible for it than the peasants. But since the peasants have eaten the leather [whip], they must pay for the cow – and they have paid double.[28] And

---

[26] Hergot may be referring to a complaint which Luther lodged with the city council of Nuremberg against Hergot and his apprentices on 26 September 1525, charging him with the unauthorized republication of Luther's September Bible. See *WA Br*, III, 577–79.

[27] A reference to the Peasants' War.

[28] The peasants tried to destroy the means of their oppression and have been doubly punished, once through their defeat and a second time through the punitive fines

they stand in the middle of the market so that all can have access to them. Suck quickly from this udder, you scribes, and teach the nobility how to leave the cow nothing in its udder, and to suck up all the milk so that there is nothing left for the children. For it is indeed true that they have sucked it so nearly dry that there is neither milk nor blood left. And many women and children starve to death. Enough has already taken place in the name of the cry, "Let whoever has hands strike and strangle to death [the peasants]; it is right and it pleases God."[29] God says, "Be merciful as my father is merciful to you" [Lk. 6:36]. If this cry is mercy to the scribes, I will leave the peasants to them and ask nothing of them. But if God is as merciful to the scribes as they are to the peasants, no scribe will ever enter his kingdom.

Therefore no one should think that insurrection comes from books or writings. Everything comes from God's power. But the scribes do not believe this. According to their lights, their wisdom is worth more than the power of God. The insane world believes them; therefore they have so blinded the whole world that no one fears God. They are incapable of anything other than guiding the world with such blindness. If they were capable of anything better, they would teach something better. They have no reason, so they cannot teach anyone. Thus, whoever they teach makes errors, and cannot find the right way, and will be destroyed everywhere, as is evident. God's wisdom completely blinds them.

I have not written this pamphlet because I am angry, or want anyone else to get angry, or because I somehow want to move the world to wrath. Rather I have written it to create benevolent peace and benevolent unity. Where there is unrest, more unrest is generated, but where there is benevolent peace, this also creates benevolent peace. The negative side of this principle has recently been demonstrated in all its repulsiveness. If the scribes had not taught so much unrest, there would not have been so much unrest. Whoever profits from unrest should clean his shoes with the gain. I would gladly give up such profits.

Nor do I want to have to share with the peasants the "profits"

imposed on them. Just below, the metaphor changes and the peasants become the "cow" that is sucked dry by the clergy and nobility.

[29] A reference to Luther's work, *Against the Robbing and Murdering Hoards of Peasants* (*Wider die räuberischen und mörderischen Rotten der Bauern*), *WA* XVIII, 357–61, written at the height of the Peasants' War in early May 1525.

which they have received on account of their insurrection. I think that they have also been well paid. Do you not think that many scribes and other people, who are a large party on earth, have done as much injustice as the peasants? And yet no one cries, "Stab them to death! Kill them!" But God, who is a true field commander, is now coming, and he will strike them more powerfully than the peasants. The scribes and others were more violent than the peasants, a thousand times more violent. God is not much concerned about buildings which are built from stone and wood, be they cities or castles. But God cannot tolerate the buildings where he resides to be destroyed, and these buildings are the poor people, peasants, and burghers[30] whom God himself created. Even though presently God does tolerate it, and allows the nobles and scribes to do whatever they want with the poor, [this will only go on] until he thinks the time is ripe [for change]. Now everyone is looking out for himself. And therefore I believe that God will never again raise up the peasants against their lords in another insurrection. For God caused the peasant upheaval for the good of the nobility and the scribes. But since they have not recognized that he did it for their good, and are ungrateful, God has raised up the Turks and all unbelievers against them, on account of the blood of the peasants which they have given him.[31] It is obvious that now the real conflict is coming. Indeed, not only with the Turks but also with our "most holy father," the pope, and all the prelates in discord with one another. Each one desires the blood of the others.

But may God not ordain Germany to suffer the fate of Italy, where the land is filled with war and the people with discord.[32] Indeed, I think that if this also comes to pass in Germany, God will take pity on us. The princes and mighty lords here are just as prone to strife in our lands as in other lands. If one whistles softly to them, they dance.

[30] *burger*, a term which in the sixteenth century referred not to the "middle classes" in an economic sense, but to residents of cities who had rights deriving from membership in the polity of the urban commune. Undoubtedly Hergot was thinking of the lower orders of the citizens, especially artisans and shopkeepers.

[31] The expansion of the Ottoman Empire in southeastern Europe in the sixteenth century was commonly regarded as a sign of divine displeasure with Christendom. Hergot, however, links God's wrath specifically to the nobility's slaughter of the peasants during the Peasants' War, and to the punishments which the nobility imposed on them after their defeat.

[32] Since 1494 Italy was the scene of endemic military conflict as France and Spain, in alliance with various Italian states and other outside powers, contended for hegemony over the Italian peninsula.

"This is good. I like to see it," [say the scribes,] who are well pleased. And they laugh behind their hands and think that if great conflict and murder occurs, it is the right course of events. They always interpret Scripture and twist it to produce quarreling and litigation. But [you should] trust completely in God. God hears the prayers of the pious and will not permit as much discord in Germany as the scribes think. The gospel should be defended with the sword, but not in this way. If God wants to have believers, there will be believers. This is my belief; others can believe what they want.

But if someone says that this pamphlet is not good and does not teach correctly, I say simply that it is good and teaches correctly. Of what concern is it to me? The rain falls from heaven, it gets muddy, and I do not like it. What does God care? It is still right, even if I do not like it. Thus, whether a know-it-all or a scribe does not care for this pamphlet is a matter of indifference to me. It has been written according to the wrath of God. If we bid God to end his wrath, he will strengthen it. But when we bid him, and are worried that he will punish and plague us, what harm does it do if this does not take place? What harm does it do if one issues a warning? Is it not better that someone tells me I am sinning against God and makes me fearful – so that I acknowledge God and bid God to forgive me – than that someone tells me I am pious while I hide in the skin of a rogue? Yes, how much would this assist me before God's judgment? What would it be worth if I said, "The world calls me pious," but through this I were not made more pious? It would be worth as much if I said, "It will occur," but it did not happen. Then I would have lost and would be called a liar. If God wills that the world becomes so pious that God is willing to remit his punishment on account of this, I will gladly set aside these words.

My pamphlet does not produce insurrection. It only reveals those who dwell in evil, so that they recognize themselves for what they are and beg God for mercy; for he will not let himself be struck as the peasants were struck. When God himself wants to duel with you, as this pamphlet clearly shows you, he who is without guilt need have no fear. But he who knows that he is guilty should run to God and beg him for mercy. For the time is at hand, and he will root out the tares [Mt. 13:25–30]. Otherwise, even if the godless devour the faithful completely, they will not know what God has said to us and proclaimed through Moses. If we believe the voice of God, we will arise and depart in blessedness. And if we believe the voice of the Lord/, what he has promised us will transpire [Dt. 28:1–14]. The subject of this work has long tormented my conscience, that of a poor man, so severely that I can no longer stand it, and so I publish this pamphlet in the name of God.

There have been three tables in the world. The first was super-fluous and had too much on it. The second had a moderate amount and enough to satisfy the needs [of those who sat at it]. The third was completely wanting. Then those from the superfluous table came and wanted to take away the bread from the table that had least. The conflict arose from this, and God will overturn the superfluous table and the table with the least, and he will uphold the middle table.

Appendices: Programs of the Peasants' War

a *The Eleven Mühlhausen Articles*

Mid-September 1524[1]

In the name of Jesus. In order to praise God, the community of Mühlhausen, [including the congregations] of St. Nicholas, St. George, St. Margaret, the linen weavers of St. Jacob,[2] and many other craftsmen of the city, have taken action themselves and derived their decisions from the word of God. Where this resolution contradicts God's word, however, it should be changed and improved.

[1] An entirely new council should be established. The reasons for this are so that it will act according to the fear of God,[3] so that old hatreds and despotism are ended, and in order to insure that those who do evil, and those who allow and approve it, receive the same punishment – Romans 1[:32], Luke 19[:20–27] on the willful servant – so that there is no confusion in the community about those who are outside it and those who are inside it. From this [confusion], harm to

---

[1] The Eleven Articles were written during a week of disturbances in the Thuringian imperial city of Mühlhausen from 19 to 26 September 1524, probably on 22–23 September. Thomas Müntzer and his Mühlhausen associate, Heinrich Pfeiffer, played a major role in their drafting, although the articles also expressed the demands of a lower-class communal movement which existed in the city well before Müntzer's arrival at Mühlhausen in mid-August 1524. The articles were evidently written to unify a radical opposition party – one which would include peasants of villages in the territory ruled by Mühlhausen as well as lesser craftsmen and shopkeepers in the city. Copies of the program were sent to these villages, but peasant support failed to materialize, for the articles did not address peasant needs. The city council regained the upper hand, and on 27 September Müntzer and Pfeiffer were expelled from the city. The translation is based on the text in *FB*, 80–82.

[2] The first three congregations were suburbs of Mühlhausen; of these, St. Nicholas' was the church where Heinrich Pfeiffer was preacher. St. Jacob's was a quarter in the inner city.

[3] The "fear of God" rather than fear of men.

the community can result, for it is difficult to accept as judges those who are themselves guilty.

[2] Judgments should be made according to the [standard of] justice in the Bible or holy word of God. This is so that the poor man is treated like the rich, as in Zechariah 17 [rather, Zech. 7:10], Leviticus 19[:15] and 26[:3], John 7[:24], Matthew 5[:19], and Luke 18[:2–8].

[3] No term of office should be imposed on the government of the [city] council, neither one year nor two.[4] This should be done to keep councilors from doing simply what they want; rather, they should issue just judgments, and not puff themselves up [with pride] and regard themselves as lords; Jude in his *canonica* [Jude 4] and 2 Peter 2[:1–2], concerning the seed of godless people, etc.; Deuteronomy 16[:18–20], on godless rulers.

[4] The council is ordered under pain of loss of life, namely hanging, to do justice and avoid injustice. This is to make sure that justice is maintained and that injustice does not go unpunished; Isaiah 5[:18–25], Luke 19[:27] on those who resist divine authority; Numbers 14[:36], Deuteronomy 4, 20 [Dt. 4:2] and 21 [Rom. 2:1–3] on unjust judges; and Numbers 25[:4] on the commandment of God to hang unjust rulers who do not want to follow God's commandment to punish evildoers.

[5] No one should be forced into the government and if someone does not want to participate, he should be replaced with another. The reason for this is so that no one may have the excuse [that he did not want to participate]; Luke 19[:20–27] on lazy servants, 1 Peter 5[:1–6] and Exodus 23[:2] on not following the mass of the godless in their injustice; Matthew 7[:24–25] on the good building; Deuteronomy 13[:7] on not even obeying father and mother when they act against God's commandment, as also Luke 14[:26].

[6] Those who are in need should be looked after. This is so that they do not have reason to be greedy for possessions, and so that they do not have to scrimp and save for survival. As is written in Exodus 18[:21], the greedy, proud, and uncomprehending liars and haters are not fit for government; it is stated in Acts 20[:28] about government, in Matthew 10[:10] that the worker is worth his wage, in 1 Corin-

---

[4] An "Eternal Council" of this kind was established in Mühlhausen in March 1525. After Müntzer and Pfeiffer were permitted to return to the city – Pfeiffer in December 1524 and Müntzer in February 1525 – political revolution took place as the Peasants' War swept Thuringia.

thians 9[:4–10] concerning assistance, and in Luke 3[:14] that you should be satisfied with your wages.

[7] Documents are to be sealed with the new or secret seal,[5] and it is to be used for the honor of God and the commonweal of the city. This is done to eliminate all deception and falsehood. As in Luke 16[:8] on the children of the world, since as a race they are cleverer than the children of light; Jeremiah 2[:13] says that people are clever in doing evil, and incapable of doing good; Genesis 6[:5] states that mankind's flesh is always inclined to evil, also Romans 6[:19].

[8] If those [in the old council] do not want to accept commands about what serves the commonweal, we will compile their evil deeds on paper – what they did through malice twenty years ago against the commonweal, and how they deceived the city, letting it fall into deception – so that it is evident what kind of people they were. The reason for this is so that everyone sees and hears how they have treated us. Then everyone will say that they have been regarded too favorably and tolerated far too long. As is written in Psalm 83[:16], "If you fill their faces with shame, they will seek your name, Lord"; Deuteronomy 6[:2], Ruth 7, and Matthew 21[:41] on the servants who did not want to give the lord his fruits, so the lord killed the evil ones in a terrible way and commended his vineyard to other workers.

[9] If everything is not ordained according to God's word, we, the above designated, will concede no legitimacy to [the old council]. Our reasoning is this. So that God's justice and equity are advanced and so that all false authorities and selfish interests are ended, we will make no agreements with either rhetoricians or councilors,[6] either craftsmen or commoners, unless they can propose something better for the commonweal, and more like God's justice and truth, than our proposal. 1 Thessalonians 5[:21], "Test everything and keep that which is best."

[10] And if our new council is not acknowledged [by the old council], as a result of manipulation on the part of our opponents [in the old council], we, the above designated, will demand compensation from this opposition. The reason is that [we will have to assume that]

---

[5] On 20 September, shortly after the outbreak of insurrection in the city, the two ruling mayors, rather than face charges from the opposition, fled the city, taking with them the city's flag, seals, and keys.

[6] *achtmann*; i.e. a member of the Council of Eight. This council had been created in 1523 as a concession to those who opposed the traditional patrician city council; by September 1524 the city's radical party felt that it had ceased to play a useful role.

they have not wanted to follow our counsel, which we have given them on the basis of the divine word, so that they could easily escape their responsibility for the damage. Exodus 21–23, Proverbs 1[:22–33].

[11] We would like to act correctly in all these matters, according to the word of God, and without any delay. The reason: If it is not permitted to carry out God's commandment, we want to know from you[7] what our good God, his only son Jesus Christ, and the holy spirit have done to you that you do not want to have God rule over you, you miserable bags of maggots. About what did God lie or deceive you, he who is certainly just? Psalms 11[:4–7] and 15[:1–5], and Deuteronomy 10[:12].

In conclusion, it is also the conviction and resolution of us all that our every work and action should be measured by God's commandments and justice, and so tested: are they harmful to God and the people? If our actions are approved by people and disapproved by God, or if God approves our work and people disapprove it, we will choose one of the two – and we would much rather have God as a friend and people as enemies than have God as an enemy and people as friends. For it is a dangerous thing to fall into God's hands. Genesis 7[:1–24], Exodus 15[:1], Romans 3[:21–31] and 9[:20–33], Matthew 14 [actually Mt. 16:27] on the Last Judgment, Luke 21[:25–28], and Matthew 10[:28], "You should fear him who has the power to throw body and soul into the fire of hell," etc.

In the name of Jesus. We write this, Christian brothers, so that you will know how to conduct yourselves accordingly.

---

[7] This exemplar of the document was directed to the village of Horsmar, near Mühlhausen, and was a response to the conservative attitude of the peasants, who had opposed earlier political developments in the city.

b The Twelve Articles of the Upper Swabian Peasants

27 February–1 March 1525

The basic and just articles of the whole peasantry and the subjects of spiritual and secular lords, by whom they feel themselves burdened.[1]

To the Christian reader, the peace and grace of God through Christ.

Because the peasants are assembled, there are many antichristians[2] who now find reason to disparage the gospel, saying, "These are the fruits of the new gospel: to be obedient to no one, to rise up and rebel everywhere, to form infantry units with great violence, to band together to reform spiritual and temporal authorities, to expel them, perhaps even to kill them." The following articles reply to all these godless, superficial critics, first, to stop them from disparaging the

---

[1] *The Twelve Articles* was the most widely circulated program produced by the rebellious peasants in 1525. It was distributed in numerous printed editions as well as in manuscript copies. The document was written at the imperial city of Memmingen in Upper Swabia by Sebastian Lotzer, a tanner and lay reformer, and Christoph Schappeler, the evangelical pastor of St. Martin's church in Memmingen. In writing it, Lotzer and Schappeler drew on a variety of grievance lists composed by the peasantry of Upper Swabia under various lordships; Lotzer and Schappeler summarized the grievances, gave them general form, and added supporting scriptural citations. *The Twelve Articles* exerted a powerful influence, direct and indirect, on other programs of the peasant insurrection in Germany. The translation is based on the text in Günther Franz, ed., *Quellen zur Geschichte des Bauernkrieges* (Ausgewählte Quellen zur deutschen Geschichte der Neuzeit, 2) (Darmstadt, 1963), 174–79.

[2] *wider christen*; i.e. followers of Antichrist and enemies of real Christians.

word of God, and second, to justify on Christian grounds the disobedience, indeed the rebellion, of all the peasants (Romans 1).[3]

First, the gospel is not a cause of rebellions or insurrections,
because it speaks of Christ the promised Messiah, whose words and
life teach nothing but love, peace, patience, and unity, so that all who
believe in Christ become loving, peaceful, patient and united. If the
basis of all the peasants' articles (as will be clearly seen) is directed
toward hearing the gospel and living according to it, how can antichristians call the gospel a cause of rebellion and disobedience?
Although certain antichristians and enemies of the gospel oppose
such demands, and want to flare up and revolt against them, the
gospel is not the cause of this, but the devil, that most pernicious
enemy of the gospel, who inspires such behavior in his followers
through lack of faith, so that the word of God (which teaches love,
peace, and unity) is suppressed and robbed.

Second, it clearly follows that since, in their articles, the peasants
want to be taught and to live by such a gospel, they cannot be called
disobedient or seditious. (Romans 11, Isaiah 40, Romans 8, Exodus 3
and 14, and Luke 18.) If God wants to hear the peasants (who are
anxiously calling for the opportunity to live according to his word),
who will blame the will of God? Who will interfere with his judgment?
Indeed, who will oppose his majesty? Did he not listen to the children
of Israel who cried out to him, and did he not free them from the hand
of Pharaoh? Is he unable to rescue his followers today? Indeed, he will
rescue them – and soon. Therefore, Christian reader, zealously read
the following articles, and then judge them.

Here are the articles

Article one

First, it is our humble desire and request, and the intention and
conviction of us all, that henceforth we want to have the full power for
a whole congregation to select and elect its own pastor; and also the
power to remove him, if he acts improperly. (1 Timothy 3, Titus 1,
Acts 14, Deuteronomy 17, Exodus 31, Deuteronomy 10, John 6, and

---

[3] Marginal references to Scripture have been enclosed within parentheses. Marginalia
which merely restate a paragraph's theme or, as with many of the following specific
articles, simply assert that they are "a fair Christian offer" have been deleted.

Galatians 2.) This elected pastor should preach the gospel to us purely and clearly, without any additional human doctrine or commandments. Rather, he should always proclaim the true faith to us, prompting us to petition God for his grace, so that he implants and confirms this same true faith in us. For if his grace is not implanted in us, we will always remain flesh and blood, which are ineffective, as is clearly stated in Scripture: only through true faith can we come to God, and only through his mercy will we be saved. Thus, such an elected leader and pastor is necessary for us and is grounded in Scripture.

Article two

Second, since a just tithe has been established in the Old Testament, and fulfilled in the New (as the whole Epistle to the Hebrews says), we will gladly pay the just grain tithe[4] to the full – but in the proper way. It should be given to God and distributed to his people, paid to a pastor who clearly proclaims the word of God. (Psalm 109, Genesis 14, Deuteronomy 18 and 12.) We are willing that henceforth our churchwardens,[5] chosen by the congregation, collect and receive this tithe. From it they shall give the parson, who has been elected by the whole congregation, enough to maintain himself and his family modestly, according to the determination of the whole congregation. And whatever is left over should be distributed to the destitute people of the village, according to their circumstances and the determination of the congregation (Deuteronomy 26). What is left over after this should be retained, in case travel is necessary for the sake of the territory. So that no land tax may be imposed on the poor, travel expenses should be taken from this surplus. (1 Timothy 5, Matthew 10, and 1 Corinthians 9.)

Also, if one or more villages, because of some necessity, have sold the rights to their tithe – and this can be proved to the villages – the tithe owner should not be paid by the whole village. Rather, we will reach an agreement with him in a proper manner according to the circumstances, and redeem the tithe rights for a reasonable amount and in a reasonable time. (Luke 6 and Matthew 9.) But if someone

---

[4] *korn zehat*, sometimes also called the "major tithe" and paid on the yield of grain and other products of the land.

[5] *Pröpst*; i.e. the administrator of ecclesiastical property in a congregation.

personally has not bought tithe rights from a village, but has inherited them from his forefathers, we shall not be, should not be, and are not obligated to pay him anything more, except what is needed to maintain our elected pastor, to change the pastor if events warrant it, and to distribute to the needy, according to Scripture. (One should not take anything from another.) This shall be the case regardless of whether the owners of rights to the tithe are spiritual or temporal lords. We will not pay the "small tithe" at all.[6] Since the lord God created cattle freely for mankind (Genesis 1), we regard it as an improper tithe which has been contrived by people. Thus, we will no longer pay it.

Article three

Third, until now it has been the custom for us to be regarded as a lord's personal property,[7] which is deplorable since Christ redeemed us all with the shedding of his precious blood – the shepherd as well as the most highly placed, without exception. Thus, Scripture establishes that we are and will be free. (Isaiah 53, 1 Peter 1, 1 Corinthians 7.) Not that we want to be completely free, with no authority over us. God does not teach us this. (Romans 13, Wisdom 6, 1 Peter 2.) We should live according to his commandments, not according to free, carnal whim. (Deuteronomy 6, Matthew 4.) Rather, we want to love God, acknowledge him as our lord in our neighbor, and we want to do everything gladly that God commanded us to do at the Last Supper (Luke 4 and 6). Although we should live according to his commandments, they do not teach us that we should not be obedient to authority, and not only to authority; rather we should humble ourselves before everyone. (Matthew 7, John 13, Romans 13.) They also show that we should gladly be obedient to our elected and established authorities (if established for us by God) in everything that is proper and Christian (Acts 5). Without a doubt, as true and just Christians, you will also gladly release us from serfdom, or show us from the gospel that we should be serfs.[8]

---

[6] The small or lesser tithe was paid on animals, especially cattle.
[7] *aigen leüt*; lit. one's "own people" – i.e. serfs or bondsmen.
[8] Something that the authors of the work plainly thought was impossible.

Article four

Fourth, until now it has been the custom that no poor man has been allowed the right to hunt game or fowl or to catch fish in flowing water. We think that this is completely improper and unbrotherly; rather, it is selfish and not compatible with the word of God. (Genesis 1, Acts 10, 1 Timothy 4, 1 Corinthians 10, Colossians 2.) The authorities in some places also maintain game [for their own hunting], to our sorrow and great detriment. And we must tolerate it that dumb animals (which God has let grow for the benefit of people) uselessly consume our crops. And we must keep silent about this, which is contrary to God's will and the needs of one's neighbors. When the lord God created man, he gave him power over all animals, birds in the air, and fish in the water. Thus it is our wish that, if someone has a body of water, and he can adequately prove in writing that the water was unknowingly sold to him, it is not to be taken from him with force. Rather, one must have Christian insight about it for the sake of brotherly love. But if someone cannot produce adequate proof of his possession, he should inform the community of this in the proper manner.

Article five

Fifth, we also have grievances concerning the use of woodlands. For our lordships alone have appropriated all the woods, and when the poor man needs wood, he must buy it at double the price. It is our conviction that, regardless of the kind of woods involved – whether possessed by spiritual or by temporal authorities who have not bought it – it should revert to the whole community. (As is shown in the first chapter of Genesis.) And, in the appropriate way, a community should be free to permit anyone in need to take wood home for burning without paying for it, or to take it for required buiding without paying. But this must be done with the knowledge of those elected by the community to supervise such matters. (Officials should see that this does not deplete the woods.)

If, however, the only woodland available is that which has been legally purchased, agreement should be reached with the owner in a brotherly and Christian way. But if originally the property was simply appropriated by some individual, and then sold, an agreement should be reached according to the circumstances of the case and of our knowledge of brotherly love and holy Scripture.

Article six

Sixth, we have a serious grievance concerning labor services,[9] which increase from day to day. We want to be granted some understanding, and accordingly not to be so severely burdened. Rather, we should be shown gracious understanding, for our forefathers served only according to the word of God. (Romans 10.)

Article seven

Seventh, henceforth we no longer want to be burdened by a lordship; rather, if a lordship has been bestowed on someone correctly, he should receive his lordship through an agreement between lords and peasants. Lords should not force or compel their peasants, seeking to get more services or other dues from them without payment. The peasant should be able to use and enjoy his property in peace, without being burdened. (Luke 3, 1 Thessalonians 4.) But if the lord is truly in need of services, the peasant should be at his disposal willingly and obediently, but at an hour and season that are not to the peasant's detriment, and the peasant should be properly paid for his services.

Article eight

Eighth, we are aggrieved, especially those that have their own land, because these lands cannot sustain the payments[10] on them, and because these peasants must then forfeit the land and are ruined. [We demand] that lords let honorable people inspect these pieces of property and establish a payment that is equitable, so that the peasant does not work for nothing. For every laborer is worth his wage (Matthew 10).

Article nine

Ninth, we are burdened by the great outrage that new laws are constantly being made, so that we are punished not according to the

---

[9] *der dyenst* (= *Dienst*), i.e. the servile obligation to perform labor services for a lord.

[10] *die gült*, a general term for monetary payments, including taxes and fees for leased or rented land.

facts of a case, but sometimes out of envy and sometimes out of favoritism. It is our conviction that we should be punished according to ancient written law, and that cases be treated that way and not on the basis of favoritism. (Isaiah 19, Ephesians 6, Luke 3, and Jeremiah 26.)

Article ten

Tenth, we are aggrieved that some have appropriated meadowland as well as fields which belong to the community (as above, Luke 6). We will take these properties into our hands again, unless they have in fact been legally bought. But if someone has bought them unfairly, the parties involved should reach a benevolent and brotherly agreement, according to the facts of the case.

Article eleven

Eleventh, we want the custom termed heriot[11] to be completely abolished. For we will never accept that the property of widows and orphans should be taken from them so shamelessly, contrary to God and honor, and that they should be robbed, as has occurred in many places (and in many forms). Those who should protect and defend us have clipped and sheared us. If they had even a slight sense of what is right, they would have realized that God will no longer tolerate it, and that the custom must be done away with. Henceforth no one should be obligated to pay the heriot, whether the amount is much or little. (Deuteronomy 18, Matthew 8 and 23, and Isaiah 10.)

In conclusion

Twelfth, it is our conclusion and final conviction that if one or more of the articles we have composed here is not in accordance with the word of God, we will retract these articles, if they can be shown to be improper according to the word of God. (Because all of the articles are contained in God's word.) We will renounce them if they are explained to be false on the basis of Scripture. If some articles are now granted us, and later it turns out that an injustice has been done,

---

[11] *den todtfall*; this feudal obligation required a dead peasant's family to make payment to a lord for the death of "his" serf.

from that moment on these articles will be null and void, no longer in force. And the same is true if other articles are found by the truth of Scripture to be against God, and a burden on our neighbors. We are also resolved and determined to give and receive according to every Christian teaching. We want to bid God the lord to grant us this, for he alone and no one else is capable of giving this to us. May the peace of Christ be with us all.

c The Memmingen Federal Constitution (Bundesordnung)

7 March 1515[1]

This Christian union and association[2] has been founded in order to praise and honor eternal, almighty God, and, by appealing to the holy gospel and the divine word, also to contribute to justice and divine law. It has not been founded in contempt of anyone or to deprive him of his rights, be he a spiritual or a secular lord. And it has been founded especially to increase brotherly love.

[1] First, the honorable territorial community[3] of this Christian association insists that the spiritual and temporal authorities are responsible for acting according to divine law, and for not violating this law in any way, but obediently maintaining it.

[2] Again, it is the honorable territorial community's will and

---

[1] This document was written by the representatives of several peasant armies of Swabia, who assembled at Memmingen in early March 1525 in a rudimentary "parliament." The text set forth the basic aims and conditions of membership in a new territorial association the peasants created at Memmingen as they formed the Christian Union of the Allgäu, Baltringen, and Lake Constance armies; it was in this sense a constitution. The work may have been influenced by a "Constitutional Draft" (*Verfassungsentwurf*) that was developed by Balthasar Hubmaier, perhaps with the help of Thomas Müntzer; unfortunately their work survives only in an incomplete report at second hand – in a pamphlet written against Hubmaier presenting evidence to justify his execution. The articles of *The Memmingen Federal Constitution*, creating a Christian federation, league, union, or convenant (*Bund*), circulated widely during the Peasants' War in manuscript form and as a printed broadsheet. The following *Document of Articles of the Black Forest Peasants* spelled out the penalties that resulted from rejecting the commoners' federal association. The translation is based on the text in *FB*, 32–34.

[2] *vereynigung und pündtnüß.*

[3] *eyn ersame landschafft*; the term *Landschaft* in southwestern Germany was more than a geographic term for a region; it also referred to the political community of a territory, sometimes having its own representative assembly. Hence, the peasants at Memmingen were claiming to speak for the territorial community as a whole.

conviction that the common peace should be maintained and that no one should violate the rights of another. But if it should occur that someone causes another to take up arms and rebel, others should not in any way assemble and form factions. And the nearest person, regardless of his social standing, should have authority to make peace among them and to request that from now on one bid the other to make peace and restrain themselves, etc. And if this peace that has been requested is not maintained, the one responsible for violating it should be punished accordingly.

[3] Again, all [feudal] dues[4] which are generally acknowledged, or for which there are documents with seals or a trustworthy record, however dilapidated, should be paid. But if someone thinks he can convince a person [who disputes an obligation], he should take the matter to court, but at his own expense, and for the sake of the common territory of this association. And this concerns debts as well as tithes; other rents and payments should be suspended pending the outcome of the lawsuits.

[4] Again, since castles are not part of this form of territorial [agreement], and since they are not joined in this Christian association, the residents of castles should be requested with friendly admonition to see to it that they do not store up provisions beyond what they reasonably need for their own use. And they should not garrison these castles with persons or arms that do not belong to this association. But if henceforth they want to garrison them, they should do this with people who are members of this association, and they should do this at their [i.e. the castle owners'] own expense and risk. The same is true of cloisters.

[5] Again, if there are servants who are serving princes and lords, they should renounce their oaths, and publicly say that they have done so; and if they do this, they should be accepted into this association. Those who do not want to do this, however, should take their wives and children and leave the territory willingly. If a lord demands [the appearance] of an official or someone else who is in this association, he should not go alone, but he should take two or three with him, and let them hear what is to be done with him, etc.

[6] Again, pastors and vicars should be requested in a friendly way to preach [only] the holy gospel. And the ones who want to do this

---

[4] *schuld.*

240

should be given what is needed to live in moderation. But those who do not want to do this should be discharged, and these pastors should be replaced with others, etc.

[7] Again, if anyone wants to make an agreement with the authorities, he should not conclude it without the prior knowledge and approval of the common territorial community of this association. And if an agreement is concluded with the approval of this said territory, the person making it should still agree to remain in this eternal covenant and Christian association.

[8] Again, a captain and four cavalrymen should be designated and dispatched from each military unit of this association. They, together with other captains and cavalry, should have the authority to negotiate suitably, so that the community does not always have to assemble.

[9] No plundered property, if it has been wrongfully expropriated, should be maintained or employed, etc.

[10] The craftsmen who want to take their work out of the territory should not oppose this Christian association to get the praise of their ecclesiastical superiors. Rather, if they hear that opposition to this territory is arising, they should inform this association and, if it is necessary, be ready to return right away and help save it. Soldiers should also be bound to do the same.

[11] Courts should proceed and laws should be applied as has been the case previously.

[12] Again, inappropriate games, blasphemy and drinking are forbidden. Whoever does not keep this article, shall be punished according to [the degree of] his guilt.

The following theologians have been designated [as competent] to determine the substance of divine law.

Doctor Martin Luther
Philip Melanchthon
Doctor Jacob Strauss at Eisleben
Osiander at Nuremberg
Billican at Nördlingen
Matthew Zell and his associates at Strasbourg
Conrad [Sam], the preacher at Ulm
[Johannes Brenz,] the preacher at Schwäbisch Hall
[Michael Keller,] the Franciscan preacher at Augsburg
[Hans Zwick,] the preacher at Riedlingen

[Sigmund Rötlin,] the preacher in the cloister at Lindau
Ulrich Zwingli and his associates at Zurich
[Matthew Alber,] the preacher at Reutlingen
[Matthew Waibel,] the preacher on the mountain at Kempten

d   The Document of Articles of the Black Forest Peasants

8 May 1515[1]

We extend to you, the mayor, council, and whole community of the city of Villingen,[2] peace and the grace of God almighty. And we admonish you to decide whether you too want to help divine justice and the holy gospel of our lord, Jesus Christ, and join our Christian brotherhood according to the terms of the articles which we are herewith sending you.[3] Accordingly, we request a written answer for our messenger without delay. Dated at Vöhrenbach on the Monday after the Feast of the Holy Cross [8 May] 1525.

The captains and council of the peasant army in the Black Forest.

The letter of articles

Honorable, wise, and favorable lords, friends and dear neighbors. In the recent past heavy burdens, much against God and all justice, have been imposed on the poor common man in the cities and in the

---

[1] The peasant army of the Black Forest, which was commanded by Hans Müller of Bulgenbach, sent the following covering letter and document to the city of Villingen. Rather than being an independent program of articles, the letter requested the city to join the Christian association proposed in *The Memmingen Federal Constitution*, and the document specified the penalties, especially the "worldly ban," for failing to adhere to this territorial federation. A version of the document, which circulated in several printed and manuscript versions, was found among the papers of Balthasar Hubmaier. Partly on the basis of the notion of a worldly or secular ban which *The Document of Articles* set forth, Hubmaier has been suggested as the most likely author of the work. The translation is based on the text in *FB*, 110–111.

[2] A small city in the territory of Freiburg im Breisgau.

[3] The text of the following *Document of Articles* fails to set forth the form and terms of this Christian brotherhood; instead it presupposes them. The articles referred to are in all probability those set forth in *The Memmingen Federal Constitution*.

countryside by spiritual and worldly lords and authorities. But these [impositions] have not touched these lords in the slightest way. The result is that these burdens and grievances can no longer be borne or tolerated, unless the common man is willing to condemn himself and his progeny to a life of begging.

Accordingly, it is the proposal and intention of this Christian association, with the help of God, to make itself independent, and to do this, so far as possible, without taking up arms and without bloodshed. This can only occur if there is brotherly admonition and agreement on all relevant matters which concern the common Christian good, as encompassed in the accompanying articles.

It is our friendly request, expectation and brotherly petition that you join us willingly, and submit as friends to this Christian association and brotherhood, so that the common Christian good and brotherly love are again established and increased. If you do this, the will of God will be realized in what you do, as you fulfill his commandment about brotherly love.

But if you reject this [petition] – which we in no way foresee – we will place you under the worldly ban.[4] And in doing so we will regard you as under the power of the ban, as set forth in this document, until the time that you repudiate your intentions and submit willingly to this Christian association. We do not want to keep this from you, who are our dear lords, friends, and neighbors of good reputation. We request a written answer from the council and community [of Villingen] to be sent with this messenger. We commend you to God.

The worldly ban is valid in this sense

All who are in this Christian association, on their honor and as their highest duty, will treat in the following way those who reject and refuse to enter the brotherly association and to further the common Christian good: they will have absolutely nothing to do with them, and this means that they will neither eat, drink, bathe, grind grain, bake, work the fields, nor harvest with them. Nor will they provide them, or allow anyone else to provide them, with food, grain, drink, wood, meat, salt, or anything else. They will neither buy anything from them

---

[4] A temporal or secular counterpart of the ecclesiastical ban of excommunication. The worldly ban excluded those affected by it from membership in the socio-political community. Its specific terms, as the peasants understood them, are taken up below.

nor sell them anything. Rather, they will let them remain as severed, dead members in [our] affairs, as those who do not wish to promote but instead hinder the Christian commonwealth and the peace of the territory.

They will also be deprived of all markets, woods, meadows, pastures, and water which are not directly under their legal power and at their disposal.[5]

And if anyone, having entered the association, then disregards it, he will also be excluded immediately and punished with the same ban. And he will be sent with wife and children to our adversaries or enemies.

Concerning castles, cloisters, and ecclesiastical foundations

Because all treachery, coercion, and corruption arise and spread from castles, cloisters, and ecclesiastical foundations, they are placed under the ban from this moment on.

But if the nobles, monks, or parsons of such castles, cloisters, or foundations want to leave them and live in normal houses like other pious people,[6] and to join this Christian association, they and their goods and property will be accepted in a friendly manner. And if they join, they will be permitted to keep, truly and honorably and without any deprivation, everything that has been conveyed to them according to divine law.

Concerning those who provision, promote and support the enemies of this Christian association

Likewise, all those who provision, promote, and support the enemies of this Christian association will be asked in a friendly way to desist from these practices. But if they do not do this, they will also be declared to be under the worldly ban and without any property.

[5] *in ihren zwingen und bännen*; i.e. areas in which a feudal lord had the right of "lower" justice and exercised the power to make binding or compulsory decisions.
[6] *wie ander frembd lüt; frembd*, "foreign," is evidently an error for *fromm*, "pious."

e   *The Forty-six Frankfurt Articles*

13 April 1525[1]

Provident, honorable, and dear wise lords, first of all we offer our obedient and due service, because God almighty has sent to many of our hearts the spirit of truth with the revelation of his holy gospel. He enlightens all who believe in him. But the clerical mob, monks and parsons, knew how to suppress this [spirit] in many ways, without having any basis in truth. Still worse, together with their tyrannical followers they keep trying to hinder it as much as they can. And they like to see disturbances, in which [the work of] the devil, with the clergy as his tools, is characterized by division among the people into different parties about how we receive the mercy of God. And all friendly requests for them to stop have been useless. Since we should owe God more obedience than man [Acts 5:29], it is highly necessary that we eliminate godless things, and that we begin to reform ourselves, to develop godly, brotherly behavior in praise of almighty God and the honor of his holy word, Christ our Lord, and to institute brotherly unity. [It is necessary to do this] so that others, foreigners, do not seek to reform us, and so that they are not able to burden us. We want to free ourselves from the grievances which need imposes on

---

[1] The radical party in the imperial city of Frankfurt am Main submitted the articles to the city council on 20 April; under popular pressure, the council accepted them shortly thereafter. While expressing many long-felt grievances of the urban lower classes, the articles also derived more immediately from an earlier list of eleven articles composed by a circle of evangelical radicals in Frankfurt and its dependency Sachsenhausen. This circle was led by Gerhard Westerburg, Karlstadt's brother-in-law and formerly his reforming associate in Saxony. *The Forty-six Frankfurt Articles* were printed shortly after their acceptance; they became one of the most influential programs of the urban popular movement in the Rhine-Main area, with discernible impact as far north as Münster and Osnabrück. The translation is based on the text in *FB*, 59–64.

us, and we want to support and maintain ourselves among one another as follows.

First, it is our request, desire and deep conviction that henceforth an honorable council and the congregation should have the power to install or remove a pastor in parish churches or in other churches. And these same elected pastors should preach nothing but the pure word of God, the holy gospel, without human additions, so that people are strengthened in right teaching and are not misled.

Second, all those who want to reside here, be they clergy or laity, should stop the great vice of prostitution; cohabitation should not be tolerated, so that no offense to one's neighbors arises from it. If people are not living chastely, they should get married, and absolutely no whoring should be permitted.

Third, all members of the clergy and those who want to be members, together with other [clerics] who live here, should assume, execute, and acknowledge the services, direct taxes, municipal fees for defense measures, indirect taxes on consumer goods, and all the other obligations of citizens.

Fourth, the monks have begged money from us poor citizens and our people, have taken it away under the guise of spirituality, and sent it to other cities, although this money was at the disposal of the community and was not theirs. Therefore, it is our conviction that the monks should be required to restore this money, or should be held in prison until they restore it. Also, no monk should be permitted to beg, preach, or hear confession any longer.

Fifth, no more monks or nuns should be accepted by the cloisters. And those who are in them should have the right to leave if they wish, though without being forced to leave. And the cloisters should be supervised so that none of their belongings can be sold, either documents or jewelry.

Sixth, all monetary dues,[2] be they to spiritual or temporal lords, which do not have documents and seals attesting to their acquisition should be abolished, and no one should be obligated to pay anything on the basis of oral testimony.

Seventh, it is known that there is an endless number of imposts on wine, grain, and other goods, and that the poor man is not able to pay them. And the reason for this is that some of the authorities employ in

[2] *gulten*, a general term for monetary payments, including taxes and fees for leased or rented land.

their households the officials who measure grain and buy up grain outside the gates. It is our view that henceforth there should be a free market in grain, and each person should be allowed to buy one eighth of a measure, or two, or three, or as much as he can afford. And those who buy in the morning, up till one or two o'clock, should not be allowed to sell again in the afternoon, so that the poor man is also able to buy grain. And if it should happen that someone has mortgaged his grain or other goods, and another who has greater need is brought to him, this one should be allowed to buy for cash, if he has it, an eighth of a measure, or two, or a half measure, according to the cash he has, and he should not be refused.

Eighth, if someone needs to make an additional set of steps, a door sill, or a cellar in his house, he should not, as up to now, be forced to pay money for it, but instead be able to do it [himself] without loss. However, the master mason should make a preliminary inspection [to determine feasibility].

Ninth, we want the high sales taxes on wine, grain, salt, oil, fish, and other goods that are used in the city to be reduced by one half, and to be completely eliminated for the poor man.

Tenth, everyone, the poor as well as the rich, should receive a decision in major legal matters within four weeks at the longest, and not be put at a severe disadvantage by advocates and lawyers. Also legal fees and the fees of lawyers, should reduced by one half.

Eleventh, all rents owed in perpetuity, even where documents and seals exist, should be redeemable like other dues. And if no documentation is presented, as encompassed in the sixth article, they should not be paid at all. Such dues should be regarded as nothing but usury, and not be tolerated as a legally valid way of obtaining an income.

Twelfth, no Jew should be allowed an insufferably great interest rate in any area in which he burdens the poor man, and he should not be allowed to buy and sell. And if something that has been stolen is discovered in the possession of Jews, they should be obliged to return it without payment. But whatever in the way of old clothes and other unredeemed pawns may be found in their possession, they may sell whole and not by the yard.

Thirteenth, an honorable city council should provision all ecclesiastical benefices which have been established by founders, whether the family is living or not. [And it should provision them] with pious, upright, and learned people, who favor the citizenry and who can instruct the people in the word of God. And benefices should not be bestowed on candidates with papal letters of provision. Benefices should be provided with an adequate tithe, namely the thirteenth. And what exceeds the personal needs of the occupants should be paid into a community chest, maintained for the honor of God, so that the destitute are looked after and do not have to beg from house to house.

Fourteenth, from now on all bequests and alms should be placed in a community chest, ordained to the honor of God, in order to feed poor people.[3] And annual commemorative feasts [for donors], confraternities, and ecclesiastical processions should not be continued, but should be totally abolished.

Fifteen, if someone has his own land, till now he has not been allowed to clear or cultivate it, unless he had previously given an official money. From now on we do not want to be forced to do this.

Sixteenth, formerly if someone raised a sow in his house, he had to pay twice its value as a fine. We no longer want to do this either.

Seventeenth, if the lord God gives us beech nuts in the forest [to feed swine], the foresters tell poor people that there are no longer beech nuts in the forest, so that they drive their animals out. Afterwards they sell off the rights to beech nuts to surrounding villages. All this results in a disadvantage to the poor and can no longer be tolerated.

Eighteenth, we no longer want to have penalties for cutting wood unless – as was traditionally the case – someone intentionally cuts down a young tree or otherwise damages the woods. For it is commonly known that surrounding villages use our forest more than we do.

Nineteenth, although it has been a customary right to gather wood [in the forest] annually, this right has been of no use unless one had a horse. For whoever owns a horse takes away what is suitable first, and the poor are miserably provided for with the stumps. Therefore it is our conviction that each should be given a definite time to bring his share home, as is the custom in other places. The poor should receive as much of the wood that is left standing as the rich.

Twentieth, we are grievously burdened by the cows, pigs, and

---

[3] In Frankfurt am Main such a community chest already existed before the Reformation.

sheep of Kelsterbach, Schwanheim, Sandhof, Neuhof, and this side of Hellershof,[4] for their grazing leads to severe damage to all parts of the meadow of our poor community and ruins the woods. Therefore, we declare that herding should be entirely abolished in the direction of Sachsenhausen.[5] And herding on this side of the outlying fortifications should be allowed, so that the butchers and all fellow citizens of Frankfurt are able to feed their own cows, pigs, and sheep.

Twenty-first, we request that in future, fees for [the use of] bridges be paid to us, but we no longer want to pay fees for transporting our own produce [over the bridges].[6]

Twenty-second, if a resident citizen takes grain, oats, wood, or other goods which he has bought in the city, over the bridges, up till now he has had to pay a toll on them. This is contrary to brotherly love and fairness, and we no longer want to pay this toll.

Twenty-third, where there are meadows inside or outside the city, we want this to be common land, belonging to the community, and to be a free meadow for the community to pasture animals, and the free use of water should be allowed.

Twenty-fourth, henceforth no citizen who can present a bailbondsman should be imprisoned, be it for debt or crime. Rather, except for thieves and evildoers, a decision should be reached as quickly as possible.[7]

Twenty-fifth, it is public knowledge that the property of some poor people has been destroyed by Jews, and this property has been partly kept by Jews and partly sold elsewhere. If the poor sue in court and no decision can be reached, we request that a decision be reached according to the law.

Twenty-sixth, henceforth we wish to pay no more than six hellers[8] for a morning vineyard guard and four hellers for a morning field guard – or whatever they may be called – as a fee for protection.

Twenty-seventh, when one's property in the fields is damaged by butchers' herders or others, the one who causes the damage should

---

[4] Kelsterbach lay southwest of Frankfurt; Schwanheim was a part of the city; Sandhof, Neuhof, and Hellershof were grazing estates of the Frankfurt patriciate near the city, Sandhof belonging to the Teutonic Order.   [5] A part of the city of Frankfurt.

[6] Bridges, especially that over the Main connecting Frankfurt and Sachsenhausen, were to become municipal property, with usage fees charged those bringing goods into the city, but not citizens taking goods out of the city.

[7] Only those charged with serious crimes were to suffer investigative detention.

[8] The heller was a coin of small denomination minted at Schwäbisch Hall.

peaceably make it good. But if the parties cannot reach agreement, they should come before the sworn Court of the Field[9] and acknowledge its assessment of the debt, and they should abide by it. They should not be responsible for paying the landlord any further fine.

Twenty-eighth, we want the day laborers in the fields to be paid two hellers more every third of the year, to improve their daily wage.

Twenty-ninth, henceforth resident citizens should not be obliged to pay the English Mark[10] on milk and other goods.

Thirtieth, attaining citizenship with a document attesting to it should cost no more than half the fee required up till now.

Thirty-first, no craftsman should be accepted as a master, regardless of the craft in question, unless he has learned his craft and proven it with his own hands.

Thirty-second, henceforth, in order to curtail expenses, we wish that no more than twelve cavalry be hired, excluding the commanding official[11] and the captain, with servants and officers. Such mercenaries are more harmful than useful to a community.

Thirty-third, it is our conviction that henceforth everyone, no matter how many houses he has, should also personally guard and protect all of them.[12]

Thirty-fourth, when a document is written to a craft guild, we want that guild to have the power to open and read it. And if there is something in it that concerns the authorities, it should then be handed over to a mayor, but not before.

Thirty-fifth, all drunkards and blasphemers should be punished without mercy, as the occasion may require and according to the orderly counsel of these articles.

Thirty-sixth, it is our conviction that henceforth, when a council member dies, a replacement should be elected who is upright, honorable, understanding, experienced, and skilled. And in the election there should be no regard for friendships or other considerations, which has been the case up till now.

Thirty-seventh, people like us should not pay more than six hellers for having the measure of a keg certified.

---

[9] The Frankfurt court which settled disputes concerning agricultural holdings.

[10] A Frankfurt market fee which was paid in a sterling silver coin minted on the model of those in England.

[11] *den schultheysen.*

[12] The wealthy should not be allowed to retain private armed squads under the guise of needing them to protect property.

Thirty-eighth, henceforth the small tithe should no longer be paid.

Thirty-ninth, it states in our guild regulations concerning an honorable city council that this council has the power to reduce and increase the articles of the guild regulations. We want to take this out of the books and replace it with this statement: an honorable council should not reduce or augment any article without the knowledge and consent of the craft guilds.

Fortieth, if it is necessary that taxes or fees be paid, then it is the community's conviction that such taxes should not be imposed without the consent of the community, so that the poor and the rich are equally affected.

Forty-first, we desire that henceforth an upright city council should maintain weights and measures. And the annual income that the officeholder has derived from this position[13] should henceforth be placed in the community chest for the good of the poor.

Forty-second, we desire that the members of the Teutonic Order[14] no longer be permitted to pasture pigs in our community fields or meadows.

Forty-third, henceforth during fairs we no longer want to pay cart taxes.[15]

Forty-fourth, the Beguines[16] who live everywhere in the city should be forced into one or two houses, and henceforth no more members be accepted, so that they die out.

Forty-fifth, all the single women who have been clerical concubines, or otherwise maintained themselves through whoring, should not be housed or provided for by anyone.

Forty-sixth and last, it is our conviction that no one should regard the articles listed above as contrived from some suspicious special interest. Rather, they have been conceived and adopted only to praise God almighty and in the best interests of the whole community. And we are determined to realize them in a Christian manner, without

[13] Previously, the warden of the Frankfurt ecclesiastical foundation of St. Bartholomew held the privilege of verifying this measure, for which he charged a fee.

[14] I.e. the house of the Order in Sachsenhausen.

[15] I.e. a market tax calculated according to carts of produce, or portion of a cart, brought to the fair.

[16] Members of a semi-cloistered association of women who led a religious life together in communal households but took no formal vows. They were not an officially recognized order of the church and were occasionally suspected of heresy.

retreating from them. We bid you honorable, provident, and wise council, for a prompt answer between tomorrow morning and one o'clock in the afternoon, with the stipulation that you may contribute something if it is necessary and according to God.

Dated Thursday the thirteenth of April in the year of our Lord 1525.

f Michael Gaismair's *Territorial Constitution for Tyrol*

This is the territorial constitution which Michael Gaismair wrote in the year 1526[1]

First, you will swear[2] to bring together body and goods, not to separate from one another, but to work and live with one another, though at all times acting after consultation with, and being obedient to your superior authorities. And in all matters you swear not to pursue selfish interests, but rather to pursue first of all the honor of God and then the common good, so that almighty God will be gracious and assist us (as he has often promised all who are obedient to his commandments). We should rely completely on God, for he is entirely truthful and deceives no one.

Second, you swear to expel all godless people, who persecute the eternal word of God, burden the poor commoner, and impede the common good.

Third, you swear to establish, and then live completely according to, laws which are wholly Christian, and which in all matters are founded only on the holy word of God.

[1] Gaismair, who was elected by the Tyrolean peasants to be their leader in May 1525, drafted a new constitution for the Tyrol when, after the suppression of the initial rebellion centered in Brixen, he fled to Switzerland and began recruiting a new army from refugees there. His plan was to invade the Tyrol from the west, to overthrow the Habsburgs, and to establish a new government and social order. He wrote the constitution in February or March 1526 as the program for recruiting an army to achieve this. The manuscript version of the constitution was given a title and contains occasional remarks by a hostile copyist. The translation is based on the text in *FB*, 139–43.

[2] *geloben und schwörn*; at the outset the presentation of Gaismair's constitutional proposals takes the form of an oath that the recruits to his army swore.

Fourth, all privileges[3] should be eliminated, for they are contrary to the word of God and falsify justice, in that no one should have an advantage over others.

Fifth, all the encircling walls around cities, castles, and fortifications in the territory should be torn down. And thereafter there should no longer be cities but only villages, so that there are no differences among people in the sense that one is higher than another or able to do wrong to another. For [with walls] there would be disorder in the whole territory, and pride and insurrection might arise. Rather, there should be complete equality in the territory.

Sixth, all images, statues, and chapels which are not parish churches should be abolished together with the Mass in the whole territory, for they are an abomination before God and completely unchristian.

Seventh, the word of God should always be preached faithfully and truthfully in Gaismair's territory,[4] and all sophistry and legalism[5] should be eliminated and the books which contain them burned.

Eighth, the courts throughout the territory should be arranged in the most convenient way and the clergy excluded from them, so that they are administered with the least cost.

Ninth, the whole population of every court district should elect a judge every year and eight jurors, to exercise legal power for that year.

Tenth, court should be held every Monday and all affairs settled on that day, not postponed to another. Judges, jurors, recorders, speakers, lawyers, and messengers should not take any payment from a private individual in legal matters, but be paid by the territory. And every Monday court officers should come before the court at their own expense to be present in court.

Eleventh, a central government should be established for the territory, for which Brixen[6] would be the best location, since it has many parsonages and other facilities, and is in the centre of the territory. And the governors should be elected from all sections of the territory, as well as some from the mines.[7]

---

[3] *freyhaitten* (= *Freiheiten*), liberties or freedoms, but in the sense of privileges, i.e. rights enjoyed by some because of their membership in a social estate or corporation (*Stand*) but denied to others who are not members.

[4] The reference to the Tyrol as "Gaismair's territory" is an addition of the copyist.

[5] I.e. scholastic theology and Roman law.

[6] Today, Bressanone in the Italian Tyrol.

[7] Gaismair makes special provision for the miners to elect representatives who will be

Twelfth, from now on legal appeals should go to the government [in Brixen] and never to Meran,[8] which causes unnecessary expense and provides no service. And from now on appeals should be decided without any delay.

Thirteenth, where the government is located [i.e., provisionally in Brixen] a university should be established where only the word of God is taught. And three learned men from this institution, who are well versed in the word of God and knowledgeable about divine Scripture (from which alone the justice of God may be expounded), should always sit in the government. They should direct and judge all matters according to the commandments of God as they pertain to a Christian people.

After consulting with one another, [the people of] the whole territory should decide whether interest payments should be abolished right away, or whether a "free year" should be established according to the law of God, and during this time the interest paid [should go, not to private persons but] into a fund for common territorial needs. For it is worth considering that the common territory will deplete the fund quickly in the event of war.

With respect to customs payments, it appears to me in the interest of the common man that customs be entirely abolished within the territory. But on the borders customs payments should be established and maintained, so that what comes into the territory is not charged customs duty, but what leaves the territory is so charged.

With respect to the tithe, each should pay it according to the commandment of God. And it should be employed in the following manner: according to the teaching of St. Paul, there should be a pastor in each congregation who proclaims the word of God. And he should be supported in his honorable needs from the tithe. And the remainder of the tithe should be given to the poor. But order should be maintained among the poor, so that no one goes begging from house to house. This is to prevent idleness among many lazy people who are clearly able to work.

Cloisters and the buildings of the Teutonic Knights should be transformed into hospitals. In some, the sick should live together and

among the officials of the central government, because miners were not included in traditional communal forms of association.

[8] Today, Merano; Meran was the old provincial capital of the county (*Grafschaft*) of Tyrol, held by the Habsburgs as a hereditary possession.

be provided with every care and medical attention. In others, old people who are no longer able to work on account of their age should live, and poor orphans, who should be taught and raised to be honorable. But where there are poor people with their own cottages, they should be helped according to the degree of their need from the tithe or from charity, according to the advice of each judge in his administrative district, where these people are best known. Where the tithe is not sufficient to maintain the pastor and the poor, each person should contribute alms in good faith, according to his capacity. And where there is a deficit beyond this, the final payment should be provided from people's incomes.[9] In every hospital there should be a director. A supervisor or governmental official should also be established over all the hospitals and over the poor. And he should do nothing but provision all the hospitals, and provide for the poor. All the judges in their administrative districts should also help him in making payments [for poor relief] with half the tithes and the alms, and in educating the people, including the poor with cottages. The poor should not only be provided with food and drink but also with clothing and all other necessities.

So that good order is maintained throughout the territory in all matters, four commanders and a commander-in-chief should be established for the whole territory. And in the event of war they should be responsible for all matters pertaining to the security of the territory. They should patrol the territory on horses – the administrative districts, the passes, the roads, the bridges, the waterways, the waterworks, and the rural roads. They should do everything that is necessary in the territory and faithfully serve the territory in all its necessities. Further, after inspection and notification they should cite all deficiencies to the government, and they should always act according to its recommendation.

The bogs, lowlands, and other unfruitful places in the territory should also be made fertile, and the common good should not be allowed to deteriorate because of some people who are selfish. All the bogs from Meran to Trent could be dried and many livestock, cows, and sheep maintained on them. Much more grain could also be cultivated in many places, so that the territory would be provided with

---

[9] Gaismair envisions an income tax as the fairest way to supplement the tithe and charity, should additional revenues be required to carry out the government's function of caring for the needy.

meat. In many places olive trees could be planted and saffron cultivated. Also, in vineyards on level ground, the vines should be grown on frames, red grapes planted, and a weaker wine made, as in Italy. And between the frames grain should be cultivated, for the territory is deficient in grain. As a result, the pestiferous moisture would be removed from the bogs and the land would be more fertile. Many sicknesses which come from wine produced on wet earth would end. Wine and grain would be cheaper and require less effort. But the hillside vineyards which are not planted with grain should be left alone.

At a convenient time each year in every district the whole community should work in the fields and the commons, clear them, and make good meadowland, thus thoroughly improving the territory. No one in the territory should practice lending,[10] so that no one is tainted by the sin of usury. So that shortages do not arise and good order be maintained, and also so that no one be overpaid or deceived, but so that fair prices and good wares be found in all matters, in the beginning one place in the territory should be designated – for which Trent would be convenient on account of its prosperity and central location – where all crafts are to be set up, and to which they are to be shifted from the countryside – crafts such as the making of silk cloth, caps, brass wares, velvet, shoes, and other things. And a general official should be established, who has charge of all these things. And what cannot be obtained in the territory, such as spices, should be ordered from outside. [And this official should see to it that] in some convenient places in the territory shops are maintained in which many things are available. And he should see to it that a profit is never made and that only the costs which have been incurred are figured into the price. This will prevent all deception and falsification; the purchaser will get true value in all things; and money will remain in the territory, which will serve the interests of the common man. This official in charge of commerce and his subordinates should be given a certain salary.

A good, solid coinage should again be established, as at the time of Duke Sigmund.[11] The present coinage should be destroyed and banished from the territory, and in addition no foreign coinage accepted, either large coins or small, so that the money is tested and

---

[10] *khaufmanschaft* = commerce or business, but here in the sense of the lending of money.
[11] Archduke Sigmund of Tyrol (1439–90).

valued; and those coins contrary to the common good of the territory should be confiscated.

All chalices and jewelry should be taken from all churches and ecclesiastical buildings, melted down, and used for the common needs of the territory.

Good relations should also be maintained with bordering countries. The Savoyards in the territory should not be allowed to wander around.[12] Henceforth a market should be maintained in the region of the Etsch river and one in the valley of the Inn.[13] The whole territory should have a single set of weights and measures and a single set of laws. The borders and passes should be maintained in good condition. A considerable sum of money should be held in reserve in case the territory becomes involved in an unforeseen war. And the buildings and property of the expelled nobility or others should be used to pay the expenses of the courts.

Concerning the Mines

First, all the refineries, collieries, ore, silver, copper and what belongs to them and are found in the territory, and which are the property of the nobility and foreign merchants and their companies – such as the Fugger, Hochstetter, Baumgarter, Bumpler,[14] and the like – should be brought into common territorial hands. For they have managed them badly and have exercised their rights by demanding unjust profits, getting money by shedding human blood. They have deceived the common man and the worker with bad wares; and by calculating the wares' value in inflated money, they have reduced wages by half. Through their engrossing they caused the price of spices and other goods to be inflated. They are the cause of devalued coinage, for all the master coiners who buy silver from them must pay them according to their falsifications. Or they take coins from the poor man and cut their wages because they do not permit smelters to purchase their ore directly [from producers], but only to buy all the wares of merchants. In this way they gather everything into their hands and inflate prices. And they have so burdened the whole world with their unchristian

---

[12] Through their peddling these Savoyards harmed the livelihood of native craftsmen.

[13] These locations for markets were apparently determined for geographic reasons; the Etsch flows south and the Inn north, thus providing convenient transportation.

[14] Famous south German commercial houses of the early sixteenth century, concentrated especially in Augsburg.

usury, through which they accumulated their princely riches, that they should be justly punished and this situation abolished.

Accordingly, a supervising manager should be established by the territory, with responsibility for controlling all the mines and all commerce and [for rendering] an annual account. And no one [i.e. a private party] should be allowed to refine metals; rather the whole territory, through this supervising official, should license the refining of all ores, determining ore purchases as fairly as possible, paying the workers in cash, and henceforth not making payment with natural products, so that in the future the rural inhabitants and the miners may live together peacefully.

This same official should maintain good order in the refineries and give the territory a considerable income from the mines. For this is the best way to support the territorial government securely in all its offices. But where a deficit appears in the territory, and it is not possible to obtain sufficient income to administer the territory, then a tax must be imposed, so that the burden is born equitably in the territory. These measures should be executed most energetically, and their costs borne by the territory, so that mines are established and developed in more places in the territory. For it is through mining that the territory is able to obtain the most income with the least hardship.

This is the territorial constitution that Gaismair would proclaim if he were a prince lazing beside a stove.[15]

---

[15] An ironic comment by the copyist.

Biographical notes

Denck, Hans (c.1500–27), was born at Heybach in Upper Bavaria and studied at Ingolstadt (1517–19) before becoming a teacher in Regensburg and Basel. On the recommendation of the Basel reformer, Oecolampadius, Denck was appointed rector of the school attached to St. Sebald's parish at Nuremberg in 1523. In 1524 he married. While in Nuremberg he came into contact with radical religious ideas and was drawn into the trial of three "godless" painters, assistants of Albrecht Dürer, who were tried for heresy. On 21 January 1525 Denck was banished for life from Nuremberg. He may then have gone to Mühlhausen to teach, at the invitation of Thomas Müntzer. According to legend, Denck, together with Heinrich Pfeiffer, Müntzer's Mühlhausen associate, and three hundred religious radicals, fled Mühlhausen on 22 May 1525, following the defeat of the peasant army at the battle of Frankenhausen. Unlike Pfeiffer, Denck eluded subsequent arrest and made his way to St. Gall, where he worked as a proofreader.

From September 1525 to October 1526 he was at Augsburg, where he was a member of radical religious circles; according to tradition, Denck baptized Hans Hut in Augsburg. There he also wrote three treatises, including *On the Law of God*. Rather than appear at a hearing, Denck fled Augsburg in October 1526. He went to Strasbourg, where in October he engaged in a public disputation with Bucer. Banished from Strasbourg, Denck was briefly in Bergzabern and Landau before moving on to Worms in early 1527. He apparently left Worms in early July, following the city's decision to exile religious radicals. Denck participated in the so-called "Martyrs Synod" of Anabaptist leaders, many of whom were later executed, at Augsburg in August 1527. Then after brief stays in Ulm and Nuremberg, he returned to Basel. Shortly before he died of the plague at Basel in late 1527, he wrote a letter to his former patron, Oecolampadius, expressing regret for the course his life had taken.

Gaismair, Michael (c.1490–1532) was born at the village of Tschöfs above Sterzing, Tyrol, to a family of prosperous peasants; his father added to familial holdings and became a mining entrepreneur. Young Gaismair was sent to school and trained to be a secretary; he married about 1507. In 1523 he was a state secretary for the vice-regent of Tyrol. Unable to clear himself of a charge of embezzling funds, he lost this position, but in May 1525 he had become the secretary of the prince-bishop of Brixen. When the Peasants' War erupted in Tyrol, Gaismair initially defended episcopal property by refusing to admit rebellious peasants into the episcopal palace in Brixen; then he suddenly accepted the position of leadership to which the peasants elected him on 13 May.

Based in Brixen, the insurgents attempted to negotiate with the Habsburg government of King Ferdinand, duke of Tyrol, at the Diet of Innsbruck in June and July. Gaismair was lured to Innsbruck and imprisoned. He escaped and fled to Zurich. With Zwingli's support, he gathered an army composed largely of refugees who had fled to Switzerland. With this army he planned to invade Tyrol and to establish a new government; his *Territorial Constitution for Tyrol* was drawn up in February 1526 as the army's revolutionary program. The invasion from Switzerland was betrayed, but Gaismair led his army across the Tyrol to assist the rebellion at Salzburg. When this rebellion was put down, he tried to invade the Tyrol from the east by marching on Brixen. Threatened by the forces of the Swabian League, Gaismair then led his army to the republic of Venice, where he was engaged as a mercenary captain. He hoped that with the support of Zurich and France (the League of Cognac), as well as Venice, a republican Tyrol could be established. These allies proved unreliable, and with the dissolution of the League of Cognac in 1529, his army fell apart. In April 1532 Gaismair was assassinated on his estate in Padua by killers seeking the price that had been put on his head by the Habsburg government.

Grebel, Conrad (1498–1526), the son of a Zurich patrician family, pursued humanistic studies at Vienna and Paris before returning to his native city. He came under Zwingli's influence and in the spring of 1522 joined the evangelical cause in Zurich; at Lent, Grebel and others openly violated fasting regulations by eating meat. That summer he was cited before the city's Small Council for interrupting sermons. By the fall of 1523 Grebel joined a group of Zurich artisans, led by Andreas Castelberger, that was meeting privately to study the Bible and to discuss religious issues. Partly because of his education and patrician background, Grebel, together with Felix Manz and Castelberger, emerged as the leaders of this circle, which soon came to differ with Zwingli over the issues of the sacrifice of the Mass, images, and tithes and interest payments. Following the Second Zurich Disputation in October 1523, in which Grebel participated, the rupture between Zwingli and his more radical followers was evident. By the end of 1523 the Zurich "brethren," as the radicals called themselves, had come to repudiate Zwingli's leadership, in large part because of his continuing reliance on the city council as the means for reform. The *Letter to Thomas Müntzer* which Grebel wrote in the name of the Zurich radicals in September 1524 provides evidence of its rift with Zwingli.

On 21 January 1525, following the Zurich council's condemnation of those opposed to infant baptism, Grebel rebaptized the priest George Blaurock at the home of Felix Manz, an event conventionally viewed as the start of the Anabaptist movement. Thereafter Grebel and his Zurich associates came together with other radicalized disciples of Zwingli who were reforming villages and small towns in the canton of Zurich. Many of these rural radicals also supported the peasantry during the Peasants' War. Grebel became an energetic missionary, travelling to Schaffhausen, Waldshut, St. Gall, and the Zurich *Oberland*. The Anabaptist movement at this time was divided between those favoring a communal Reformation, which could legitimately be defended with force, and those like Grebel who advocated nonviolence and a separatist church. On 8 October 1525 Grebel was arrested for fomenting unrest in the Zurich *Oberland*. The authorities decided to keep him in prison until he was willing to recant. Through a guard's negligence he escaped on 21 March 1526. Later that spring, in May or June 1526, Grebel died of the plague at Maienfeld in the Gray Leagues, Switzerland.

Hergot, Hans (?–1527), about whom little is known, was an apparently self-educated Nuremberg printer and colporteur. In October or early November 1524 Thomas Müntzer's *Special Exposure of False Faith* was printed in Hergot's shop. When city officials discovered and confiscated the publication, Hergot claimed it was printed in his absence and without his knowledge by shop apprentices. He was not punished by the city council, but he may have left Nuremberg soon thereafter. It is not known where he was during the Peasants' War. In 1526 his wife was allowed to complete a business transaction in Nuremberg in his absence. In May 1527 Hergot was arrested in Zwickau for distributing a "seditious" pamphlet he evidently wrote, *The New Transformation of the Christian Life*. Although Hergot's authorship is open to question, the bulk of the evidence supports it. A contemporary referred to the tract as his, and two students at the university of Leipzig who were also arrested for distributing the work – and who may have given the authorities Hergot's name – were punished with only a brief imprisonment. Hergot was beheaded at Leipzig on 20 May 1527. After his death his wife married an apprentice and continued to run the Nuremberg print shop.

Hubmaier, Balthasar (c.1484–1528) was born at Friedberg, near Augsburg. After taking minor orders, he enrolled at the university of Freiburg im Breisgau (1503–10), where he studied theology with Johann Eck. In 1510 Eck accepted a professorship at Ingolstadt; in 1512 Hubmaier, now ordained a priest, followed him. Hubmaier received his doctorate in theology at Ingolstadt, where he remained as a professor and preacher. Having ascended the academic hierarchy to prorector of the university, he left Ingolstadt in January 1516 for unexplained reasons and became a cathedral preacher at Regensburg. While at Regensburg (1516–20) Hubmaier was a leader of an anti-Jewish movement in the city.

In 1520 he left Regensburg, again for unexplained reasons, to become pastor of the church of St. Mary at Waldshut, a small provincial town in

Habsburg lands in the Breisgau. Here, in the early 1520s, he became an adherent of the evangelical movement, having contact with Zwingli and others, denouncing traditional practices, and calling for religious reform. In October 1523 he attended the Second Zurich Disputation on images and the Mass. Secular and ecclesiastical authorities demanded Hubmaier's extradition, but the city council at Waldshut supported him. He married Elizabeth Hügeline, the daughter of a citizen of Reichenau. When Ferdinand of Austria threatened to use force, Hubmaier left Waldshut on 1 September 1524 for Schaffhausen. Feeling unsafe in Switzerland, he returned to Waldshut in October 1524, where he continued his reform program and became a leader of the city's resistance to its Austrian overlord. At Easter 1525, following growing contact with Swiss radicals, Hubmaier was baptized by Wilhelm Reublin, one of the first Zurich Anabaptists.

During the Peasants' War, Hubmaier supported the peasants and was aided by them. He and Müntzer may have written a "Constitutional Draft" (*Verfassungsentwurf*), ideas for a new popular government, that influenced *The Memmingen Federal Constitution* and *The Document of Articles*. After the defeat of the peasants at Griessen, Waldshut was conquered by Austrian troops; Hubmaier fled the city on 5 December 1525 just before it was occupied. He found refuge in Zurich, which refused to extradite him, but in order to remain there, he recanted his position on baptism. He also repudiated his earlier support for the Peasants' War. Fearful for his safety, he secretly left Zurich, travelled to Constance and Augsburg, and in the summer of 1526 moved on to Moravia.

In July 1526 he settled at Nikolsburg, Moravia. Under Hubmaier's leadership and with the protection of the local lord, Leonhard von Leichtenstein, Nikolsburg became an early Anabaptist center (1526–28), attracting many immigrants. Conflicts arose among the radicals in Nikolsburg. Hubmaier opposed the views of both Hans Hut, who rejected paying war taxes and accepted the legitimacy of forceful resistance, and the separatist and nonresisting "people of the staff" (*Stäbler*), who disagreed with Hubmaier's support for the government. Hubmaier wrote *On the Sword*, one of many tracts he published at Nikolsburg, in June 1527, as a refutation of the *Stäbler* position. Shortly thereafter Hubmaier was arrested at Nikolsburg at the behest of the new Habsburg government of Moravia. His political past in Waldshut had caught up with him. Convicted of heresy and insurrection, on 10 March 1528 he was burned at the stake in Vienna. Three days later his wife was executed by drowning.

Hut, Hans (c.1490–1527), in the early 1520s was an itinerant bookseller, residing at his native village of Bibra, near Meiningen, and traveling between Nuremberg and Wittenberg. He was a married layman, apparently self-educated. He may have met with Karlstadt in Orlamünde as well as Müntzer in Allstedt; he certainly came under the influence of the latter. When Müntzer was expelled from Mühlhausen in September 1524, he entrusted the publication of his *Special Exposure of False Faith* to Hut, who knew Nuremberg printers. In Nuremberg Hut also came to know Hans Denck. Early in 1525 Hut was expelled from Bibra for refusing to have the last of his three children baptized. In the spring of 1525 he was with Müntzer at Mühlhausen, where his name appears on the membership list of Müntzer's "Eternal Covenant" or "League" (*Ewiger Bund*).

Hut was present at the disastrous battle of Frankenhausen on 15 May 1525, but managed to escape; for a time he continued to preach resistance, arguing that the final apocalyptic conflict remained imminent. With the end of the Peasants' War, Hut became a wanted man. By the spring of 1526 he had made contact with Anabaptists, and on Pentecost 1526 was baptized by Denck; thereafter he became a secretive missionary, seeking to spread radical religious ideas especially among former participants in the Peasants' War in Franconia. When Franconian authorities began the persecution of religious radicals in the spring of 1527, Hut was unable to return after a stay in Augsburg. Instead he travelled to Nikolsburg in Moravia, where Hubmaier was established. Following public debate with Hubmaier, Hut was imprisoned and threatened with extradition. Instead he fled. Late in the summer of 1527 Hut and some of his followers met at Augsburg at the so-called "Martyrs Synod," where disagreements appeared between his views and those of Upper German and Swiss Anabaptists; Hut rejected the nonresisting separatism expressed in *The Schleitheim Articles*. A few weeks later Hut was arrested at Augsburg. Investigation and torture revealed Hut's radical background and commitments, and he was sentenced to death. In December 1527 he died as a result of a mysterious fire in his cell. The authorities said the fire broke out during an attempt to escape; Hut's son said a candle was accidentally tipped over as Hut lay in his cell after a session on the rack.

Karlstadt, Andreas Rudolf Bodenstein von (1486–1541), came from a patrician family of the small town, Karlstadt am Main. He studied at Erfurt and Cologne before receiving his M.A. (1505) and doctorate in theology (1510) from Wittenberg. In 1510 he was ordained, and from 1511 he was a professor of theology at Wittenberg. After initially criticizing Luther's new theological ideas, on 26 April 1517 Karlstadt publicly supported him with 152 "Theses on nature, law and grace," and thereafter Karlstadt was one of the most important exponents of the new Wittenberg theology.

By 1521 Karlstadt was opposed to the veneration of images, priestly celibacy, and monastic vows, and during Luther's absence at Wartburg castle, Karlstadt assumed leadership of the Wittenberg reform movement. On Christmas 1521 Karlstadt celebrated the first evangelical Mass when he dispensed with vestments and distributed communion in both forms to the laity. On 19 January 1522 he married Anna von Mochau, the orphaned daughter of one of the Saxon elector's military officers. In January his demand that a Wittenberg council resolution against religious images be acted upon touched off iconoclastic disturbances. The unrest contributed to the elector's decision to slow the reform movement; Karlstadt's preaching activities were curtailed to lessen his influence on the laity. In March Luther returned to Wittenberg and preached against the pace and scope of Karlstadt's reform program. After this, Karlstadt was denied permission to publish his works.

When his activities were restricted by the university, Karlstadt began to criticize academic life.

In February 1523 he received a leave of absence from the university to take up pastoral duties at the small town of Orlamünde am Saale. At Orlamünde Karlstadt had an opportunity to carry out his Reformation program unhindered, but only briefly. In the summer of 1524 the university ordered him back to Wittenberg. His congregation, against the will of the authorities, urged him to remain as pastor, and on 22 July he resigned his archdeaconship. In August he and Luther had a fruitless discussion at Jena, following which his congregation defended him against Luther. In September 1524 Karlstadt was banished from Saxony.

On a trip through southwestern Germany, Karlstadt came into contact with religious radicals who were interested in the issue of infant baptism. In Basel, Gerhard Westerburg, his brother-in-law, and Felix Manz arranged for the publication of some of his writings, including *Whether One Should Proceed Slowly*. In December 1524 Karlstadt arrived at Rothenberg ob der Tauber, where he remained, despite an expulsion order from the city council, until May 1525. During the Peasants' War, Luther branded him a rebel, despite the fact that Karlstadt's *Letter from the Community at Orlamünde to the People of Allstedt* (July 1524) rejected the revolutionary violence of Müntzer. In fact Karlstadt attempted to persuade the rebellious Franconian peasantry to renounce violence. In the immediate aftermath of the Peasants' War, he was hunted as an insurrectionary. In July 1525 Luther secretly gave him protection – in exchange for Karlstadt's promise to give up further preaching and writing. The terms of his asylum also restricted him to the region around Wittenberg, where he fell into poverty despite working as a peasant and retail trader. His covert efforts to maintain contact with fellow radicals were discovered and he was confined to house arrest. Despite Luther's pressures, Karlstadt refused to write against Zwingli, and when threatened with imprisonment, he fled Wittenberg early in 1529. After travels which took him to Kiel and East Friesland, Karlstadt traveled south through Strasbourg and Basel to Zurich, where Zwingli helped him obtain a position. By the end of 1530 Karlstadt was a supporter of the Reformation in Zurich. In June 1534 he returned to academic life, accepting a professorship at Basel. He died of the plague on 24 December 1541.

Lotzer, Sebastian (c.1490–?), came from a learned family in Horb, in the Württemberg territory of Hohenberg. Rather than pursuing a university education, as his father and brother did, he became a furrier. His travels as a journeyman took him to the imperial city of Memmingen, where he married the daughter of the shopkeeper Weigelin and became a citizen. He joined the evangelical movement in 1522, almost as soon as it came to Memmingen, and was a close friend of one of the city's leading evangelical preachers, Christoph Schappeler. During the Peasants' War the city of Memmingen became an urban center of the insurrection in southwest Germany. Lotzer and Schappeler helped write the petition which the Memmingen peasants submitted to the city council on 24 February 1525, and which became the basis of *The*

Twelve Articles, published on 19 March. The work was based on earlier grievance lists compiled in Upper Swabia, but Lotzer may have been mainly responsible for the final formulation of the articles and Schappeler for the biblical citations.

The Twelve Articles became the program of the peasant armies that assembled on 27 February at Memmingen to form the Christian Union of the Allgäu, Baltringen, and Lake Constance armies. Lotzer worked for this broad alliance of rebellious peasants and held the position of "field secretary" (*Feldschreiber*) in the Baltringen army under Ulrich Schmid. Both Lotzer and Schmid advocated a peaceful settlement of peasant grievances through negotiations with the princes – a futile strategy, given the Swabian League's determination to crush the rebellion with military force. Following the defeat of the Baltringen army and the Treaty of Weingarten (17 April), which sealed the fate of the peasant movement in upper Swabia, the Swabian League ordered Memmingen to arrest Lotzer. But he was no longer in the city. With the peasants' defeat, Lotzer and Schmid fled to St. Gall, Switzerland, the hometown of Schappeler. Here Lotzer was concealed and presumably lived out the remainder of his life under an assumed name.

Manz, Felix (c.1498–1526), the son of a Zurich canon, received some education and was an early lay supporter of Zwingli's reform movement at Zurich. Like Conrad Grebel, Manz broke with Zwingli in late 1523, especially when Zwingli left the decision about abolishing the Mass to the city council. The circle of Zurich radicals around Grebel, Manz, and Castelberger frequently met at the home of Manz's mother. On 17 January 1525 the city council held a public disputation on infant baptism, with Grebel and Manz speaking against it. In his *Protest and Defense*, written shortly before the disputation, Manz submitted his position to the Zurich council in writing and insisted that Zwingli do likewise. When the council decided the disputation in favor of Zwingli, and on 18 January threatened to banish those who refused to have their children baptized, the Zurich "brethren" instituted a rite of adult or believer's baptism.

The movement of the brethren spread quickly in the city and canton of Zurich. Manz was repeatedly arrested for zealously propagandizing in favor of adult baptism. The city council held a second and a third public disputation on infant baptism on 20 March and 6–8 November 1525; at both, Manz again argued against it. With each arrest, the Zurich council imposed severer punishments on Manz and other members of the movement. On 7 March 1526 Manz, Grebel, Blaurock, and fifteen others were sentenced to life imprisonment on bread and water, and the council made future "rebaptism" subject to the death penalty. By an act of clemency the prisoners were released, but they soon resumed their radical preaching and baptisms. On 3 December 1526 Manz and Blaurock were arrested at a meeting in the region of Grüningen and taken to prison at Zurich. On 5 January 1527 Manz was sentenced to death by drowning for his radical activities, and Blaurock, not a citizen, to whipping and expulsion. Manz was executed in Lake Zurich on the day of sentencing.

Müntzer, Thomas (c.1489–1525), was born at Stolberg in the Harz mountains. Little is known about his family background. He studied at the universities of Leipzig (1506) and Frankfurt am Oder (1512), but it is not known from what university he obtained the degrees of master of arts and bachelor of theology. In 1515 he became a chantry priest at Brunswick. Between 1517 and 1519 he was at Wittenberg, where he had contact with Luther and Karlstadt. Sermons he gave in 1519 at Jüterbog led a hostile witness to describe him as a "Lutheran." In 1520–21 he preached at Zwickau, where he sided in city politics with the disenfranchised and with those in the council seeking to repudiate outside ecclesiastical authority; following disturbances in the city he left Zwickau. Later in 1521 he travelled to Bohemia. He preached at Prague, where he was also viewed as a follower of Luther, and in November wrote his *Prague Protest*.

After a year of hardship and travel following his expulsion from Bohemia in early 1522, Müntzer arrived at the small market town of Allstedt in electoral Saxony at Easter 1523. The town council appointed him pastor of the church of St. John without the approval of the patron, the Saxon elector, Frederick the Wise. In Allstedt, Müntzer introduced the first vernacular liturgy of the German Reformation. He married the former nun Ottilie von Gersen. His reform program was a success in Allstedt, and he soon enjoyed a wide following in the surrounding countryside. Due to Müntzer's influence, Count Ernst of Mansfeld attempted to prohibit his subjects from attending services in Allstedt. This Müntzer protested. In November 1523 Müntzer's activities at Allstedt were investigated by the university of Wittenberg, but no action was taken against him. In March 1524 a group of Müntzer's followers, members of a secret covenant or league (*Bund*) which may have been formed as early as 1523, burned the small pilgrimage chapel of Mallerbach, near Allstedt. Müntzer defended the deed and worked to hinder its investigation by electoral officials. On 13 July 1524 he preached the *Sermon to the Princes* at the Allstedt castle before Saxon rulers and officials. On 31 July–1 August, Müntzer and the Allstedt council were interrogated in Weimar by ducal officials, and Müntzer was ordered to end his radical agitation.

A week later he fled Allstedt and went to Mühlhausen, a Thuringian imperial city, where he joined another radical reformer, Heinrich Pfeiffer. Between 19 and 26 September Mühlhausen was shaken by rebellion; Müntzer and Pfeiffer contributed to *The Eleven Mühlhausen Articles* which were written at this time. On 27 September both were expelled from the city. Later in the fall of 1524 both of Müntzer's final treatises against Luther, *A Special Exposure of False Faith* and *A Highly Provoked Defense*, were secretly printed at Nuremberg. Müntzer travelled at this time to southwestern Germany, where he made contact with fellow-radicals, preached to the peasants who had risen in Klettgau and Hegau, and may have written with Hubmaier "some articles drawn from the gospel on how one should govern," a draft constitution that influenced *The Memmingen Federal Constitution* and *The Document of Articles*.

In late February 1525, Müntzer returned to Mühlhausen and rejoined Pfeiffer, who had been readmitted to the city two months earlier. In March a revolution in Mühlhausen led to the formation of a new government, the Eternal Council, and a more radical association which Müntzer developed, the Eternal League of God. When the Peasants' War swept Thuringia in April, Mühlhausen became an urban center of the insurrection, Muntzer and Pfeiffer campaigned with peasant troops and worked assiduously to promote the uprising. On 11 May a Mühlhausen military contingent under Müntzer marched to join the peasants assembled at Frankenhausen while Pfeiffer remained behind to defend the city. Following the devastation of the peasant army at the battle of Frankenhausen on 15 May, Müntzer was arrested. After interrogation and torture he was executed by beheading outside the walls of Mühlhausen on 27 May 1525.

Pfeiffer, Heinrich (?–1525), also known as Heinrich Schwertfeger, Müntzer's associate at Mühlhausen, was a native of that city. He became a Cistercian monk at the monastery of Reifenstein in the region of Eichsfeld, but in 1522 renounced the cloister. By early 1523 he was again at Mühlhausen and soon became a popular evangelical preacher at the suburban church of St. Nicholas. The city council's efforts to have him removed resulted in demonstrations that led to changes in city government and the adoption of ordinances in favor of the Reformation. In August 1523 Pfeiffer was briefly banished from the city, but he returned in December. Early in 1524 his preaching led to new disturbances in the city.

With Müntzer's arrival at Mühlhausen in mid-August 1524, he and Pfeiffer worked together to further the Reformation there. Insofar as *The Eleven Mühlhausen Articles* (22–23 September) represented long-standing grievances, Pfeiffer may have contributed more to their formulation than Müntzer did. Some articles also show traces of Müntzer's distinctive ideas. As a result of the agitation in the city which led to the framing of the articles, Pfeiffer and Müntzer were both expelled from Mühlhausen on 27 September after the council regained control. Pfeiffer then travelled to Nuremberg, where he engaged in public debate and attempted to have two pamphlets published. Expelled from Nuremberg, he returned to Thuringia and took up his cause in the countryside around Mühlhausen. In December 1524 he was readmitted to the city. In January 1525 altarpieces were removed from Mühlhausen churches, and the mendicant cloisters came under attack. In late February Müntzer, too, was readmitted to Mühlhausen, and in March the two radical preachers worked together to bring about a revolution in the city that resulted in the installation of a new council, the Eternal Council, which had been envisioned in the Mühlhausen Articles. Neither Pfeiffer nor Müntzer was a member of this council.

When the Peasants' War broke out in Thuringia in April 1525, Pfeiffer worked with Müntzer to make Mühlhausen a center of the insurrection. In late April the two preachers participated in campaigns with a military contingent from Mühlhausen. There is scant evidence of a disagreement between the two, although Pfeiffer remained in Mühlhausen when Müntzer led a military unit to join the peasants at Frankenhausen. Rather, Pfeiffer remained to guard their strategic base. Following the defeat at Frankenhausen, as princely armies prepared for the subjugation of Mühlhausen, Pfeiffer and three hundred radicals fled the city on 22 May. Pfeiffer was captured near Eisenach. On 27 May Müntzer and Pfeiffer were beheaded outside the city walls of Mühlhausen.

Sattler, Michael (c. 1490–1527), was born at Staufen in the Breisgau. He became a Benedictine monk, and perhaps prior, of the monastery of St. Peter's in the Black Forest, fifteen kilometers east of Freiburg, where he learned Latin. Sometime in the mid-1520s he left the monastery, possibly because of sympathy he felt for the peasants protesting dues they owed the monastery; in May 1525 the monastery was invaded by the army of the Black Forest peasants. In late 1525, Sattler, by this time married, was at Zurich in the company of Anabaptists; on 18 November he was expelled from the city. He learned weaving in the Zurich *Unterland*, north of the city, and evidently joined the Anabaptist movement in the summer of 1526. Later in 1526 he was in Strasbourg.

Following his participation at the Schleitheim conference in February 1527, where he was the principal author of *The Schleitheim Articles*, he was arrested in March while engaged in missionary and pastoral activity at Horb. He was tried at Rottenberg am Necker on 17–18 May and executed there on 20 May. The sentence specified that Sattler should be handed over to the hangman, "who shall lead him into the square and cut off his tongue, then chain him to a wagon, there tear his body twice with red hot tongs, and again when it is brought before the city gate, five more times. When this is done he is to be burned to powder as a heretic." Two days after Sattler's execution, his wife, Margaretha, was executed by drowning.

Schappeler, Christoph (c.1472–1551), an evangelical preacher in Memmingen and, with Sebastian Lotzer, a main contributor to *The Twelve Articles of the Upper Swabian Peasants*. Schappeler received a licentiate at St. Gall, Switzerland, his native city. He must have known Karlstadt early, for the latter's first work (1508) was dedicated to Schappeler. He was appointed preacher at St. Martin's church at Memmingen in 1513. His sermons frequently expressed a critical stand on social issues. In 1521 he protested the way the judicial system put the poor at a disadvantage. From 1522 on, he joined the evangelical movement and attacked papal authority, the clergy's manner of life, the Mass, and canon law.

In October 1523 Schappeler was among those who presided over the Second Zurich Disputation, and the influence of Zwingli on his religious ideas seems more important than that of Luther. Schappeler's ideas made an impression on the Memmingen journeyman furrier, Sebastian Lotzer, perhaps because of Schappeler's view that the laity needed to be liberated from clerical domination, and the two became friends. In February 1524 Schappeler was excommunicated for his radical views. He remained popular in Memmingen and the surrounding villages, and the city council took no action against him. In the second half of 1524, the council abolished clerical privileges. Schappeler introduced a German liturgy at Memmingen, and on 7

December he distributed Communion in both forms. Early in 1525 a public debate took place in Memmingen between Schappeler and the priest, Megerich, who had opposed Schappeler's evangelical views. Schappeler was declared the winner, which cleared the way for the adoption of further reforms at Memmingen.

When the Peasants' War reached Memmingen, Schappeler, like Lotzer, combined his evangelicalism with support for the uprising. Between 28 February and 3 March 1525, Schappeler cooperated with Lotzer in the formulation of the grievances of the Baltringen peasants, a petition which in its later published version became known as *The Twelve Articles*, the most widespread and influential program of the Peasants' War. But on 2 May 1525 Schappeler wrote Zwingli a letter in which he regretted the violent course the Peasants' War had taken. Following the defeat of the Baltringen peasants by the army of the Swabian League, Schappeler barely escaped from Memmingen when the League army occupied the city on 9 June 1525. Schappeler fled to his native St. Gall, where he again came into contact with Lotzer, who had also sought refuge there. Schappeler held a variety of positions in and near St. Gall until his death on 25 August 1551.

Westerburg, Gerhard (1490s–1558), from a patrician family of Cologne, studied at Cologne (1514–15) and Bologna (1515–17), where he received a doctorate in both civil and canon law. He was drawn to the Reformation by Nikolaus Storch, one of the so-called "Zwickau prophets," with whom Westerburg visited Wittenberg in 1522. Westerburg soon became a supporter, and then reforming associate, of Andreas Karlstadt in Wittenberg and later at Orlamünde. He married Karlstadt's sister and was expelled from Saxony with Karlstadt in September 1524. In November of that year Westerburg, assisted by Felix Manz, saw to the publication at Basel of several of Karlstadt's writings, including *Whether One Should Proceed Slowly*.

Westerburg then settled at Frankfurt am Main, where he became a leader in radical religious circles, and where he influenced *The Forty-six Frankfurt Articles* (13–20 April 1525). When the Swabian League suppressed the popular cause in Frankfurt, Westerburg was banished from the city on 17 May 1525. He returned to his native Cologne, where in 1526 he was condemned for heresy but allowed to remain. By the end of the 1520s, Westerburg was drawn to the emergent Anabaptist movement in Cologne. He formally joined the movement during the Anabaptist revolution at Münster, where in January 1534 he was baptized at the home of Bernard Knipperdolling, a revolutionary leader in the city. Much of Westerburg's later life was spent in northern Germany – Prussia, Emden, and East Friesland – where his religious views became more conservative. He joined the Reformed Church and in 1542 he became a counselor to the duke of Prussia.

Index of subjects

abbot 68, 91
abomination xxii, 14, 16, 18, 44, 60,
    147, 174–76, 255
accusation 74, 89, 95, 184, 194
admonition xxiii, 38, 41, 44–47, 97, 99,
    119, 126, 155, 176, 177, 240, 243,
    244
adultery 51, 53, 58, 62–64, 81, 138,
    139, 177, 193
alliance (allies) xv, xxviii, 33, 34, 71,
    262, 267; see also covenant,
    federation, league
alms 249, 257; see also charity
altar 29, 41, 70, 71, 85, 115
anarchy xiii
angel 23, 27, 31, 47, 89, 184, 186, 189,
    200
anger 26, 29, 65, 75, 117, 140, 144,
    201, 204
antichristians 232
anticlericalism xii
antinomianism xxii, 173n
apocalypticism xii, xxv
apostles 9, 12–14, 23, 24, 29, 35, 40,
    44, 46, 51, 59, 96, 97, 98, 100, 137,
    142, 150–55, 157, 165, 174, 179,
    219
arbitrariness (arbitrary opinion, power)
    xx, 38, 51, 76, 116, 118, 120, 122,
    127, 155, 185
armies, peasant xix, xxi, xxix, xxx, 127–
    29, 239n, 243, 254n, 261, 262, 267,
    269–71
arrogance 3, 14, 39, 75, 111, 206

artisan xii, 81, 262; see also crafts
assembly xxiv, 51, 56, 62, 91, 122, 123,
    127, 176, 180, 239
authority, authorities xiii, xv–xix, xxi–
    xxv, xxviii, 1, 11n, 14, 25, 27, 28,
    49n, 51, 72, 80, 86, 88, 101, 102–
    12, 118, 120–22, 124, 127, 128,
    161, 174, 177, 178, 182, 183, 186,
    187, 191–94, 196–98, 201–9, 212,
    214, 216, 217, 228, 229, 231, 234,
    235, 239–41, 244, 247, 251, 254,
    263–66, 268, 270

ban xxiv, 8, 42n, 174, 176, 177, 180,
    191, 193, 194, 243, 244, 245; see also
    excommunication, exile
baptism xvi, xvii, xxiii, xxiv, xxix, 37, 38,
    43, 44, 46, 47, 95–100, 130, 152,
    155, 161–63, 165, 166, 167–71, 174,
    175, 191, 214, 263, 264, 266, 267;
    see also infant baptism
begging 211, 213, 224, 247, 249; see
    also mendicants
behavior xviii, xxii, 37, 147, 164, 218,
    232, 246; see also conduct
belief xv, 95, 148, 152, 224; see also faith
benefice 33n, 41, 248, 249
benefit 59, 106, 116, 133, 149, 153,
    178, 209, 235
biblicism xvii, 40n; see also literalism
bishops xxviii, 110, 113, 115, 192, 203,
    262; see also prelates
blasphemy xx, 51–53, 62, 85, 86, 90,
    121, 208, 241

blessedness 121, 158, 161, 192, 196, 225

bloodshed 110, 205, 244

boasting (bragging) 34, 77, 88, 89, 92, 111, 121, 128, 137, 151, 155, 156, 169, 182, 220

body of Christ, church as 39, 135, 158, 162, 165, 174–76, 178, 200, 201, 202

bond 39, 57, 152, 163, 164, 214

bondage 12, 90n

books 5, 8, 13, 66, 77, 131, 157, 215, 220, 222, 252, 255

brotherhood 36, 107, 116, 243, 244

brotherly love 39, 53–56, 64–66, 104, 106, 117, 121, 190, 198, 208, 235, 236, 239, 244, 250

brotherly unity 108, 109, 126, 246

Bund xx, 239, 265, 268; *see also* alliance, covenant, federation, league

burdens 2, 107, 108, 113, 137, 166, 192, 231, 236, 238, 243, 244, 246, 248, 249, 254, 259, 260

burgher 223n; *see also* citizen

calling 45, 127, 164, 187, 232, 264

canon law 86n, 103n, 270, 271

castle xxvii, xxviii, 11, 28, 49, 221, 240, 265, 268

ceremonies 15, 34, 37, 96, 99, 137, 159, 160, 168, 191

chalice 9, 131; *see also* cup

chantry 128, 268

charity xviii, 257; *see also* love

chastisement 79, 128

chronicles 24, 30, 34, 72, 110, 127, 131, 190, 200, 203

circumcision 56, 73, 97–99

citizen (citizenry) 46, 95, 100, 248, 250, 264, 266, 267

citizenship 96, 178, 251

city councils xiii, xxix, 94, 95, 99, 221, 227, 229, 246, 248, 252, 262–64, 266, 267, 269, 270

civil equality xx, xxi

civil law 99, 103n, 271

clergy xii, xiii, xviii, xxiii, 2, 3, 7, 9, 11, 13, 14, 25, 26, 47, 52, 84, 86, 96, 98, 109, 113, 212, 219, 221, 246, 247, 255, 270; *see also* minister, parson, pastor, preacher

cleverness 25, 26, 89, 124

cloister 88, 92, 210–13, 215, 217, 240, 242, 245, 247, 256, 269

coercion xix, xxiv, 25, 80, 125, 176, 183, 204, 208, 245

cohabitation 247

coins 137, 139, 214–17, 250, 251; *see also* money

coinage 216, 258, 259; *see also* minting

command, commandment 39, 42, 44, 53, 54, 56, 58, 62–64, 72, 78, 81, 84, 85, 97, 100, 102, 108, 114, 127, 133, 137, 151, 154, 155, 157, 161, 171, 174, 175, 177, 178, 186, 187, 191–93, 197, 198, 200–3, 205, 208, 209, 228, 230, 244, 256

commerce 72, 81, 258, 260

common chest (common fund) 106, 109, 118

common good 106, 108, 109, 121, 207, 210–18, 254, 257, 258

common land (commons) 250, 258

common man, the commoner xii, xiii, xxi, xxii, xxiii, xxv, xxvi, 110, 116, 118, 132, 157, 243, 244, 254, 256, 258, 259

commonweal xviii, xxvi, 213, 229, 245

Communion xxvii, 7n, 40, 214, 265, 271; *see also* Eucharist, Lord's Supper

community (commune) xv, xvi, xvii, xviii, xx–xxviii, xxxi, 12, 13, 29, 33, 39–42, 49, 56, 57, 58, 61, 74, 75, 80, 87, 99, 112, 114, 115, 117–19, 122, 135, 152, 156, 161–63, 168, 174, 175, 176, 181, 183, 188, 189, 191, 211–15, 227, 228, 235, 237, 239, 241, 243, 244, 247, 249–52, 255, 258, 263; *see also* congregation

conduct 41, 44, 50, 58, 131, 132, 135, 136, 153, 159, 164, 191, 212, 213, 219, 230; *see also* behavior

confession 44, 88, 214, 247

congregation xvi, 33, 35, 38, 49, 56, 181, 212, 232, 233, 247, 256, 266; *see also* community

conscience 8, 20, 127, 147, 172, 190, 207, 209, 225

consciousness 18, 24, 143, 167

consolation (consoling) xxiii, 43, 44, 77,

83, 112, 129, 140, 145, 148, 163–
  66, 172, 178
contemplation 21, 82
contrived faith xvi, 6, 12, 36, 42, 76,
  154, 166
conversion 7, 130, 140
corruption xii, xvii, xix, 9, 16, 26, 40,
  82, 83, 107, 245
counsel 3, 17, 39, 42, 84, 99, 123, 178,
  179, 206, 208, 230, 251
courage 32, 132, 165
covenant xx, 34, 39, 52, 56–59, 62, 67,
  71, 76–78, 142, 146, 161–63, 239,
  241, 265, 268; *see also* alliance,
  federation, league
crafts (craftsmen) 210, 213, 227, 229,
  241, 258, 259; *see also* artisan
creation 156–58
"creaturely" desires, things xx, xxii, 16,
  22, 136, 143, 144, 148, 159, 160,
  166, 167, 168
creatures xxiii, 2, 5, 16, 66, 76, 81,
  133, 136, 144, 145, 148, 149, 156–
  62, 170, 171, 175, 187, 197, 199
crime (criminals) xxiii, xxxi, 118, 119,
  128, 185, 194, 250; *see also* villainy,
  villain
crucifixion (crucify) 14, 22, 76, 82, 152,
  156, 164, 165, 169, 174
cunning 76; *see also* cleverness,
  deception, trickery
cup 39, 175; *see also* chalice
custom 44, 58, 96, 137, 147, 174, 212,
  234, 235, 237, 249; *see also* tradition
customary law 80, 108, 147–50, 249
customs dues 102, 104, 106–8, 118,
  192, 208, 256

damnation 5, 39, 43, 141
damned, the 4, 7, 10, 200; *see also*
  godless
death (dying) 10, 29, 30n, 35, 42, 43,
  100, 104, 113, 174, 177, 184–86,
  193, 201, 205, 214, 222, 237n
debt 61, 250, 251
defense xi, xiii, xvii, xix, xxiv, xxv, xxix,
  9, 74, 95, 101, 123, 183, 186, 190,
  247, 267, 268; *see also* resistance
demagogues 182
democracy xxi
deposing 109, 118–20, 122

desires 2, 21, 22, 85, 118, 141, 159,
  160, 166, 167, 174, 184, 204, 213,
  223
despotism 227; *see also* tyranny
devil xxii, 3, 4, 6, 8, 9, 12, 18, 19, 21,
  22, 25, 27, 66, 71, 75, 76, 78,79, 82,
  83, 89, 90, 92, 93, 109, 113, 114,
  116, 117, 118, 122, 123, 154, 156,
  166, 173–75, 178, 182, 183, 184,
  187, 195, 196, 210, 220, 232, 246
dignity 75, 112, 127
diligence 1, 10, 16, 145, 147, 192
disciple 54, 75, 79, 163, 169, 182; *see*
  also follower
discipleship xxiv
discipline 123, 164, 166
discord 221, 223, 224; *see also* division
disloyalty 105, 126
disputation xxviii, 91, 96, 261, 262,
  264, 267, 270
disputing 86, 100, 119, 189, 203, 221
divine law xviii, xxii, 21, 31, 34, 37, 60,
  61, 69, 104, 107, 119–22, 130,
  132n, 133–44, 147–51, 153n, 160,
  166, 178, 193, 194, 200, 202, 239,
  241, 245
division xxvi, xxviii, 13, 131, 178, 181n,
  246; *see also* sect
document 1, 145, 229, 240, 243, 244,
  247, 248, 251
domination 109, 270; *see also*
  oppression
dream (dreaming) xix, 17–19, 21–26,
  151; *see also* visions
dues xvi, 102, 108, 113, 209, 236, 240,
  247, 248, 270
duty 1, 45, 62, 94, 103, 113, 176, 209,
  244, 256, 266; *see also* office,
  obligation

egalitarianism xvi
Eigennutz xviii; *see also* selfish interest
elect, the xv, xix, 1–4, 7–10, 12, 16–19,
  24, 27, 28, 30, 31, 75, 79, 81, 115,
  138, 146, 149, 154, 163, 167, 168,
  209, 212, 214, 215, 217, 232, 255
elective office, government xx, xxvi, 9,
  111, 112, 114, 115, 121, 212n, 214,
  215, 217, 232, 233, 247, 251, 255;
  see also republicanism
emperor 102, 105, 107, 112–14, 121,

122, 127, 128, 181, 182, 206, 217, 221
envy 75, 76, 99, 154, 197, 207, 237
equality xx, xxi, 48, 168, 210–12, 218, 219, 225, 255
equity 110, 229, 250
error 3, 12, 24, 37, 41, 50, 52, 60, 71, 131, 133, 148, 153, 160, 174, 179, 186, 210, 245
estate, social xxi, 45, 107, 113, 203, 211, 218, 255
eternity 4, 5, 10, 29, 50, 81, 94, 104, 134, 148, 150
Eucharist 72n
evangelicalism xi, xii, 87n, 271
evil xxiv, 6, 14, 16, 19, 25, 27, 42, 43, 53, 64, 82, 83, 90, 94, 97, 102, 105, 107, 113, 117, 120, 122, 130, 131, 132, 134, 135, 138, 142, 143, 146, 162, 166, 168, 175–77, 179, 180, 183, 184, 187, 192, 193, 194–99, 202–9, 220, 224, 227, 229; *see also* vice, wickedness
evildoer 28, 81, 117, 183, 190, 191, 194, 198, 203
excommunication xxiv, 8, 174, 244; *see also* ban
executioner 58, 84, 201n, 202
exile xxiv, 95, 100, 261; *see also* ban
experience xiv, 5, 7, 19, 23, 26, 51, 52, 59, 69, 115, 139

faith xii, xiii, xvii, xviii, xxii, xxiii, 1–3, 5–10, 14, 15, 18, 19, 21, 27, 28, 30, 34–39, 42–46, 69, 71, 75, 76–79, 88, 89, 91, 96, 103–5, 110, 116, 119, 123, 128, 129, 134, 135, 137, 138, 145, 148, 153, 154, 155, 162, 163, 165, 166, 171, 173–76, 178, 195, 199, 205, 206, 214, 232, 233, 257, 263, 264, 268; *see also* contrived faith
fanatic (fanaticism) xvi, 78, 87, 154, 155, 157
fasting xxviii, 55, 182, 212, 262
fate 75, 91, 94, 213, 223, 267
favoritism 219, 237
fear 23, 29, 32, 42, 47, 59, 67, 116, 129, 131, 132, 140, 142, 146, 166, 168, 185, 192, 194, 205, 206, 218, 219, 221, 224, 230

fear of God 2, 4–6, 15, 16, 19, 28, 78, 81, 105, 117, 123, 127, 152, 190, 227
federation (confederation) xx, xxix, xxx, 109, 128, 239, 243, 264, 268; *see also* alliance, covenant, league
fees 102, 106, 108, 192, 212, 213, 236, 247, 248, 250, 252
fellowship 18, 53, 68, 175
fidelity 33, 111, 123, 126, 155, 171
figure xi, 3, 29, 92; *see also* image, symbol
fines 14, 85, 86, 93, 102, 108, 221, 249, 251
flattery 5, 25, 83, 84, 87, 91
Flur xxvi, 211–14
follower 89, 147, 268; *see also* disciple
force xviii, xxiv, xxv, 7, 33, 56, 90, 113, 128, 134, 176, 181, 195, 217, 221, 235, 236, 238, 263, 264, 267; *see also* coercion, violence
fortresses 128; *see also* castle
freedom 112, 122, 149, 164, 173
freedom of the will 90
foundations, ecclesiastical 92, 210, 212, 213, 218, 245

game, game laws 116, 117, 125, 235
Gelassenheit 59n, 170n
Gemeinde 80n; *see also* community, congregation
Gemeinnutz xviii; *see also* common good, commonweal
glory 75, 76, 87, 141, 191, 200
godless, the xix, 12–17, 30, 31, 58, 77–79, 83, 84, 90, 94, 99, 111, 115, 116, 118, 127, 128, 171, 182, 224, 228
"godless" painters at Nuremberg xxix, 261
goodness 17, 31, 123, 165, 169
government xii, xvii, xviii, xx, xxi, xxvi, 9, 11, 27, 28, 32, 75, 111, 112, 114–16, 176, 181, 183, 191, 196, 197, 206, 212, 216, 228, 254–57, 260, 262, 264, 268, 269
grace 2, 3, 20, 36, 45, 47, 59, 82, 101, 103, 107, 110, 118, 129, 132, 141, 144, 152, 155, 163, 172, 173, 180, 181–83, 185, 203, 205, 209, 231, 233, 243, 265

grief 42, 111, 115, 116, 124–26, 154, 158, 162, 163, 165, 166, 167, 168, 170, 172
grievance 192, 231, 236, 266; *see also* burdens
guild 112, 251, 252

harvest xii, 10, 31, 108, 158, 244
hate (hatred) 6, 38, 54, 66, 75, 84, 86, 99, 122, 137, 154, 183, 197, 199, 200, 207
heathen 3, 12, 15, 17, 23, 27, 29, 42, 44, 55, 67–72, 77, 79, 87, 97, 103, 109, 114, 115, 135, 137, 149, 160, 191, 209
heaven 4, 18, 20, 23, 32, 53, 97, 99, 102, 106, 109, 119, 127, 129, 133–35, 140, 143, 147, 157, 161, 178, 179, 186, 188, 191, 196, 197, 224
hell 2, 5, 8, 9, 66, 104, 105, 119, 163, 165, 184, 201, 202, 207, 210, 230
hereditary rule, power xx, 111, 114–16, 121, 123, 256
heresy xxix, 7, 31, 87, 90, 155, 182, 252, 261, 264, 271
heriot 102, 108, 113, 125, 237
history xii, xix, 24n, 40, 70, 210n
history, written 9n, 13n, 23, 100, 131; *see also* chronicles
holy spirit 1–3, 6, 7, 13, 14, 18–22, 24, 31, 35, 75, 77, 79, 82, 89, 97, 98, 136, 142, 152, 163, 165, 170, 184, 210, 218–20, 230
honor; of authorities 52, 107, 124, 128, 154, 162, 192, 203, 237; of God xx, xxvi, 1, 16, 59, 66, 75, 87, 106, 111, 129, 149, 157, 173, 174, 210–15, 217, 221, 229, 239; personal 1, 99, 127, 166, 182, 244
honey 5, 92
honors 79, 87, 145, 160, 165
hospital 213, 257
household (householder) xxi, 57, 58, 106, 119, 136, 159, 166, 182, 214
human nature 102, 148
humility 90, 208
hunger 6, 45, 132, 155, 163, 202
hunting 110, 116, 235
hymns (psalms) 38, 39, 87; *see also* singing
hypocrisy xvi, 87, 143

idols 14, 15, 72, 99, 103, 115, 117, 145, 146
idolatry 12, 19, 29, 30, 40, 42, 46, 58, 64, 66, 69, 72, 88, 114–16
ignorance 12, 50, 53, 89, 103
images xvi, 13, 14, 28, 62, 88, 114, 115, 137, 215–17
imperial cities 127
impudence 3, 90, 108
infant baptism xvi, xvii, xxix, 44, 95, 99, 100, 171, 174, 263, 266, 267
infantry 101, 214, 231
injustice 81, 124, 132, 147, 176, 180, 189, 190, 194, 219, 220, 221, 228, 237
innocence xxiv, 43, 75, 77, 79, 80, 82, 86, 100, 103, 116, 117, 127, 147, 184–87, 196
insolence 75, 113, 117, 168
insurrection xvii, xix, xxi, 34, 80, 81, 83, 86, 92, 101, 122, 123, 192, 217, 222, 224, 229, 231, 255, 264, 266, 269; *see also* rebellion, revolt, revolution
interest payments 41, 256, 262; *see also* usury

judges xxiv, 57, 62, 120, 123, 147, 188–90, 194, 199, 201, 202, 219, 228, 255, 257
judgment, divine 9, 51, 53, 80, 90, 91, 102, 154, 155, 198, 201, 220, 224, 232; human xxiv, 18, 20, 28, 53, 78, 80, 82, 83, 86, 148, 153, 169, 177, 185, 288–90, 198, 200, 220, 228
jurisdiction 93, 215
jurists 56, 120, 121; *see also* lawyers
justice xviii, 4, 34, 62, 67, 82, 90, 108, 110, 112, 117, 123–25, 134, 143, 152, 153, 155, 166, 167, 169, 178, 197, 198, 208, 219, 220, 228–30, 239, 243, 245, 255, 256
justification (justify) xxii, 78n, 82, 87, 96, 100, 107, 123, 132, 134, 139, 142, 153n, 154, 162, 164–66, 169, 232, 239

king xxxi, 17, 18, 21, 22, 26, 27, 31, 34, 63, 74, 106, 107, 109, 114–16, 123, 124, 127, 128, 177, 181, 192, 200, 262

kingdom of God xix, 54, 132, 138, 139, 145, 147, 149, 158, 163
kingship 116; *see also* hereditary rule, monarchy
knowledge 1, 6, 7, 15, 19, 20, 25, 37, 39, 43, 52, 61, 75, 79, 85, 90, 98, 107, 111, 134, 144, 145, 148, 156, 160, 173, 174, 195, 211, 235, 236, 241, 250, 252, 263

labor (toil) xxiii, 53, 108, 123, 125, 129, 208, 236; *see also* work
laity (laymen) xi, 13, 25, 64, 66, 84, 195, 247, 264, 265, 270
landlord 203, 251
Landschaft 239n; *see also* territory
law, canon xxviii, 8, 86n, 100, 103n, 270, 271; civil xvi, xxiii, xxv, 96n, 103n, 105, 177, 190, 192, 219, 220, 237, 241, 250, 254–56, 259; natural xix, 270
lawyers 107, 122, 248, 255; *see also* jurists
laziness 12, 22, 54, 56, 60, 130, 228, 256, 260
league xx, xxix, xxx, 93, 239, 262, 265, 267–69, 271; *see also* alliance, covenant, federation
learned, the xxiii, 14, 18, 42–44, 46, 50, 51, 133, 157; *see also* scholars, scribes, theologians
learning xxiii, 42, 133
legalism 7, 49, 255
legitimacy xiii, xvi, xvii, xix, xxiv, 173, 229, 264
liberty xi; *see also* freedom
literalism xiii, xiv, 7n, 76, 143; *see also* biblicism
liturgy xxviii, 9, 37, 38, 84, 182, 268, 270
Lord's Supper xxiv, 36n, 37, 39, 40, 42, 47, 96n, 174, 201; *see also* Mass, Eucharist, Communion
lords xix, 6, 25, 51, 80, 81, 91, 93, 95, 96, 99–103, 106, 108, 109–14, 117–20, 122–25, 128, 129, 154, 203, 204, 211, 215–17, 222, 223, 228, 231, 234, 236, 240, 243, 244, 246, 247
lordship 107, 115, 116, 236
love xxii, xxiii, 6, 19, 37, 39, 40, 42, 45, 47, 48, 52–56, 58, 60, 61, 64–67, 86, 104–7, 117, 121, 123, 127, 132, 133, 137, 139–41, 143, 145–49, 151–53, 155, 162–67, 172, 173, 175, 177, 182, 190, 195, 197–99, 207, 208, 218, 232, 234, 235, 236, 239, 244, 250; *see also* brotherly love, charity
lowly, the 80, 91; *see also* common man, poor, needy
lusts 22, 159, 160, 162, 165–67, 170, 174, 180, 184; *see also* "creaturely" desires

magisterial reformers xii–xxii, xxiv, 132n, 176n
magistrates xiii, xxiv, xxv, 178, 203; *see also* judges, officials
mankind xxiii, 87, 90, 104, 130, 134, 137, 158, 162, 197, 213, 229, 234; *see also* human nature
market 6, 15, 110, 222, 248, 251, 252, 259, 268
martyrs xxxi, 1, 30, 82, 87, 261, 265
Mass 15, 38–40, 44, 61, 64, 255, 262, 264, 267, 270
masses, the 50, 53, 57, 93, 216
mendicants 113, 211, 212, 269
merchants 88, 91, 259
mercy 16, 30, 36, 62, 89, 90, 103, 134, 140, 141, 150, 153, 154, 163, 165, 169, 172, 173, 177, 212, 222, 224, 233, 246, 251
mighty, the 31, 80, 86, 91, 108, 124, 155
military service 206, 214, 240, 257; *see also* armies
millenarianism xix, 210n
mines (miners) 80, 255, 259, 260
ministers xvi, 12, 39, 174, 176
minting 214–17; *see also* coinage
miracles 58, 118, 150, 218, 221
mockery 3, 17, 76, 89, 92, 129, 147, 201
monarchy 25; *see also* hereditary rule, kings, kingship, princes
monastery 68, 88, 269, 270
monasticism 3, 18n, 19; *see also* monks
monks xii, 2, 84, 86, 87, 90, 92, 93, 109, 247, 269, 270
Mosaic Law 23, 142, 149

murder 52, 53, 62, 63, 109, 110, 112–
14, 125, 197, 221, 224
mysteries 16, 27
mysticism xxii, xxiii, 2n, 130n, 167n,
170n

needy, the xxi, 80, 234, 257
negotiation xix, 227, 233, 235–38, 240,
241
nobility 91, 92, 109, 117, 211–13, 218,
220–23, 259
nobles 219, 223, 245
non-Christians 8; *see also* unbeliever,
heathen
nonresisting separatism xxiv, xxv, 172n,
265

obedience xvii, 103, 106, 107, 110,
111, 161, 162, 166, 175, 187, 206,
211, 246
offense xvi, 45, 55, 64, 65, 69–71, 73,
173, 247
office 7, 27, 30, 31, 76, 83, 92, 105–8,
112, 122, 126, 176, 183, 187, 188,
190–94, 198, 203, 205, 207, 212,
217, 228; *see also* duty, calling
officials 11, 74, 93, 108, 109, 211, 220,
235, 247, 255, 263, 268; *see also*
magistrates
oppression xx, 221
original sin 81
outlaw 46, 93

papists 47, 66, 83, 119
parables 4, 157–59, 161
parish 110, 212, 247, 255, 261; *see also*
congregation, community
parliament, peasant 239n
parson 2, 15, 163, 233
pastor xv, xxiv, 33, 41, 176, 181, 182,
231–34, 247, 256, 257, 263, 266,
268
patience 25, 59, 82, 129, 173, 196, 232
payments 145, 236, 237, 248, 255, 257,
260; *see also* taxes, fees, dues
peace xviii, xxvi, 27, 30, 33, 35, 36, 45,
57, 88, 89, 101, 102, 122, 124, 125,
129, 131, 138, 152, 163, 167, 172,
173, 178, 180, 181, 187, 189, 194–
96, 201, 206, 208, 209, 222, 231,
232, 236, 238, 240, 243, 245

peasantry xix, xx, xxx, 101, 107, 117n,
124, 125, 231, 263, 266
peasants xii, xix, xx, xxi, xxii, xxiii, xxiv,
xxvi, xxviii, xxx, 14, 25, 88, 93, 111,
117, 124, 126, 128, 130, 152, 157,
182, 184, 210, 218, 221, 222–24,
227n, 230–32, 236, 237n, 239n, 243,
244n, 254n, 261–71
perfection 2, 161, 171, 177, 178
persecution xxiii, xxv, 25, 27, 33, 42,
44, 47, 84, 85, 89, 93, 114, 125,
167, 168, 197, 200, 254, 265
perseverance 26, 172
piety xii, 126, 196, 213
pleasure 23, 31, 44, 45, 48, 67, 79, 85,
105, 109, 110, 114, 118, 125, 130,
153–56, 159, 160, 169
polity xvii, xx, xxi, xxiv, xxv, 99n, 173n,
174, 223n
pomp (pompousness) 5, 14, 76, 111,
112, 120, 154, 160, 196
poor, the 4, 6, 14, 16–18, 25, 28, 61,
78, 80, 81, 83, 84, 86, 88, 93, 106,
108, 109, 113, 114, 116, 117, 120,
122–24, 129, 153–57, 161, 164, 199,
219, 223, 228, 233, 235, 243, 247–
50, 252, 254, 256, 257, 259,
270
pope 8, 54, 83, 84, 88, 92, 95, 100,
101, 103, 105, 121, 122, 154, 174,
202, 223
popular Reformation xii, xvi, xviii
popular sovereignty xx, xxi, 30n
poverty 118, 199, 266
power xiii, xvii, xx, xxii, xxv, 1, 6, 7,
13–16, 19, 22, 26, 28, 30–32, 35,
38, 47, 75, 77, 80, 88, 94, 97, 103,
105, 107–10, 112–19, 121, 122, 125,
127, 128, 133, 136, 138, 143, 144,
150, 151, 156–59, 161, 163, 169,
170, 173, 176, 179, 181, 184, 185,
186, 190–92, 196, 203, 205, 207,
208, 219, 221, 222, 230, 232, 235,
244, 245, 247, 251, 252, 255
prayer 42, 55, 124, 176, 180
preacher 41, 47, 89, 92, 183, 227, 241,
242, 263, 269, 270
preaching xii, xv, 11, 15, 41, 42, 46,
49, 55, 56, 72, 78, 84, 85, 92, 144,
152, 157, 162, 203, 265–67, 269
prelates xii, 101, 113, 223

pride 8, 83, 105, 110, 112, 114, 126, 195, 206, 228, 255
priests xii, 6, 95, 263, 268, 271
priesthood xi, 41
princes xiii, xvi, xvii, xxv, xxviii, 6, 8, 11, 16, 24, 26, 27, 30, 46, 49–51, 53, 59, 74, 75, 79–81, 83–85, 87–89, 91, 92, 93, 101, 105, 107–9, 111, 121, 122, 124, 125, 128, 177, 192, 196, 203, 208, 211, 218, 220, 221, 223, 240, 260, 262, 267, 268
principalities xx, 88
prison xxxi, 24, 53, 111, 116, 123, 125, 126, 247, 263, 267
privilege xx, xxvi, 252
profit 6, 139, 153, 163, 258
property xxi, 81, 92, 109, 116, 122, 127, 129, 160, 211, 218, 233–37, 241, 245, 250, 251, 259, 262
prophecy (prophesying) xxvi, 6, 11, 13, 19, 24, 31, 63, 77, 92, 124, 125, 128, 144, 152, 153
prophet 11, 16, 17, 20, 65, 83, 92, 115, 118, 123, 127, 129, 140, 143, 150, 165
prostitution 50, 51, 247; *see also* whoring
publishers 220, 221
pulpit 10, 47, 182
punishment 17, 28, 53, 60, 62, 79, 86, 90, 102, 105, 109, 115, 118, 163, 176, 185, 190, 193, 206, 208, 214, 218, 224, 227

raka 201
radical Reformation xi, xii, xiv, xv, xvi, xvii, xix, xxi, xxii, xxiii, xxiv, xxv, xxvi, 173n
radical reformers xii, xv, xvi, xvii, xviii, xix, xx, xxi, 132n
reason (rationality) 6, 15, 20, 21, 27, 53, 59, 67, 78, 90, 136, 161, 170, 218, 222
rebaptism xxiii, xxxi, 100n, 267
rebel 95, 123, 182, 231, 240, 266
rebellion xvii, xix, xxvi, xxix, xxx, 1, 28, 34, 80, 85, 86, 89, 92, 95, 96, 101, 123, 124, 128, 182, 206, 232, 254, 262, 267, 268; *see also* insurrection, revolt, revolution
reformation 24

rent 88, 113, 211, 212, 214, 218, 240, 248
repentance 116, 140, 141, 146, 174, 213
repression xxii, 125
republicanism xx, xxi, xxvi, 112, 114, 115, 262
resignation 59, 169
resistance (resisting) xix, xxii, xxiv, xxv, 33, 82, 93, 96, 138, 147, 176, 179, 193, 194, 196, 206, 228, 264, 265
revenge 15, 194, 204
revelations xiv, 2n, 3–8, 14n, 16–21, 24, 26, 30, 148, 153n, 210n
revolt 101, 109, 126, 232
revolution xii, 83n, 117n, 228n, 268, 269, 271
riches 133, 260
righteous, the 6, 7, 77, 94
righteousness xvi, 18, 26, 50, 52, 81, 134, 165, 195, 205
rights xvi, 57, 107, 134, 223, 233, 234, 239, 240, 249, 255, 259
Rottengeister 87n; *see also* fanatic
rulers xiii, xvi, xvii, xviii, xix, xxii, 11, 13, 18, 25, 26, 27, 28, 30, 31, 58, 79, 82, 84, 87, 88, 108, 109, 114–16, 119, 121, 154, 185, 206, 211, 216, 219, 228, 268

sacrament xvii, 2, 39, 44, 85, 99, 147, 153, 214
sacrifice xxvii, 50, 62, 149, 159, 162, 170, 212, 262
sacrilege 71, 102, 134
saints 27, 30, 35, 62, 64, 66, 93, 162, 189, 213, 214
salvation 3, 6, 7, 14, 18, 37, 38, 45, 46, 78, 104, 121, 124, 138, 141, 162, 173, 178, 186, 195, 206, 215
sanctification 4n
scholars 5, 38, 210, 218; *see also* the learned, scribes, theologians
scribes 7, 14, 16–18, 20, 28–30, 41, 50, 75–78, 83–85, 92, 103, 107, 111, 143, 145, 153–57, 161, 163, 218, 219, 220–24; *see also* the learned, scholars, theologians
sect xxiv, 34, 85, 210; *see also* division
self-defense xix, xxiv, xxv

selfish interest xxii, 13, 147, 150, 206, 213, 218, 229, 252, 254
separatism xxiv, xxv, 172n, 173n, 265
serf 109, 113, 114, 125, 234, 237
serfdom 109, 115, 234; *see also* bondage, servitude
sermon xiii, xvi, xvii, xxviii, 11, 62, 80, 268
servitude 164, 176
shame 17, 19, 24, 26, 66, 81, 87, 189, 190, 214, 218, 229
sign 4, 10, 39, 60, 150, 161, 163, 165, 166, 168, 171, 179, 223
simple people 69, 75, 171, 196
simplicity 85, 90, 179, 180
sin xx, 12, 15, 19, 43, 53, 67, 69, 70, 73, 80, 81, 85, 97, 98, 110, 132, 138–40, 143, 144, 147, 151, 166, 168, 170, 174, 176, 177, 184, 189, 190, 192–94, 198, 199, 202, 204, 207, 213, 258
sinner 3, 90, 114, 133, 140, 198
singing 36, 38–40, 46, 106
slavery 14, 119, 120, 125
social contract xvii
socialism xxi
soul 2, 5, 6, 9, 10, 20–23, 51, 57, 71, 104, 106, 114, 121, 165, 167, 168, 170, 195, 205, 215, 217, 230
spirit xxviii, 1–3, 5–7, 10, 13–25, 29, 31, 35, 38, 39, 41, 43, 46–48, 51, 65, 69, 71, 74–79, 82, 84, 89, 90, 97, 98, 105, 107, 119, 121, 122, 134, 136–38, 141, 142, 143, 148, 152, 157, 159, 160, 163, 165, 167, 169–73, 175, 176, 178, 184, 186, 187, 191, 195, 196, 205, 206, 210, 218–20, 230, 246
state xviii, 1n, 99, 211n
subjects xiii, 25, 53, 93, 106, 112, 122, 124, 201, 206, 207, 208, 216, 231, 268
suffering xxiii, 2, 5, 15, 28, 34, 42, 43, 59, 76, 83, 89, 97, 104, 135, 146, 156–58, 161, 164–66, 168–71, 175, 212
superstition 19; *see also* idolatry
sword, the xx, xxiv, xxv, xxxi, 26–28, 30, 42, 80, 102, 109, 110, 120, 148, 174, 176, 177, 181, 183–88, 190, 191, 192–98, 201, 203, 205–8, 224, 264

symbol 94, 98, 117, 147, 152, 162, 163, 168
synteresis 9n

tax collector (publican) 42, 164, 191, 220
taxes xxiv, 102, 104, 106–8, 118, 174, 206, 208, 212, 236, 247, 248, 252, 264
teaching 18, 29, 35, 38, 41, 56, 57, 59, 60, 63, 69, 72, 78, 80, 85, 86, 90, 98, 120, 132, 153, 169, 182, 205, 238, 247, 256
temporal goods 81, 82, 189, 194, 205
temptation 28, 37, 138
territory xx, xxi, xxv, 84, 88, 89, 109, 116, 118–20, 207, 208, 214, 215, 227, 233, 239–41, 243, 255–60, 266
testament 3, 38, 39, 41, 43, 71, 78, 98, 139, 143, 179, 193, 194, 198, 201, 210, 233
testimony xxvi, 4, 6, 20, 22, 35, 52, 75, 77, 89, 124, 143, 144, 145, 147, 154–56, 160, 162, 174, 176, 183, 190, 194, 198, 247
theologians xiii, 1, 2, 7, 8, 41, 66; *see also* the learned, scholars, scribes
tithes xvi, xxviii, 41, 53, 233, 234, 240, 249, 251, 256, 257, 262
titles 9, 14, 36, 38, 70, 75, 79, 87, 95, 101, 105, 106, 112, 254
torture (torturing) 105, 109, 111, 121, 125, 265, 269
tradition 55, 167, 172, 261; *see also* custom
transgression (transgressor) 80, 82, 115, 117
treachery 113, 245
tribulation 5, 22, 23, 59, 168
trust 34, 116, 123, 124, 145, 165, 171, 224
tyranny xx, xxv, 35, 82, 94, 109–12, 114, 116, 117, 246
tyrants 17, 34, 82, 93, 102, 108, 123, 124, 183, 207

unbeliever 5, 8, 119, 189; *see also* non-Christian
unchristian xxii, 37, 105, 109, 115, 117–19, 196, 208, 255, 259
understanding xi, xxii, xxiii, xxvi, 18,

19, 21, 38–40, 46, 52, 58–61, 69,
78, 82, 89, 96, 100, 107, 134, 143,
155, 165, 179, 203, 236, 251
unity xiv, xv, xix, xxii, xxvi, 27, 40, 108,
109, 111, 126, 131, 162, 173, 218,
222, 232, 246
university xiii, 33, 66, 215, 216, 256,
263, 265, 266, 268
unrest xxvii, 130, 222, 263, 265
usury 41, 81, 113, 248, 258, 260
utopianism xxvi

vestments xxvii, 40, 265
vice 51, 53, 121, 247, 262
victory 122, 127, 129
violence xix, xx, xxii, 34, 46, 64, 66,
111, 177, 183, 184, 194, 205, 231,
266; *see also* coercion, force
virtue 7, 31, 112, 141, 218
visions 16, 18, 21–24, 58, 210n; *see also*
dream

war 43, 46, 106, 110, 123, 127, 132,
178, 202, 203, 205, 207, 214, 223,
256, 257, 259

weak, the xvi, 45, 46, 49–52, 54–56,
61–68, 71, 73, 86
weakness 168, 169
whore 4, 9, 64, 103, 154
whoring 3, 50, 121, 154, 247, 252
wickedness 15; *see also* evil
wife 53, 54, 86, 103, 106, 108, 109,
112, 128, 129, 160, 198, 200, 240,
245, 263, 264, 270
wisdom 15, 16, 31, 42–44, 50, 58, 59,
68, 78, 85, 95, 96, 107, 134, 141,
150, 152, 154, 155, 157, 185, 218,
219, 220–22, 234
women xxi, 20, 55, 81, 86, 87, 149,
158, 167, 177, 193, 212, 222, 252
work 12, 56, 69, 147, 157, 158, 160,
198, 212, 213n, 214, 236, 241, 244,
254, 256–58; *see also* labor
worship 99, 212, 215
wrath 3, 7, 29, 81, 93, 118, 121, 129,
131, 132, 139, 140, 144, 192, 204,
206, 221–24

zeal xv, 10, 12, 15, 26, 31, 74, 122,
173, 180

Index of proper names

Aaron 24, 46, 99, 124
Abednego 72
Abel 127
Abijah 34, 200
About Two Martyrs of Christ at Brussels
    87n
Abraham 23, 82, 86, 115, 178, 179,
    186, 188, 192, 199, 200
Absalom 29
Achab 115
Adam 43, 85, 103, 114, 137, 163, 168,
    186n, 191, 192
Adonijah 202
Adrammelech 127
Adrian VI, pope xxvii, xxviii
Advent 214
Aesop 115, 192
Agag 115, 118
*Against the Perverted and False Imperial
    Mandate* 86n
*Against the Robbing and Murdering
    Hoards of Peasants* 222n
Ahab 118, 123
Alber, Matthew 242
Albertine or ducal Saxony 89n
Albrecht of Mansfeld, count 47n
Allgäu xxix, 239n, 267
Allstedt xvi, xxviii, xxix, 11n, 29n, 33,
    36, 41n, 44n, 45, 74, 84, 88, 93n,
    94, 264, 266, 268
Alsace xxx
Amaziah 127
Anabaptism xiv, xxi–xxv, xxxi, xxxii,
    95n, 100n, 130n, 172n, 181n, 261,

263, 264, 265, 270, 271
Ananias 98
Antichrist 5, 10, 30, 38, 40, 44, 54, 71,
    84n, 95, 119, 231n
Apocalypse xxii, 10n, 152n; *see also* Last
    Days, Last Judgment, Judgment Day
Arkleb of Bozkovic 181
Asmodeus 8
Assyrian empire 114n
Athenians, the 29
Augsburg xxxi, 91, 130n, 152n, 188n,
    241, 259n, 261, 263–65
Augustine, St. 43, 44, 90
Augustinian order 87n, 91n, 211n
Augustus 112; *see also* Octavian
Austria xxxi, 264

Baal 7, 9, 30, 71, 104, 115, 118
Babel 7, 46, 114
Babylon, whore of 86, 103, 154
Babylonian captivity 17, 108, 110, 118,
    120, 123, 126
Babylonian empire 25, 114, 115, 175
Bach, Bartel 49, 50n, 68n
Baden 99n, 111
Baltringen xxix, 239n, 267, 271
Barnabas 72
Basel xxix, xxxi, 41n, 49n, 95n, 181n,
    261, 266, 271
Baumgarter, firm of 259
Bavaria 261
Beelzebub 6, 75
Beguines 252
Behemoth (behemoths) 108, 109, 114

Index

Belial 175
Benaiah 202
Benedictine order xxv, 270
Bergzabern 261
Bern 152n
"Biberius" 112; see Tiberius
Bibra 264
Billican, Theobald 241
Black Forest xx, xxviii, xxx, 239n, 243, 270
Blaurock, George xxxi, 95, 263, 267
Böblingen, Battle of xxi, xxx
Boethius 112
Bohemia xxvii, xxxi, 49n, 181n, 268
"Bohemian gifts" 92
Bohemians, the 1
Bologna 271
Booklet on the Papacy 119
Bregenz 104n
Breisgau 264
Brenz, Johannes 241
Brixen (Bressanone) 254–56, 262
Brötli, Hans 47
Bruno, St. 213n
Brunswick 268
Brussels 87n
Bucer, Martin 44n, 261
Budapest 152n
Bumpler, firm of 259
Bundschuh 117, 124

Caesar 102, 182, 218
Caesar, Julius 112, 114
Caiaphas 83
Cain 118
Cajetan, cardinal 91
Caligula, emperor 113
Canaanites, the 30
Capito, Wolfgang 44n
Carmelite order 211n
Carniola 126n
Carthusian order 213
Castelberger, Andreas 36n, 45–47, 262, 267
Charlemagne 114
Charles V, emperor xxvii
Christendom xii, xvii, xix, 11–13, 16, 24, 26, 64, 75, 81, 86, 89–91, 113, 116, 152, 156, 171, 216, 222
Christian League, at Allstedt 93n
Christian Union of the Allgäu,

Baltringen and Lake Constance peasant armies xxix, 267
Cistercian order 88n, 269
Claudius, emperor 113
Clement V, pope 103
Clement VII, pope xxviii
Cologne 265, 271
Columbanus, St. 104
Consolation of Philosophy, The 112
Constance xxviii, 264
Constance, Lake xxix, 239, 267
"Constitutional Draft"
(*Verfassungsentwurf*) 239n, 264, 268
Corinth 24
Cornelius 23, 55, 73, 97
Council of Constance 1n, 9n
Court of the Field 250
Cyprian, St. 43, 44
Czech language 1n, 3n, 5n
Czech nation 1n

Damascus 98
Danube 127
David 4, 7, 24, 28, 62, 94, 106, 110, 116, 124, 129, 139, 148, 154, 158, 159, 162, 163, 165, 196, 200, 203
Denck, Hans xiv, xv, xxii, xxiii, xxxi, 130, 134, 147n, 261, 264, 265
Diocletian, emperor 114
Document of Articles, The xx, xxx, 239n, 243–45, 264, 268
Doeg 201
Dominican order 211
Domitian, emperor 114
Dózca, György 126n
Duke of Prussia 271
Dürer, Albrecht 261

East Friesland 266, 271
East Prussia xxx
Easter 264, 268
Eck, Johann 91, 263
Eden, garden of 86n
Egypt 21, 23, 71, 114n, 124, 150, 175
Egyptians, the 63, 166, 188
Eichsfeld 269
Eisenach 41n, 270
Eleven Mühlhausen Articles, The xxix, 227–30, 268, 269
Elijah 30, 74, 123, 186
Emden 271

283

Index

Emser, Jerome 66
English Mark 251
Erastianism xiii
Erfurt xxii, 41n, 265
Ernestine or electoral Saxony xxviii,
   xxix, xxxi, 11n, 89n, 268; *see also*
   Saxony
Ernst of Mansfeld, count 268
Erzgebirge 49n
Esau 23, 91
Eternal Council at Mühlhausen 228n,
   269
Eternal League or Covenant (*Ewiger
   Bund*) at Mühlhausen 265, 269
Etsch 127, 259
Eusebius of Caesarea 9, 13
Eve 186, 191, 192

Ferdinand of Austria xxxi, 181n, 262,
   264
Formula Missae et Communionis 84n
Forty-six Frankfurt Articles, The xxi, xxx,
   246–53, 271
France 202, 223n, 262
Franciscan order 210n, 211n, 241
Franconia xxviii, xxx, 128, 265, 266
Frankenhausen, Battle of xxi, xxx,
   152n, 261, 265, 269
Frankfurt am Main 246n, 249n, 250n,
   251n, 252n, 271
Frankfurt am Oder 268
Frederick the Wise, elector of Saxony
   xxx, 89n, 111n, 268
Freiburg im Breisgau xxx, 243n, 263
Friedberg 181, 188n, 263
Fritz, Joss 117n
Fugger, firm of 259

Gad 24
Gaismair, Michael xx, xxi, xxx, 254,
   255n, 257n, 260–62
Galba, emperor 113
George, duke of Saxony 89n
German language 1n, 38, 39, 44, 84,
   102, 106, 182n, 208, 259, 268, 270
German mystics 2n, 59n, 167n
German Mass 84
Germany xi, xii, xv, xx, xxiii, 46, 101,
   172n, 182n, 223, 224, 231n, 239n,
   266, 268, 271
Gersen, Ottilie von 268

Gideon 71, 72, 128, 192
Goliath 94
Gray Leagues xxxi, 263
Grebel, Conrad xiv, xvi, xxviii, xxix,
   xxxi, 36, 37n, 38n, 42, 44n, 45, 46n,
   47, 95n, 262, 263, 267
Greek language 216
Greeks, empire of the 25
Griessen 264
Grüningen 267

Habsburgs 181n, 254n, 256n, 262, 264
Halle 42n, 46, 47
Harz 36, 45, 90n, 267
Hebrew language 60, 63, 216
Hegau 268
Hegesippus 9, 13
Hellershof 249
Hergot, Hans xv, xviii, xxi, xxii, xxv,
   xxvi, xxxi, 210, 211n, 212n, 213n,
   214n, 216n, 217n, 220n, 221n,
   223n, 263
Herod 23, 24
Heshbron 63
Heybach 261
Hezekiah 30, 72, 196
Highly Provoked Defense, A xiii, xxix, 74–
   94, 101n, 268
Historia ecclesiastica 9n
Hochstetter, firm of 259
Hohenberg 266
Holy Roman Empire 1n, 25, 92, 192n,
   216n
Hölzel, Hieronymous xxix, 74n, 101n
Horb 266, 270
Horsmar 230n
Hottinger, Klaus 99n
Hubmaier, Balthasar xv, xvi, xxii, xxiv,
   xxv, xxxi, 130n, 177n, 181, 182n,
   183, 186, 188n, 239n, 243n, 263–65,
   268
Hügeline, Elizabeth 264
Hujuff, Hans 42n, 46, 47
Hungary xxxi, 126, 181n
Hus, Jan 1, 9
Hussite Wars 1n
Hut, Hans xiv, xv, xvii, xxi, xxii, xxiii,
   xxx, xxxi, 152, 153n, 156n, 160n,
   167n, 183n, 191n, 261, 264,
   265
Hutten, Ulrich von xxviii

India 114n
Ingolstadt xxx, 91n, 261, 263
Inn 259
Innsbruck, Diet of 262
Invocavit Sermons xxviii, 49n
Israel 34, 63, 70, 109, 137, 148, 150,
    159, 166, 179, 232
Israelites, the 69, 115, 188; *see also*
    Jews
Italian Tyrol 255
Italians, the 38
Italy 104n, 202, 223, 258

Jacob 23, 41, 44, 47, 91, 227, 241
Jehoshaphat 72
Jehu 26, 72
Jena 266
Jeroboam 115, 192, 196
Jerusalem 55, 178, 179, 185
Jews, the 7, 8, 14, 15, 38, 51, 55–57,
    61, 67–73, 77, 79, 81, 82, 85, 86,
    97, 136, 137, 149, 151, 183, 185,
    190, 194, 248, 250, 263
Joab 202
Joachim of Fiora 210n
Joachimstal 49
John, duke of Saxony 11n, 93
John Frederick, crown prince of Saxony
    11n
John the Baptist 25, 97, 98, 168
Jordan, river 163
Joseph 21, 23
Josiah 27, 30, 34
Jud, Leo 41n, 44, 47
Judaism 210n
Judea 150
Judgment Day 187, 197, 208
Junker 204
Justinian, emperor 103
Jüterbog 268

Karlstadt, Andreas xiv, xv, xvi, xxviii,
    33, 41, 44–47, 49, 50n, 51n, 60,
    62n, 63n, 66n, 69n, 71n, 72n, 74n,
    87n, 91n, 95n, 101n, 246n, 264,
    265, 266, 268, 270, 271
Karlstadt am Main 265
Keller, Michael 241
Kelsterbach 249
Kempten 242
Kiel 266

Klettgau 268
Knipperdolling, Bernhard 271

Lamech 118
Landau 261
Last Days xix, 24, 31; *see also*
    Apocalypse, Judgment Day
Last Judgment 93, 230
Latin language 1n, 9n, 38, 40, 74n,
    106, 110, 172n, 216, 270
Lawrence, St. 89n
Lawrence of Nordhausen 89
League of Cognac 262
Leipsig xxxi, 68n, 91n, 119n, 263, 268
Lent xix, xxviii, 262
Leo X, pope xxvii
Letter from the Community at Orlamünde
    33–35, 266
Letter to the Princes of Saxony xxviii, 46n,
    74n, 75n, 88n, 91n, 92n
Letter to Thomas Müntzer xiv, xxix, 36–
    48, 262
Leviathans 80
Levite 57
Liechtenstein, Leonhard von 181n, 264
Lindau 242
Lot 17, 54, 188
Lother, Melchior 91
Lotzer, Sebastian xxi, 231n, 266, 267,
    270, 271
Louis II of Hungary and Bohemia xxxi,
    181n
Lucerne 99n
Lucifer 8, 103, 186
Luther, Martin xi, xiii, xvi, xviii, xxii,
    xxvii, xxx, 14n, 23, 27n, 28n, 33n,
    39, 44–48, 49n, 51n, 55n, 62n, 66n,
    69n, 74–84, 86–94, 111n, 119, 134n,
    153n, 154n, 214n, 221n, 222n, 241,
    265, 266, 268, 270

Macedonia 23, 24
Maienfeld 263
Main 246n, 250n
Mallerbach xxviii, xxix, 88, 93n, 268
Manz, Felix xiv, xvi, xvii, xxviii, xxix,
    xxxi, 36n, 45, 47, 95, 96n, 99n,
    100n, 262, 263, 266, 267, 271
"Martyrs Synod" at Augsburg xxxi,
    261, 265
Mary 88, 179

Maximian, emperor 114
Medes, empire of the 25
Megerich, priest 271
Meiningen 264
Melanchthon, Philip 241
Memmingen xx, xxix, xxx, 231n, 239, 264, 266–68, 270, 271
Meran (Merano) 256, 257
Meshach 72
Middle Ages 66n, 124n
Minerva 87
Moab 109, 115, 118
Moabites, the 109
Mochau, Anna von 265
Mohács, Battle of xxxi, 181n
Moravia xxv, xxxi, 181, 264, 265
Moses 20, 24, 26, 29, 30, 46, 51, 55–59, 62–66, 69, 70, 76, 78, 90, 124, 135, 136, 142, 149–51, 159, 160, 188, 192, 224
Mount of Olives 185
Mount Zion 129
Mühlhausen xxviii, xxix, xxx, 74n, 227, 228, 230, 261, 264, 265, 268–70
Mühlhausen Recess xxviii
Münster 246n, 271
Müntzer, Thomas xii, xiii, xiv, xv, xvi, xvii, xix, xx, xxii, xxiii, xxviii, xxix, xxx, 1, 2n, 3n, 4n, 7n, 9n, 10n, 11, 13n, 14n, 15n, 16n, 18n, 19n, 21n, 24n, 25n, 26n, 28n, 29n, 30n, 33n, 36, 38n, 41n, 42n, 44, 45, 46n, 47, 74, 75n, 78n, 80n, 83n, 84n, 86n, 88n, 89n, 91n, 92n, 93n, 94n, 101n, 130n, 152n, 153n, 154n, 167n, 227n, 228n, 239n, 261, 262, 263–70

Nathan 24
Naundorf 88n
Nebuchadnezzar 17, 22, 25, 26, 31, 187
Nero 8, 113, 118
Neuhof 249
Nicodemus 76
Nikolsburg xxxi, 181n, 183n, 264, 265
Nimrod 3, 114
Ninus 114
Noah 79, 150, 166, 221
Nordhausen 89
Nördlingen 241
Nuremberg xv, xxvii, xxix, xxx, 44n, 74n, 86n, 101n, 210n, 220n, 221n, 241, 261, 263, 264, 268, 269
Nuremberg Edict xxvii, 86n, 88n

Oath of Ruetli 128n
Octavian 14, 112; *see also* Augustus
Oecolampadius, Johann 261
On Commerce and Usury 81n
On Contrived Faith 36n
On the Abolition of Images 66n
On the Law of God 130–51, 261
On the Mystery of Baptism 152–71, 191n
On the New Transformation of the Christian Life xxv, 210–25, 263
On the Papacy of Rome 119n
On the Sword xxiv, xxxi, 177n, 181–203, 264
Orlamünde am Saale xvi, xxviii, 33n, 35, 49, 56, 87n, 264, 266, 271
Osiander, Andreas 44n, 241
Osnabrück 246n
Otho, emperor 113
Ottoman Empire 233n

Padua 262
Paris 154, 262
Passover, feast of 60
Peasants' War xii, xix, xx, xxi, xxii, xxiii, xxiv, xxvi, xxviii, 130n, 152n, 182n, 184n, 207n, 210n, 214n, 221n, 222n, 228n, 239n, 262–66, 269, 271
Pegau 68
Pelagius II, pope 103
Pentecost 265
Persian empire 25
Pfeiffer, Henrich xxix, xxx, 227n, 228n, 261, 268–70
Pharaoh 35, 124, 166, 168, 232
Pharisees 77
Philip, Margrave of Baden 111
Phineas 188
"Poor Conrad" 126
Prague 1, 10, 268
Prague Protest xi, xxvii, 1–10, 13n, 268
Protest and Defense xxix, 95–100, 267
Protest or Offering 36n, 38n, 46n
Prussia, duke of 271
Pur, Bartholomew 45

Red Sea 35, 166

Index

Reformation xi–xix, xxi–xxvi, xxviii,
    xxxi, 37n, 38n, 45n, 94n, 132n,
    173n, 213n, 214n, 249n, 263, 264,
    266, 268, 269, 271
Regensburg 261, 263
Rehoboam 192, 196, 200
Reichenau 264
Reifenstein 269
Reublin, Wilhelm 264
Reutlingen 242
Rhine 127, 246
Riedlingen 241
Roman Catholicism 1n, 37n, 154n,
    176n
Roman civil law 103n, 255
Roman empire 25, 112ff., 216
Rome xi, xxxi, 8, 106, 113, 114
Römer, Hans xxii
Rothenburg ob der Tauber 266
Rötlin, Sigmund 242
Rottenberg am Neckar 270
Rufinus 9n

Saale 33n
Sabaoth, Lord of 118
Sabbath 55, 60, 62, 73, 76, 79
Sachsenhausen 246, 250, 252
Salzburg xxxi, 262
Sam, Conrad 241
Samaria 55
Samaritans, the 55, 78, 83
Sandhof 249
Satan 8, 75, 77, 83, 109, 182, 196
Sattler, Michael xxii, xxiv, xxv, 172,
    173n, 177, 183n, 270
Sattler, Margaretha 270
Saul 94, 116, 196, 202, 203
Savoyards, the 259
Saxony xiv, xv, xviii, 26, 29, 80, 88n,
    89n, 246, 266, 271; see also Albertine
    Saxony, Ernestine Saxony
Schaffhausen 172, 173, 263, 264
Schappeler, Christoph xxi, xxix, xxx,
    231n, 266, 267, 270, 271
Schleitheim 172n
Schleitheim Articles, The xxiv, xxxi, 172–
    80, 183n, 265, 270
Schmid, Ulrich 267
Schwäbisch Hall 137n, 241, 250n
Schwanberg mountain 128
Schwanheim 249

Schwertfeger, Heinrich 269; see
    Pfeiffer
Schwertler 183n
Second Zurich Disputation xxviii, 262,
    264, 270
Semiramis, queen 114n
Senate, Roman 112
Seneca 113
Sennacharib 127
September Bible 221n
Sermon to the Princes xiii, xvi, xvii, xxviii,
    11–32, 80n, 268
Shadrach 72
Sharezer 127
Shimei 202
Sibylline Prophecies 124n
Sickengen, Franz von xxviii
Sigmund, Archduke of Tyrol 258
Sihon 63
Slavic 126n
Small Council, Zurich 262
Solomon 78, 107, 121–23, 125, 127,
    154, 185, 200, 201
Sorg, Simprecht 181
Spain 223n
Special Exposure of False Faith 263, 264,
    268
Speyer xxxi, xxxii
Spiritualists xiv
St. Gall 36, 263, 267, 270, 271
Stäbler xxxi, 183n, 264
Stadelhofen 99
Staufen 270
Staupitz, Johannes von 91
Stephen, St. 73
Sterzing 261
Stiefel, Michael 47
Stolberg 1, 267
Storch, Nicholas 92n, 271
Strasbourg 241, 261, 266, 270
Strauss, Jacob 41, 47, 241
Stübner, Markus, see Thomae
Stühlingen 182n
Stumpf, Simon xxviii
Sturm, Jacob 44
Süsse, Lawrence 89n
Swabia 231, 239, 266, 267
Swabian League xxx, 262, 267, 271
Swiss, the 101, 128–30
Swiss Brethren 183n
Swiss Confederation 109, 128

Index

Switzerland xi, xi, xv, xxiii, xxxi, 104n,
  128, 172n, 254n, 262, 263, 264,
  267, 270

Tabernacles, feast of 60
Ten Commandments 57n, 63
Territorial Constitution for Tyrol xxx,
  254–60, 262
Tertullian 43
Theophylactus 43
"Theses on nature, law and grace" 265
Thomae, Markus (Stübner) 92n
Thuringia xv, xxix, xxx, 152, 227n,
  228n, 268, 269
Tiberius, emperor 106, 112
Tiburtine Sibyl 124n; *see also* Sibylline
  Prophecies
Tileman 109
To the Assembly of the Common Peasantry
  xix, xx, 101–29, 192n
Trebitz 181
Troas 23
True Warning to All Christians . . . A 92n
Tschöfs 261
Turks, the 8, 10, 15, 103, 119, 125,
  216, 222
*Twelve Articles of the Upper Swabian
  Peasants, The* xxi, xxix, 231–38, 266,
  267, 270, 271
*Two Contradictory and Opposed Imperial
  Commands* 86n
Tyrol xx, xxi, xxx, 41, 254–56, 258,
  261, 262

Ulhart, Philip 130n
Ulm 241, 261

Vadian 36n
Venetian soup 112
Venice 262
Vienna xxxii, 181n, 262, 264
Villingen xxx, 243, 244
Vitellius, emperor 113

Vöhrenbach 243
Vulgate, the 11n

Waibel, Matthew 242
Waldshut xvi, xxx, 181n, 182n, 263,
  264
Wartburg xxvii, 49n, 265
Weigelin, shopkeeper 266
Weimar xxix, 93n, 94n, 268
Weingarten, Treaty of xxx, 267
Wendish lands 126
Westerburg, Gerhard 246n, 266, 271
Whether One Should Proceed Slowly xv,
  xxix, 49–73, 266, 271
Whitsun 214
Wittenberg xi, xxvii, xxviii, 33n, 41, 43,
  47, 49n, 51n, 55n, 56, 66n, 74, 76,
  78, 84, 85, 91n, 92n, 154, 264–66,
  268, 271
Worms 261
Worms, Diet of xi, xxvii 92, 93n
Württemberg xxx, 126, 266

Zabern, Battle of xxi, xxx
Zacchaeus 164
Zedekiah 72
Zell, Matthew 241
Zeus 115
Zurich xi, xiii, xiv, xvi, xvii, xxiii, xxiv,
  xxviii, xxix, xxx, xxxi, 36, 38n, 40n,
  41n, 42n, 44n, 45, 47, 95, 96, 99n,
  100n, 182n, 242, 262–64, 266, 267,
  270
Zurich *Oberland* 263
Zurich *Unterland* 270
Zwick, Hans 241
Zwickau 89, 92n, 263, 268, 271
"Zwickau prophets" xxvii, 271
Zwingli xi, xiii, xxiv, xxviii, 36n, 41n,
  44n, 47, 95n, 96n, 99, 100, 172n,
  182n, 242, 262–64, 266, 267, 270,
  271

Index of biblical references

Old Testament
Genesis
  Chapter 1 114n, 234, 235
  Chapter 2 137
  Chapter 3 85, 148, 192
  Chapter 4 118
  Chapter 6 102, 166, 221, 229
  Chapter 7 230
  Chapter 8 43, 79, 102, 105
  Chapter 10 3n, 114n
  Chapter 14 188, 233
  Chapter 15 23
  Chapter 17 23
  Chapter 19 17, 54
  Chapter 22 186, 200
  Chapter 25 91
  Chapter 28 23
  Chapter 32 23, 199
  Chapter 37 23
  Chapter 39 21, 23
  Chapter 40 21, 23
  Chapter 41 23

Exodus
  Chapter 2 188
  Chapter 3 124, 232
  Chapter 4 24
  Chapter 7 124
  Chapter 12 63
  Chapter 14 35, 232
  Chapter 15 230
  Chapter 17 115
  Chapter 18 228
  Chapter 19 170

  Chapter 20 146, 186, 199
  Chapter 21 230
  Chapter 22 28, 230
  Chapter 23 31, 50, 66, 67, 69, 70,
    71n, 228, 230
  Chapter 31 232

Leviticus
  Chapter 1 90
  Chapter 4 12, 50
  Chapter 5 53
  Chapter 10 150, 170
  Chapter 11 23, 25, 90, 159, 200
  Chapter 16 57
  Chapter 19 228
  Chapter 20 139
  Chapter 24 194
  Chapter 25 60
  Chapter 26 59, 228

Numbers
  Chapter 14 32
  Chapter 15 51, 80
  Chapter 16 150
  Chapter 19 5, 20
  Chapter 22 29, 118
  Chapter 24 118
  Chapter 25 115, 228
  Chapter 26 188

Deuteronomy
  Chapter 1 19, 43, 194
  Chapter 2 30, 63

Deuteronomy (*cont.*)
  Chapter 4 52, 56, 57, 58, 59, 60,
    64, 66, 135, 154, 170, 228
  Chapter 5 52, 56, 57, 132, 155,
    199
  Chapter 6 56, 57, 199, 229, 234
  Chapter 7 29, 68, 69, 70, 71n
  Chapter 8 56
  Chapter 10 230, 232
  Chapter 11 56, 60, 61, 64
  Chapter 12 50, 57, 72n, 108, 155,
    233
  Chapter 13 17, 28, 58, 65, 76, 80,
    122, 150
  Chapter 14 61, 159
  Chapter 15 61
  Chapter 16 57, 228
  Chapter 17 57, 58, 80, 200, 232
  Chapter 18 76, 122, 150, 233,
    237
  Chapter 19 170
  Chapter 20 26, 228
  Chapter 21 228
  Chapter 22 139
  Chapter 26 57, 233
  Chapter 27 57, 71
  Chapter 28 57, 225
  Chapter 29 56, 58, 59, 60, 63, 66,
    150
  Chapter 30 20, 43, 90, 136, 142
  Chapter 31 43, 145
  Chapter 32 19, 141, 166, 204
  Chapter 33 65
  Chapter 34 150
  Chapter 36 19

Joshua 192, 196
  Chapter 1 69, 119, 155
  Chapter 2 69
  Chapter 3 69
  Chapter 5 30
  Chapter 11 32
  Chapter 23 68

Judges
  Chapter 3 69, 109n
  Chapter 6 71
  Chapter 7 128
  Chapter 8 128, 158, 163

Ruth, Chapter 7 229

1 Samuel
  Chapter 8 115, 192
  Chapter 12 146
  Chapter 15 115
  Chapter 22 202

2 Samuel
  Chapter 1 202
  Chapter 11 139
  Chapter 12 200
  Chapter 15 29
  Chapter 18 29

1 Kings
  Chapter 2 163, 201
  Chapter 3 107, 185
  Chapter 8 80
  Chapter 11 115, 200
  Chapter 13 115
  Chapter 15 72n
  Chapter 16 115
  Chapter 17 94
  Chapter 18 30, 123, 182
  Chapter 19 74, 123

2 Kings
  Chapter 9 26, 123
  Chapter 10 26, 72n
  Chapter 15 72
  Chapter 19 127
  Chapter 22 27n
  Chapter 23 27n, 30, 34
  Chapter 24 34, 72n

1 Chronicles, Chapter 14 30

2 Chronicles
  Chapter 11 200
  Chapter 12 72
  Chapter 13 34
  Chapter 17 72n
  Chapter 19 190, 202
  Chapter 21 127
  Chapter 25 127
  Chapter 29 24, 72n
  Chapter 36 30

Ezra, Chapter 4 13

Nehemiah, Chapter 4 129

Job
Chapter 25 102n
Chapter 27 78
Chapter 28 23, 78
Chapter 40 108n
Chapter 41 80

Psalms
Psalm 1 79, 145
Psalm 2 25, 125, 158
Psalm 4 110
Psalm 5 3, 75
Psalm 6 167
Psalm 7 81
Psalm 10 84
Psalm 11 154, 230
Psalm 15 79, 230
Psalm 17 200
Psalm 18 28, 146
Psalm 19 16, 21, 78, 79, 83, 145
Psalm 22 14
Psalm 23 129
Psalm 25 129
Psalm 27 89
Psalm 31 162, 165
Psalm 34 60
Psalm 36 84
Psalm 37 16, 77, 85, 162n
Psalm 40 26, 62, 144
Psalm 44 30, 158
Psalm 46 14
Psalm 48 20
Psalm 49 22
Psalm 50 53, 159
Psalm 51 159
Psalm 55 77, 162
Psalm 58 31
Psalm 62 207
Psalm 63 77
Psalm 64 77
Psalm 68 75, 79
Psalm 69 14, 15, 29
Psalm 73 91
Psalm 77 165
Psalm 78 158
Psalm 79 80
Psalm 80 12, 13
Psalm 83 229
Psalm 85 90
Psalm 87 7
Psalm 89 3n, 12

Psalm 91 83
Psalm 93 22, 75
Psalm 94 146
Psalm 103 200
Psalm 109 233
Psalm 111 16, 89
Psalm 115 106, 129
Psalm 118 13, 14, 26
Psalm 119 20, 22, 74n, 77, 200
Psalm 125 129
Psalm 139 20
Psalm 140 27
Psalm 141 3
Psalm 143 167
Psalm 145 81
Psalm 146 124
Psalm 192 3

Proverbs
Chapter 1 16, 166, 230
Chapter 2 121n
Chapter 3 207
Chapter 4 16, 155
Chapter 5 15
Chapter 6 26, 28
Chapter 7 87
Chapter 9 15, 90
Chapter 16 162
Chapter 17 60
Chapter 18 78, 151
Chapter 24 22, 78, 140, 142
Chapter 25 204
Chapter 28 127
Chapter 30 89

Ecclesiastes
Chapter 3 20, 60n
Chapter 7 131
Chapter 8 15
Chapter 9 60
Chapter 10 22
Chapter 27 158
Chapter 33 158
Chapter 34 17
Chapter 38 158

Isaï·h 64, 150
Chapter 1 12, 159, 186, 207
Chapter 2 199
Chapter 4 158
Chapter 5 12, 19, 59, 81, 228

Index

Isaiah (cont.)
  Chapter 6 83
  Chapter 10 80, 237
  Chapter 11 78
  Chapter 19 237
  Chapter 22 4
  Chapter 24 3
  Chapter 28 13, 20, 59
  Chapter 29 4, 12, 20, 50
  Chapter 30 158
  Chapter 33 20
  Chapter 40 90, 232
  Chapter 41 158
  Chapter 42 87
  Chapter 44 65n, 71
  Chapter 53 158, 234
  Chapter 55 7, 146
  Chapter 58 18, 75, 151
  Chapter 59 27, 102
  Chapter 60 7
  Chapter 64 19, 205
  Chapter 65 20
  Chapter 66 16

Jeremiah 14, 70, 81, 150
  Chapter 1 93, 158
  Chapter 2 20, 146, 158, 229
  Chapter 3 200
  Chapter 4 6, 71, 158
  Chapter 5 18, 82
  Chapter 7 147
  Chapter 8 5, 18, 20
  Chapter 15 12
  Chapter 18 158
  Chapter 20 17
  Chapter 21 186, 207
  Chapter 22 186
  Chapter 23 2, 3, 51, 136, 143,
    144, 146
  Chapter 26 237
  Chapter 31 41, 136, 144, 160
  Chapter 32 146
  Chapter 38 182
  Chapter 45 20
  Chapter 48 60

Lamentations
  Chapter 3 81
  Chapter 4 14

Ezekiel 4, 12, 63
  Chapter 3 3, 144
  Chapter 12 91
  Chapter 13 91, 94
  Chapter 18 136, 140, 199
  Chapter 23 17, 93
  Chapter 33 136, 140, 144
  Chapter 34 6, 63, 91, 158
  Chapter 36 12, 41
  Chapter 37 158

Daniel
  Chapter 2 11, 13, 14, 17–22, 24–
    26, 31
  Chapter 3 31, 72n
  Chapter 6 30
  Chapter 7 30, 80
  Chapter 9 9

Hosea
  Chapter 4 3, 12, 14, 163
  Chapter 10 128

Joel
  Chapter 2 7, 24
  Chapter 3 158, 163, 199

Amos
  Chapter 2 115
  Chapter 3 149

Obadiah, Chapter 1 20

Jonah 165

Micah
  Chapter 3 16, 77, 81, 91
  Chapter 6 207
  Chapter 7 65

Nahum, Chapter 3 207

Habakkuk 208

Zechariah
  Chapter 7 146, 207–8, 228
  Chapter 11 3, 158
  Chapter 17 228

Malachi
  Chapter 1 16

Chapter 2 12
Chapter 3 29, 31

Apocrypha
Tobit
Chapter 3 8n
Chapter 4 60

The Wisdom of Solomon
Chapter 6 234
Chapter 9 154
Chapter 12 43

Baruch, Chapter 3 20

1 Maccabees, Chapter 3 127

New Testament
Matthew 164, 170
Chapter 1 23, 158, 165
Chapter 2 23
Chapter 3 25, 97, 158
Chapter 4 158, 196, 234
Chapter 5 xxiv, 29, 76, 82, 121,
    132, 134–36, 142, 147, 175,
    176, 178, 179, 182, 188, 193,
    194, 197, 198, 199, 201, 228
Chapter 6 16, 34, 78, 136, 160,
    184
Chapter 7 13, 15, 28, 85, 104,
    120, 124, 136, 199, 228, 234
Chapter 8 237
Chapter 9 83, 158, 233
Chapter 10 27, 55, 75, 88, 89,
    182, 191, 196, 221, 228, 230,
    233, 236
Chapter 11 115, 145, 146, 166,
    200
Chapter 12 12, 28, 54, 139, 158
Chapter 13 10, 12, 31, 78, 83,
    150, 157, 158, 224
Chapter 14 230
Chapter 15 73n, 91, 221
Chapter 16 26, 50, 177, 199, 230
Chapter 17 74, 102, 158, 182
Chapter 18 27, 30, 31, 40, 42, 43,
    65, 66, 92, 121n, 147, 161, 174,
    191, 198, 200
Chapter 19 43, 123, 198–200, 219
Chapter 20 122, 158, 162, 169,
    177

Chapter 21 14, 72n, 229
Chapter 22 102, 104, 106, 123,
    132, 182, 218
Chapter 23 7, 15, 19, 28, 78,
    86, 89, 102, 122, 179, 199, 237
Chapter 24 12, 15
Chapter 25 140, 142, 200
Chapter 26 34, 39, 184, 185, 199,
    200
Chapter 28 32, 97, 174, 199
Chapter 29 179

Mark 121
Chapter 1 97
Chapter 2 158
Chapter 4 12, 21, 31, 150, 157
Chapter 9 43, 120, 136, 170
Chapter 10 43, 179
Chapter 12 14, 218
Chapter 14 39, 200
Chapter 15 168
Chapter 16 97, 156, 157, 174,
    199

Luke
Chapter 1 14, 74, 88n, 140
Chapter 2 14, 78, 179
Chapter 3 97, 158, 229, 236, 237
Chapter 4 83, 234
Chapter 6 2, 122, 193, 199, 222,
    233, 234, 237
Chapter 7 21
Chapter 8 5n, 12, 22, 31, 83, 150,
    157
Chapter 9 87, 186
Chapter 10 27, 158
Chapter 11 4, 86, 139, 184
Chapter 12 14, 16, 53, 120, 163,
    170, 177, 187, 188
Chapter 13 6n, 120, 158
Chapter 14 54, 199, 228
Chapter 15 50
Chapter 16 158
Chapter 17 54, 120, 121n
Chapter 18 31, 43, 141, 228, 232
Chapter 19 4n, 31, 35, 104, 118,
    125, 227, 228
Chapter 20 13, 14, 158, 218
Chapter 21 12, 13, 230
Chapter 22 39, 185, 200, 202,
    219

Luke (*cont.*)
  Chapter 23 182
  Chapter 24 76n

John
  Chapter 1 75, 77, 87, 97, 199
  Chapter 2 15, 29, 72n
  Chapter 3 3, 5, 46, 75, 117
  Chapter 4 20, 55, 97
  Chapter 5 52, 76, 77, 152, 198
  Chapter 6 7, 14, 15, 39, 40, 77,
    177, 232
  Chapter 7 28, 76, 82, 143, 228
  Chapter 8 3, 22, 75, 78, 81, 82,
    86, 87, 90, 92, 133, 177, 193,
    198
  Chapter 9 76
  Chapter 10 14, 76, 84, 85, 91,
    133, 158, 200, 211
  Chapter 11 83, 185
  Chapter 12 118, 157, 170
  Chapter 13 60, 135, 200, 234
  Chapter 14 135, 184, 200
  Chapter 15 28, 158
  Chapter 16 20, 79
  Chapter 18 183
  Chapter 20 191
  Chapter 21 29, 54

Acts of the Apostles
  Chapter 2 2, 24, 39, 158, 165, 174
  Chapter 3 153
  Chapter 5 120, 234, 246
  Chapter 7 63
  Chapter 8 174
  Chapter 9 55
  Chapter 10 23, 55, 97, 98, 159,
    235
  Chapter 11 159
  Chapter 12 158
  Chapter 14 158, 232
  Chapter 15 2, 137
  Chapter 16 23, 174
  Chapter 17 2, 29
  Chapter 18 24
  Chapter 19 168, 174
  Chapter 20 13, 199, 228
  Chapter 21 55
  Chapter 22 98
  Chapter 25 87
  Chapter 27 24

Romans
  Chapter 1 20, 43, 157, 160, 227,
    232
  Chapter 2 43, 79, 81n, 147, 160,
    208, 228
  Chapter 3 25, 105, 140, 230
  Chapter 5 59, 141–43, 168
  Chapter 6 98, 138, 168, 229
  Chapter 7 43, 79, 140, 144, 148,
    184, 200
  Chapter 8 3, 14, 18, 20, 75, 121,
    135, 142, 158, 163, 177, 232
  Chapter 9 158, 200, 230
  Chapter 10 20, 43, 90, 142, 236
  Chapter 11 17, 154, 165, 199
  Chapter 12 78, 135, 158, 159,
    162, 200, 204
  Chapter 13 27, 28, 30, 80, 102,
    104–6, 121, 137, 185–87, 190,
    192, 194, 195, 198, 202–4, 206,
    208, 218, 234
  Chapter 15 148

1 Corinthians 154
  Chapter 1 76, 157
  Chapter 2 21, 82, 163, 199
  Chapter 3 75, 158
  Chapter 4 163
  Chapter 5 31, 80, 139, 158
  Chapter 6 189, 194, 199
  Chapter 7 120, 198, 234
  Chapter 8 61, 67
  Chapter 9 176, 233, 228–29
  Chapter 10 14, 61, 148, 163, 170,
    235
  Chapter 11 39, 61, 200
  Chapter 12 158
  Chapter 13 2, 22
  Chapter 14 4, 30, 42, 43, 92, 173,
    200
  Chapter 15 168, 191

2 Corinthians
  Chapter 1 75, 192
  Chapter 3 4, 41, 77
  Chapter 6 21, 53, 82, 175, 198
  Chapter 8 199
  Chapter 9 60
  Chapter 10 107, 119, 195
  Chapter 11 12, 78, 85, 90

Index

Galatians 56
    Chapter 1 51, 76, 199
    Chapter 2 29, 233
    Chapter 3 104
    Chapter 4 4, 106
    Chapter 5 22, 158

Ephesians
    Chapter 1 75, 141, 143, 199, 204
    Chapter 3 163
    Chapter 4 2, 104, 135, 158, 163,
       200, 204
    Chapter 5 12, 16, 38, 59, 139,
       158, 163, 191, 204
    Chapter 6 34, 105n, 106, 195,
       196, 237

Philippians
    Chapter 2 13, 75, 153
    Chapter 3 15, 18, 28

Colossians
    Chapter 1 141, 143, 157, 158,
       204
    Chapter 2 19, 85, 90, 147, 204,
       235
    Chapter 3 29, 38, 42

1 Thessalonians
    Chapter 2 113
    Chapter 3 19
    Chapter 4 236
    Chapter 5 19, 229

1 Timothy
    Chapter 1 79, 80, 105, 142, 147,
       200
    Chapter 2 196, 199, 200, 208
    Chapter 3 176, 232
    Chapter 4 16, 235
    Chapter 5 119, 233

2 Timothy
    Chapter 2 46n, 159, 203
    Chapter 3 12, 16, 31, 158

Titus
    Chapter 1 3, 30, 232
    Chapter 2 180
    Chapter 3 163

Hebrews 233
    Chapter 1 87
    Chapter 3 136, 160
    Chapter 4 148
    Chapter 6 139, 179
    Chapter 7 142
    Chapter 8 41, 136
    Chapter 10 139, 147, 204
    Chapter 11 199
    Chapter 13 158

James
    Chapter 1 59, 200
    Chapter 2 199
    Chapter 4 199
    Chapter 5 118

1 Peter
    Chapter 1 27, 31, 200, 234
    Chapter 2 43, 102, 109, 110,
       111n, 149, 163, 178, 234
    Chapter 3 30, 168, 183
    Chapter 4 183
    Chapter 5 228

2 Peter
    Chapter 1 27, 148
    Chapter 2 13, 15, 136, 139, 140,
       228

1 John
    Chapter 1 138, 199
    Chapter 2 148
    Chapter 3 138, 167
    Chapter 4 142
    Chapter 5 137, 139, 142, 148

Jude, Chapter 4 13, 228

Revelation of John
    Chapter 2 148
    Chapter 3 4
    Chapter 5 153
    Chapter 6 7, 80
    Chapter 11 74
    Chapter 13 6
    Chapter 16 13
    Chapter 18 86, 175
    Chapter 22 145

CAMBRIDGE TEXTS IN THE HISTORY OF POLITICAL THOUGHT

Titles published in the series thus far

Aristotle *The Politics* (edited by Stephen Everson)

Bakunin *Statism and Anarchy* (edited by Marshall Shatz)

Bentham *A Fragment on Government* (introduction by Ross Harrison)

Bossuet *Politics Drawn from the Very Words of Holy Scripture* (edited by Patrick Riley)

Cicero *On Duties* (edited by M. T. Griffin and E. M. Atkins)

Constant *Political Writings* (edited by Biancamaria Fontana)

Filmer *Patriarcha and Other Writings* (edited by Johann P. Sommerville)

Hegel *Elements of the Philosophy of Right* (edited by Allen W. Wood and H. B. Nisbet)

Hobbes *Leviathan* (edited by Richard Tuck)

Hooker *Of the Laws of Ecclesiastical Polity* (edited by A. S. McGrade)

John of Salisbury *Policraticus* (edited by Cary Nederman)

Kant *Political Writings* (edited by H. S. Reiss and H. B. Nisbet)

Leibniz *Political Writings* (edited by Patrick Riley)

Locke *Two Treatises of Government* (edited by Peter Laslett)

Luther and Calvin on Secular Authority (edited by Harro Höpfl)

Machiavelli *The Prince* (edited by Quentin Skinner and Russell Price)

J. S. Mill *On Liberty*, with *The Subjection of Women* and *Chapters on Socialism* (edited by Stefan Collini)

Milton *Political Writings* (edited by Martin Dzelzainis)

Montesquieu *The Spirit of the Laws* (edited by Anne M. Cohler, Basia Carolyn Miller and Harold Samuel Stone)

More *Utopia* (edited by George M. Logan and Robert M. Adams)

Nicholas of Cusa *The Catholic Concordance* (edited by Paul E. Sigmund)

Paine *Political Writings* (edited by Bruce Kuklick)

Pufendorf *On the Duty of Man and Citizen according to Natural Law* (edited by James Tully)

The Radical Reformation (edited by Michael G. Baylor)

Vitoria *Political Writings* (edited by Anthony Pagden)